AF521913

An American Focus

THE ANDERSON

GRAPHIC ARTS COLLECTION

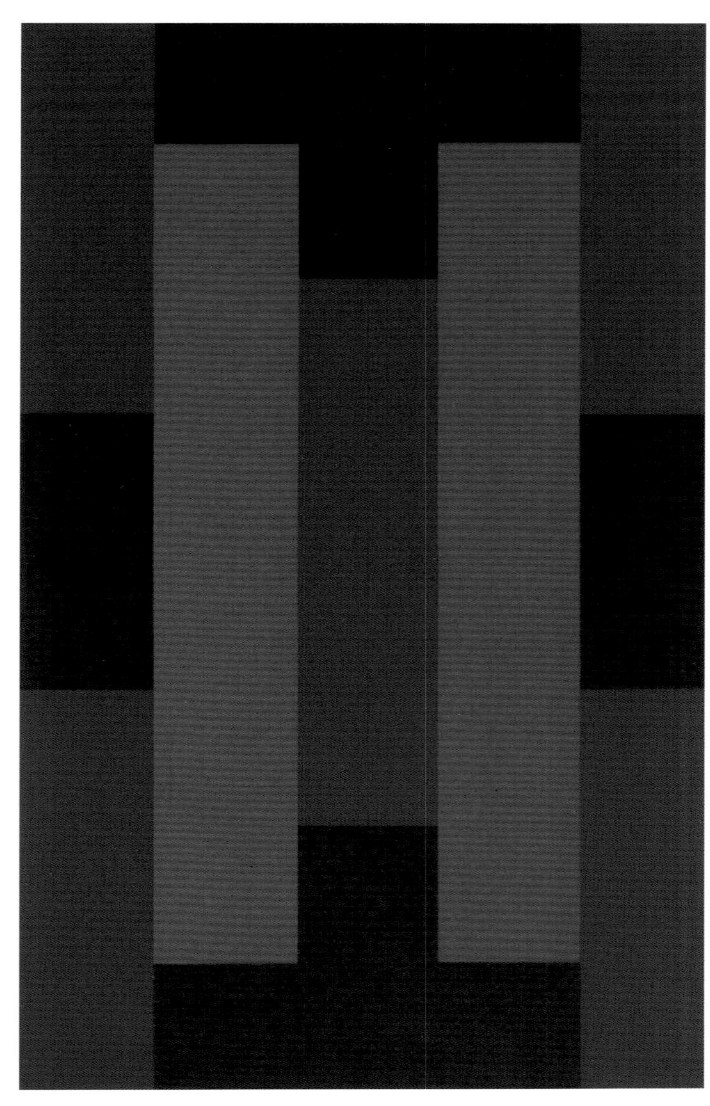

An American Focus

THE ANDERSON GRAPHIC ARTS COLLECTION

Karin Breuer

FINE ARTS MUSEUMS OF SAN FRANCISCO
UNIVERSITY OF CALIFORNIA PRESS Berkeley Los Angeles London

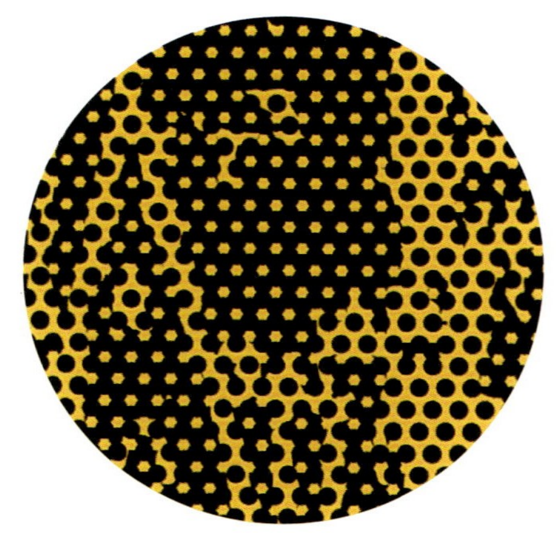

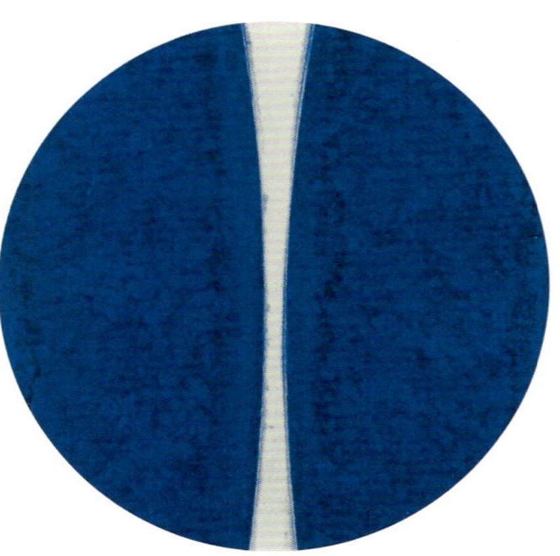

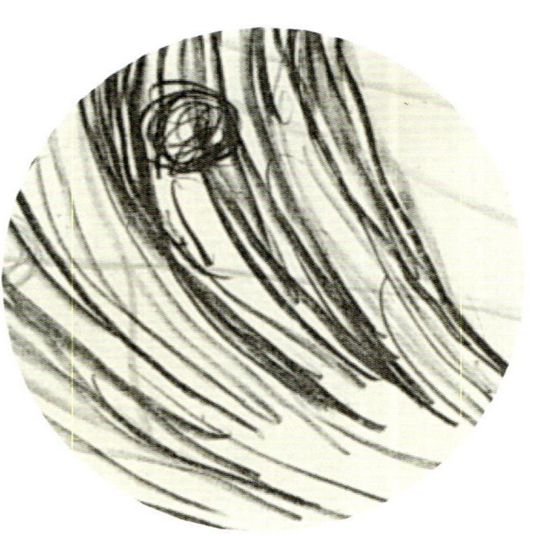

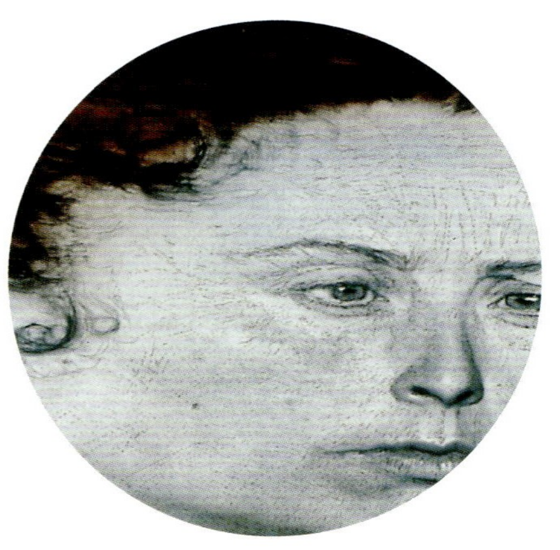

Contents

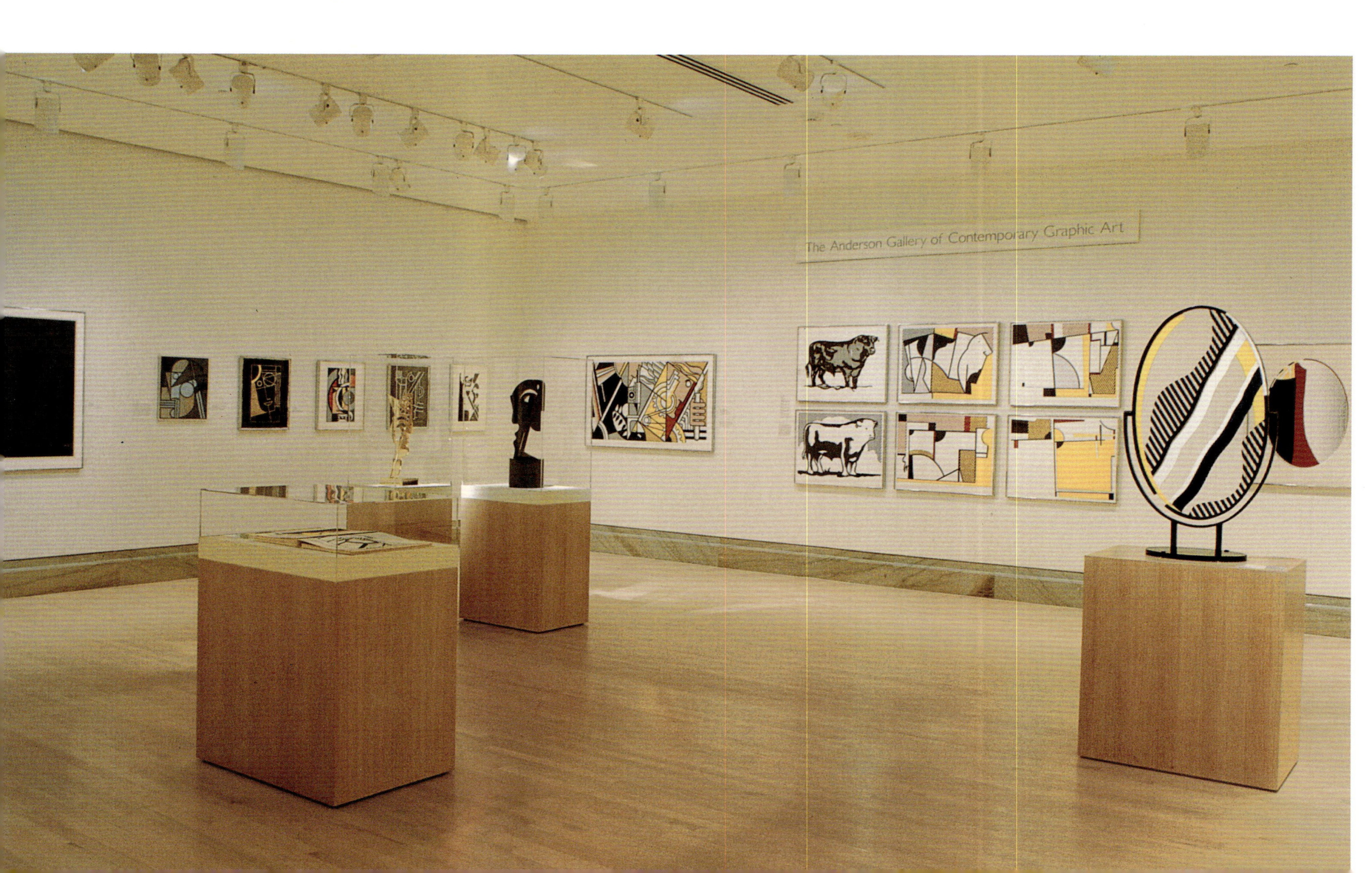
The Anderson Gallery of Contemporary Graphic Art

Foreword

Mr. and Mrs. Harry W. Anderson, known to all by their nicknames, "Hunk" and "Moo," have been associated with the Fine Arts Museums of San Francisco from the time they began collecting art in the mid-1960s. In fact, one of their early contemporary art acquisitions, the 1964 publication of Pop Art prints entitled *1 ¢ Life*, was purchased from the Patrons of Art and Music at the California Palace of the Legion of Honor.

As well as being lifetime members of the Museums, Hunk and Moo are longtime supporters of its programs. They have been lenders to its exhibitions (most notably the 1971 exhibition of their Gemini G.E.L. print collection) and donors to its prints and drawings department, the Achenbach Foundation for Graphic Arts.

The exhibition *An American Focus: The Anderson Graphic Arts Collection* is a celebration of the donation in 1996 of 656 contemporary American prints by the Andersons and their daughter, Mary Patricia Anderson "Putter" Pence. This generous gift gave new impetus to efforts to extend the Museums' collection into the twentieth century, particularly the prints and drawings collection, which had been previously stimulated by the acquisition of the Crown Point Press archive in 1991. Today the Fine Arts Museums of San Francisco can boast that its contemporary American print collection is one of the most extensive in the country.

To showcase the extraordinary Anderson Graphic Arts Collection, the Anderson Gallery of Contemporary Graphic Art was unveiled at the Legion of Honor in 1997. The gallery, which features selections from the Anderson Collection in regularly scheduled exhibitions, will move to the new M. H. de Young Memorial Museum in 2005, where it will greatly enhance the presentation of American art.

Hunk, Moo, and Putter remain actively involved in the activities generated by the Anderson Collection at the Museums, including the Collection Sharing Program (which is described in a separate section of this catalogue) and the annual Anderson lecture series. They also participate in the Anderson Collection Management Committee meetings that provide focus for the curatorial effort of Karin Breuer, curator of the Anderson Graphic Arts Collection.

It was a suggestion by the Andersons at one of these meetings that prompted this auspicious, first-time cooperative effort of the Fine Arts Museums and the San Francisco Museum of Modern Art in presenting the best of the Anderson Collection in concurrent exhibitions at both museums. I join with SFMOMA director David Ross in saluting Hunk and Moo Anderson and Putter Pence for providing us with such a splendid opportunity to celebrate their longtime commitment to modern art and their contributions to the cultural life of the San Francisco Bay Area.

Harry S. Parker III
Director of Museums

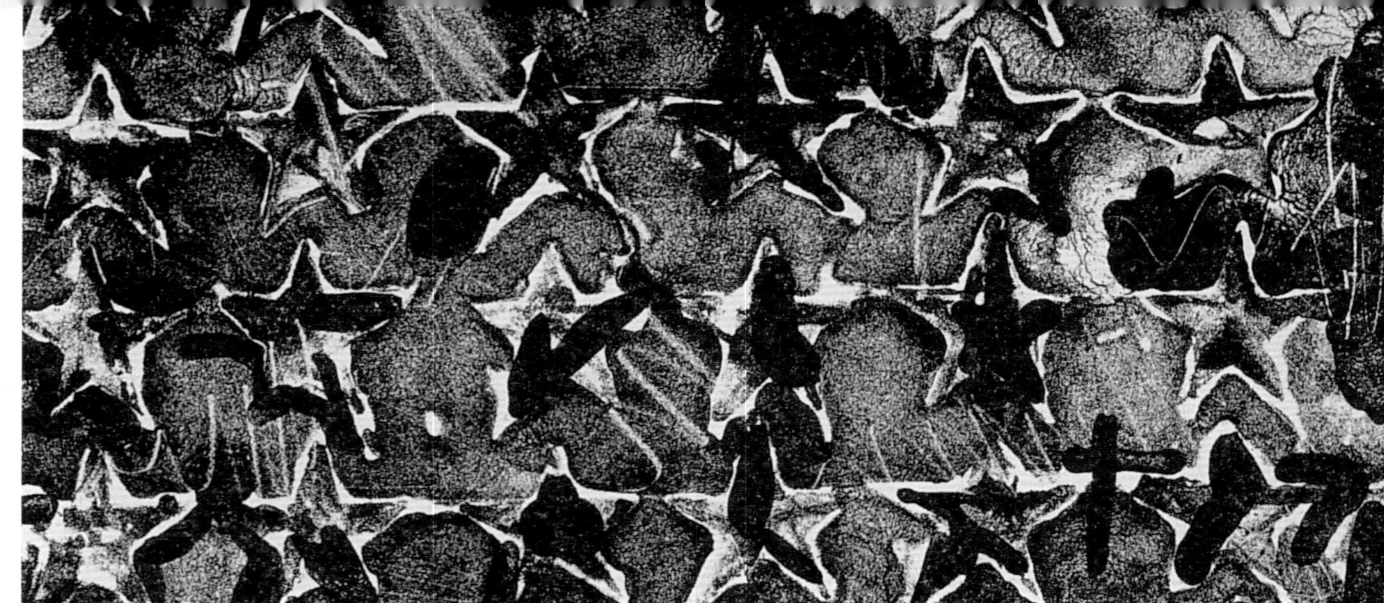

Acknowledgments

Although they have long been associated with the Fine Arts Museums of San Francisco, it has been my pleasure to work with Hunk and Moo Anderson and their daughter, Putter Pence, since 1996, the year of their generous gift to the Museums. At this time I was fortunate to have been selected as the curator who would manage their collection for the Museums. Working with this important group of prints, many of which are considered icons of twentieth-century art, has been a labor of love.

It was obvious to me from the beginning of my collection research that the Anderson Collection is a personal one, reflecting the taste, interests, and enthusiasms of a family of art lovers. As a whole, and even with individual objects, the collection speaks of passionate involvement. If it's true, as the Andersons have claimed, that their passion for the art is addictive, I thank them for so willingly sharing the addiction.

In getting to know the Andersons and the collection I was aided from the start by their curatorial staff. Dee Weldon White, administrative director from 1988 to 1998, and the current staff—Rachel Teagle, curator; Molly Hutton, collection manager; and Nancy Bennett, registrar—have been a pleasure to work with.

My curatorial efforts also have been greatly assisted by the Anderson Collection Management Committee. In addition to the Andersons, I acknowledge committee members Harry S. Parker III, director of Museums; Sylvia S. Kingsley, Museums trustee; and Steven Nash, associate director and chief curator, who is ex-officio, for their continued guidance.

The staff of the Museums has been enthusiastic from the start with all aspects of exhibition planning. I thank my colleagues Robert Flynn Johnson, Maxine Rosston, and Mark Garrett of the Achenbach Foundation for Graphic Arts; Debra Evans of the Museums paper conservation laboratory; Kathe Hodgson,

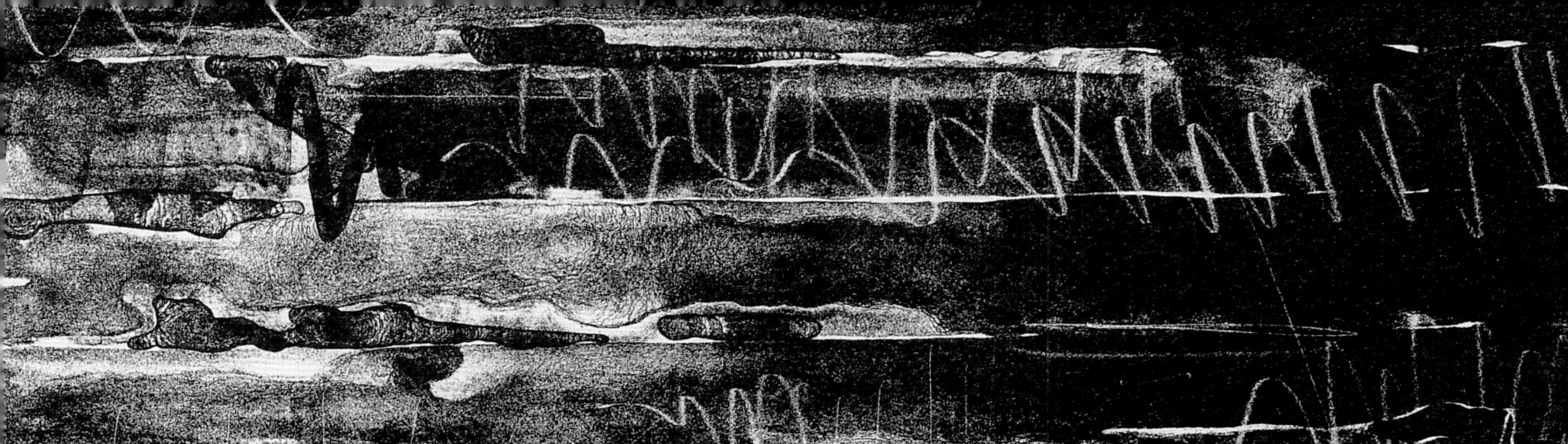

director of exhibition planning; Vas Prabhu, director of education; Jennifer Williams, coordinator of adult education programs; Barbara Traisman and Andrew Fox in media relations; Steven Lockwood in registration; Couric Payne of the Museum Stores; and Joseph McDonald, photographer. Thanks also to Deborah Gangwer, volunteer research assistant, who compiled information for the many versions of the exhibition checklist.

I owe a debt of gratitide also to Ann Karlstrom and Karen Kevorkian of the publications department for their attention to all aspects of the catalogue production. I also thank Tracey Shiffman for her beautiful catalogue design.

Others who have been tremendously helpful in all aspects of our joint presentations are deputy director Lori Fogarty and chief curator Gary Garrels at the San Francisco Museum of Modern Art. Finally, I thank curators Katherine Plake Hough of the Palm Springs Desert Museum and Ellen Landis at the Albuquerque Museum for their enthusiastic participation in the traveling exhibition of *An American Focus*.

Karin Breuer, Curator
Achenbach Foundation for Graphic Arts and
the Anderson Graphic Arts Collection

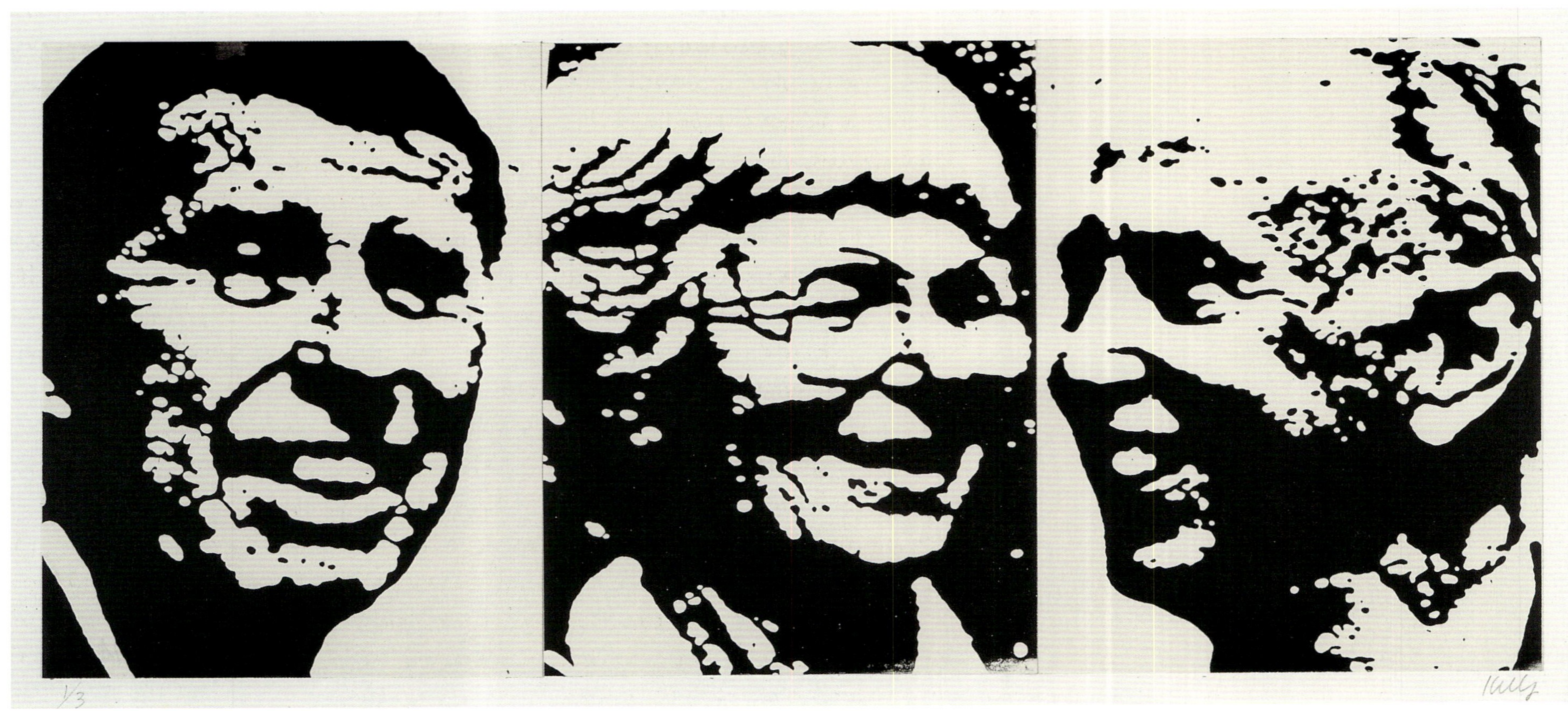

Journey to the New: Four Decades of Print Collecting

In 1968 Mary Margaret "Moo" Anderson and art dealer Helen Heninger walked into the Poindexter Gallery in New York City. There they saw Richard Diebenkorn's *41 Etchings Drypoints,* a bound volume of forty-one prints that had been published by Crown Point Press, then in Berkeley, California, in 1965.

Heninger, director of Gump's Gallery in San Francisco, advised Mr. and Mrs. Anderson on building an art collection and was instrumental in introducing them to a variety of galleries. Mrs. Anderson remembers that "Helen and I regularly met in San Francisco to look for art books [artist-illustrated books], which were an interest of mine. We'd found some things locally. So, on a trip to New York we went to the Poindexter Gallery where Diebenkorn's book was available. Helen was very encouraging. She knew Dick [Diebenkorn] and she also knew something about the [printmaking] process he was using. I remember bringing it back with me on the plane, and telling Hunk that I'd found a really great thing."[1]

"By 1968 there were already indications that we were headed in the direction of collecting contemporary art," Harry W. "Hunk" Anderson explains. "This was our first contemporary art purchase, but it didn't stay with us for long. Moo had told me that *41 Etchings Drypoints* was also available in loose portfolio, and that the individual prints could be framed. That seemed a better idea and so we traded the bound volume for the loose set [cat. 5–8] and had it framed immediately."[2]

The Andersons, who moved to the San Francisco Bay Area from upstate New York in 1962, had collected art since the mid-1960s, initially focusing on French Impressionist paintings and then, later, on European and American modernist paintings, drawings, and sculpture.[3] Their purchase of the Diebenkorn portfolio in 1968 set them on a new course of collecting contemporary art, and contemporary prints in particular. It also established a pattern of buying that the Andersons soon recognized as a collecting strategy: they initially introduced themselves to an artist's work through his or her prints. If their interest was sustained, further purchases of prints followed, and perhaps also drawings, paintings, or sculpture.

The journey towards collecting new, contemporary art that began with the Diebenkorn print purchase continued at a rapid pace in 1968, spurred by Mr. Anderson's business interests. The Saga Corporation,[4] which he had cofounded with two partners, was located in Menlo Park in a two-building complex designed by Cliff May in his legendary style that incorporated elements of landscape with early California ranch architecture. With high ceilings, thick white stucco walls, paved tile floors, and skylights that allowed the large rooms and corridors to fill with natural light, the corporate offices at Saga were ideal for the display of contemporary art (fig. 1). Mr. Anderson's proposal to mount installations of his art collection in the corporate offices met with approval from his Saga partners.

ELLSWORTH KELLY
Hunk, Moo, and Ellsworth, ca. 1990
Xerographic print
10⅞ x 25 in. (overall)

At about the same time, one of the partners, William Laughlin, arranged for a business meeting in Aspen, Colorado, that serendipitously brought the Andersons together with John and Kimiko Powers. The Powerses were contemporary art collectors based in Colorado who had been instrumental in helping Tanya Grosman promote her successful subscription program for purchasing prints by artists at Universal Limited Art Editions (ULAE) in West Islip, New York. The Powerses had recently become involved in a similar program offered by Gemini G.E.L. in Los Angeles.[5] Upon learning of the Andersons' interest in contemporary art, they urged the young couple to investigate.

Within months of their initial introduction to Gemini, in December 1968 the Andersons purchased numerous works with their new subscription, including Jasper Johns's *Black and White Numeral Series* (cat. 22–31), six prints by Robert Rauschenberg, and the *V Series* of prints (cat. 16–19) by Frank Stella.[6] In 1969 the Andersons continued the subscription program at Gemini and added a second, which entitled them to buy two impressions of each print produced at Gemini for that year. Mr. Anderson notes that "At the time, it was not a foregone conclusion that this was the beginning of a golden age of printmaking. It was a risk to take one subscription, let alone two."[7]

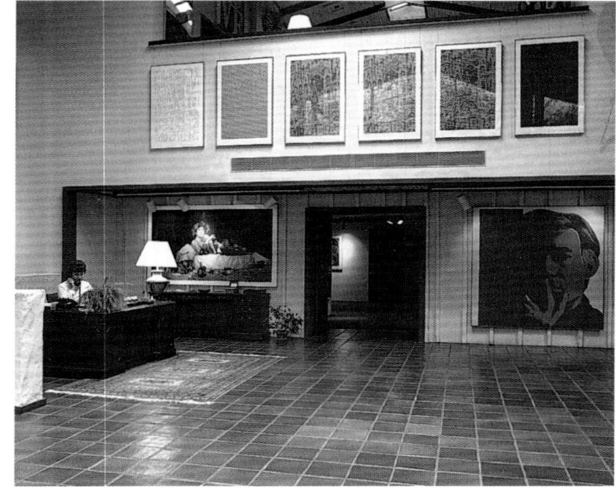

1

It was a risk that the Andersons obviously enjoyed as they purchased numerous prints by Johns, including the *Color Numeral Series* (cat. 32–41) and the *Lead Reliefs* (cat. 51–55), and editions of prints by Josef Albers and Roy Lichtenstein, all in a six-month period. These purchases provided an initial introduction to the three artists that, in keeping with the Andersons' collecting strategy, later led to further purchases. For example, in 1971 they purchased important paintings by Lichtenstein (*Rouen Cathedral Set V,* 1969) and Johns (*Two Flags,* 1959). Mr. Anderson credits the print workshops for this exposure: "Through the print workshops, we were exposed to new artists. They acted as a kind of filter for us, enabling us ultimately to select certain key artists. From there we would purchase prints and then perhaps paintings or drawings. With some artists, we were content to buy only their prints."[8]

Gemini was not the only source for print purchases in 1969 as the Andersons traveled to New York in March and purchased Wayne Thiebaud's print series *Delights* (cat. 1–2) and his painting *Candy Counter* (1963) from the Allan Stone Gallery. Mrs. Anderson found two Albers screenprint portfolios at Wittenborn, an antiquarian bookstore that also sold artists' books and portfolios. Two of Barnett Newman's etchings, *Untitled Etching #1* (cat. 42) and *#2* were purchased from M. Knoedler & Company on the same trip. In all cases, these were "catch-up" purchases in that the prints had been made and published earlier, but the Andersons recognized that they would be important additions to the complete collection they were trying to put together. The Newman prints, for example, had been published that same year by ULAE, but because the Andersons did not have a subscription with ULAE, they sought them from a New York dealer.

In fact, the Andersons never obtained a subscription directly from ULAE. Instead they committed to buy ULAE prints from John Berggruen, a young art dealer who had just opened up his gallery in downtown San Francisco in 1970. (Berggruen was fortunate enough to have become acquainted with ULAE in its early days when he worked in New York. He was later one of a chosen few who were offered a subscription opportunity.) Berggruen remembers that his early success in selling ULAE prints was due in large part to the Andersons' commitment to buy "one of everything" from his gallery. "There weren't a lot of people in

San Francisco buying prints by contemporary artists in those days."[9] The Andersons developed a strong relationship with Berggruen that resulted in purchases not only of ULAE prints but other works as well. Mary Patricia "Putter" Anderson Pence recalls that Berggruen became a friend of the family, often presenting works for sale from a portfolio on the Andersons' living room floor after a game of tennis with her father.[10]

Other local galleries, Albert Smith's Atherton Gallery and Gump's Gallery in San Francisco in particular, continued to be a source for acquisitions in 1970 and 1971, especially for works by California artists and also for the Andersons' growing collection of Pop Art prints. The deluxe, multi-artist edition of *1¢ Life* (cat. 3) was purchased from the bookstore at the California Palace of the Legion of Honor and several screenprints from Andy Warhol's *Campbell's Soup II* series were purchased from Gump's.[11] Although it was unusual for them at the time, in 1971 the Andersons also acquired prints directly from artists, including *Blue Meander* (cat. 56) from Anni Albers and the *To Edgar Allen Poe* portfolio of lithographs (cat. 71) from Nathan Oliveira.

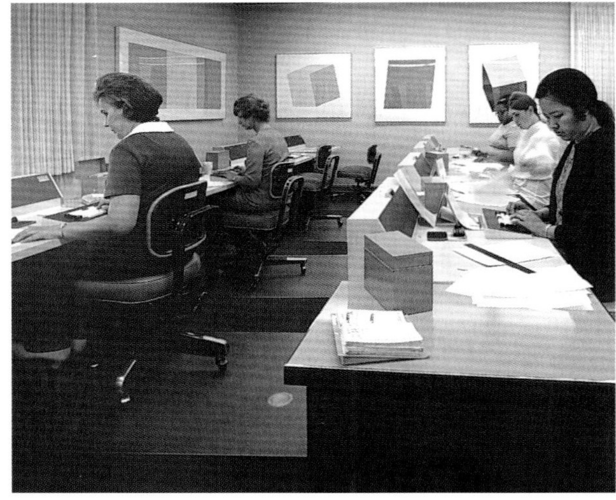

2

It became established practice for the Andersons to frame and install new print purchases at their home or at Saga in the lobbies, conference rooms, hallways, and offices. The installations at Saga were always directed by Mr. Anderson, and each work was identified with a museum-style wall label. Generally the installations were well-received by Saga employees, although Mr. Anderson tells the story of one that was not (fig. 2):

> In those days of early computers, the work of a keypunch operator was a laborious activity. The operators worked at desks in long rows in large open rooms. One weekend we had installed a group of Jasper Johns's prints (*Souvenir, Device, Evion, Zone,* and *Fool's House* [cat. 68]) in the keypunch room. All the prints featured backgrounds in various shades of gray. Well, after about a week, a delegation from the keypunch room came to see me. They explained that while they enjoyed the art program, they weren't growing fond of the Johns prints. After all, their work consisted of punching cards at a keyboard all day. Couldn't they have something a little more lively? I had the "gray" prints taken down and more colorful prints by Ellsworth Kelly were installed in their place![12]

The Andersons' sensitivity to art in the Saga offices blossomed in the 1970s into an educational program for employees as well as members of the nearby communities of Stanford and Palo Alto. The Andersons arranged for an art library to be available to employees in one office building and sponsored talks on prints by artists.[13] Such ambitious programs eventually necessitated additional management, even as the Andersons functioned as their own curators in the selection and placement of art in their home and at Saga. In 1975, encouraged by their good friend Professor Albert Elsen at the nearby Stanford University Department of Art, the Andersons invited Stanford graduate students to intern at the collection, which by then included a considerable number of paintings, drawings, and sculpture as well as over 300 prints. Despite the obvious emphasis on prints, the students were encouraged to use the entire collection as their laboratory. Over the years, student investigations of the collection greatly enhanced the educational program for employees, with didactic labels and brochures on a variety of art topics available throughout the office complex.

1
An art installation in the lobby of the Saga Corporation office complex, ca. 1974. The six prints of Lichtenstein's *Cathedral Series* [cat. 44–49] are featured on the balcony wall.

2
The keypunch office at Saga with an installation of Ellsworth Kelly's prints, ca. 1973.

During the early 1970s, the Gemini publications continued to impress the Andersons. Gemini was a main source for print acquisitions with the Andersons retaining their two subscriptions through 1972. Gemini's marketing and publicity was informative and friendly. Casual notes passed between Gemini director Sidney Felsen and Mr. Anderson. Ordering prints was made easy through subscriber information sheets, slides, and lists with prices and selection options. Gemini also kept the Andersons abreast of developments in the print market with frequent mailings of "Current Fair Market Values" for Gemini prints published since 1966. Reprints of magazine articles on topics such as the print market, contemporary art appreciation, and connoisseurship were also sent, courtesy of Gemini.[14]

The quality of the Anderson collection of Gemini prints soon came to the attention of the San Francisco museum community. In 1971 Ian White, director of the Fine Arts Museums of San Francisco, asked the Andersons about the possibility of an exhibition featuring their collection at the M. H. de Young Memorial Museum. The Andersons agreed and Gunter Troche of the Museums' Achenbach Foundation for Graphic Arts was assigned as curator. The exhibition, *American Graphics, Reliefs, and Sculptures from the Gemini G.E.L. Workshop: The Collection of Mr. and Mrs. Harry W. Anderson*, opened on 10 June 1971 and featured 140 works by eight artists: Joseph Albers, Jasper Johns, Ellsworth Kelly, Roy Lichtenstein, Claes Oldenburg, Kenneth Price, Robert Rauschenberg, and Frank Stella. It was reviewed favorably by the local press and the Andersons were pleased by this first major exposure of their collection. True to their wishes, however, and duly noted in newspaper reviews, the emphasis of the exhibition was to provide insight into the creativity of artists at an innovative print workshop, rather than on the collecting efforts of the Andersons.[15]

Other exhibitions drawn from the print collection soon followed and paved the way for the establishment of a private collection-sharing program that brought the Anderson Collection into many museums and galleries. The Andersons provided access to their collection with public tours, generously underwriting loans to museums in order to share their contemporary art. Mrs. Anderson was particularly involved with a program she initiated at the Sacred Heart School in Menlo Park, where she was a trustee and daughter Putter was a student. With permission from the principal, Sister Nancy Morris R.S.H., to install art in the attractive corridor of the school's main building, Mrs. Anderson organized several exhibitions with Kit Pravda, a friend who had many connections in the Bay Area art community. Among Mrs. Anderson's favorites were an exhibition of Frank Stella's work that included paintings, prints, drawings, and assemblages from the Anderson Collection, and a Diebenkorn monotype exhibition with works borrowed from the John Berggruen Gallery. Mrs. Anderson remembers that the installations were a labor of love, involving family and friends. (Mr. Anderson often adjusted the lighting and Bob Mahoney and Charlie Strong from Gump's frequently offered assistance.) The program continued for many years and the exhibition space became known as the Art Corridor. Later it was directed by professional curators who presented art from other sources in addition to the Anderson Collection.

By the late 1970s, with exhibition spaces at the Andersons' home and the Saga complex nearly filled, the Andersons' print collecting activity slowed considerably. Nevertheless, they continued to add selectively to the print collection with purchases from fine art presses and galleries, in addition to Gemini G.E.L., that had begun to flourish at mid-decade: Crown Point Press, Cirrus Editions, Institute for Experimental Printmaking (later Experimental Workshop), Pace Editions, Inc., Tyler Graphics, Ltd., and many others.[16]

Their passion for collecting art remained strong, the "visual experience" or the one-on-one experience with an artwork that took on new importance at this time continuing into the 1980s. The Andersons (including teenaged Putter) were indefatigable museum- and gallery-goers, making annual trips to New York to see new work at previews. Just as it was important for them to receive pre-publication notices for prints, it also became important for them to attend gallery openings so that they could see the work and select the best for their collection. Acquisition records show that they would sometime purchase several works from a single gallery show, often visiting artists' studios and in many cases becoming friends with the artists as well as patrons. A visit to Ellsworth Kelly's studio and the purchase of his major painting *Black Ripe* (1955) led to a friendship that resulted in Kelly's creation of a limited edition (of three) printed portrait of *Hunk, Moo, and Ellsworth* (p. 10). Kelly had used photographs taken by Leo Holub at a University Art Museum, Berkeley, opening of a Kelly print show in 1989 and, unbeknown to the Andersons, transformed them into an artistic record of the friendship.

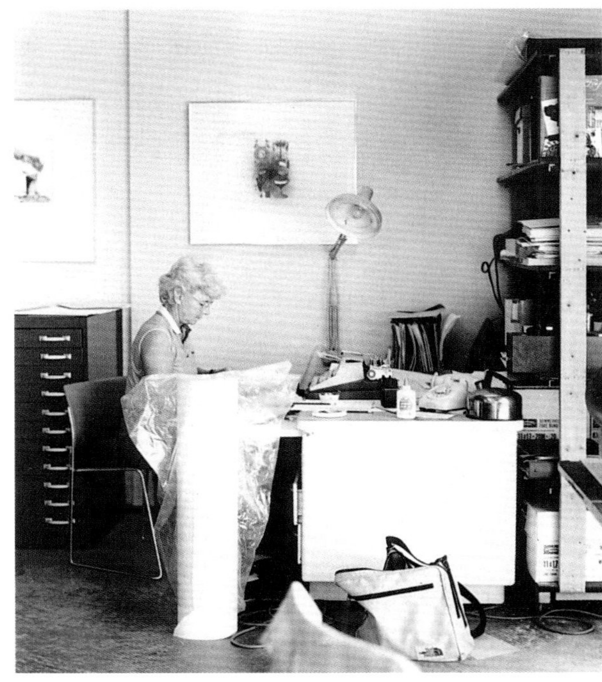

3

In addition to artists' studios, the Andersons also visited workshops of fine art presses where they observed firsthand and with great interest the practices of contemporary printmaking. In 1978 they visited the Bedford Village studios of Kenneth Tyler, who had left Gemini in 1973 to found his own press, Tyler Graphics, Ltd. There they saw the "Handmade Paper Project" (colored, pressed paper pulp monoprints) by Kenneth Noland and were intrigued by this new form of art making. Only a few months before, they had purchased similar pieces by Noland produced at Garner Tullis's Experimental Workshop in San Francisco. At Tyler, they purchased several works by Noland from the *Circle I* and *II* series, and later, *Paper Pool 14: Sprungbett mit Schatten* (1978) by David Hockney, which had been created using the same process.

The Andersons identify the visit to Tyler and observing this new process as influential in their decision to become involved in collecting innovative forms of printmaking. At about the same time, they also became interested in monotypes through Paula Kirkeby, whose Smith Andersen Gallery had exhibited examples by Nathan Oliveira in 1970 and 1973. "Paula and I talked about how we'd like to encourage more artists to make monotypes," said Mrs. Anderson, "and maybe we'd start a business publishing them. Before long we had convinced Joe Goldyne to join us. He was an artist who had done some beautiful monotypes and really understood the process."[17] The three formed 3EP, Ltd.,[18] in Palo Alto with the specific idea of publishing unique prints, primarily monotypes, and also intaglio prints. Over the course of five years, the press hosted twenty artists, many of them from the Bay Area, but also a large number who were active in Southern California. "Hunk and I were buying a lot of work by Southern California artists, and Paula had always shown work by Sam Francis and others, so it was natural to want to invite them to work with us. I loved working there and, even though I was pretty much the official 'bill-payer' and administrator, I learned so much about how artists work"(fig. 3).[19]

The first monotype published by the press in 1978 was *Asparagus* by Goldyne. The Andersons greatly admired the piece and asked Goldyne if he would create a group of monotypes in portfolio form on the subject of fruit and vegetables as a privately commissioned work. The result was the *Produce* portfolio,

3
Mrs. Anderson in the office
at 3EP, Ltd., ca. 1979.

twelve monotypes, each with a different fruit or vegetable as its subject, printed on elegant, unbound folio sheets and encased in a box, also designed by Goldyne (cat. 113–124). (The Andersons also acquired the cognates [second impressions] that Goldyne had hand-colored (cat. 125–136). Goldyne's twelve images on the subject of food made them a natural choice for illustrations in the 1979 Saga Corporation calendar. It was the first of two Saga calendars featuring prints from the Anderson Collection. The second was the 1981 calendar featuring selections from Wayne Thiebaud's *Delights* series of prints, also on the subject of food (fig. 4).

The press thrived through the following five years, with publications by Laddie John Dill, Sam Francis, David Gilhooly, Ed Moses, Miklos Pogany, Matt Phillips, and many others.[20] In 1983, however, the original partnership was restructured with Mrs. Anderson and Putter Anderson, who was living in Southern California, continuing to publish prints as 3EP.[21] Putter Anderson, who had graduated with a business degree from the University of Southern California, wanted to combine her interest in art with her expertise in business; the print publishing enterprise was a natural fit for her. Their first project together, begun in 1984 and published in 1985, was with Laddie John Dill, who had previously worked at 3EP and had expressed an interest in working with molded paper. For this project Charles Hilger, an artist and teacher with tremendous expertise in cast paper technology, created paper that was molded to Dill's specifications. The sheets of molded paper were then sent to Dill's Los Angeles studio, where he painted them (cat. 154).

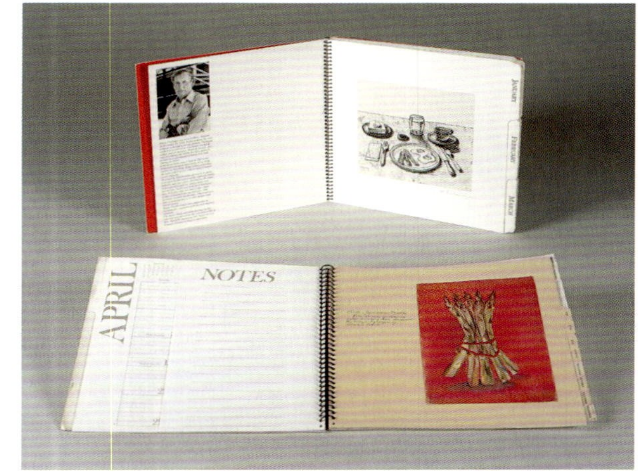

4

By 1986 Putter had married businessman J. Blair Pence II and begun to immerse herself in the Los Angeles art scene (an internship with curator Maurice Tuchman at the Los Angeles County Museum of Art, a job with Sam Francis organizing his personal collection of photographs, and a position at the Melinda Wyatt Gallery). She decided to open her own gallery, the Pence Gallery, in Santa Monica and hired Christopher Ford from New York as director. The Pence Gallery exhibited prints from the 3EP inventory and various other American presses, as well as prints by emerging artists. The Andersons credit their daughter with providing opportunities for them to see new work by familiar and unfamiliar artists through her gallery. "We've extended our interest on her initiative," Mr. Anderson explains.[22] Over a four-year period prints by Susan Rothenberg, Kiki Smith, Robert Therrien, Tim Rollins + K.O.S., and Elizabeth Murray were added to the Anderson Collection as a result of Putter's introduction.

In 1986 the Saga Corporation was acquired by the Marriott Corporation, and in 1987 the Saga building complex (which had grown from two to five buildings, including one dedicated to art storage) was sold to the Henry J. Kaiser Family Foundation and was renamed Quadrus. Under an agreement reached with the foundation, the art collection remained and its programs continued for the new tenants. That same year Dee Weldon White was appointed administrative director of the Anderson Art Collection at Quadrus and over the next ten years she ably assisted Mr. Anderson with the management of the ever-growing collection with its inventory of over 700 prints. During the 1980s, prints from the Anderson Collection were frequently seen at the Stanford University Museum of Art in exhibitions organized by Betsy Fryberger, curator of prints and drawings.[23]

The decade of the 1990s brought significant changes to the contemporary art market and to the Anderson Collection as well. The Pence Gallery was closed in 1992 with Putter Pence's decision to devote her

4
The Saga Corporation calendar for 1979, featuring reproductions of Joseph Goldyne's *Produce* monotypes (foreground), and the calendar for 1981 featuring reproductions of Wayne Thiebaud's *Delights* etchings (background).

full time to family. That same year the Andersons announced the major gift of six paintings and one sculpture to the San Francisco Museum of Modern Art, which had just broken ground on a new museum building. Four years later in July 1996, the Andersons made another major donation, a group of 656 prints, to the Fine Arts Museums of San Francisco. This re-gifting (the collection had previously been donated to the Stanford Museum in 1991) was met with great excitement by the Bay Area art community. The collection was titled the Anderson Graphic Arts Collection at the Fine Arts Museums of San Francisco and was transferred to the newly remodeled California Palace of the Legion of Honor with its state-of-the-art exhibition, conservation, and storage facilities. In February 1997 the Anderson Gallery of Contemporary Graphic Art was unveiled at the Legion of Honor accompanied by the Fine Arts Museums' commitment to exhibit works from the Anderson gift and other important contemporary graphics from the prints and drawings department (the Achenbach Foundation for Graphic Arts) and its Crown Point Press archive.[24]

In addition, the Fine Arts Museums announced the continuation of the Anderson Collection Sharing Program, begun at Stanford in 1992, which would allow small and mid-sized institutions to access the collection for exhibition loans at nominal cost. This was important to the Andersons as it guaranteed the continuation of their own generous lending policy and meant that the collection could potentially be enjoyed by a larger audience.

The Andersons and Putter Pence have been extremely active with the collection at the Fine Arts Museums, providing financial assistance for acquisitions of a print by Roy Lichtenstein (cat. 190), renovation of frames, and support for the annual Anderson lecture series, which has featured speakers Riva Castleman (1997), Frank Stella (1998), and Bill Goldston (2000).

Making sure that the collection continues to grow and that its programs thrive at the Museums has been a major interest of the Andersons. At the same time, they still enjoy searching for new work by familiar names and, with their daughter's ongoing help, new work by new names. Over the years, they have developed various collecting strategies, some of which continue to work for them. One of the early plans that is no longer used was modeled on a Saga business plan entitled "Management by Objective." In the late 1960s, Helen Heninger with Mr. Anderson adapted that plan and the managment style of Saga to the Andersons' art collecting efforts by defining "Key Result Areas" (of art) and rating artists within each area by collection priority. It provided a way for the Andersons to focus their collecting as the art scene exploded with activity in the late 1960s and early 1970s. Later that decade the approach was amplified by the print subscription plans that provided immediate exposure to new trends and further advantageous acquisition opportunities. All along, the Andersons continually developed an eye for great art by seeing as much of it as possible and by including their daughter, Putter Pence: "We've always been interested in new ideas that drive us to take the next step in collecting. It might be another step in the present, or a leap into the future. We make a decision and we don't wait for validation before continuing on. We are passionate collectors and the journey is just too exciting."[25]

Notes

1 Mrs. Anderson, conversation with author, 21 September 1999.

2 Mr. Anderson, conversation with author, 21 September 1999.

3 For an in-depth history of the Anderson Collection, see Rachel Teagle's essay, "A Modern Touch: The History of the Anderson Collection" in *Celebrating Modern Art: The Anderson Collection,* exh. cat. (San Francisco: San Francisco Museum of Modern Art, 2000).

4 Saga Corporation was a leading food-service company with operations throughout the United States and Canada.

5 The subscription program at Gemini, begun in 1968, consisted of a one-year contract in which the subscriber committed to buy one print from each edition published in that year at a special subscriber's price (a discounted publication price).

6 Gemini G.E.L. had published prints since its founding in 1966. The Andersons decided to purchase important works published from 1966 to 1968 that were sold-out editions. Prints such as Josef Albers's *White Line Square* series (1966), Rauschenberg's *Booster* (1967), and Claes Oldenburg's *Notes* portfolio (1968) had to be purchased through the secondary market. The Andersons were successful in finding the necessary impressions to complete the Gemini collection by 1982.

7 Mr. Anderson, conversation with author, 28 July 1999.

8 Mr. Anderson, conversation with author, 28 July 1999.

9 John Berggruen, conversation with author, 19 August 1999.

10 Putter Pence, conversation with author, 6 October 1999.

11 The Warhol prints remained in the collection until they were sold in 1989. The Andersons never pursued Warhol's work as avidly as other Pop artists. Today, there are no works by Warhol in the collection.

12 Mr. Anderson, conversation with author, 21 September 1999.

13 For a more complete description of the employee programs, see Teagle, "A Modern Touch," 24.

14 Three such articles that remain in the Andersons' "Gemini" file are: Frank Whitford,"You're the Tops," a summary of Dr. Willi Bogard's survey of the top twenty artists in contemporary world art in *Capital*, a German business magazine, in *Studio International* (February 1973): 211–12; Jacob Kainen,"Quality in Edition Prints," *Art News* (March 1974); and "On Art: The Revival of Lithography," *Architectural Digest* (March-April 1971): 4, 68–77.

15 Marilyn Crawford, "American Graphics, Reliefs, and Sculptures," *Artweek* (7 August 1971): 12; Arthur Bloomfield, "A Carnival of Pop Art," an undated, unattributed newspaper article; Charles Long, "Major Showing of Contemporary Graphics, Reliefs, and Sculpture," an undated press release from the M. H. de Young Memorial Museum.

16 The Andersons never acquired works from the Tamarind Institute, Albuquerque, although many artists whose prints they collected had worked at the Tamarind Lithography Workshop in Los Angeles. Mr. Anderson believes this may have been because they were not aware they could acquire prints directly from Tamarind. Tamarind's own publishing program was not active until after its move to New Mexico in 1970.

17 Mrs. Anderson, conversation with author, 21 September 1999.

18 The name for 3EP, Ltd., is derived from the "3 Equal Partners": Anderson, Goldyne, and Kirkeby, who each invested $2,500 in the enterprise.

19 Mrs. Anderson, conversation with author, 21 September 1999.

20 The Andersons had two sets of works produced by 3EP. Mr. Anderson was an early subscriber and Mrs. Anderson, as a partner, received one from every published set or series. Currently, one set resides at the Stanford University Hospital, where it is exhibited as a long-term loan.

21 Kirkeby subsequently established Smith Andersen Editions in 1984. Goldyne left the press prior to 1980.

22 Mr. Anderson, conversation with author, 6 October 1999.

23 The Stanford Museum exhibitions with publications were: "From the Collection of Mr. and Mrs. Harry W. Anderson: Selected Prints by Robert Motherwell," 9 May–17 August 1986; "From the Collection of Mr. and Mrs. Harry W. Anderson: Selected Prints by Richard Diebenkorn," 5 May–16 August 1987; "The Anderson Collection: Two Decades of American Graphics, 1967–1987," 29 September 1987–3 January 1988.

24 The gallery at the Legion of Honor is temporary and will move to a larger space at the new M. H. de Young Memorial Museum when it opens in 2005.

25 Mr. Anderson, conversation with author, 6 October 1999.

From top to bottom:
Mary Margaret Anderson
Harry W. Anderson
Mary Patricia Anderson Pence

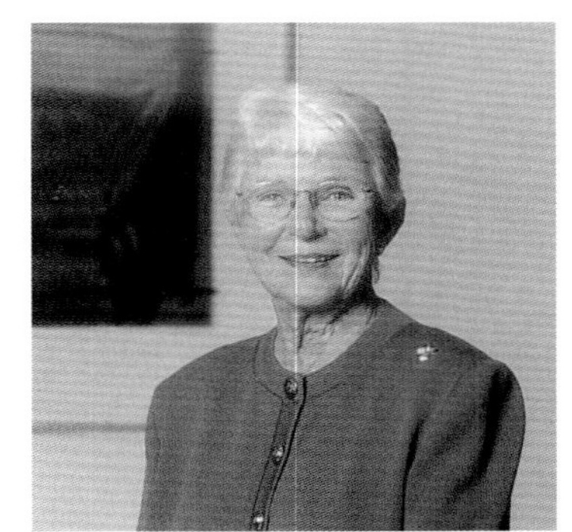

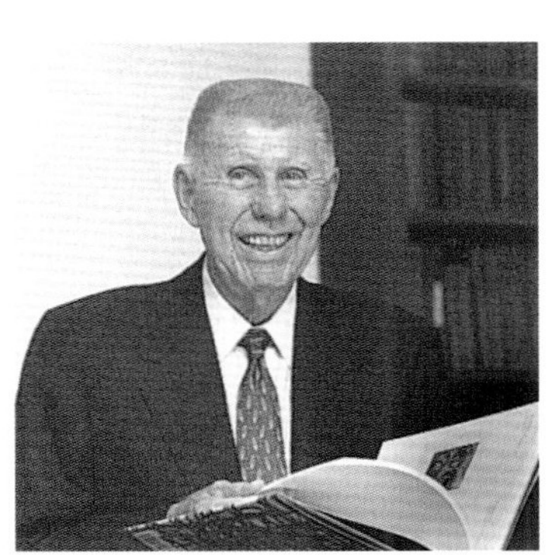

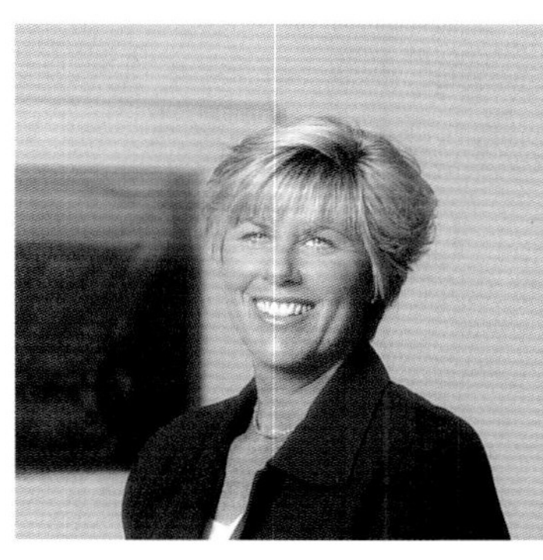

The decade of the 1960s has often been described as "explosive" for the development of the contemporary print as a primary art form in America. Yet, by today's standards, the appearance of most prints made in the early 1960s seems relatively tame. Tentative though these early efforts may appear today, prints made in the early to mid-1960s were revolutionary enough to change the face of American printmaking. Given the fairly representative selection in the Anderson Graphic Arts Collection, a visual review of these early works and their workshop origins reveals innovation and subtle change that prepared the way for the truly "explosive" prints that would appear later in the decade.

Previously considered a fairly commercial process, screenprint was utilized in a number of print projects in the early 1960s. With its ability to provide flat, pure, unmodulated color, it was the choice of many artists who were involved in the Pop and Op art movements that dominated the decade. Essentially a non-collaborative process (the artist provides a design for the print and is rarely involved in the cutting and inking of stencils) screenprint was the obvious vehicle for artists Josef Albers and Ad Reinhardt with their geometric, hard-edged, abstract compositions, and Robert Indiana with his optically charged color numeral subjects. While the screenprints of these artists were not especially large, they packed tremendous visual power with bold color combinations and Precisionist rendering that appealed directly to hip, young, educated American audiences eager to collect art.

Artists were also drawn to collaborative printmaking, especially when New York and California emerged in the 1960s as centers for printmaking by virtue of their being homes to revivals of lithography and etching. Many young artists, among them Lee Bontecou, Jasper Johns, and Robert Rauschenberg, were introduced to lithography through Universal Limited Art Editions (ULAE) in West Islip, New York, and Tamarind Lithography Workshop in Los Angeles, founded in 1957 and 1962 respectively. Other artists were introduced to new ways of etching at Crown Point Press, founded in 1962 in the San Francisco Bay Area.

The initial publications of these presses, east and west, were modest from the start. Many reflected, for the most part, an artist's simultaneous efforts in painting. Some examples were very successful, such as Robert Motherwell's *Summertime in Italy* and Richard Diebenkorn's *41 Etchings Drypoints*, but they brought no great innovation to classic printmaking traditions. Even Joseph Albers's translation of his *Homage to the Square* paintings to the *White Line Squares* lithographs seems conservatively executed. However, these three print projects and others like them shared one thing: they were expertly printed and technically pristine in appearance. As such, they are examples of the high quality of printing guaranteed by master printers (in these examples—Irwin Hollander, Kathan Brown, and Kenneth Tyler) that would become common in the workshop production at American fine art presses.

It was not until Gemini G.E.L.'s publication of Rauschenberg's *Booster* in 1967 that the contemporary standard for new and different work took hold in a way that we can recognize today. *Booster*, at six feet high, was a very large print for the time. It combined lithography and screenprint, two processes not usually paired together, for dramatic effect. To make *Booster*, Rauschenberg collaborated with Tyler, a Tamarind-trained master printer, who established his lithographic print workshop, Gemini G.E.L., in Los Angeles and pushed accepted practice to more high-tech levels of production. *Booster* set the precedent for new contemporary prints that would emanate from the Gemini shop and from other print workshops soon thereafter. Prints that were to follow *Booster* at Gemini were large scale, bold and colorful, and technically ambitious. Johns's *Color Numeral Series* and Roy Lichtenstein's *Cathedral Series* are prime examples.

By the end of the decade, Rauschenberg, Johns, and Lichtenstein were considered the pioneers of a new kind of printmaking that involved stretching the limits of technique and production. Workshops and publishers eagerly adjusted their practice to the demands of artists with new and different ideas. In the 1970s, attracted by these accommodations, more artists became involved in printmaking and continued to innovate.

Looking at Prints: The 1960s

I

The 1960s

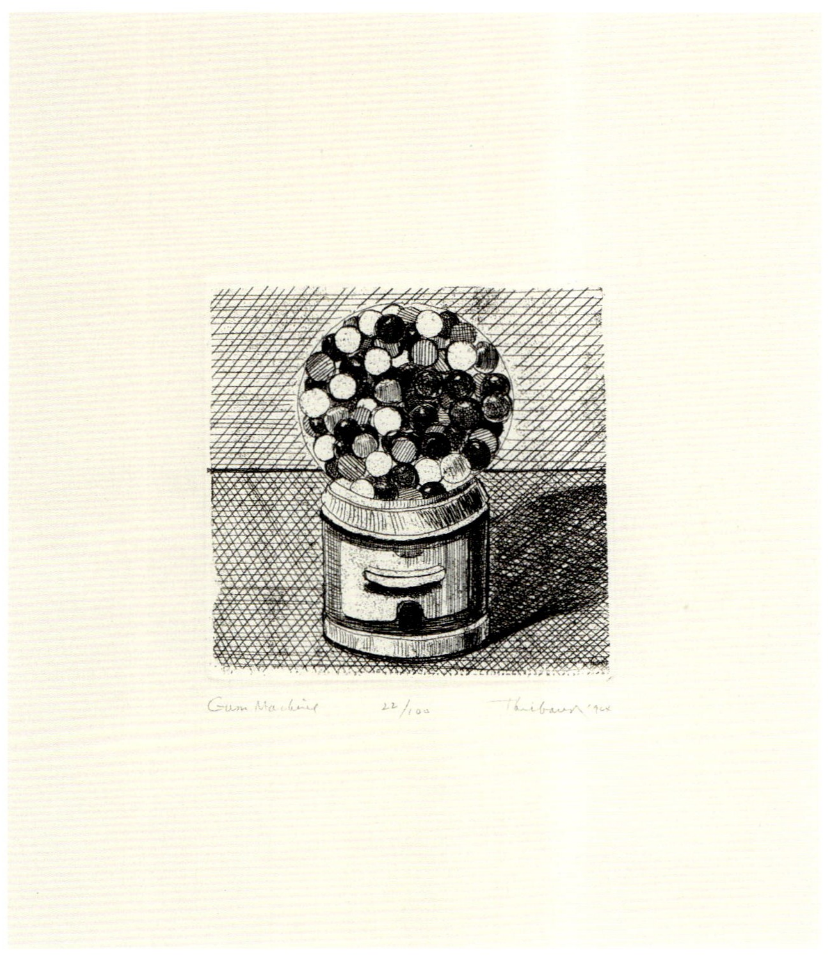

1

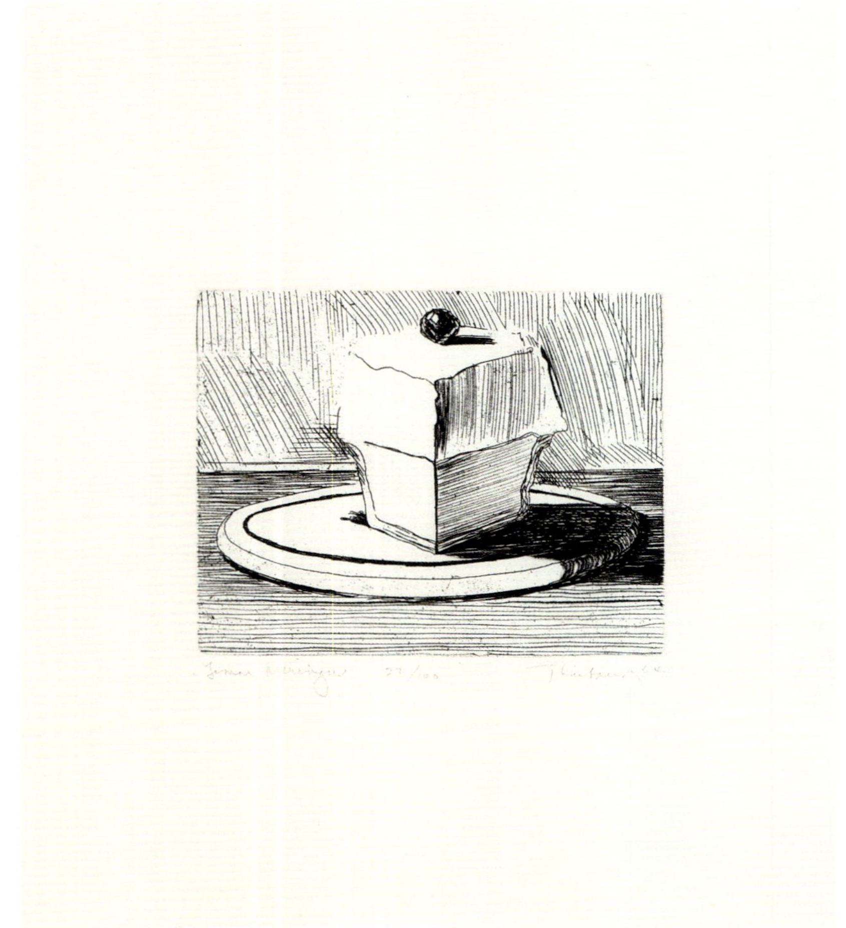

2

1
WAYNE THIEBAUD
Gum Machine,
from the portfolio *Delights,* 1965
Etching
$12\frac{7}{8}$ x $16\frac{7}{8}$ in. (sheet)

2
WAYNE THIEBAUD
Lemon Meringue,
from the portfolio *Delights,* 1965
Etching
$12\frac{7}{8}$ x $16\frac{7}{8}$ in. (sheet)

3
SAM FRANCIS
Pink Venus Kiki, in the book *1¢ Life,*
by Walasse Ting, 1964
Color lithograph
$16\frac{1}{16}$ x $11\frac{5}{15}$ in. (each page)

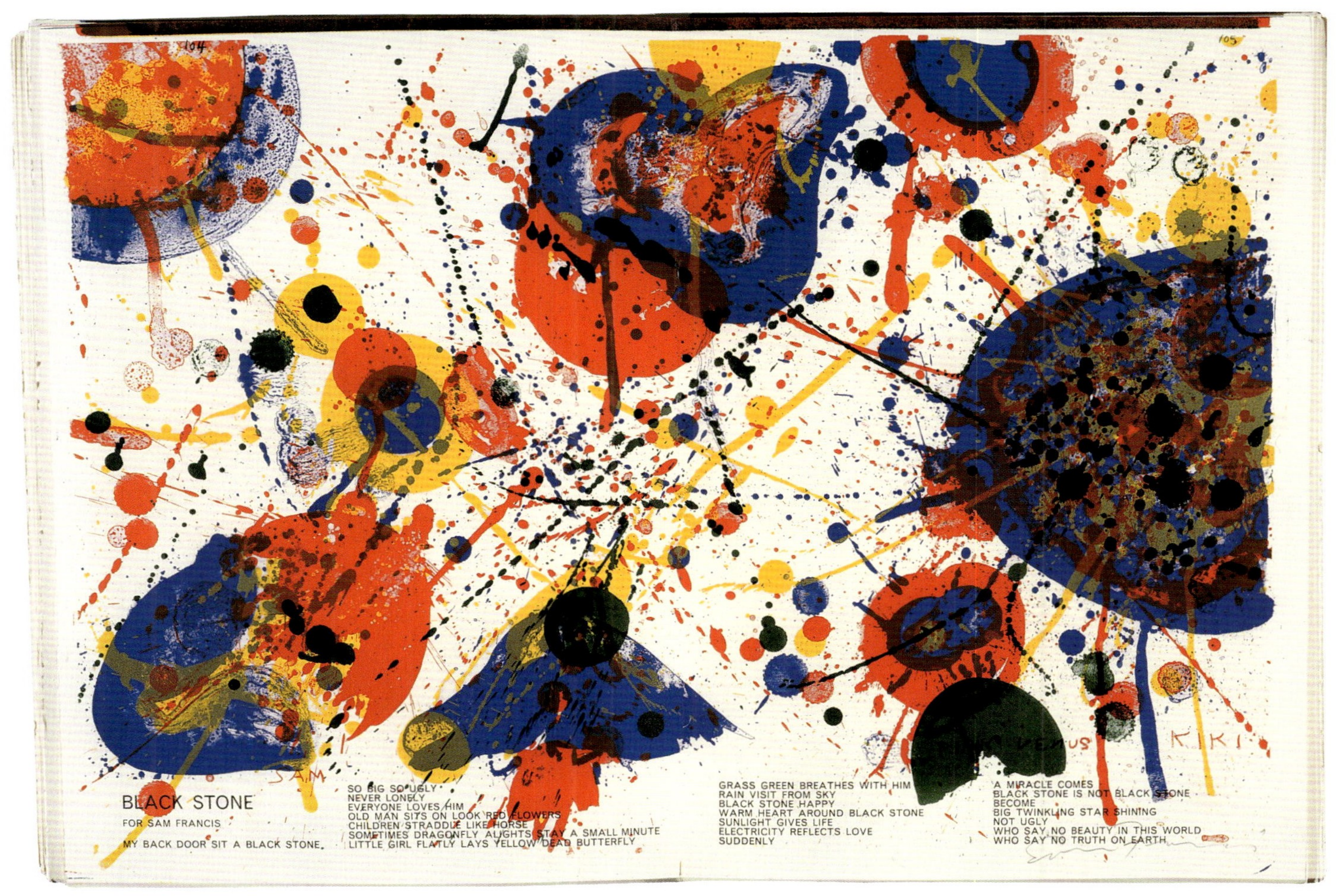
BLACK STONE
FOR SAM FRANCIS
MY BACK DOOR SIT A BLACK STONE.
SO BIG SO UGLY
NEVER LONELY
EVERYONE LOVES HIM
OLD MAN SITS ON LOOK RED FLOWERS
CHILDREN STRADDLE LIKE HORSE
SOMETIMES DRAGONFLY ALIGHTS STAY A SMALL MINUTE
LITTLE GIRL FLATLY LAYS YELLOW DEAD BUTTERFLY
GRASS GREEN BREATHES WITH HIM
RAIN VISIT FROM SKY
BLACK STONE HAPPY
WARM HEART AROUND BLACK STONE
SUNLIGHT GIVES LIFE
ELECTRICITY REFLECTS LOVE
SUDDENLY
A MIRACLE COMES
BLACK STONE IS NOT BLACK STONE
BECOME
BIG TWINKLING STAR SHINING
NOT UGLY
WHO SAY NO BEAUTY IN THIS WORLD
WHO SAY NO TRUTH ON EARTH

3

4
ROBERT MOTHERWELL
Summertime in Italy (with blue), 1965–1966
Color lithograph
30 x 22 in. (sheet)

5
RICHARD DIEBENKORN
Pl. 18 from the portfolio
41 Etchings Drypoints, 1965
Etching and drypoint
17¾ x 14¾ in. (sheet)

6
RICHARD DIEBENKORN
Pl. 26 from the portfolio
41 Etchings Drypoints, 1965
Aquatint, drypoint, and etching
17¾ x 14¾ in. (sheet)

7
RICHARD DIEBENKORN
Pl. 31 from the portfolio
41 Etchings Drypoints, 1965
Aquatint and etching
17¾ x 14¾ in. (sheet)

8
RICHARD DIEBENKORN
Pl. 33 from the portfolio
41 Etchings Drypoints, 1965
Aquatint, etching, and drypoint
17¾ x 14¾ in. (sheet)

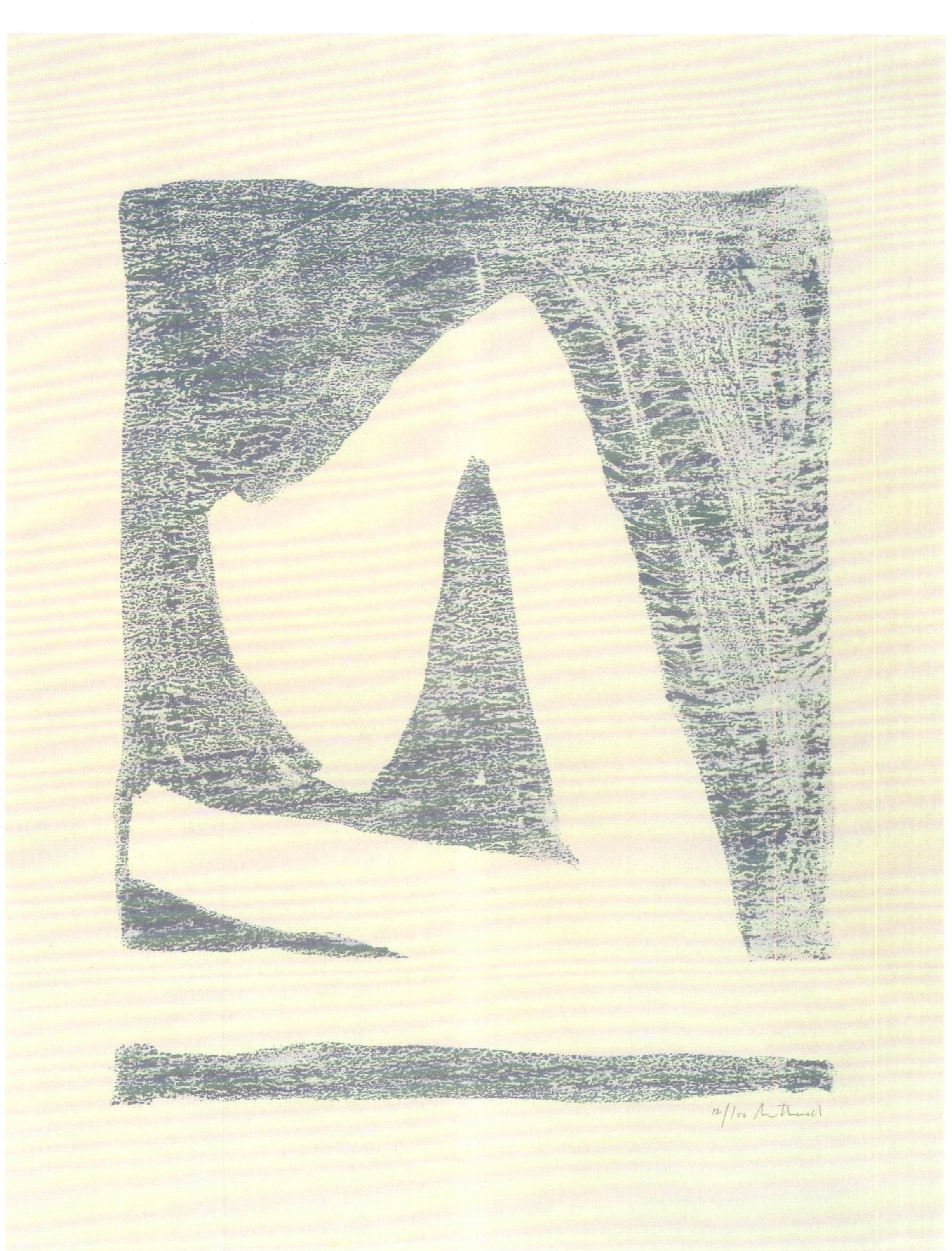

4

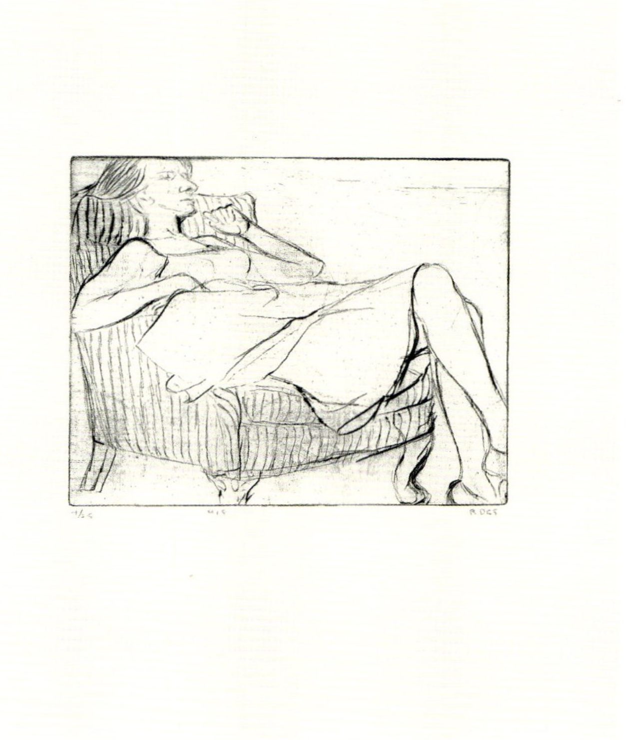

5

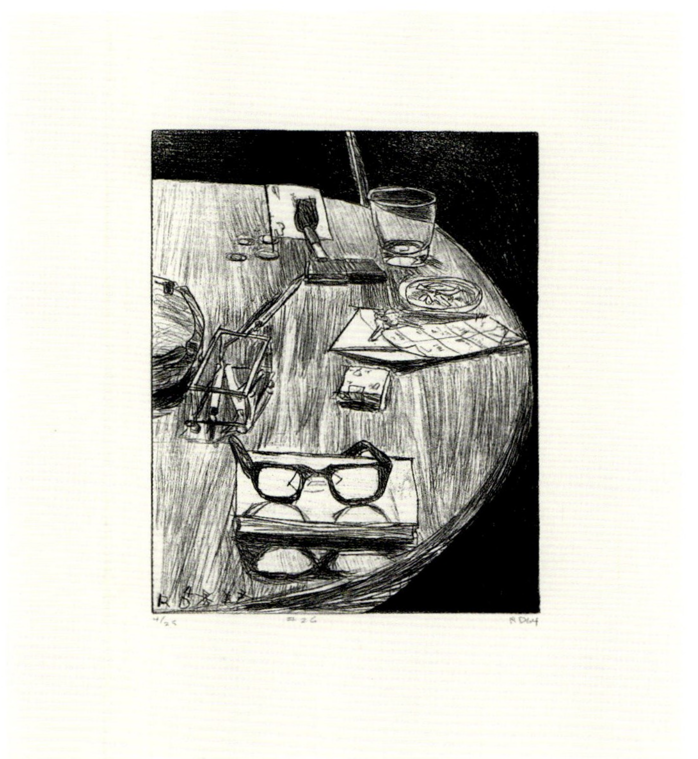

6

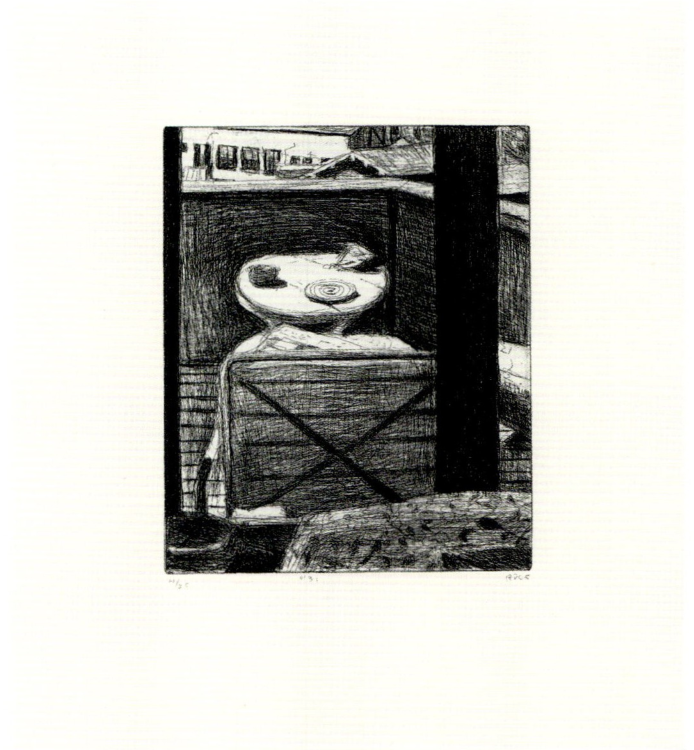

7

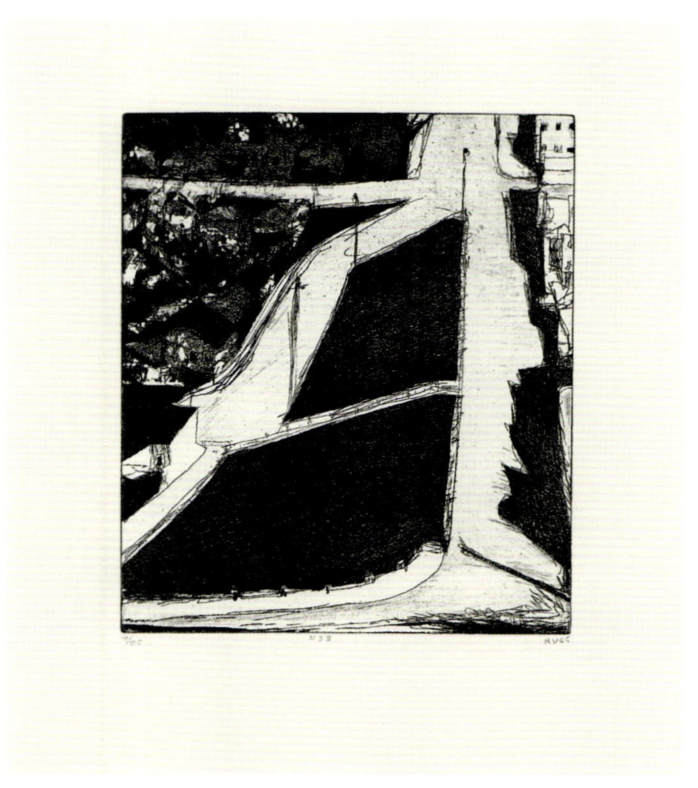

8

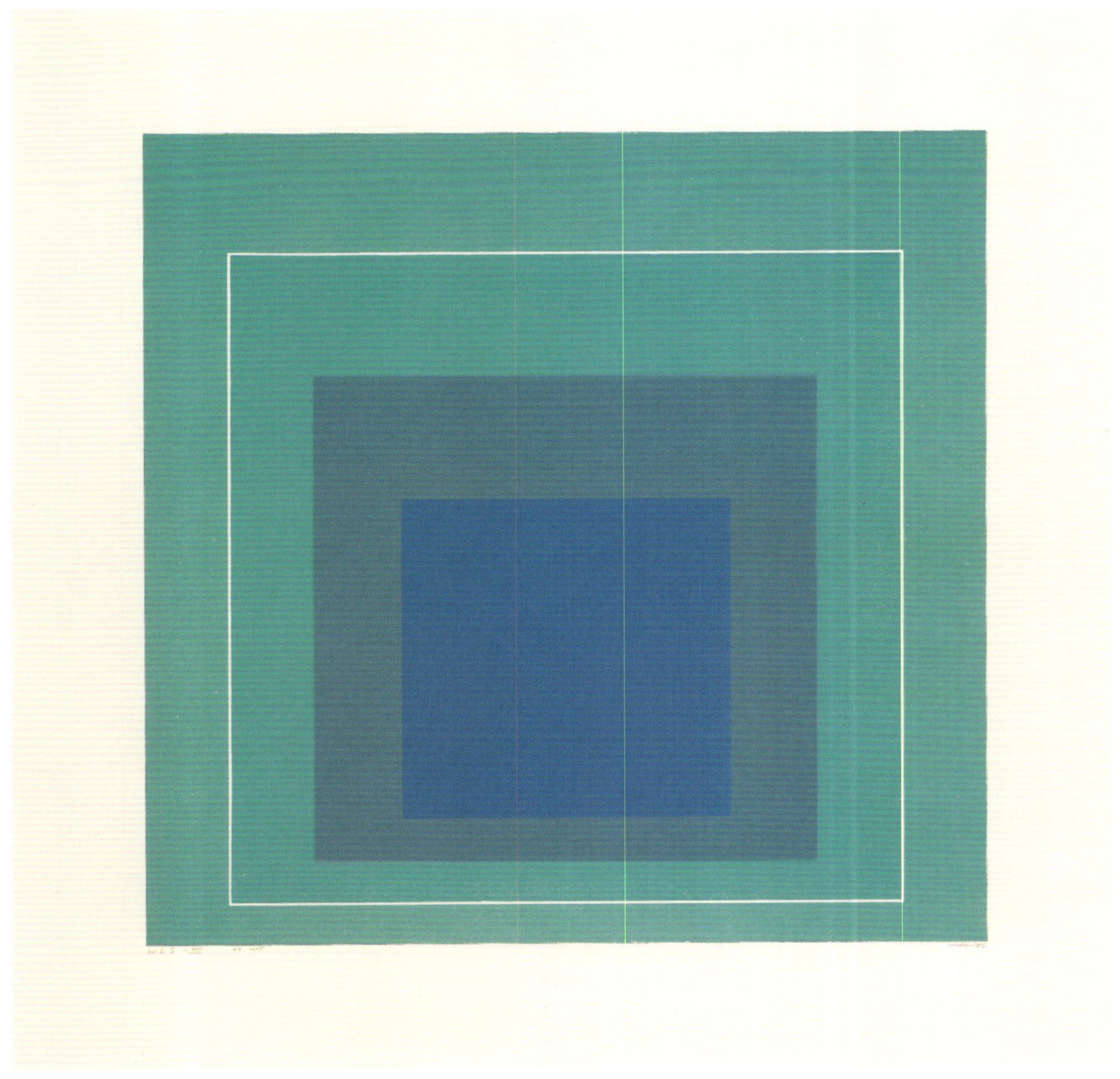

9

9
JOSEF ALBERS
White Line Square III,
from the series *White Line Squares,* 1966
Color lithograph
21 x 21 in. (sheet)

10
JOSEF ALBERS
White Line Square IV,
from the series *White Line Squares,* 1966
Color lithograph
21 x 21 in. (sheet)

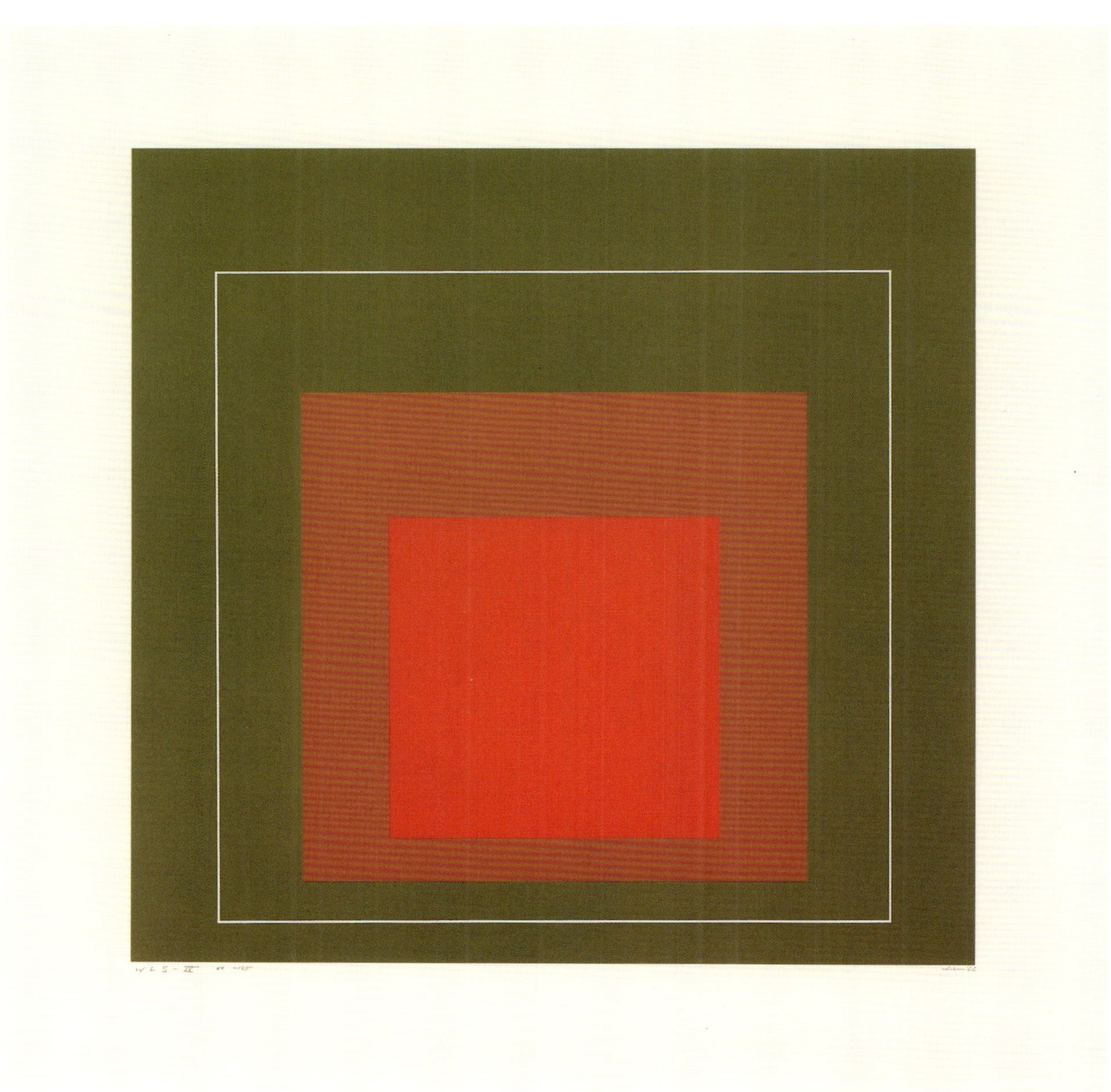

10

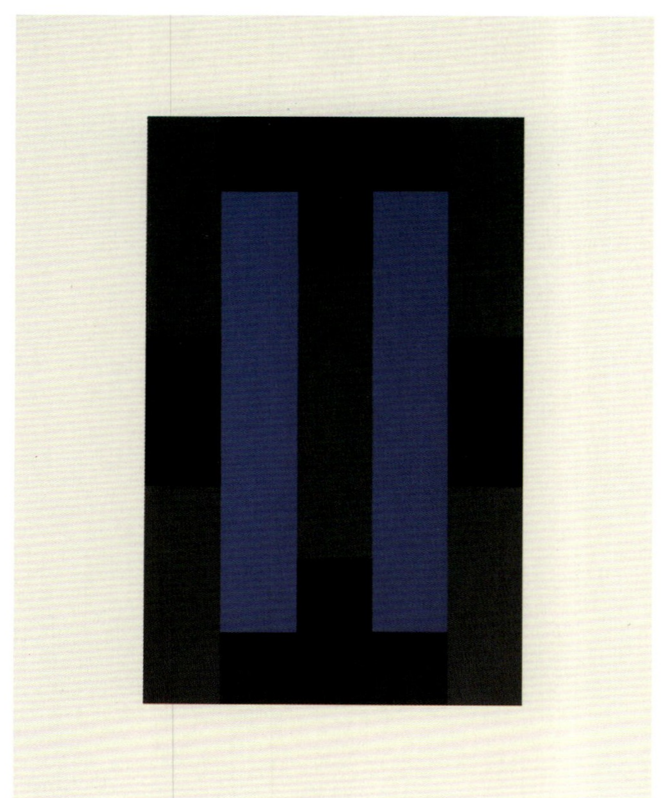

11

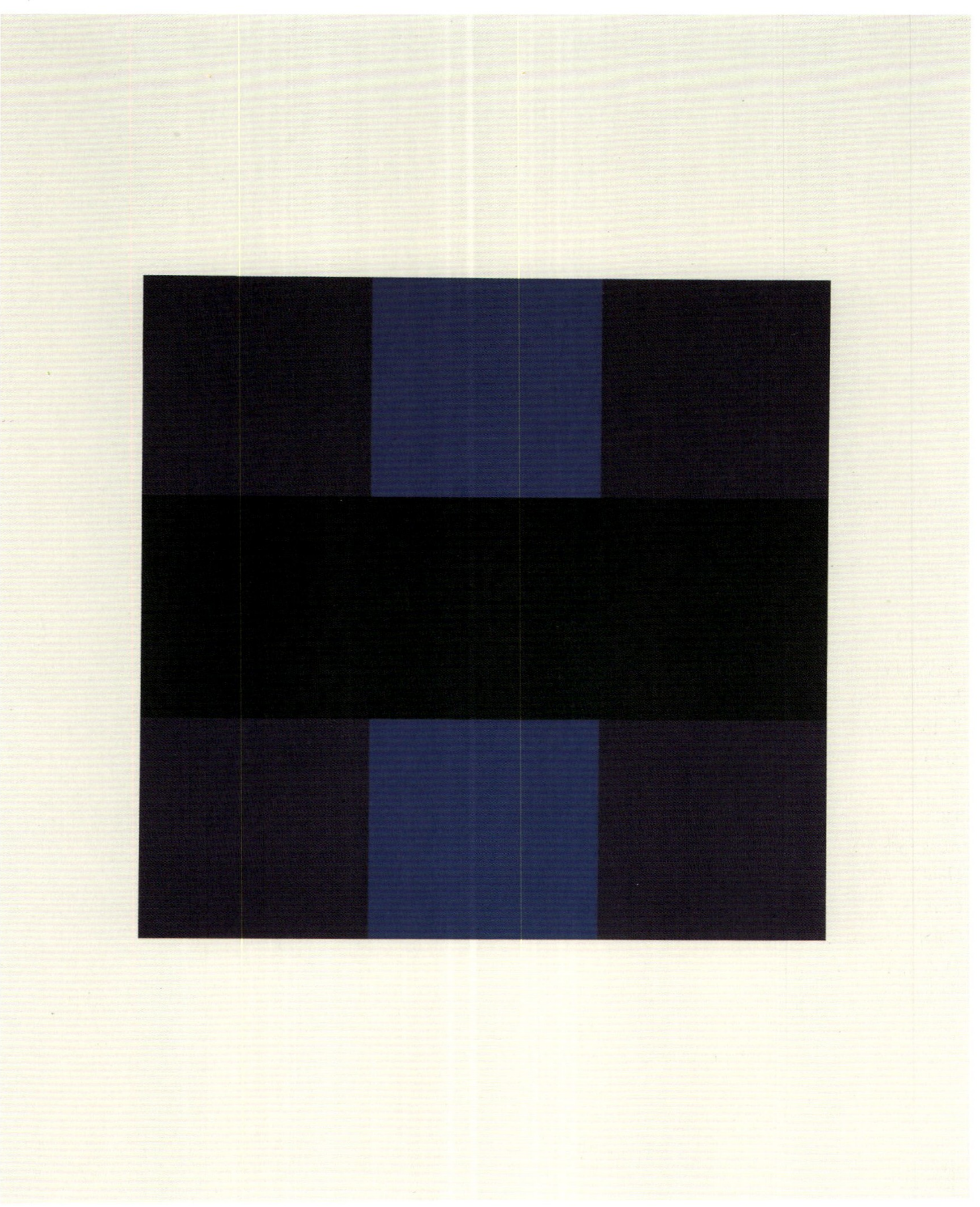

12

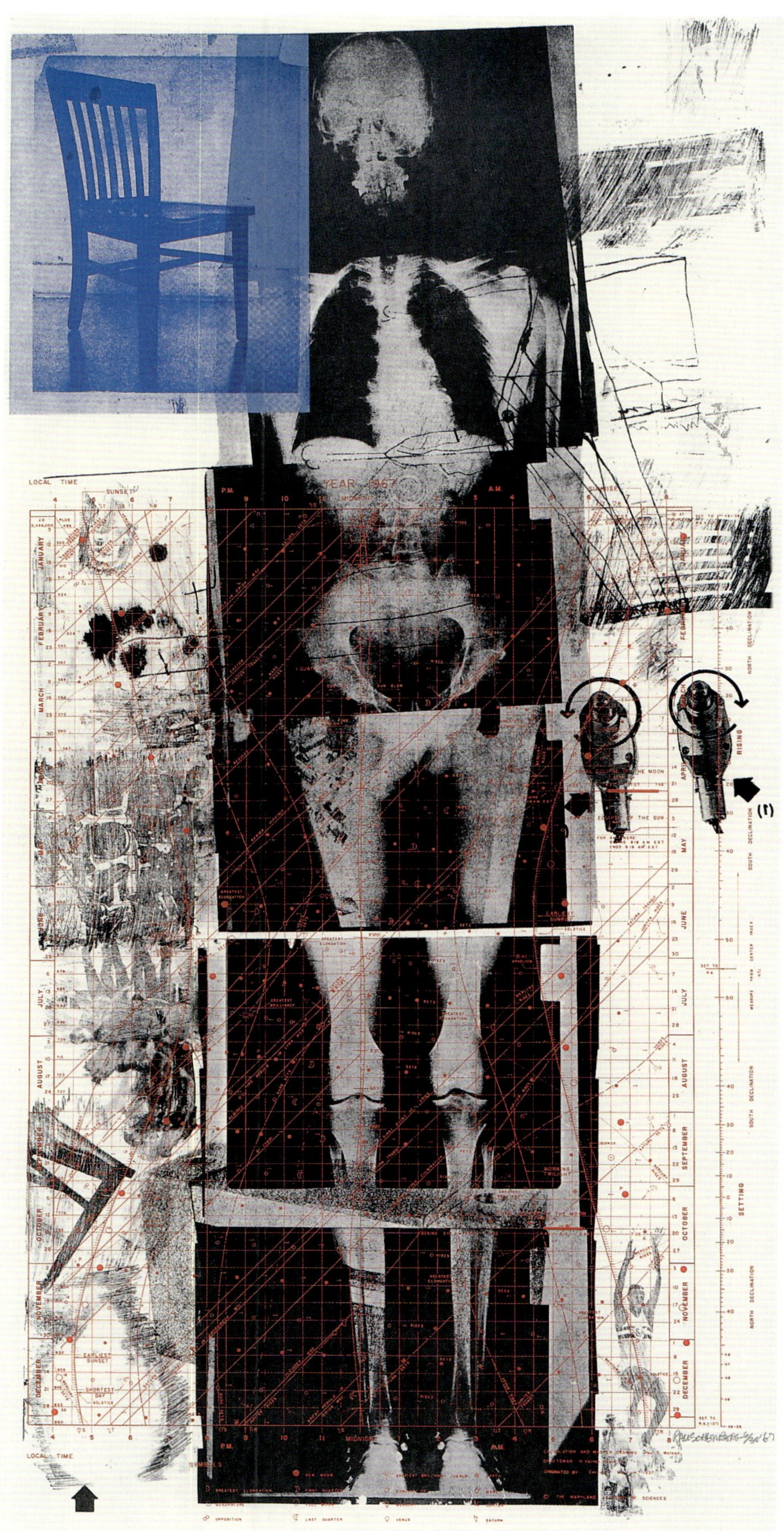

13

11
AD REINHARDT
Untitled #5,
from the portfolio *10 Pieces,* 1966
Color screenprint
$21\frac{3}{4}$ x $16\frac{13}{16}$ in. (sheet)

12
AD REINHARDT
Untitled #6,
from the portfolio *10 Pieces,* 1966
Color screenprint
$21\frac{3}{4}$ x $16\frac{13}{16}$ in. (sheet)

13
ROBERT RAUSCHENBERG
Booster, 1967
Color lithograph and screenprint
72 x 36 in. (sheet)

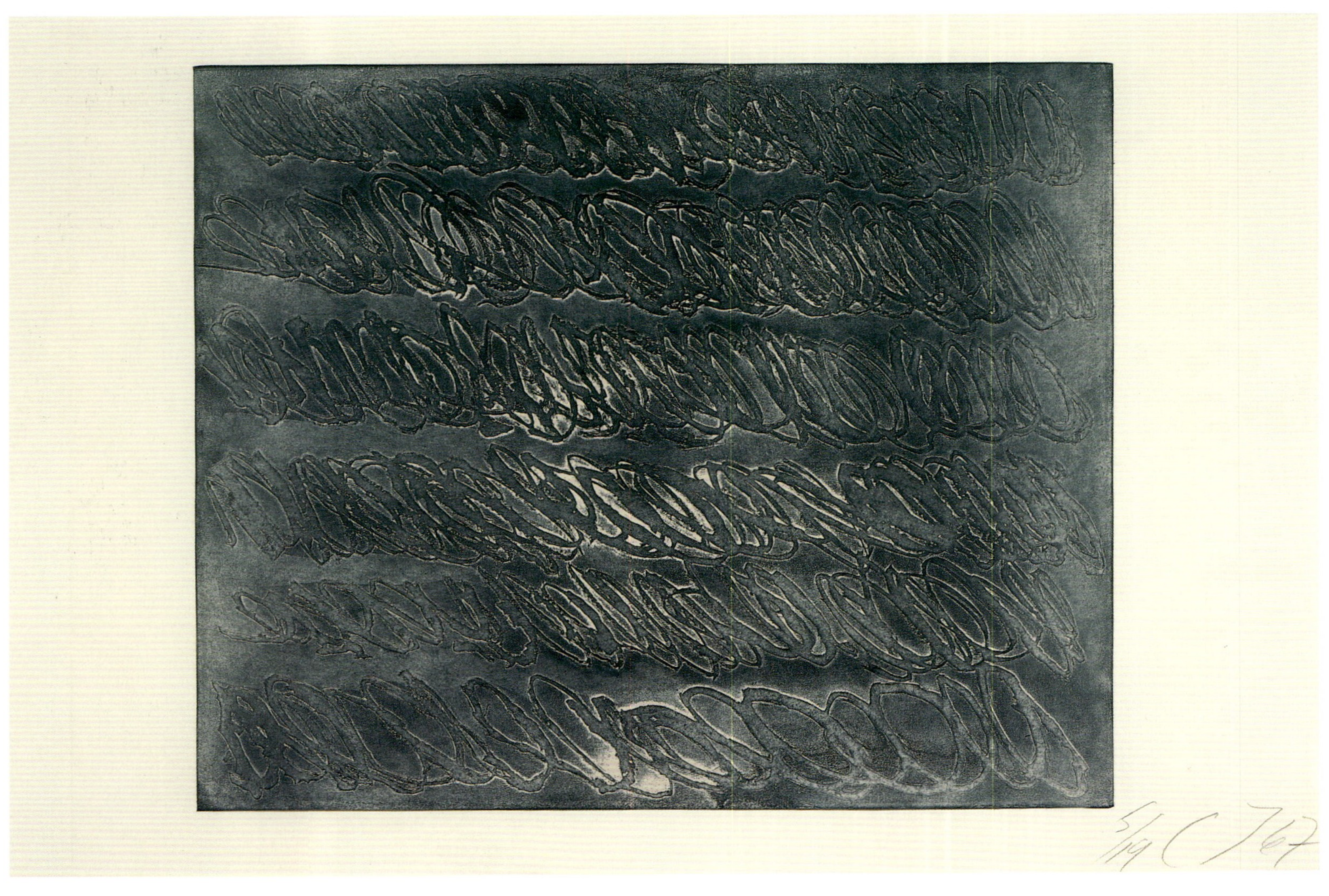

14

14
CY TWOMBLY
Untitled I, 1967–1974
Open-bite aquatint and aquatint
27$\frac{9}{16}$ x 40$\frac{5}{8}$ in. (sheet)

15
FRANK STELLA
Irving Blum Memorial Edition,
from the *Star of Persia Series,* 1967
Lithograph on English vellum graph paper
25$\frac{3}{4}$ x 31$\frac{3}{4}$ in. (sheet)

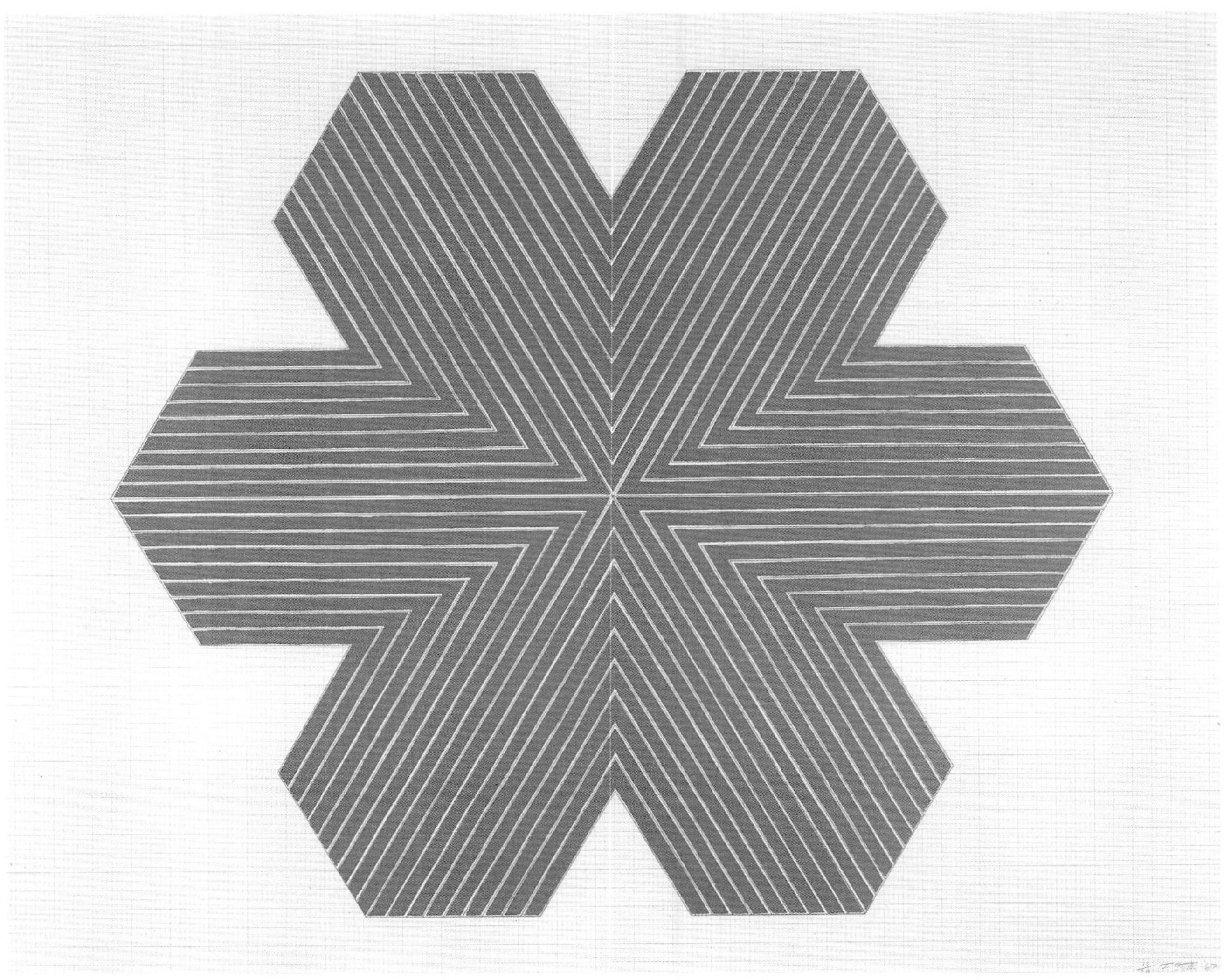

15

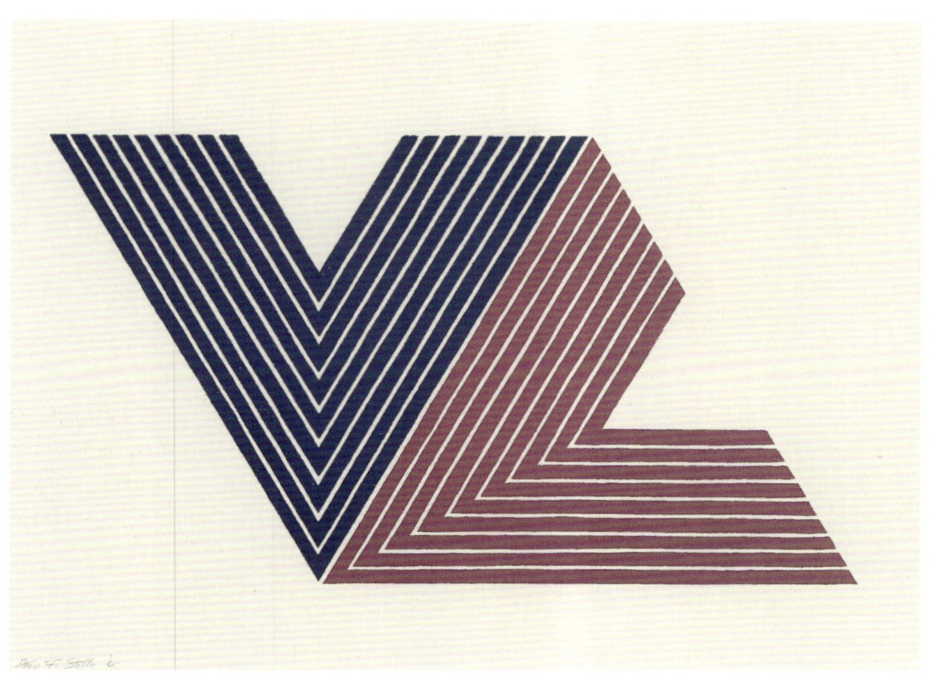

16

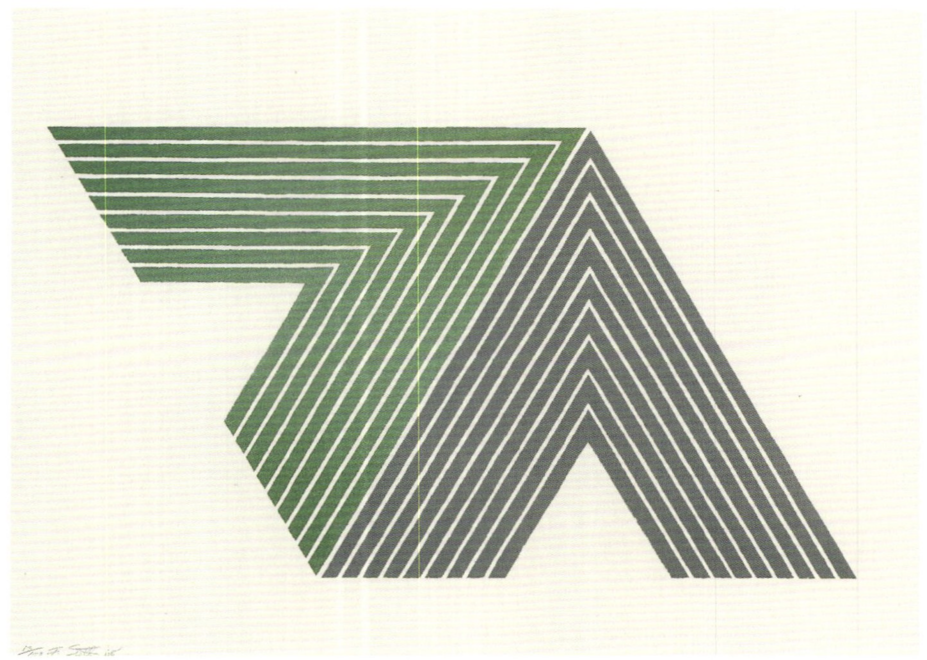

17

16
FRANK STELLA
Ifafa I,
from the *V Series,* 1968
Color lithograph
$16\frac{1}{4} \times 22\frac{3}{8}$ in. (sheet)

17
FRANK STELLA
Ifafa II,
from the *V Series,* 1968
Color lithograph
$16\frac{1}{4} \times 22\frac{3}{8}$ in. (sheet)

18
FRANK STELLA
Quathlamba I,
from the *V Series,* 1968
Color lithograph
$16\frac{1}{4} \times 28\frac{7}{8}$ in. (sheet)

19
FRANK STELLA
Quathlamba II,
from the *V Series,* 1968
Color lithograph
$16\frac{1}{4} \times 28\frac{7}{8}$ in. (sheet)

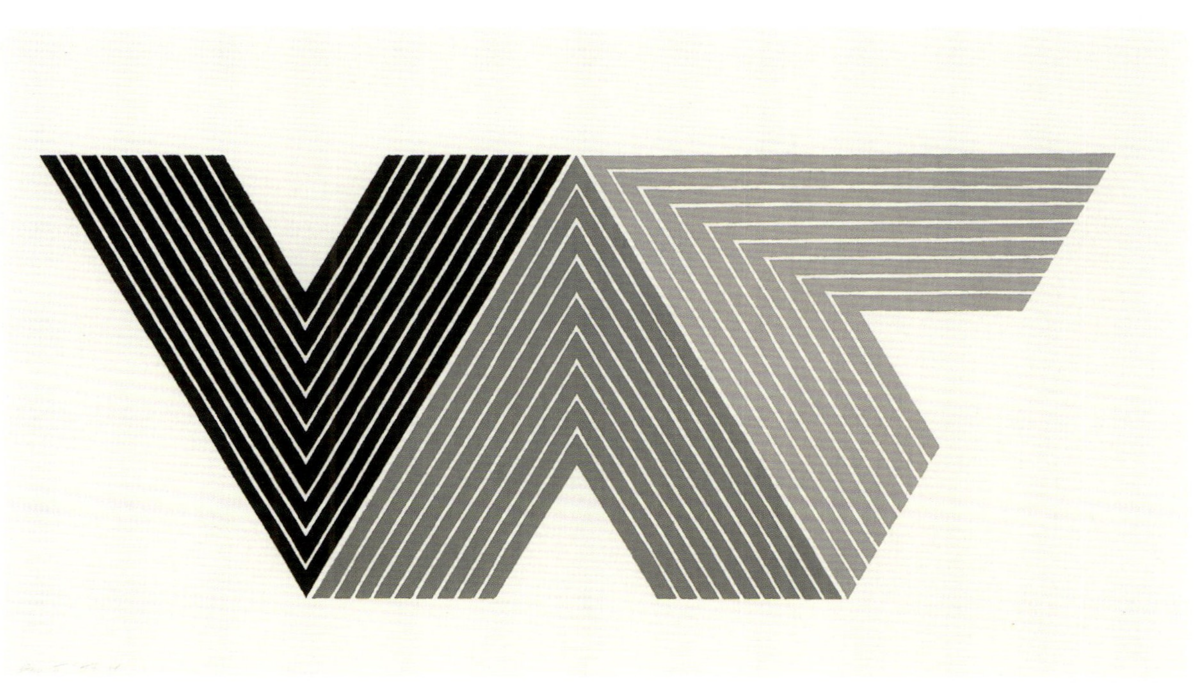

18

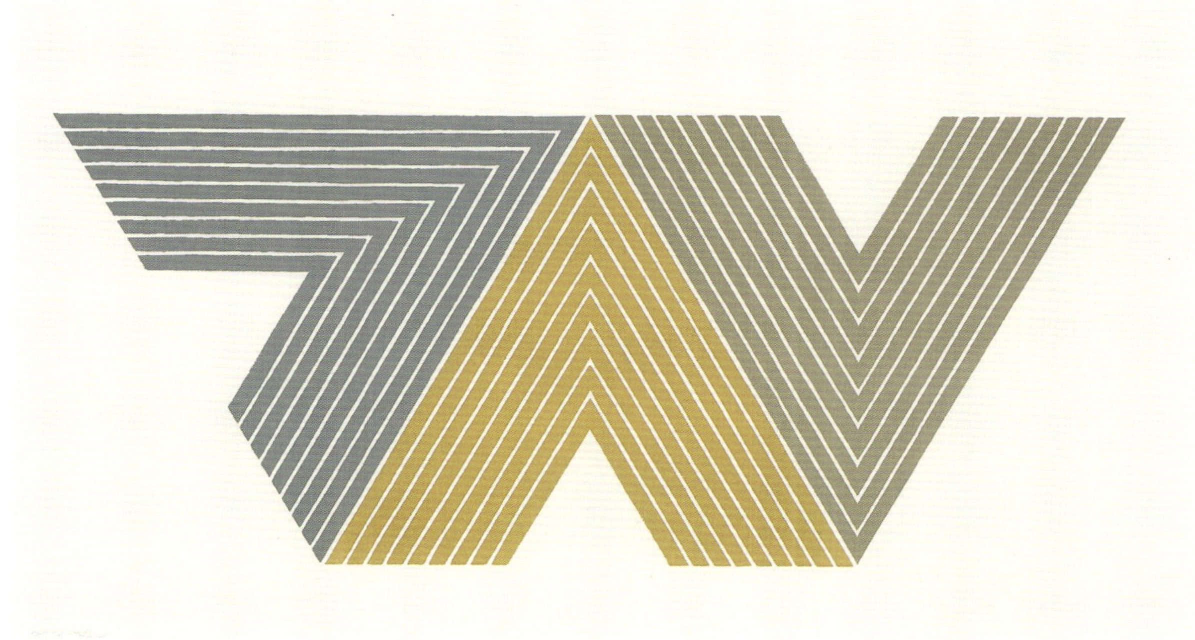

19

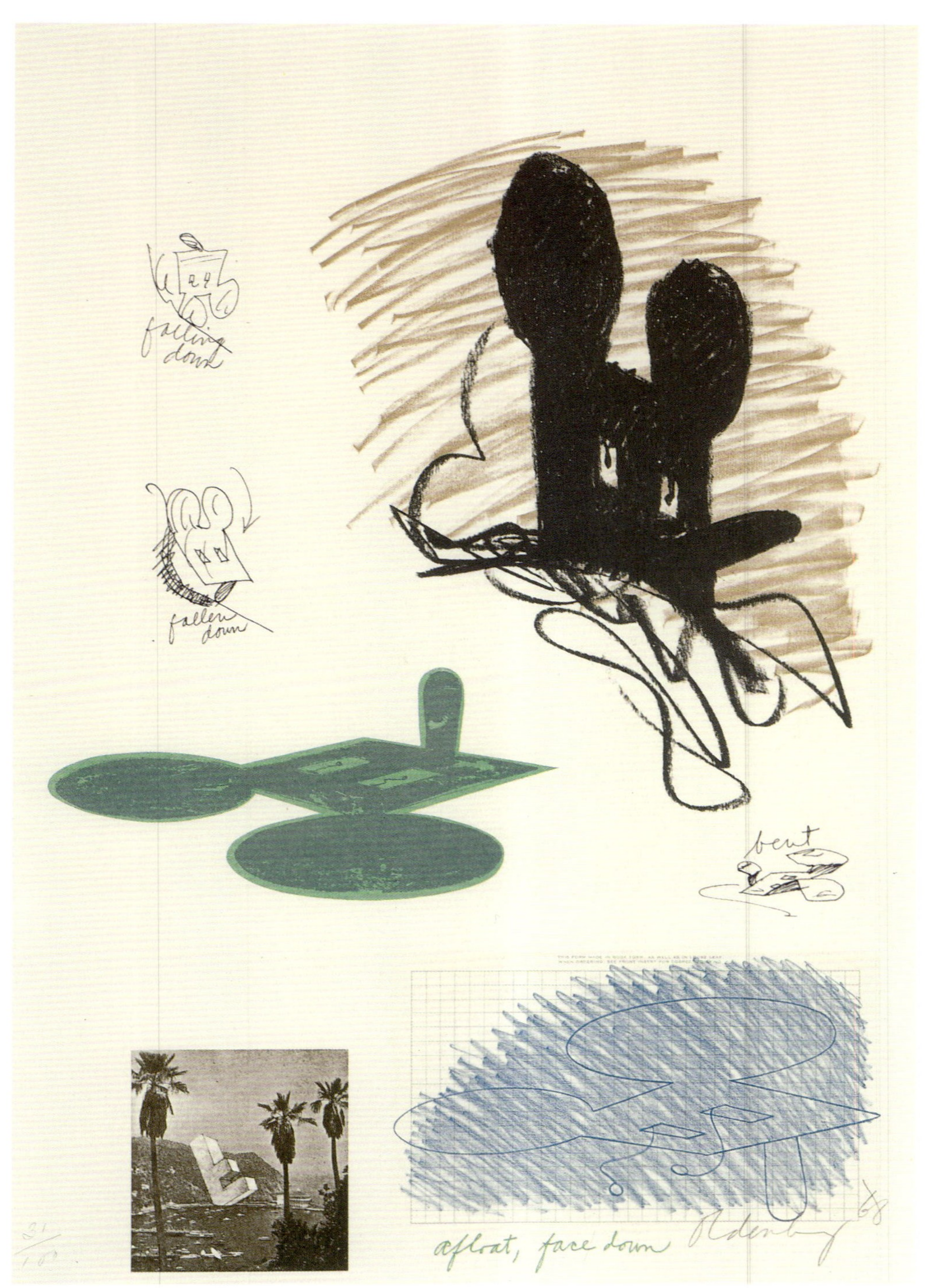

20

20
CLAES OLDENBURG
Untitled [geometric mouse],
from the portfolio *Notes*, 1968
Color lithograph
22 11/16 x 15 3/4 in. (sheet)

21
ROBERT INDIANA
One,
from the portfolio *Numbers*, 1968
Color screenprint
25 9/16 x 19 5/8 in. (sheet)

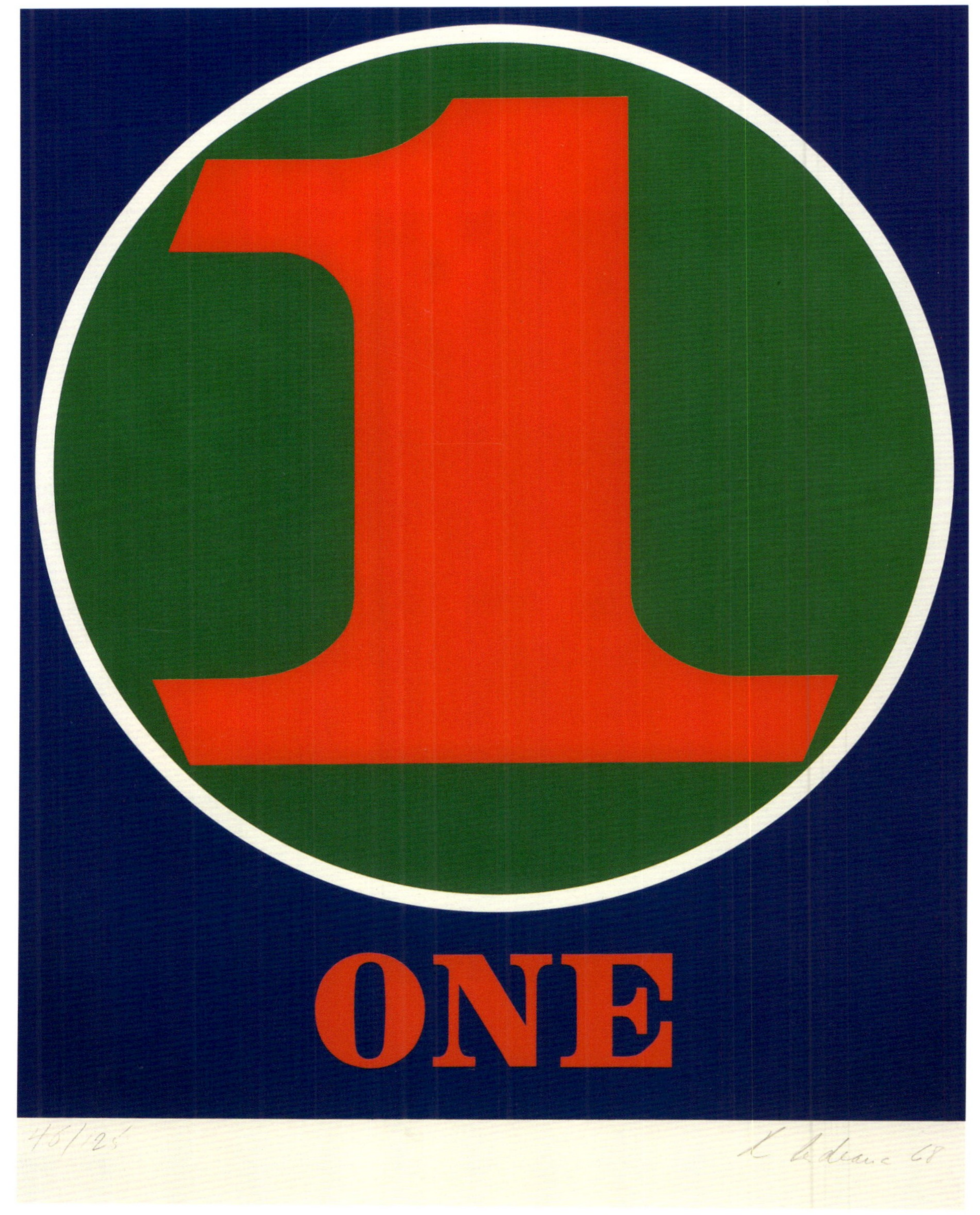

21

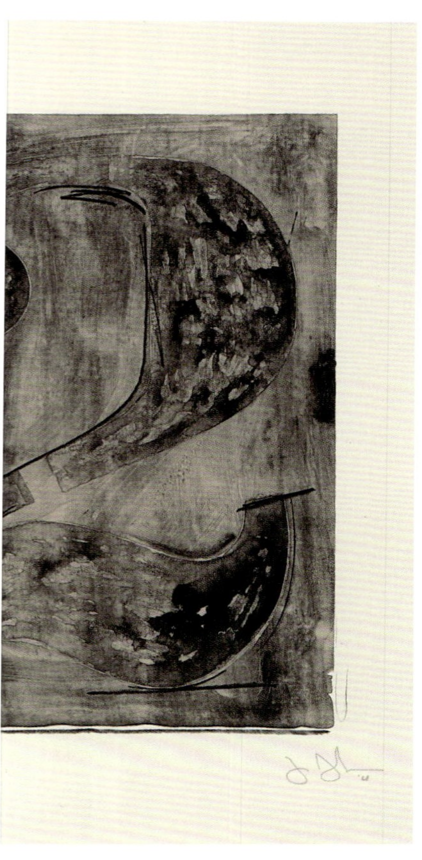

24

28

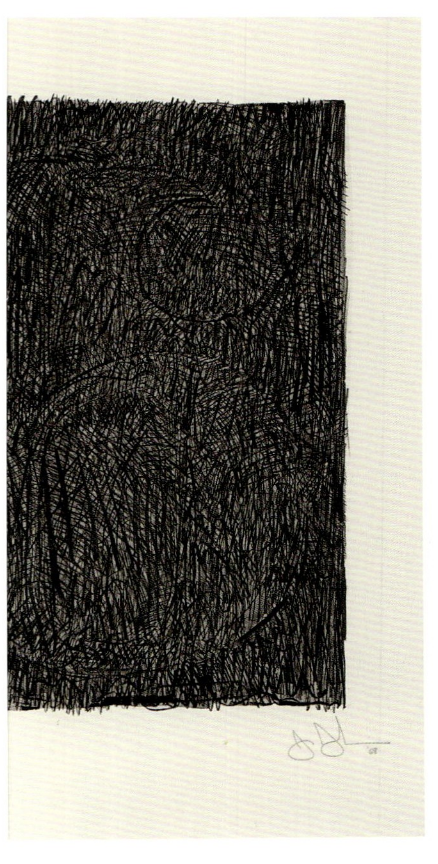

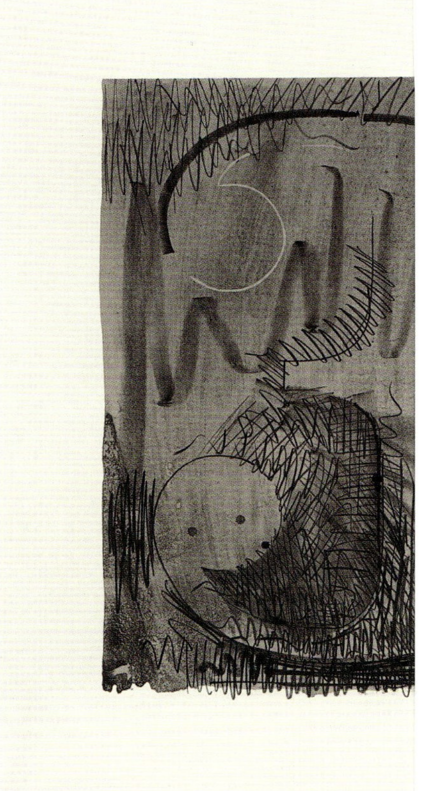

JASPER JOHNS

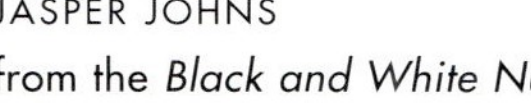

from the *Black and White Numeral Series,* 1968

Lithographs

37 x 30 in. (sheet)

22 *Figure 0*
23 *Figure 1*
24 *Figure 2*
25 *Figure 3*
26 *Figure 4*
27 *Figure 5*
28 *Figure 6*
29 *Figure 7*
30 *Figure 8*
31 *Figure 9*

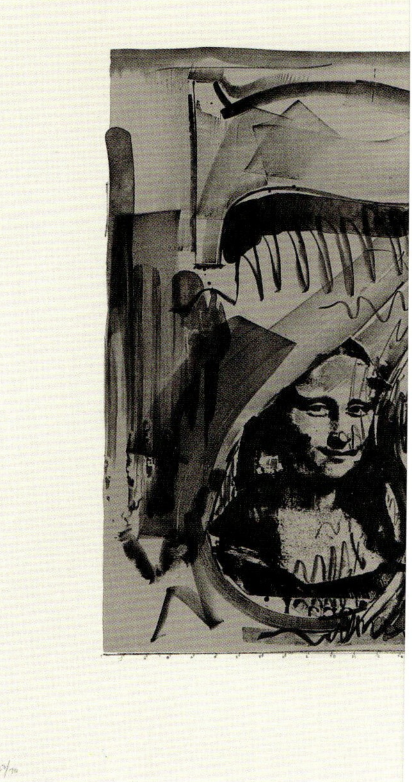

JASPER JOHNS

from the *Color Numeral Series,* 1968–1969

Color lithographs

37 x 30 in. (sheet)

32 *Figure 0*
33 *Figure 1*
34 *Figure 2*
35 *Figure 3*
36 *Figure 4*
37 *Figure 5*
38 *Figure 6*
39 *Figure 7*
40 *Figure 8*
41 *Figure 9*

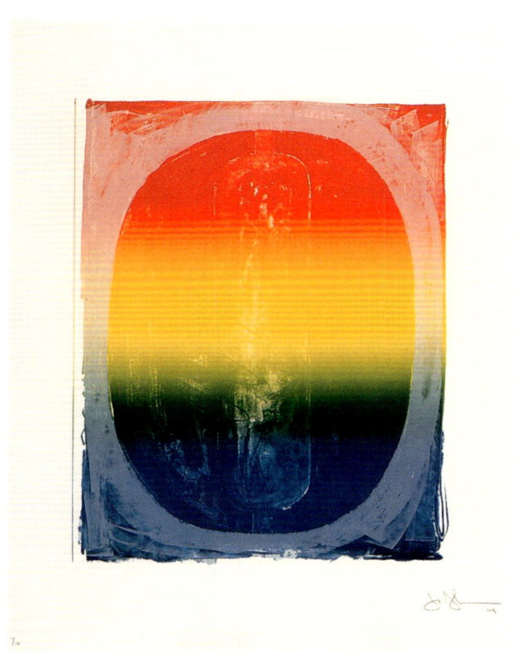

32

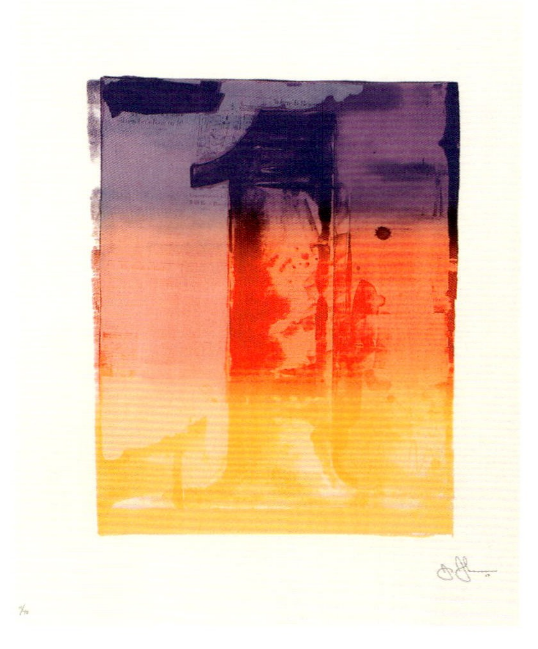

33

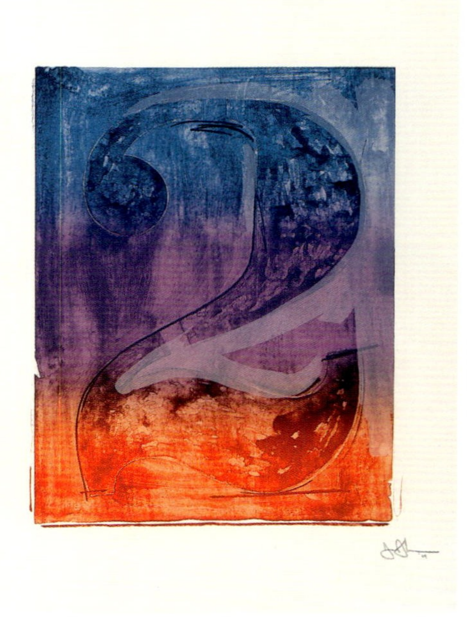

34

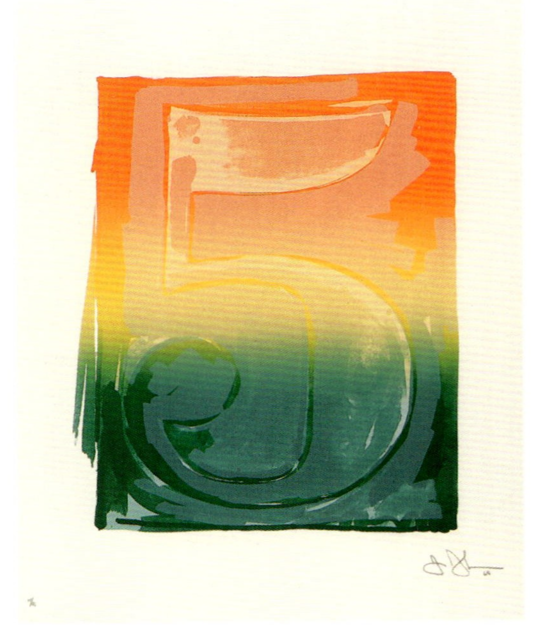

37

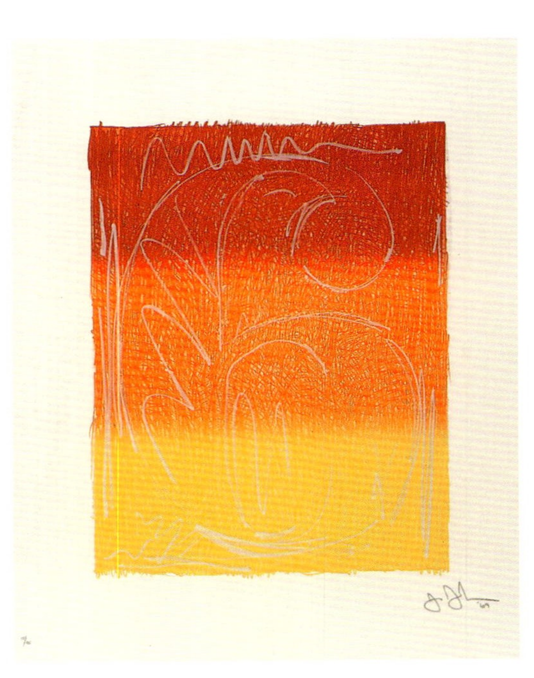

38

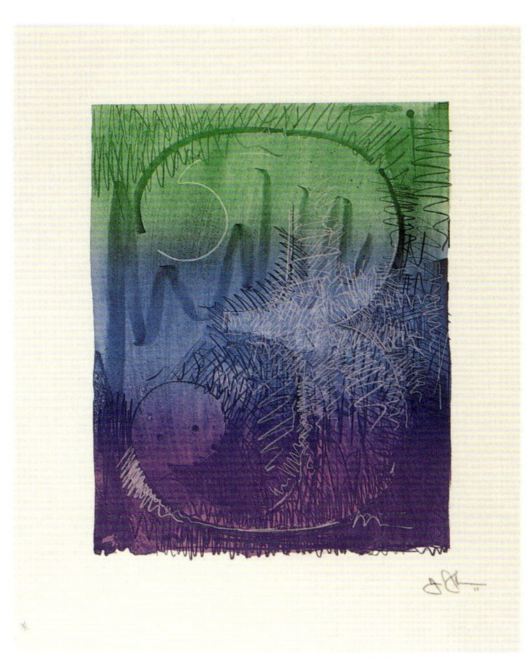

35

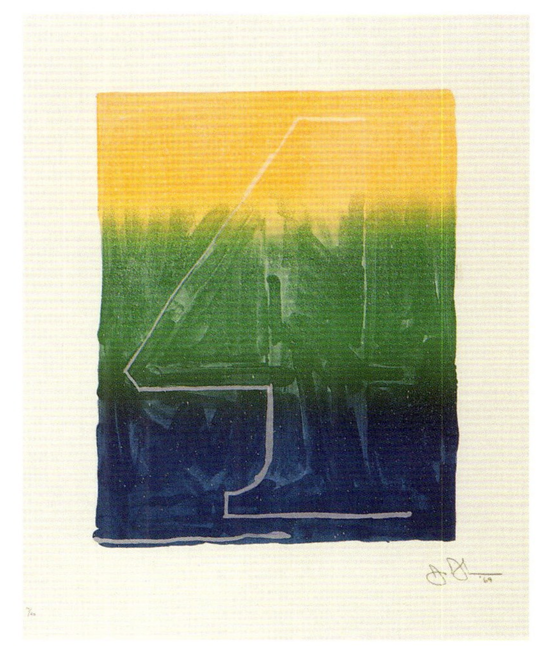

36

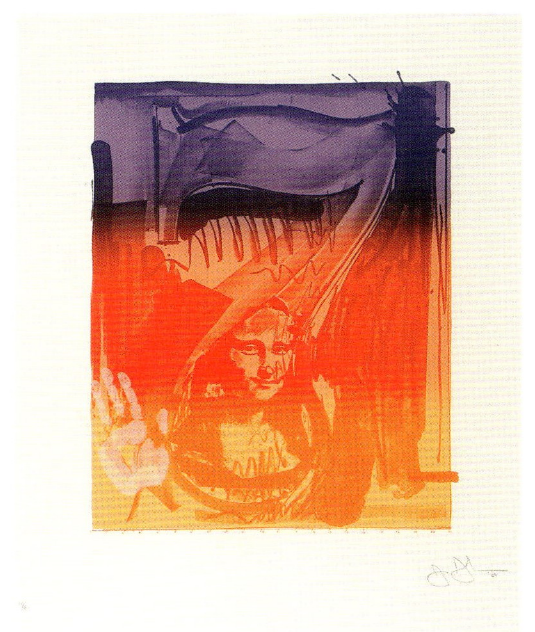

39

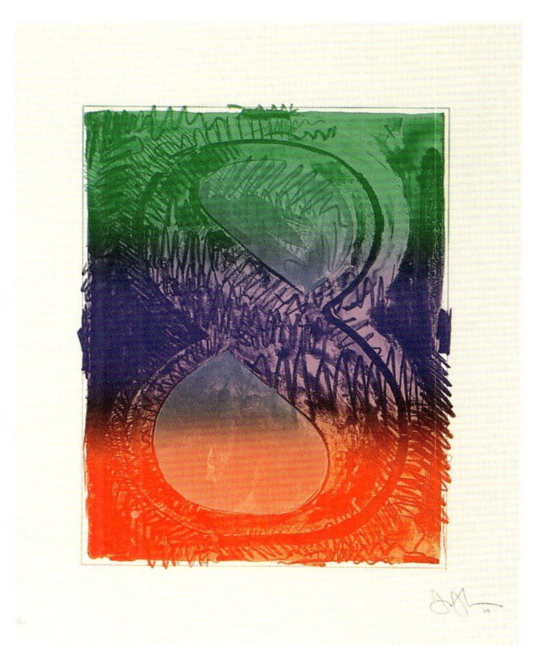

40

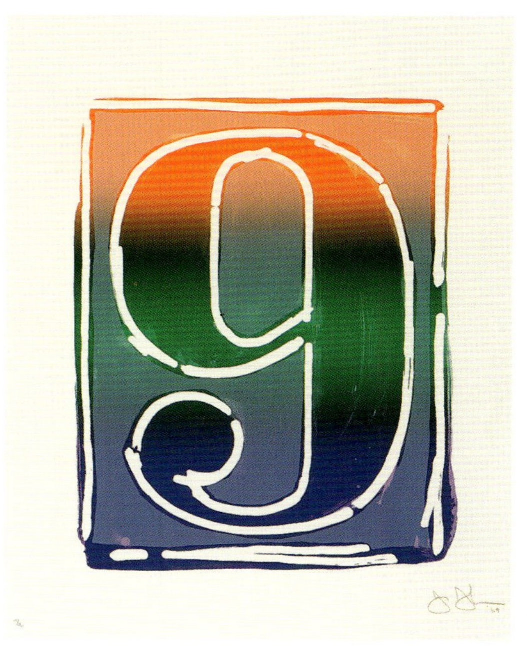

41

42★
BARNETT NEWMAN
Untitled Etching #1, 1968–1969
Etching and aquatint
22½ x 31¾ in. (sheet)

43
LEE BONTECOU
Thirteenth Stone, 1968–1972
Lithograph
22⅜ x 28⅝ in. (sheet)

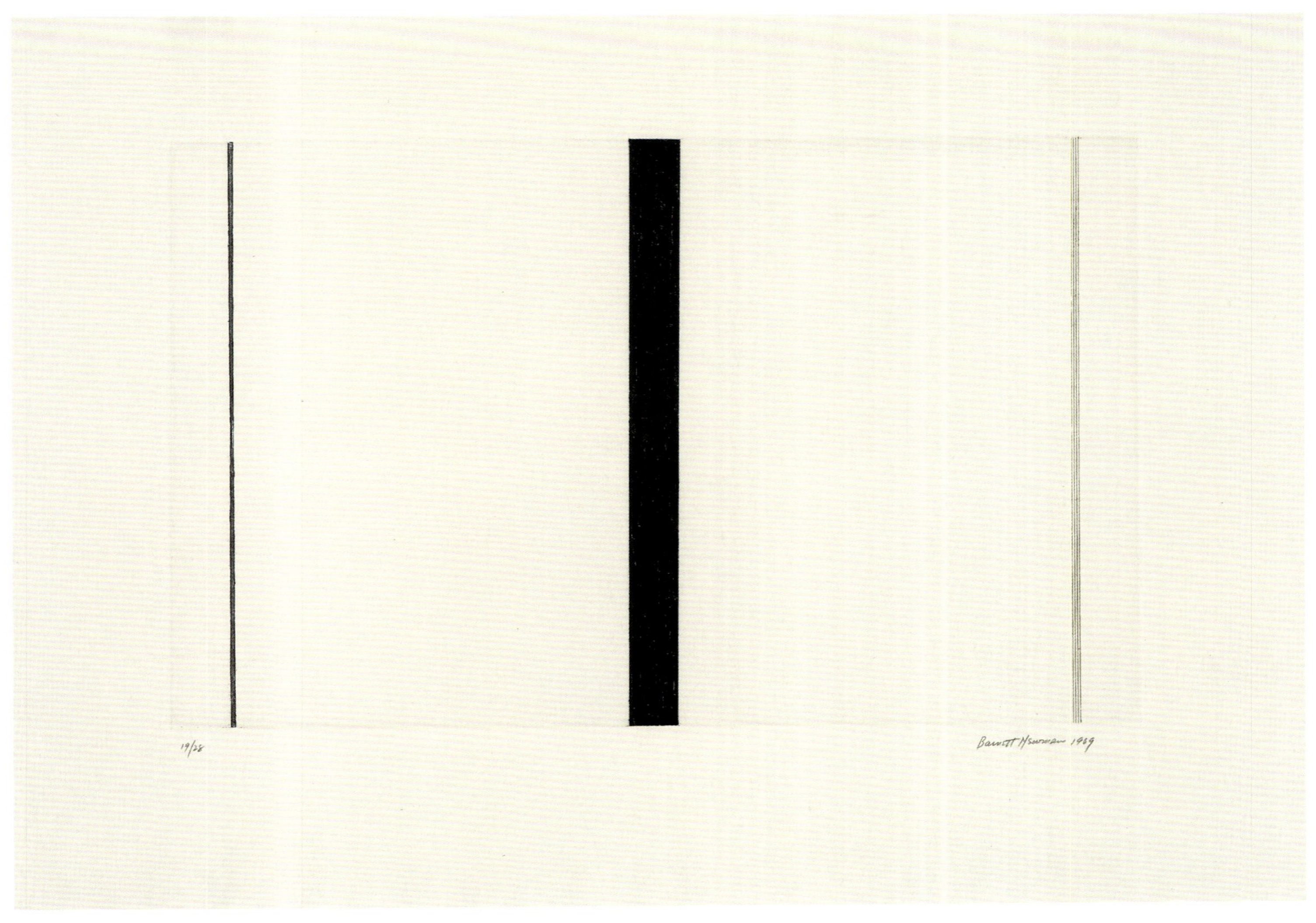

42

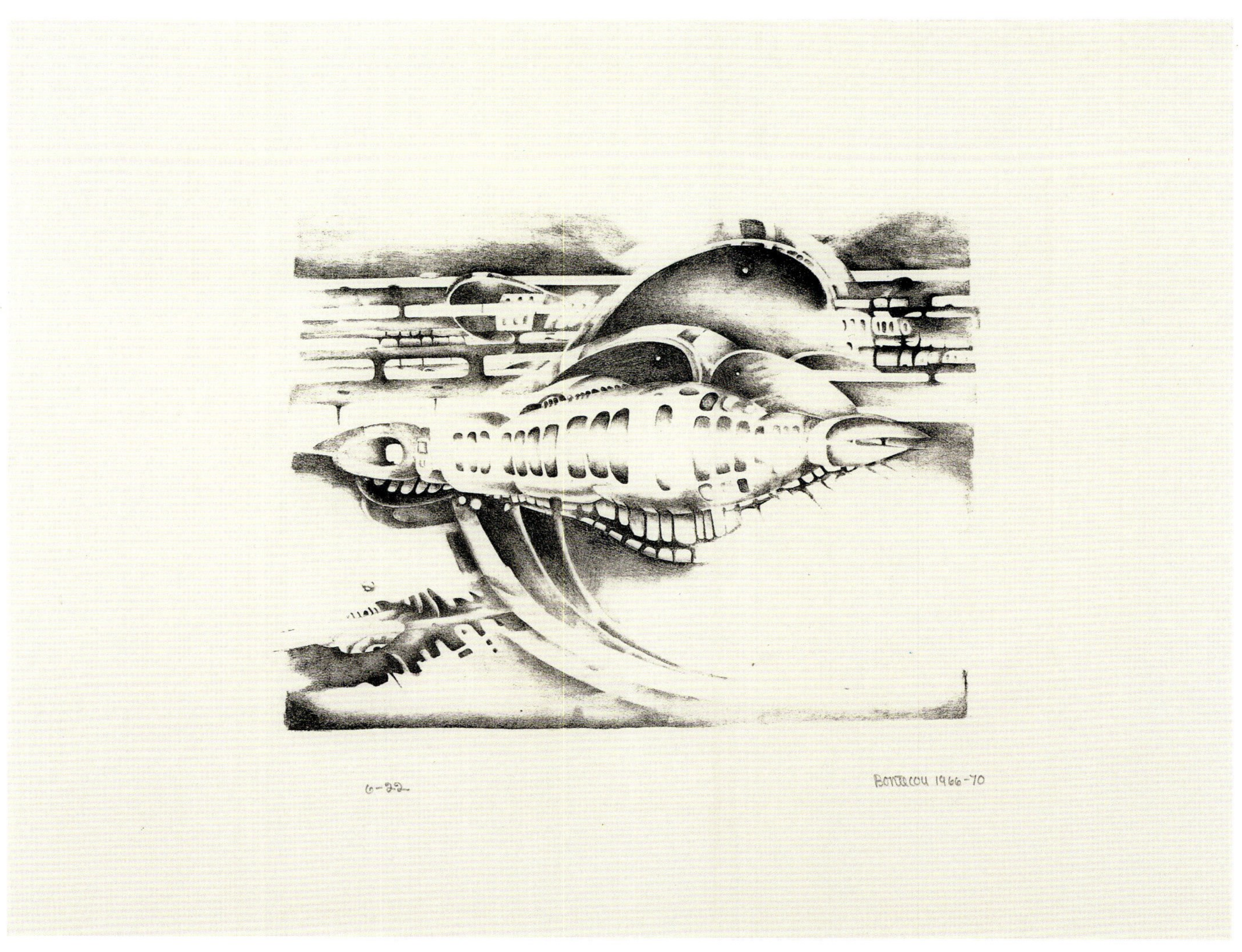

41 Looking at Prints: the 1960s

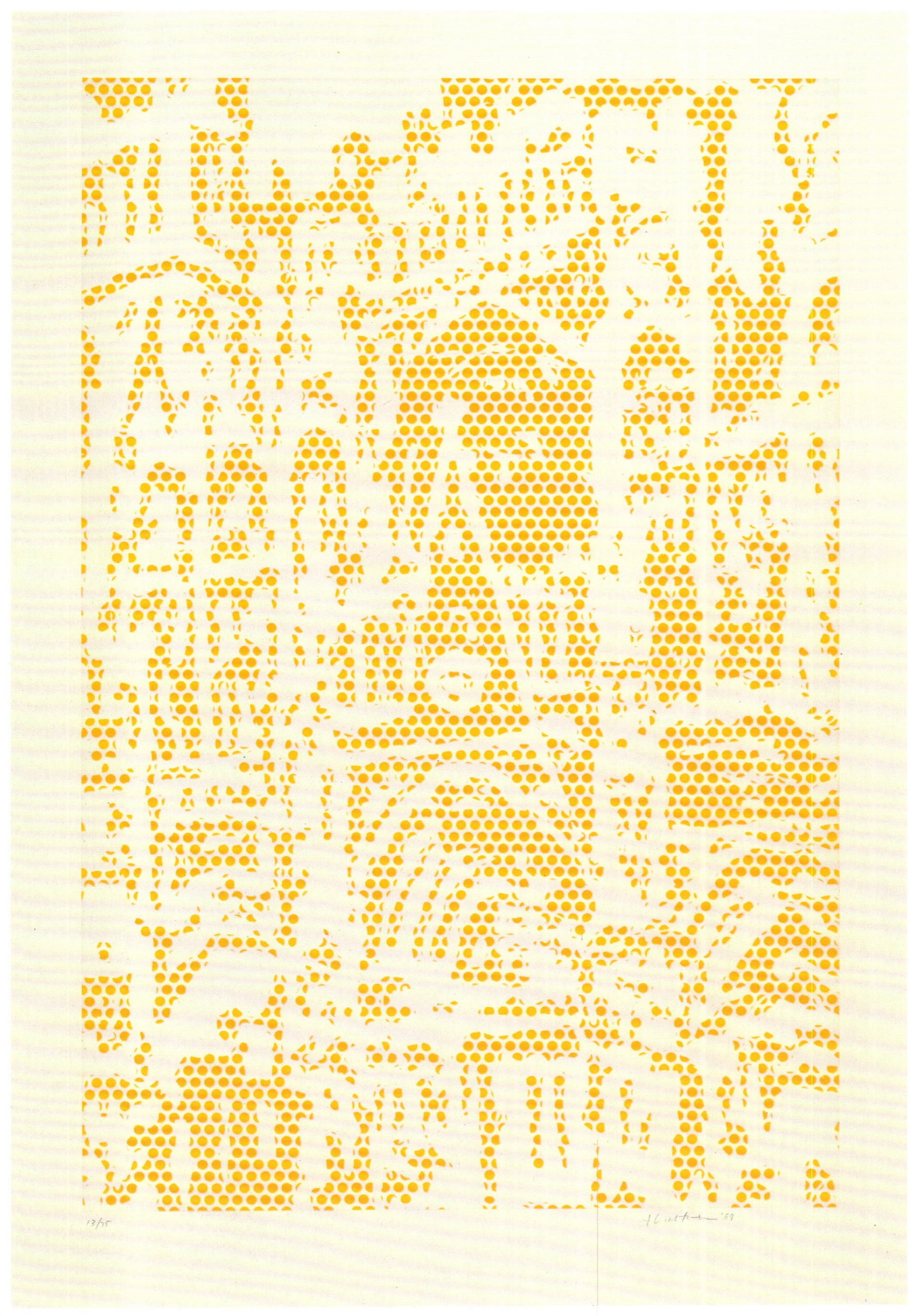

42

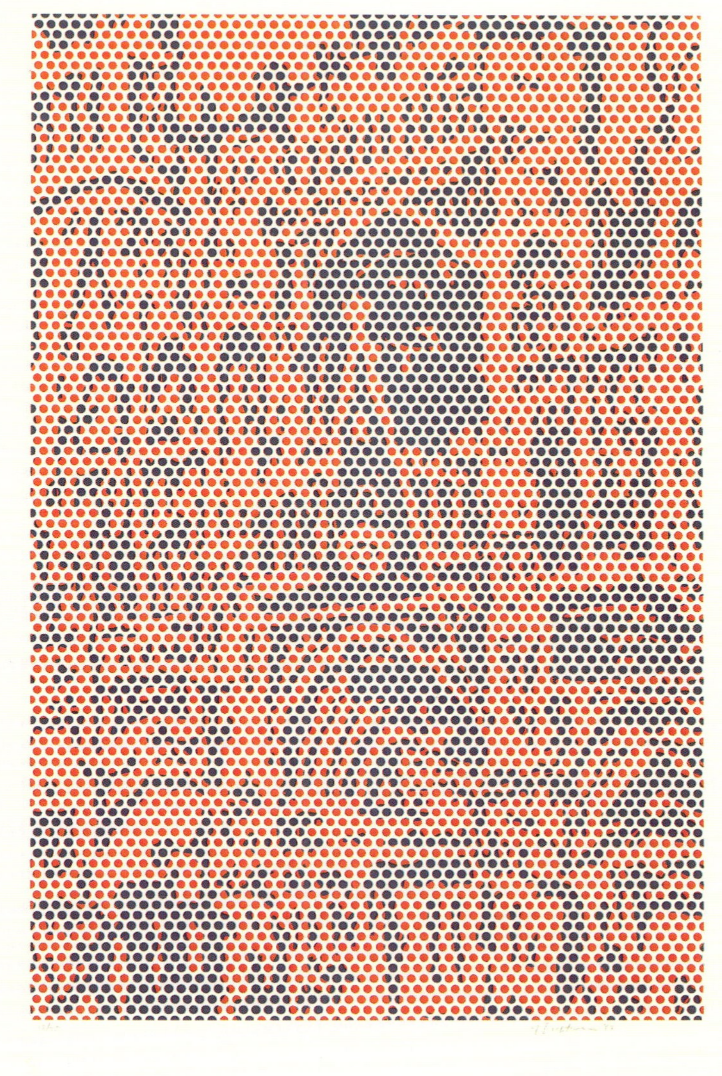

45

44
ROY LICHTENSTEIN
Cathedral #1,
from the *Cathedral Series,* 1969
Color lithograph and screenprint
$48\frac{1}{2}$ x $32\frac{1}{2}$ in. (sheet)

45
ROY LICHTENSTEIN
Cathedral #2,
from the *Cathedral Series,* 1969
Color lithograph and screenprint
$48\frac{5}{16}$ x $32\frac{3}{8}$ in. (sheet)

46
ROY LICHTENSTEIN
Cathedral #3,
from the *Cathedral Series,* 1969
Color lithograph and screenprint
$48\frac{1}{2}$ x $32\frac{1}{2}$ in. (sheet)

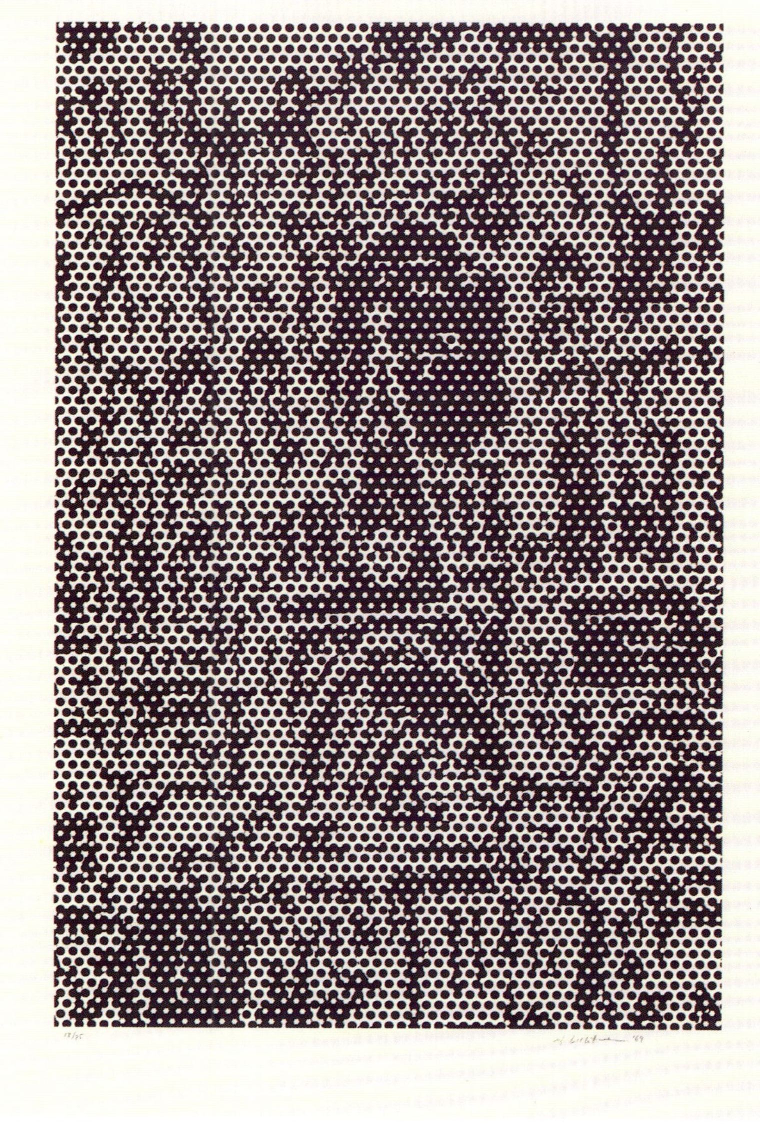

46

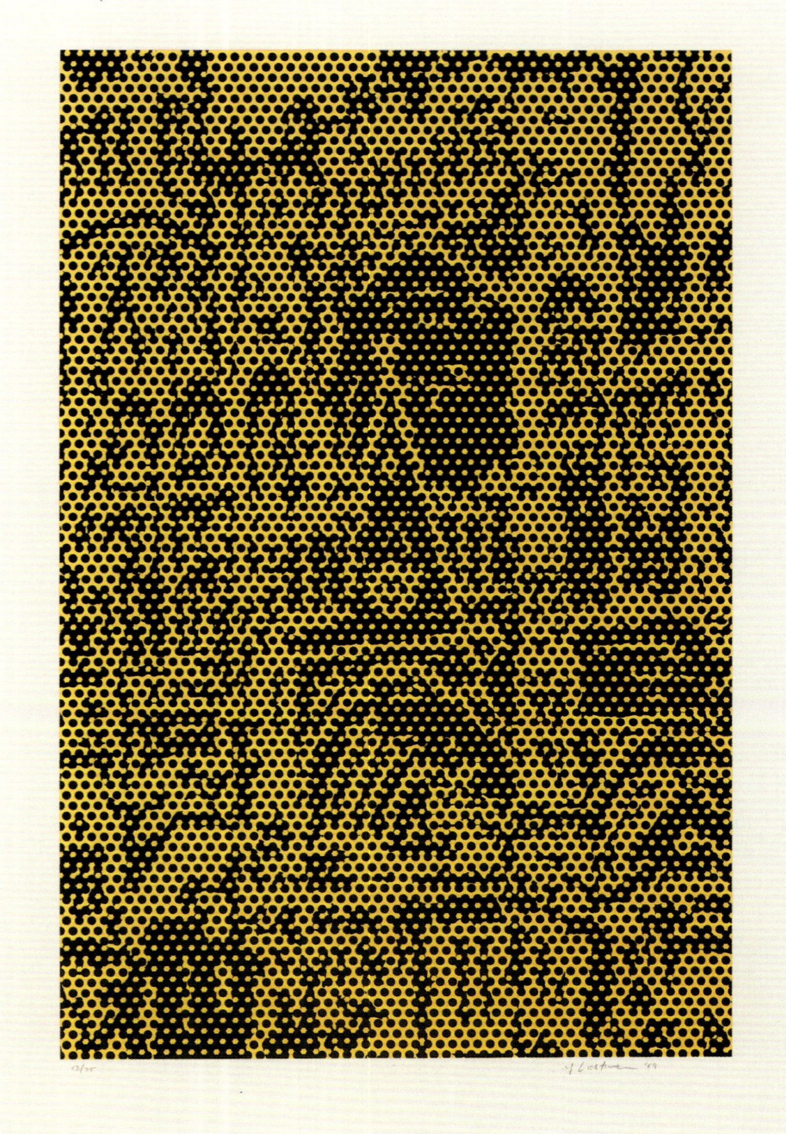

48

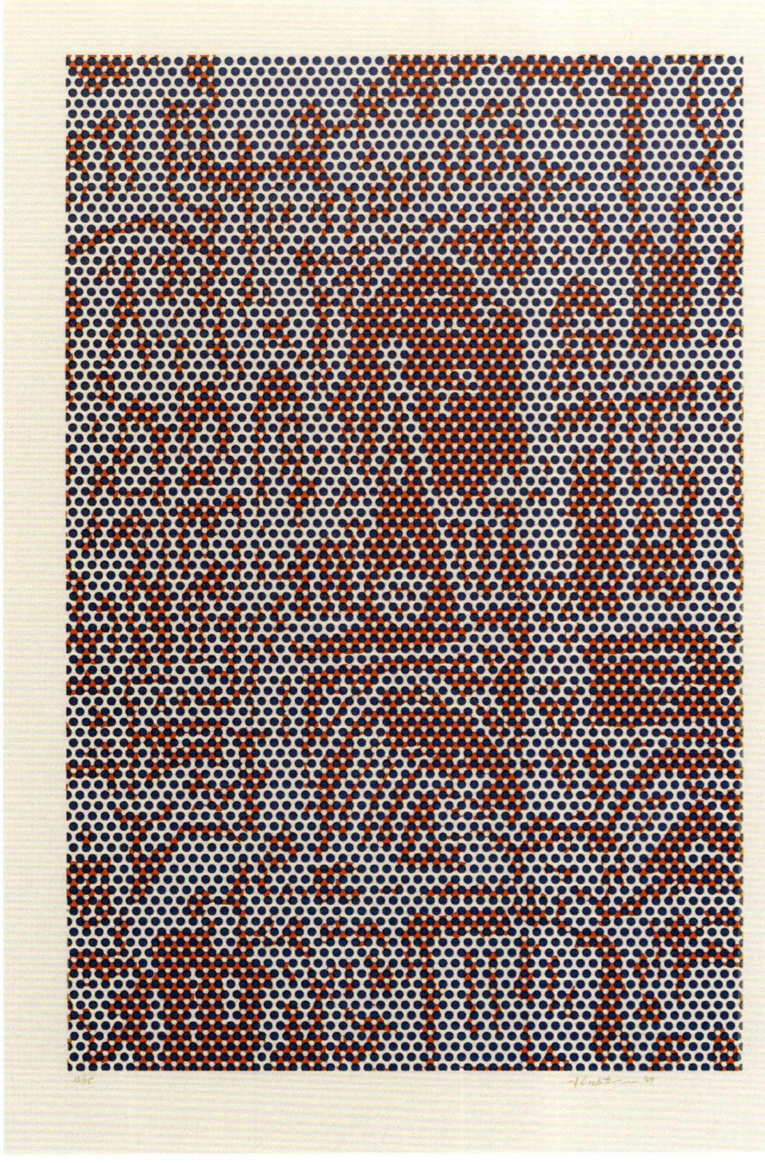

47

47
ROY LICHTENSTEIN
Cathedral #4,
from the *Cathedral Series,* 1969
Color lithograph and screenprint
48 3/8 x 32 3/8 in. (sheet)

48
ROY LICHTENSTEIN
Cathedral #5,
from the *Cathedral Series,* 1969
Color lithograph and screenprint
48 5/8 x 32 1/2 in. (sheet)

49
ROY LICHTENSTEIN
Cathedral #6,
from the *Cathedral Series,* 1969
Color lithograph and screenprint
48 5/16 x 32 5/16 in. (sheet)

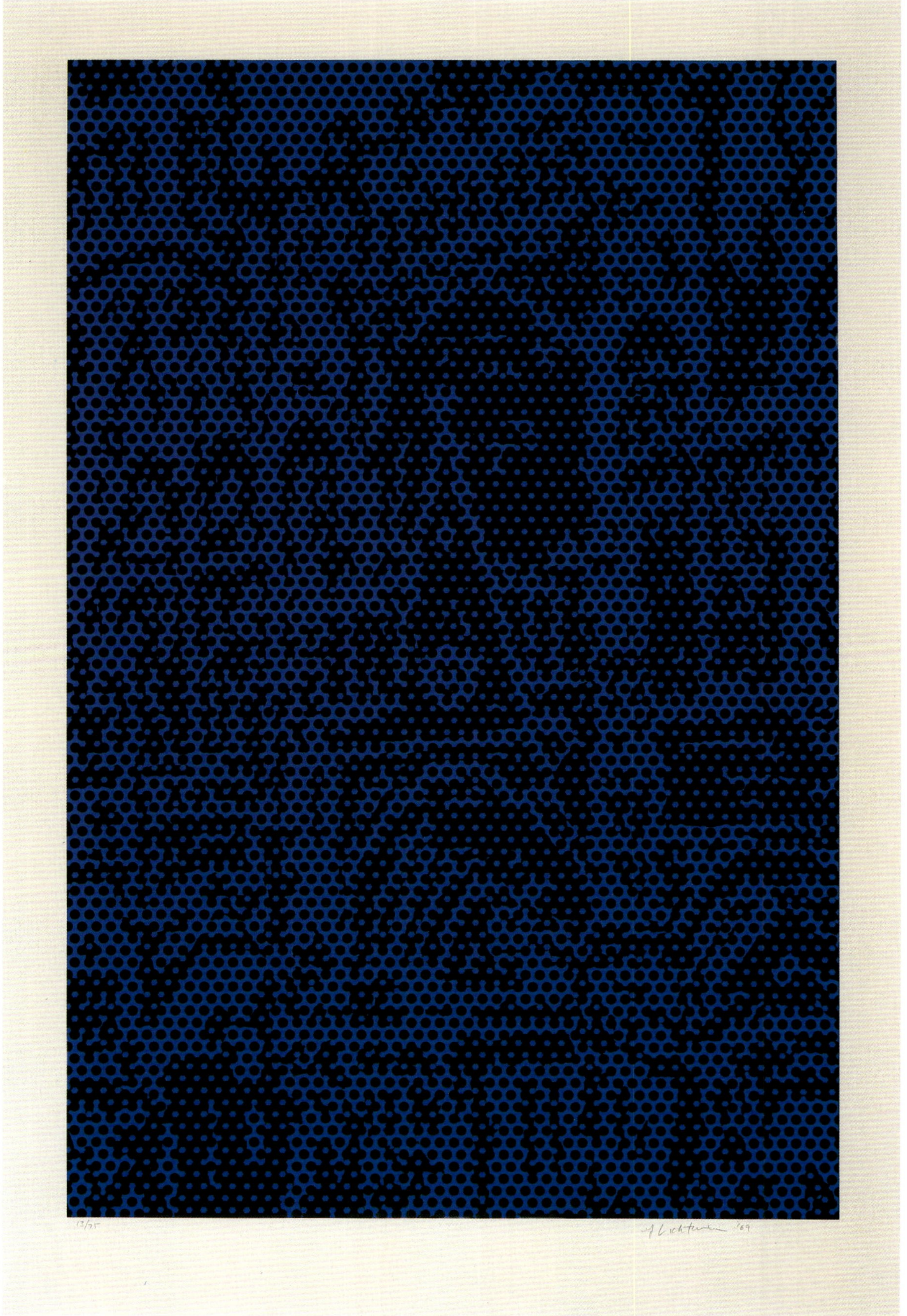

49

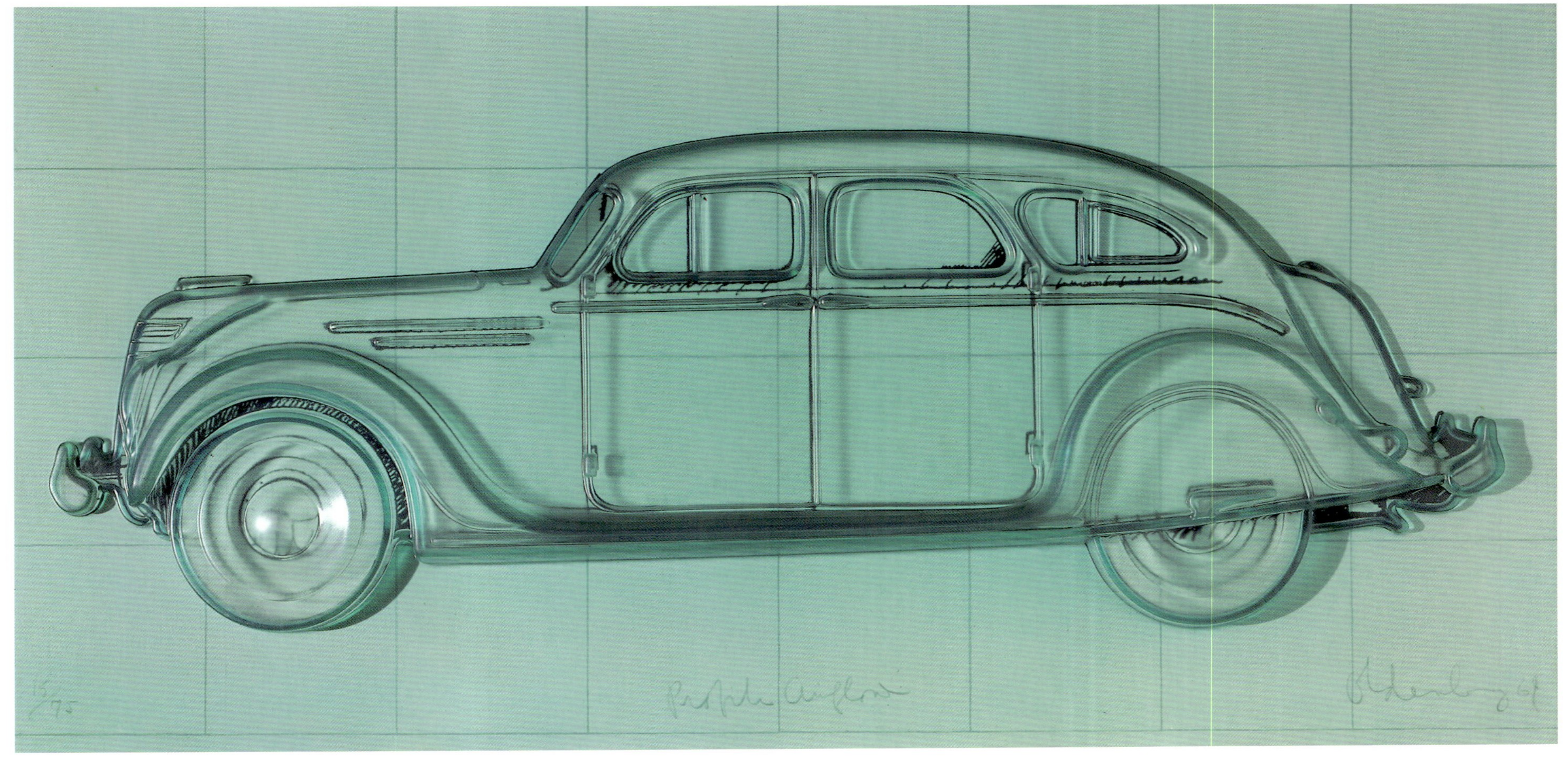

50

50
CLAES OLDENBURG
Profile Airflow, 1969
Cast-polyurethane relief over lithograph
$33\frac{1}{2}$ x $65\frac{1}{2}$ x 4 in. (overall)

51
JASPER JOHNS
High School Days,
from the series *Lead Reliefs,* 1969
Sheet-lead relief with mirror
23 x 17 in. (overall)

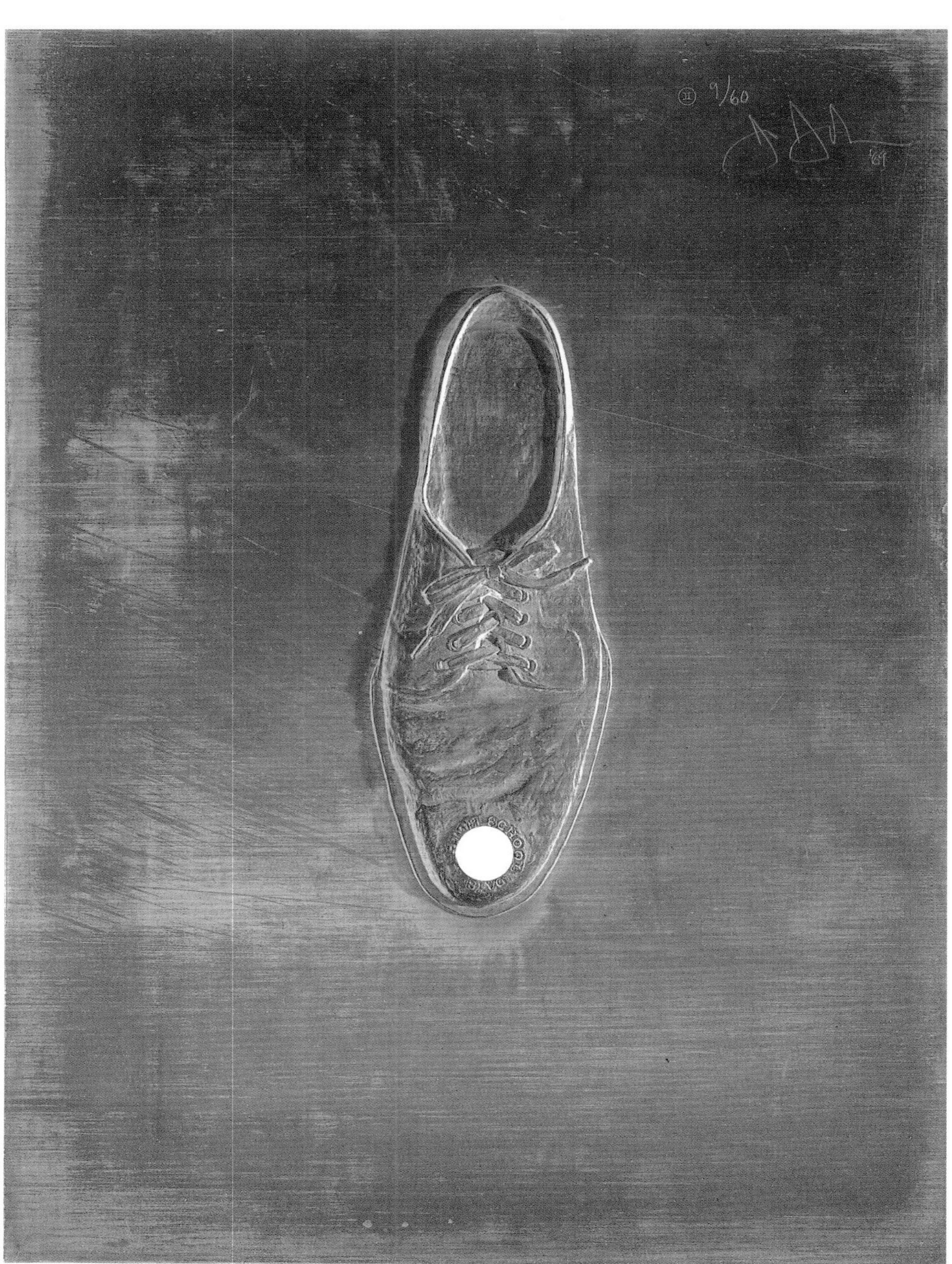

51

52
JASPER JOHNS
The Critic Smiles,
from the series *Lead Reliefs,* 1969
Sheet-lead relief, cast gold, and tin leaf
23 x 17 in. (overall)

53
JASPER JOHNS
Flag,
from the series *Lead Reliefs,* 1969
Sheet-lead relief
17 x 23 in. (overall)

52

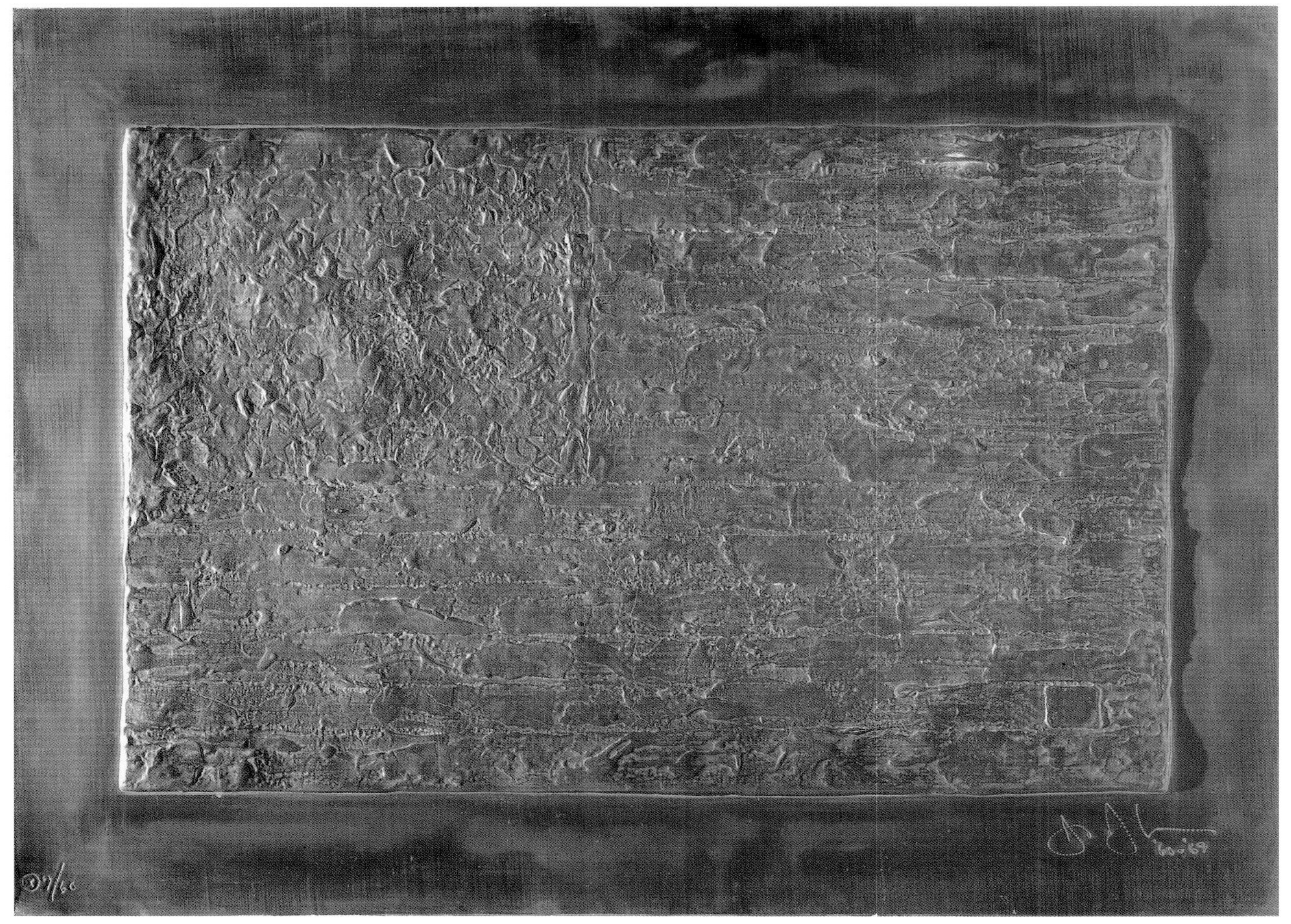

53

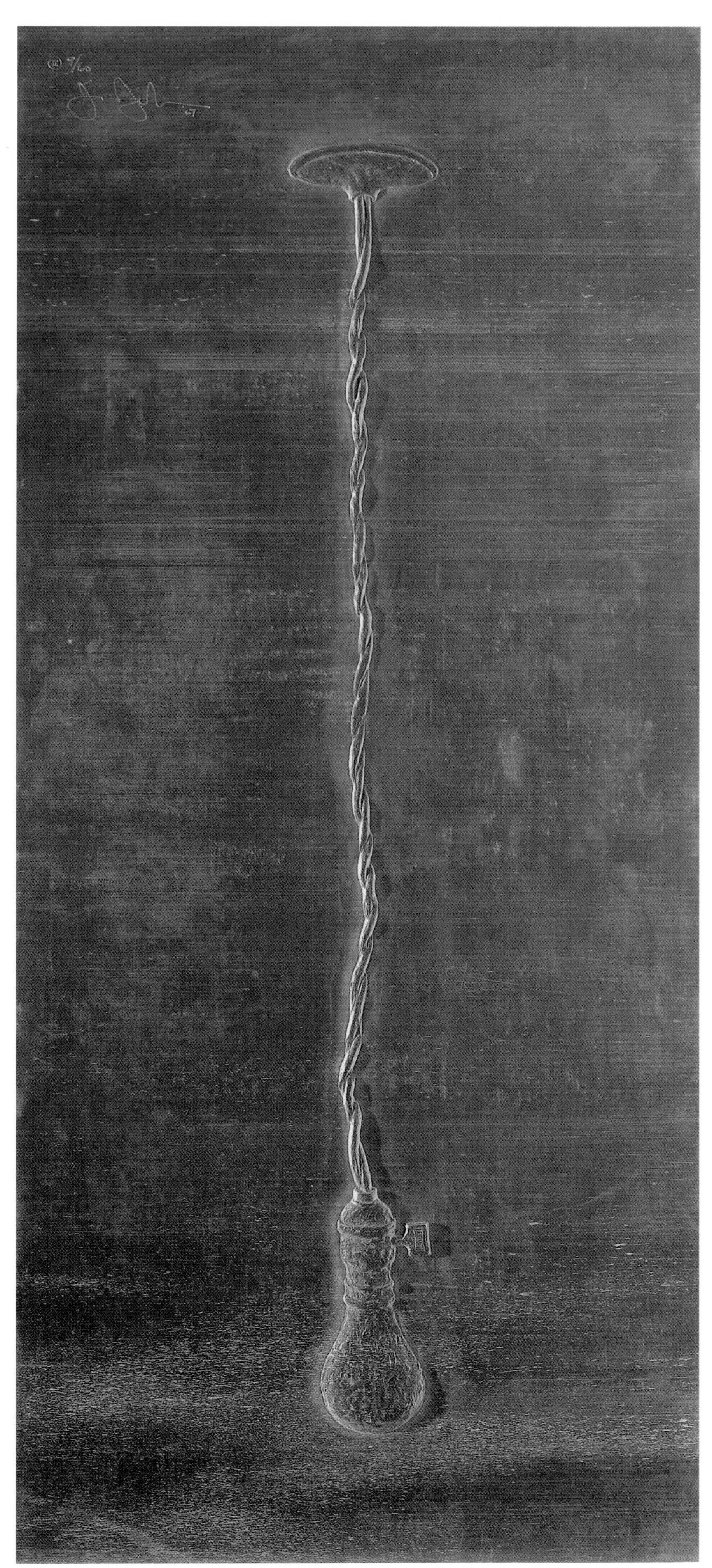

54

54
JASPER JOHNS
Light Bulb,
from the series *Lead Reliefs,* 1969
Sheet-lead relief
39 x 17 in. (overall)

55
JASPER JOHNS
Bread,
from the series *Lead Reliefs,* 1969
Sheet-lead relief and embossed rag paper
23 x 17 in. (overall)

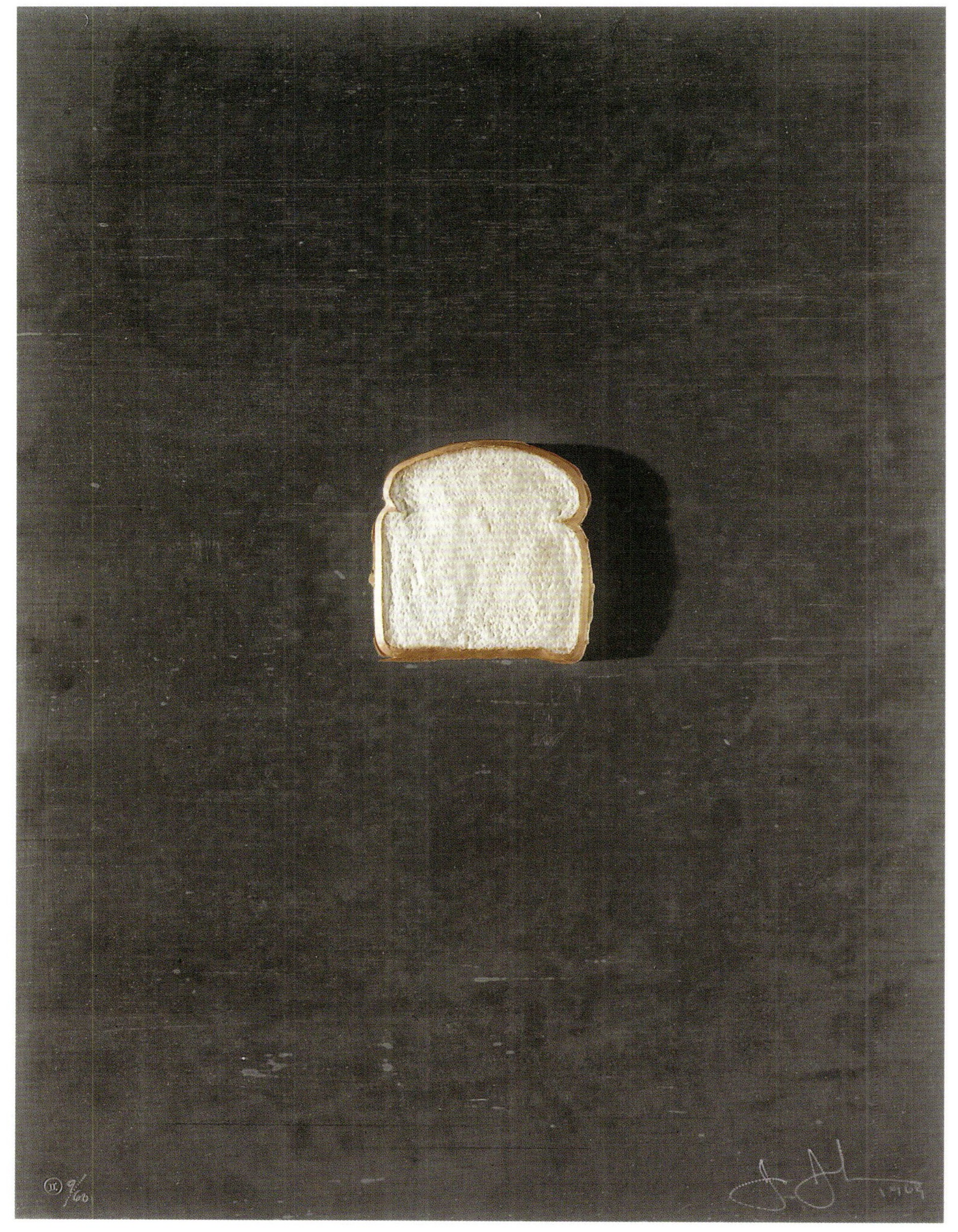

55

If the 1960s can be characterized as an explosive decade in terms of the contemporary print's entry into the mainstream of fine art, the 1970s can be viewed as expansionist for the dazzling array of styles and techniques that proliferated over ten years.

Lithography continued to be the dominant print medium in the early 1970s, particularly through the aggressive efforts of ULAE and Gemini G.E.L. in attracting well-known artists, such as Ellsworth Kelly and Richard Serra, to make prints for the first time, and in encouraging those who had made prints in the 1960s, such as Jim Dine, Marisol, and James Rosenquist, to continue making them. The prints they created were large (Rosenquist's *Off the Continental Divide*, which surpassed Robert Rauschenberg's *Booster* in size, was considered a watershed for big print production) and colorful, with sometimes as many as twenty-five colors employed in a single print.

In addition, the contemporary print also became more complicated in its appearance. Inspired by the layered approach inherent in printmaking processes and encouraged by proficient master printers, artists frequently combined multiple techniques in a single print. The combination print, or "combo print" as it came to be known, was a feat of technical excellence. To the average viewer, who likely knew little about printmaking techniques, combo prints appeared sleek, sophisticated, and visually exciting. Roy Lichtenstein's *Bull Profile Series*, with its combination of lithograph, screenprint, and line-cut is one example, while Wayne Thiebaud's prints combining etching and color aquatint from his *Recent Etchings I* of 1979 is another.

The extreme manifestation of the "can do" attitude of print workshops towards its artists' creative desires was probably no better seen than in Gemini G.E.L.'s production of small-scale sculptures produced in large editions, better known as "multiples." In 1968 and 1969 Gemini produced precursors to the multiple, Jasper Johns's *Lead Reliefs* and Claes Oldenburg's *Profile Airflow*, both of which were three-dimensional bas-reliefs. In 1970 Roy Lichtenstein experimented with embossed, dye-cut, and engraved printing surfaces in his *Peace through Chemistry* and *Modern Head* series. These eventually led to his executing relief sculptures and three-dimensional multiples, *Untitled Head I* and *II*, that same year. In 1971, one year later, Oldenburg created the three dimensional multiples *Ice Bag—Scale B* and *Geometric Mouse—Scale C* at Gemini.

Except for Oldenburg and Lichtenstein, artistic interest in Pop and Op forms waned in the early 1970s when new art forms such as photorealism, minimalism, and conceptual art emerged with different aesthetic and intellectual concerns.

Photorealism found its way from canvas to print immediately on its acceptance as a mainstream art form in the early 1970s. Chuck Close, an early practitioner, chose intaglio processes for his black-and-white prints at Crown Point Press, not so much for their kinship with black-and-white photography, but because of the way etching techniques corresponded to his way of working. Vija Celmins, who began making prints at Gemini in the early 1980s, responded to intaglio techniques, particularly drypoint and mezzotint, because of the directness of application (neither requires the use of acid) and the effective translation of her graphite drawings of deserts, oceans, and galaxies. Richard Estes's impersonal prints from *Urban Landscapes I*, with their cold, antiseptic views of city streets, found an immediate printmaking counterpart in screenprint.

Artists whose work was identified with minimalism and conceptual art movements also made prints. Some, like Bruce Nauman, worked at Cirrus Editions, Ltd., in Los Angeles under the direction of Jean Milant. Milant, a Tamarind-trained master printer, cultivated West Coast-based artists such as Joe Goode, Ed Moses, and Edward Ruscha. At Cirrus, Ruscha's *Evil*, Goode's untitled work, and Moses's *Wedge Series* were printed on wood veneer, two paper layers, and silk tissue respectively, illustrating the lively mood of experimentation at Cirrus with alternatives to the standard paper vehicle. At about the same time at Gemini, Robert Rauschenberg was making prints on silk fabric and cardboard. In 1973–1974 he made *Link*, a combination of screenprint and colored paper pulp.

Experimentation with paper pulp was a trend embraced almost simultaneously by presses east and west in the 1970s. Garner Tullis at his Institute for Experimental Printmaking and Ken Tyler at his Tyler Graphics, Ltd. (established after he left Gemini in 1974), worked with artists Kenneth Noland, Louise Nevelson, Ellsworth Kelly, David Hockney, and others in paper pulp casting. In the hands of these different artists, paper pulp prints varied widely in appearance, from softly colored and textured flat paper pieces to radically sculptured and cast paper reliefs. The process captivated artists throughout the decade. Some, like Hockney, continued to work with paper pulp projects well into the 1980s.

The reemergence of the monotype was perhaps the most outstanding development to affect the look of prints from the mid-1970s onwards. Many artists were challenged to take up the form because of excitement generated by an exhibition of the nineteenth-century artist Edgar Degas's monotypes at the Fogg Art Museum in 1968. Artists from across the country responded to the spontaneity offered by the process and the ease with which images could be produced. The result was a proliferation of monotype styles, from relatively controlled, delicately colored works by Nathan Oliveira and Joseph Goldyne to broadly handled, gestural works by Jim Dine, Michael Mazur, and Mary Frank. Like paper pulp prints, monotype was a process that would continue to captivate artists through the late 1970s into the 1980s and 1990s.

Looking at Prints: The 1970s

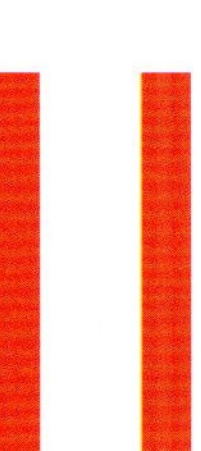

The 1970s

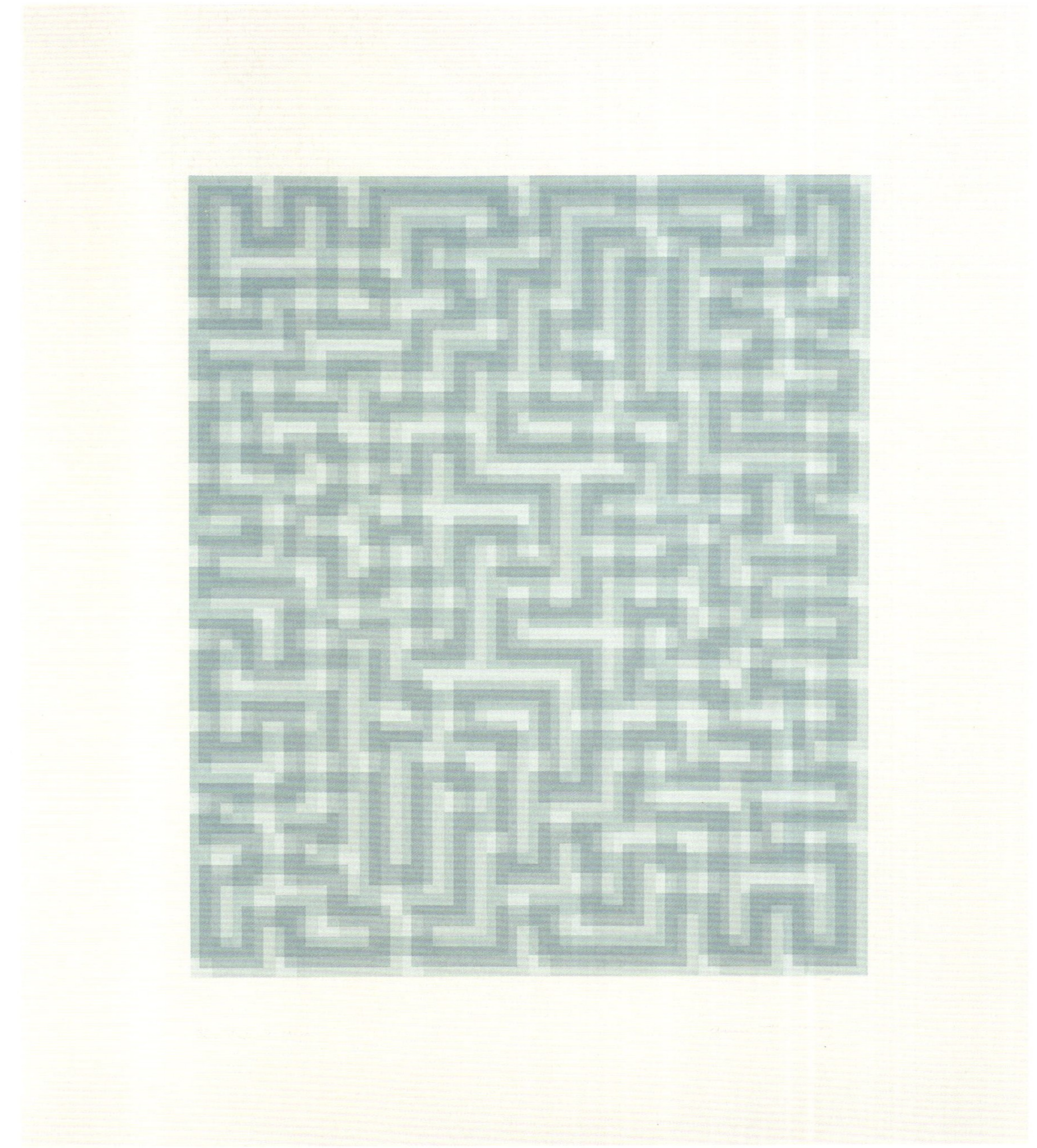

56

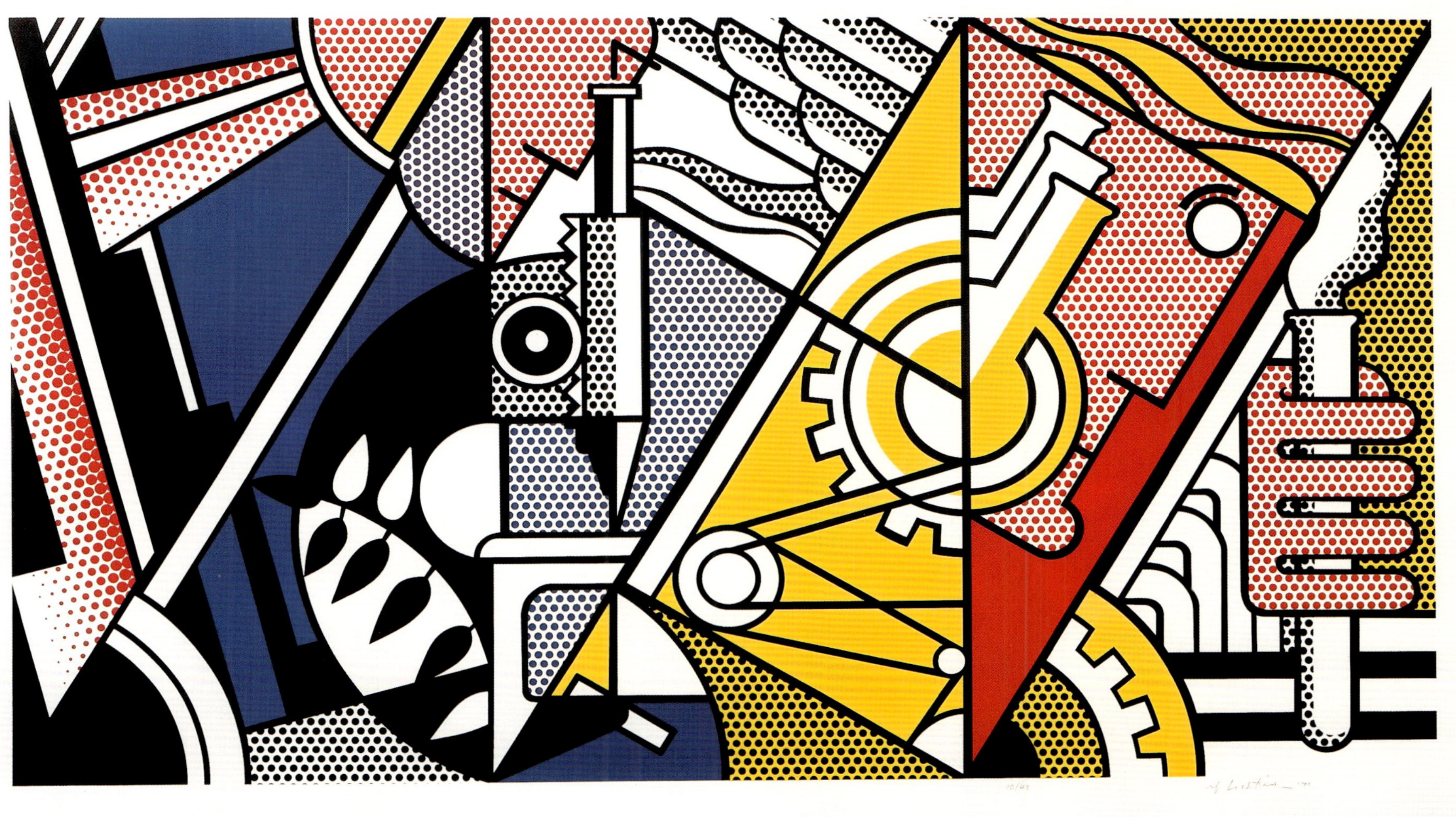

57

56
ANNI ALBERS
Blue Meander, 1970
Color screenprint
$27^{3}/_{4}$ x $23^{7}/_{8}$ in. (sheet)

57
ROY LICHTENSTEIN
Peace through Chemistry II,
from the *Peace through Chemistry Series,* 1970
Color lithograph and screenprint
$37^{3}/_{8}$ x 63 in. (sheet)

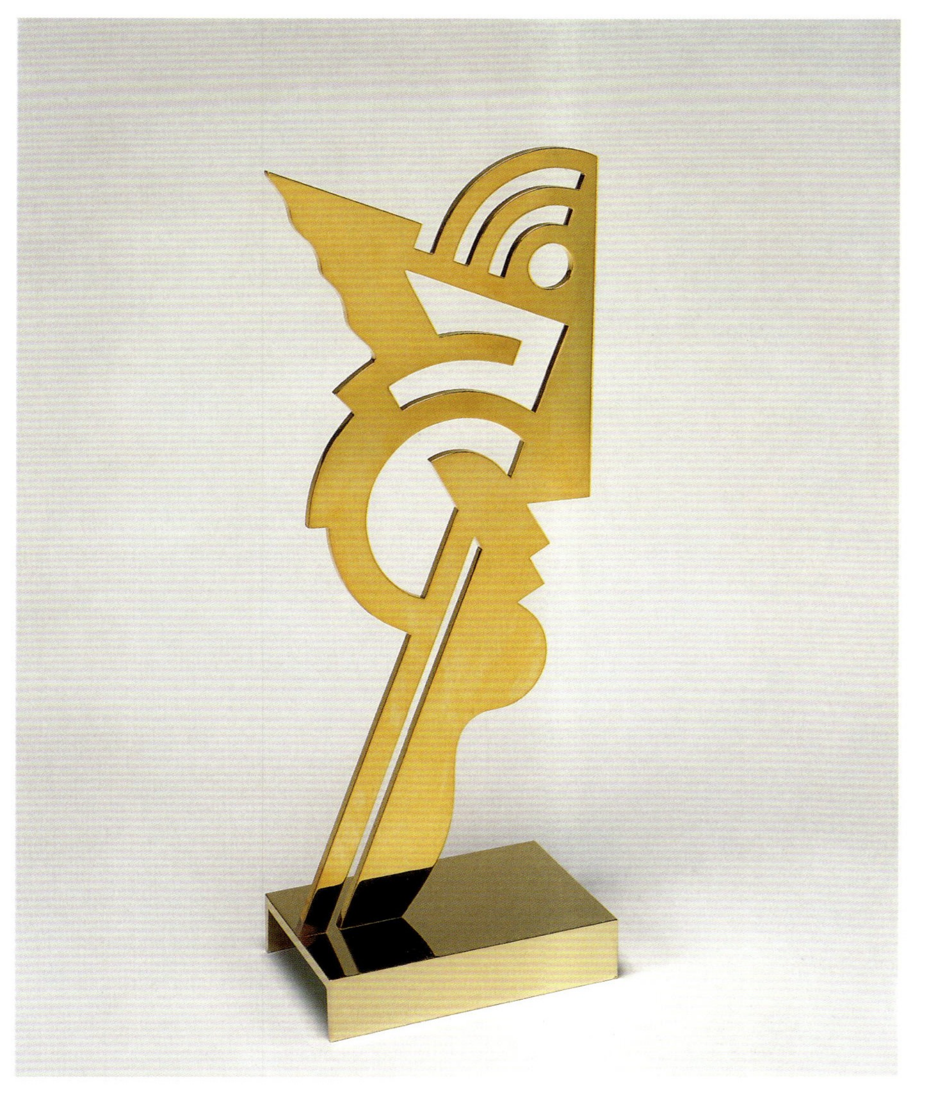

58

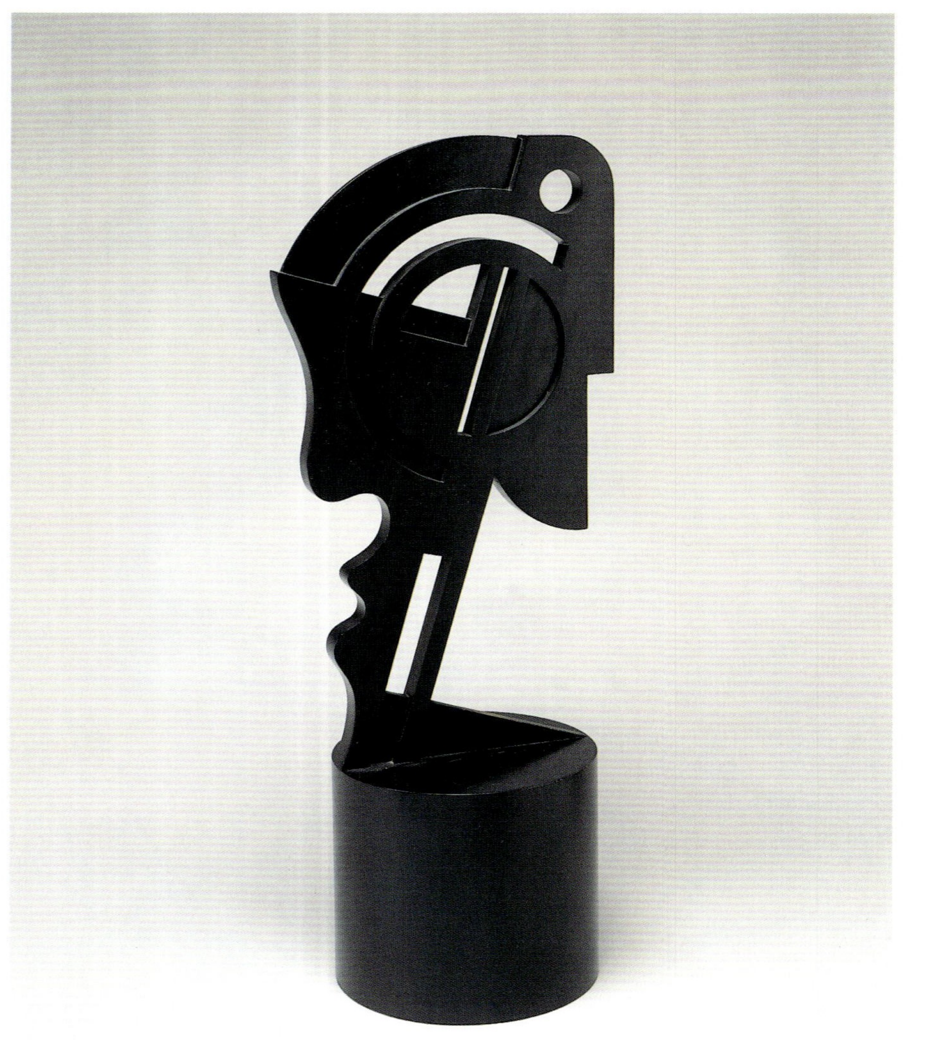

59

58★
ROY LICHTENSTEIN
Untitled Head I, 1970
Solid brass on a brass-plated steel base
25 5/8 in. (height)

59★
ROY LICHTENSTEIN
Untitled Head II, 1970
California English walnut wood
30 in. (height)

60
HELEN FRANKENTHALER
Lot's Wife, 1971
Color lithograph
135 1/2 x 36 in. (overall)

60

61
ROBERT MOTHERWELL
The Black Douglas Stone, 1970–1971
Color lithograph
48 x 32 in. (sheet)

62
ROBERT RAUSCHENBERG
Cardbird II,
from the *Cardbird Series,* 1971
Cardboard, tape, steel staples,
photo-offset lithograph, and screenprint
54 x 33½ in. (overall, irregular)

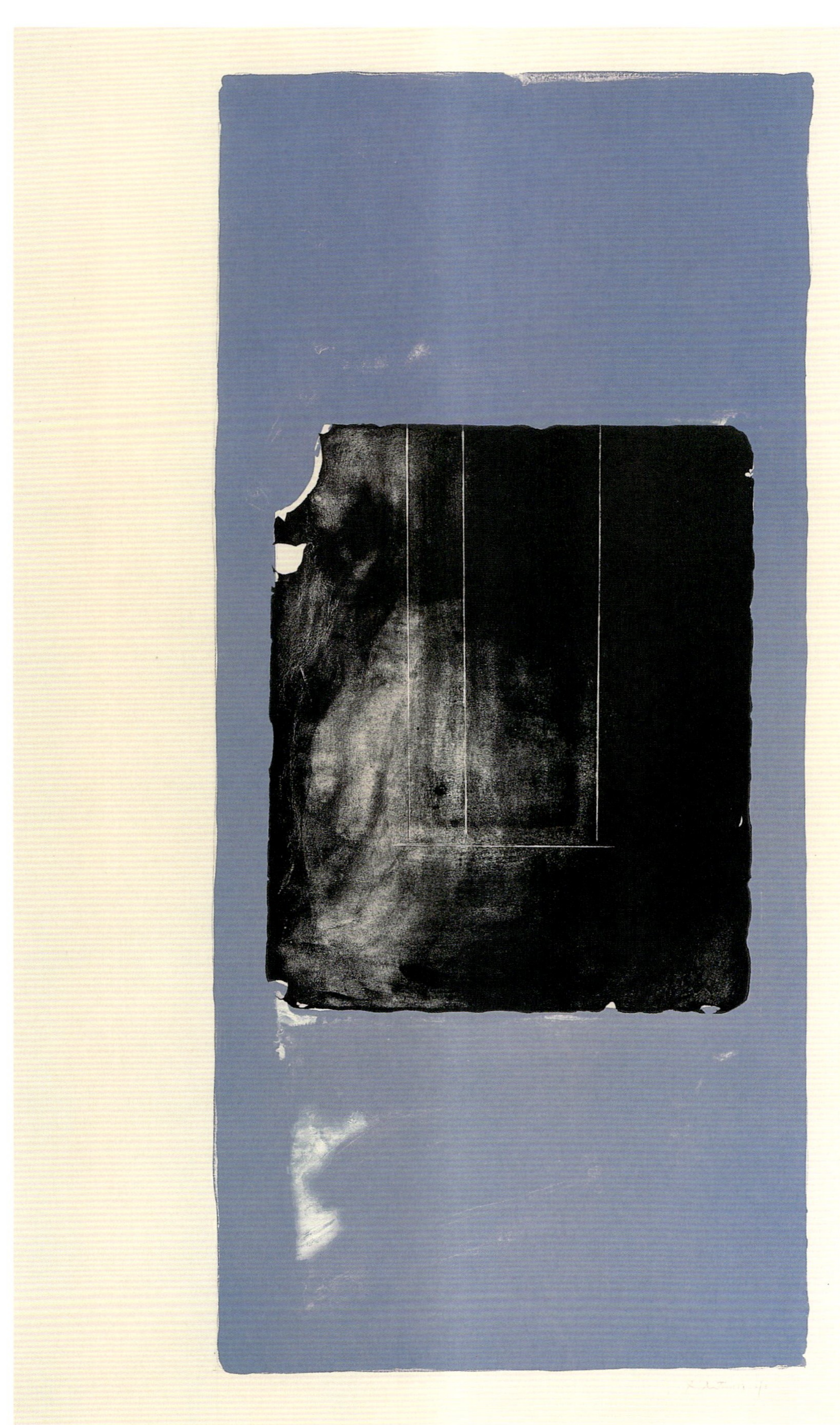

61

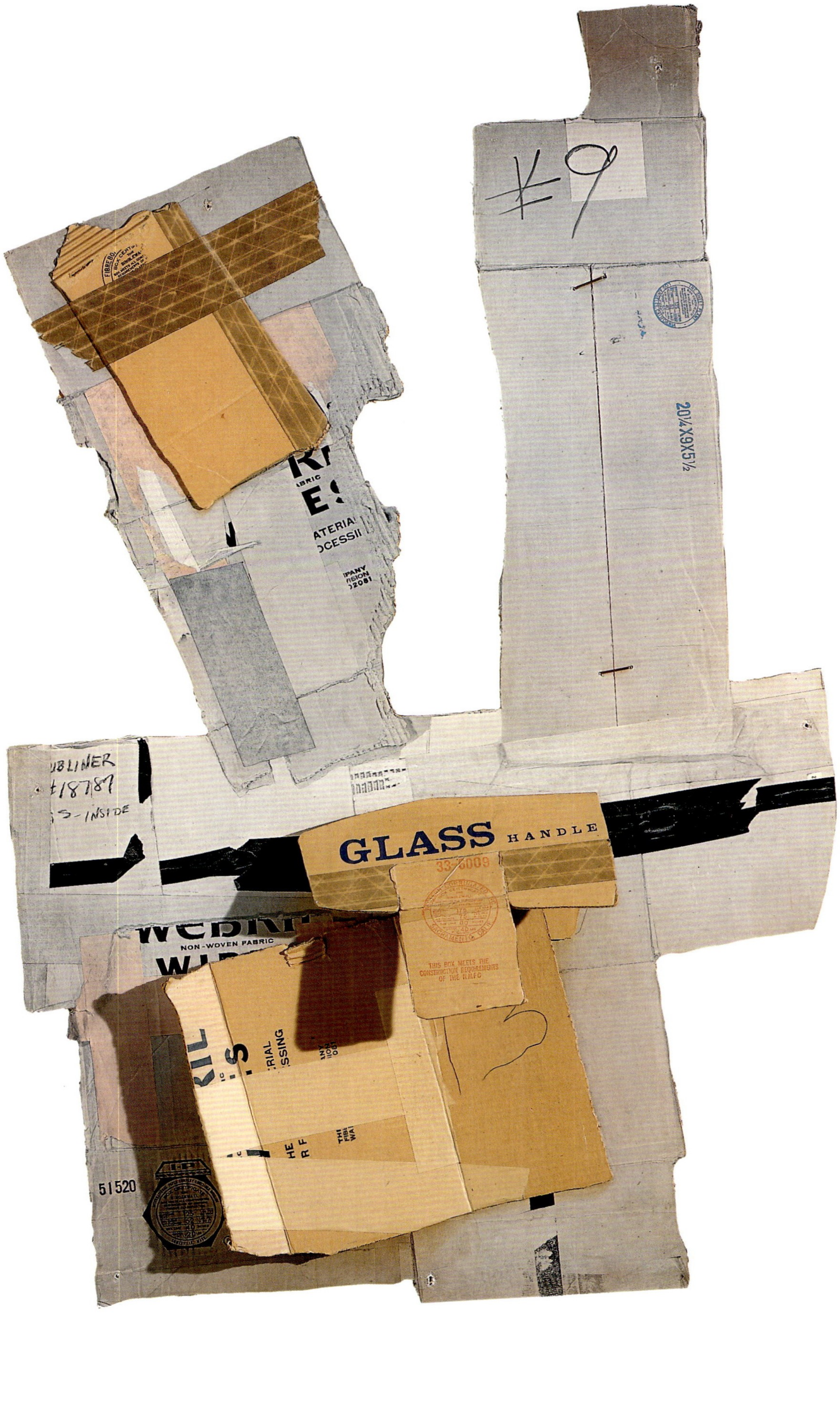

62

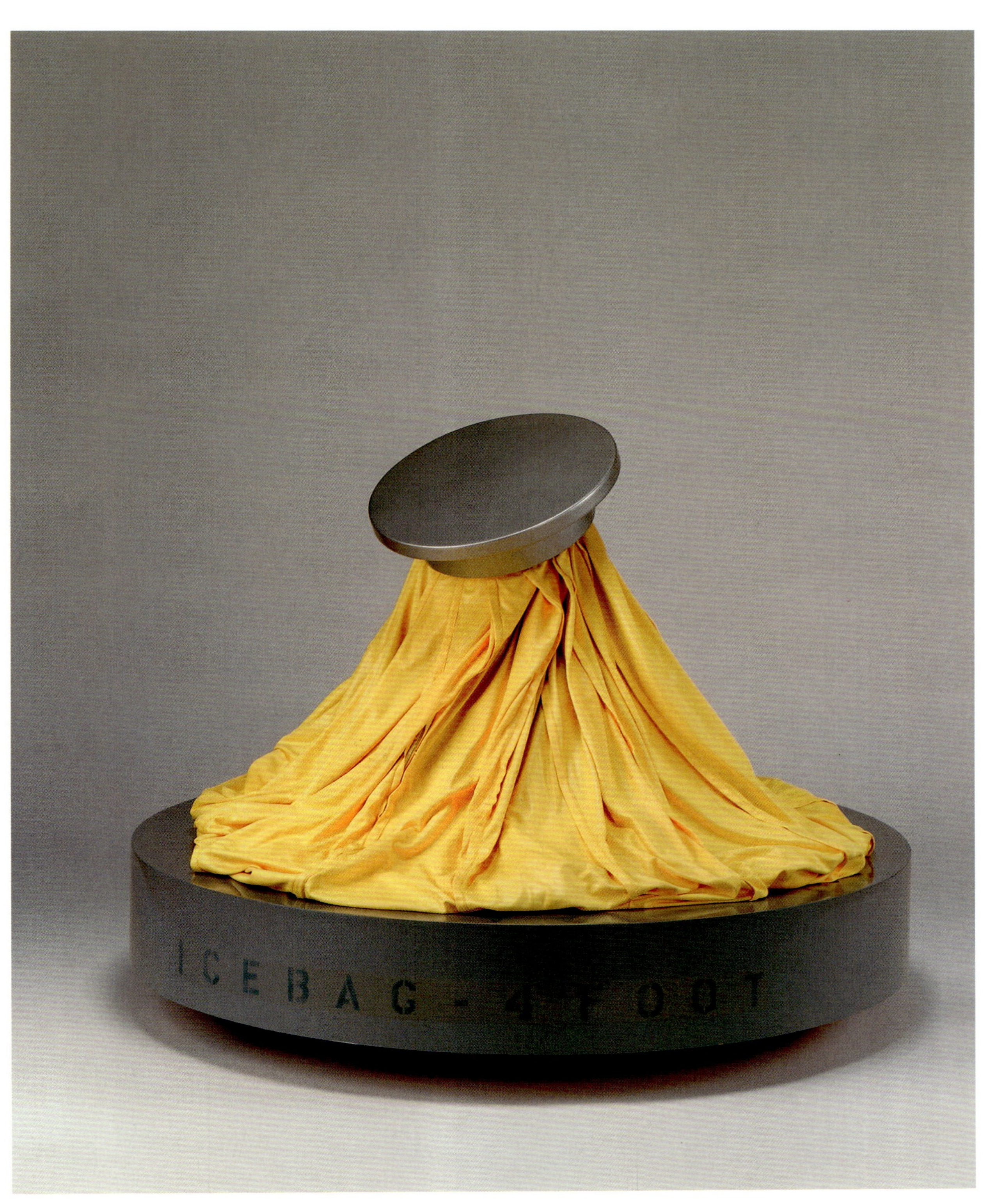

63

63
CLAES OLDENBURG
Ice Bag—Scale B, 1971
Programmed kinetic sculpture
40 in. (height) x 48 in. (diameter)

64★
CLAES OLDENBURG
Geometric Mouse—Scale C, 1971
Black anodized aluminum
24½ x 20 in. (face), 9 in. (ears)

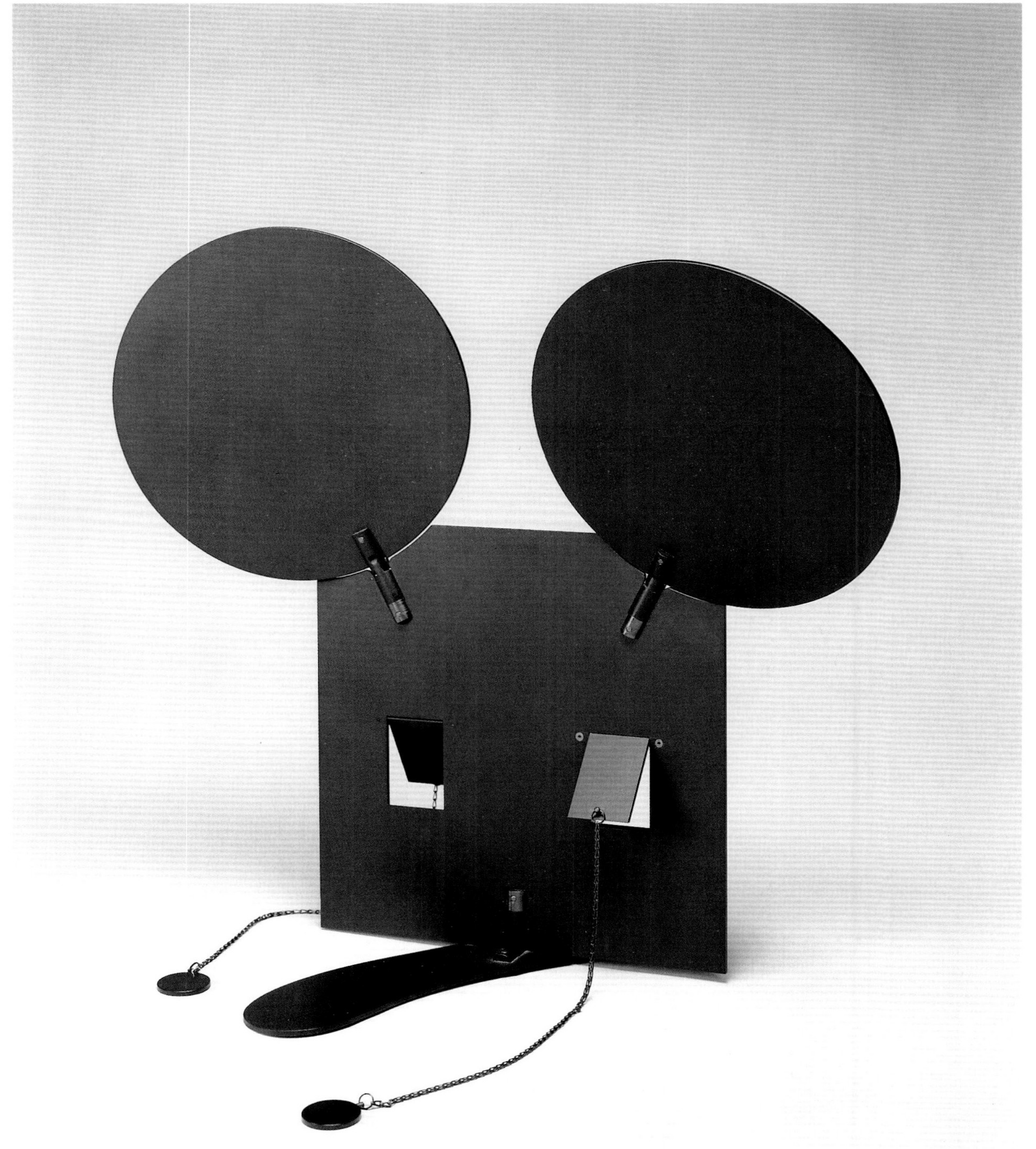

64

65
FRANK STELLA
River of Ponds IV,
from the *Newfoundland Series,* 1971
Color lithograph
38 x 38 in. (sheet)

66
FRANK STELLA
Bonne Bay,
from the *Newfoundland Series,* 1971
Color lithograph and screenprint
38 x 70 in. (sheet)

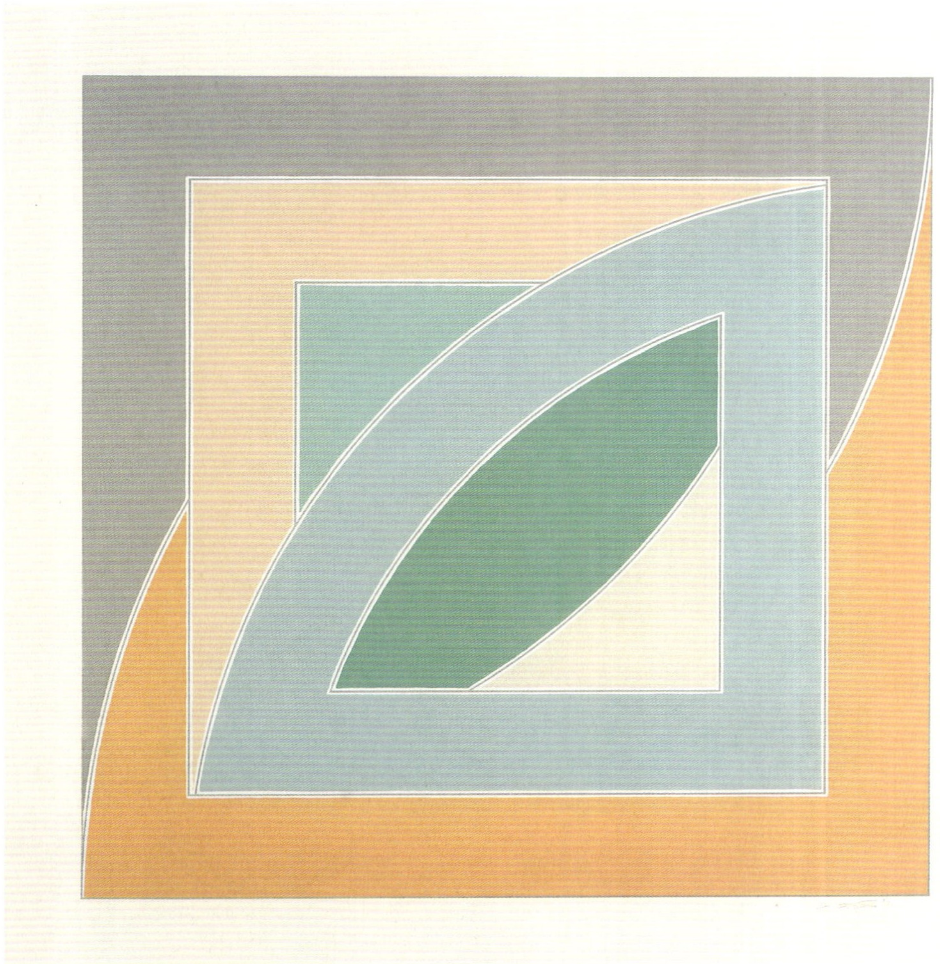

65

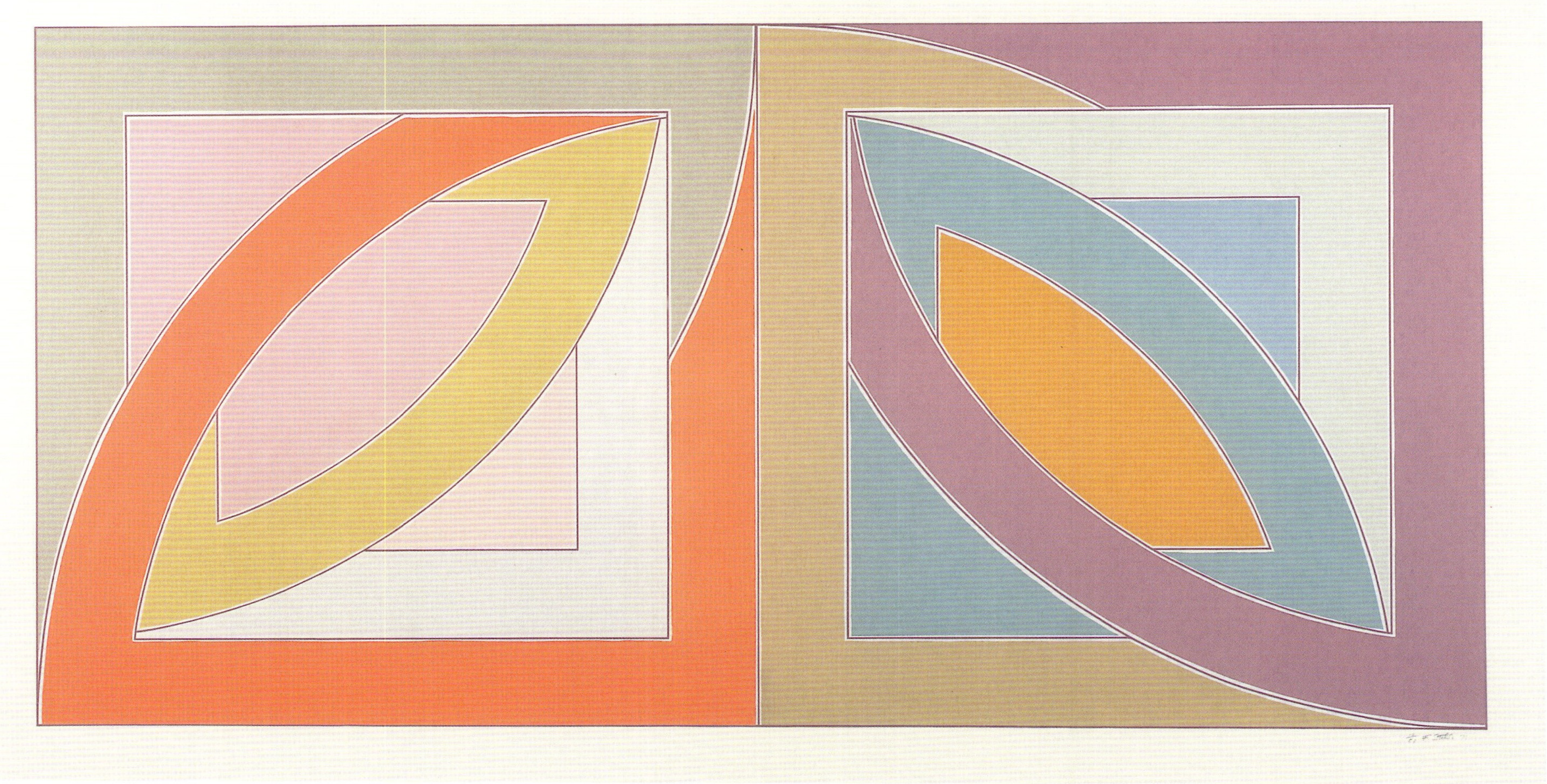

66

67★
JASPER JOHNS
Decoy, 1971
Color lithograph
41 x 29 in. (sheet)

68
JASPER JOHNS
Fool's House, 1971
Color lithograph
44 x 29 (sheet)

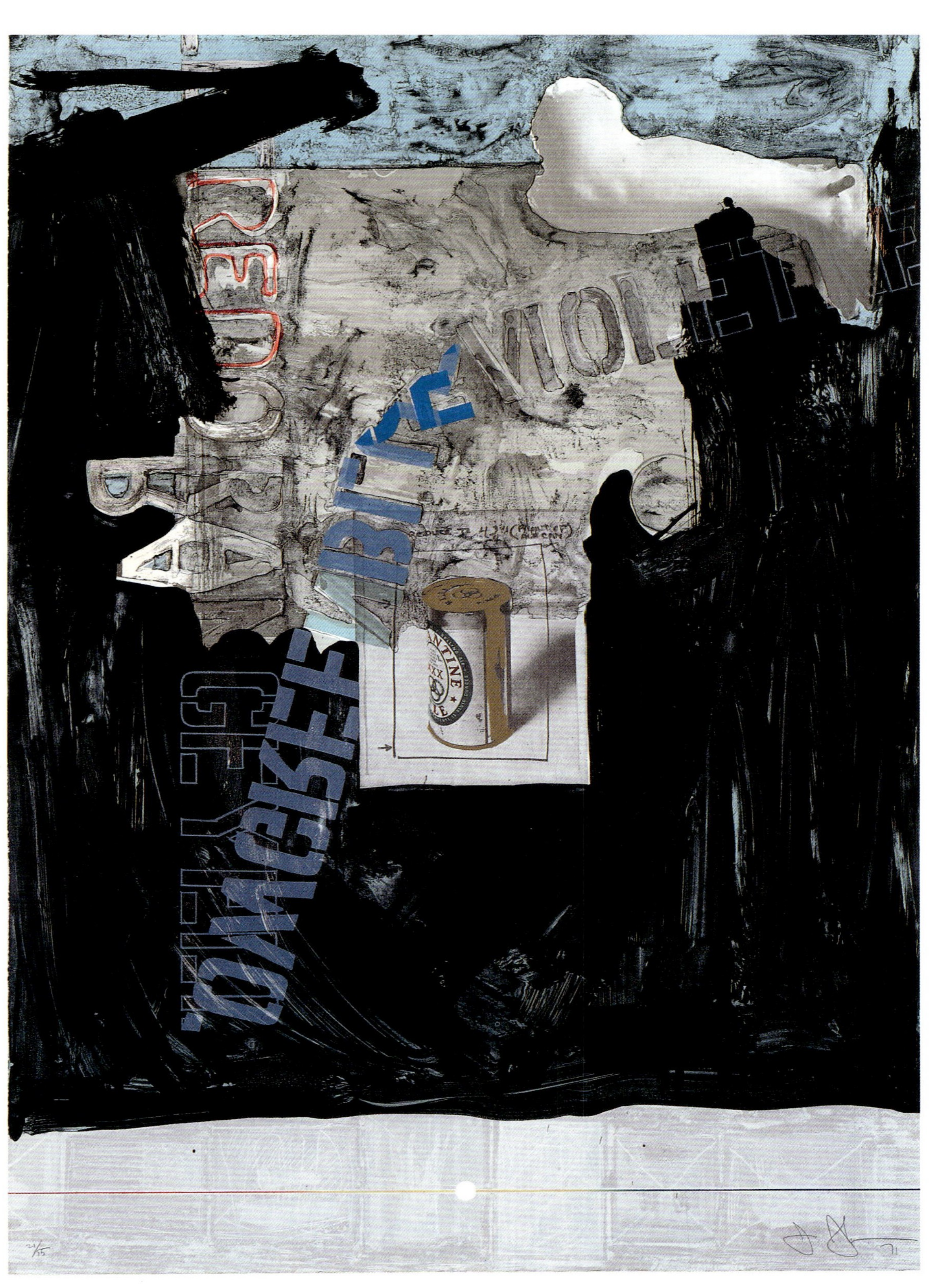

67

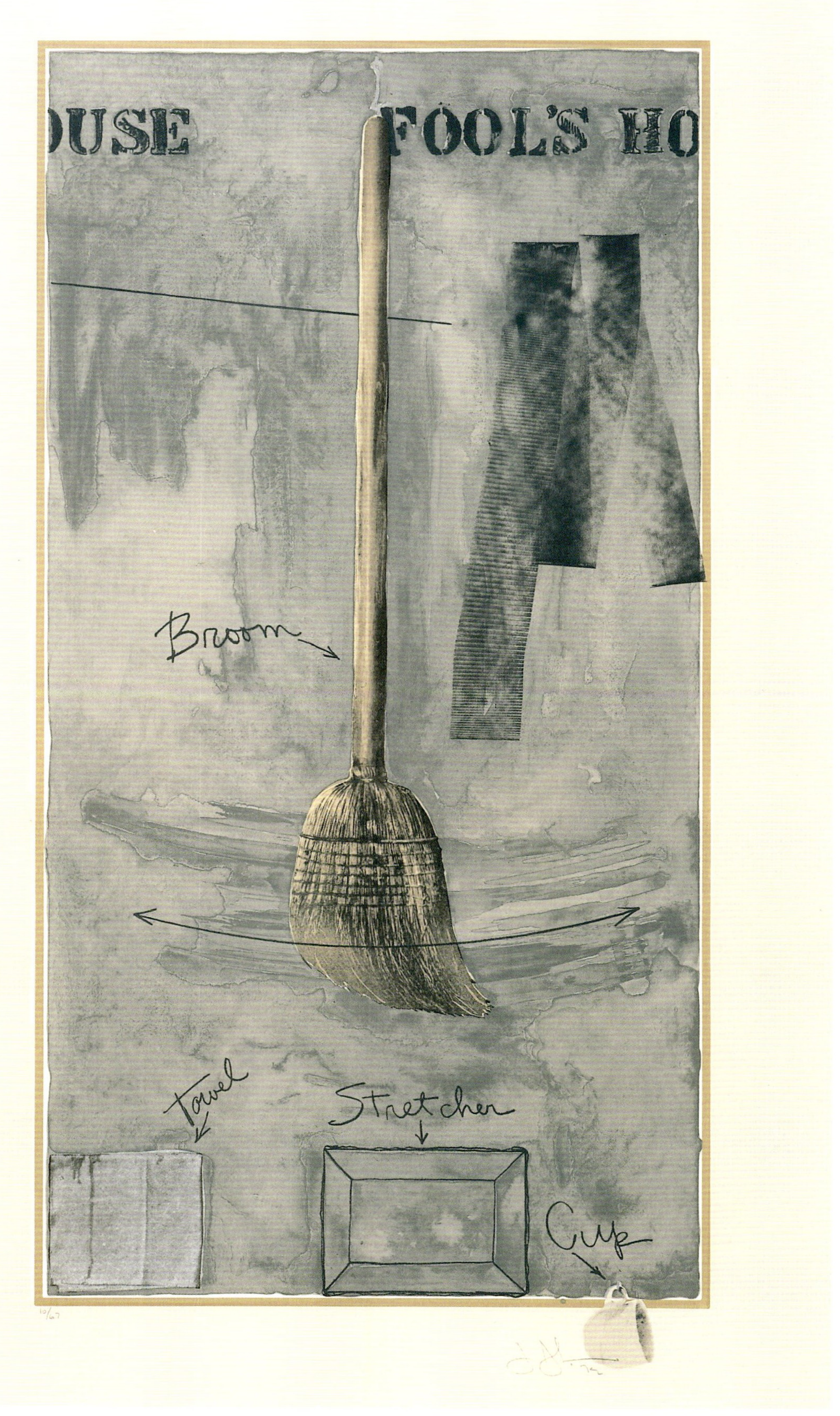

68

69
JASPER JOHNS
Two Flags (Black), 1970–1972
Lithograph
31½ x 23 in. (sheet)

70
MARISOL [MARISOL ESCOBAR]
Diptych, 1971
Lithographs
95½ x 31⅝ in. (overall)

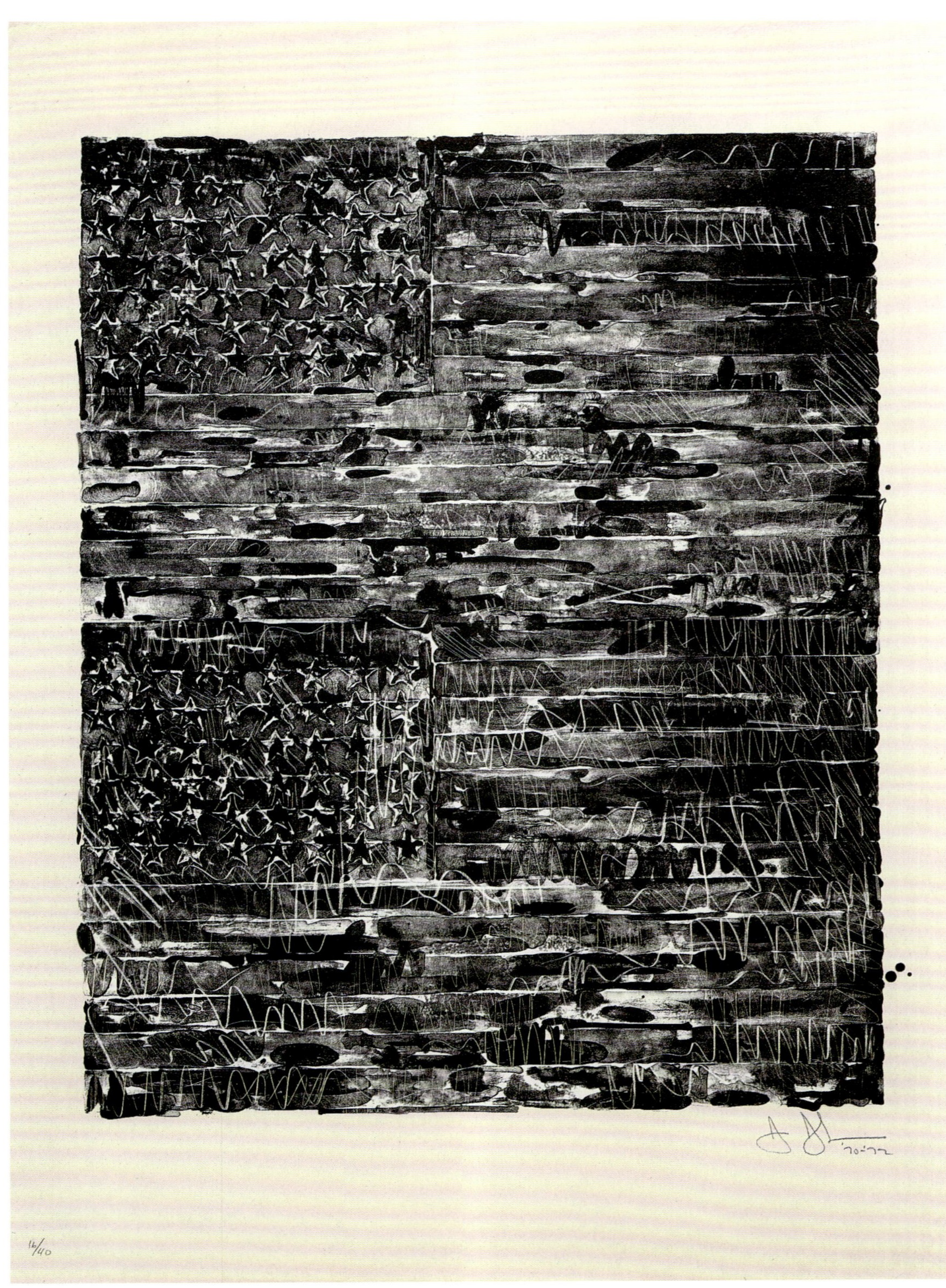

69

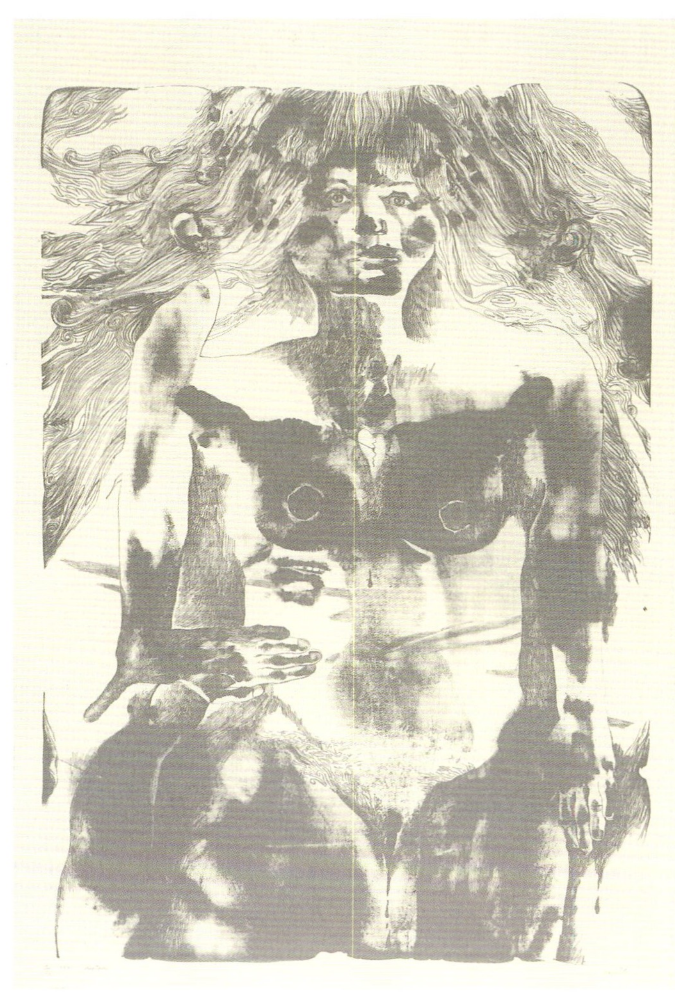

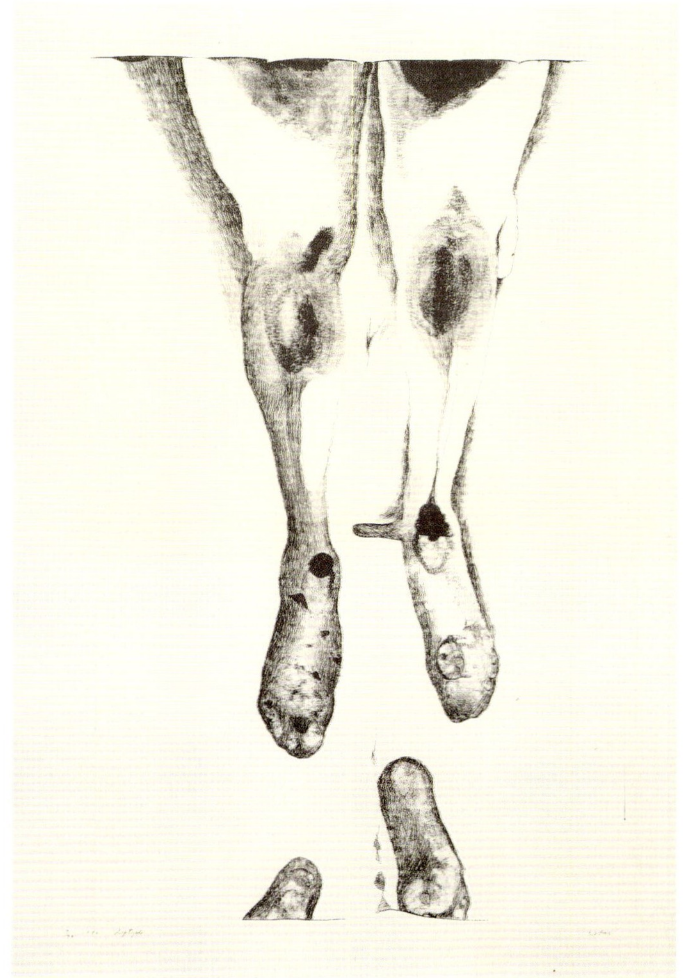

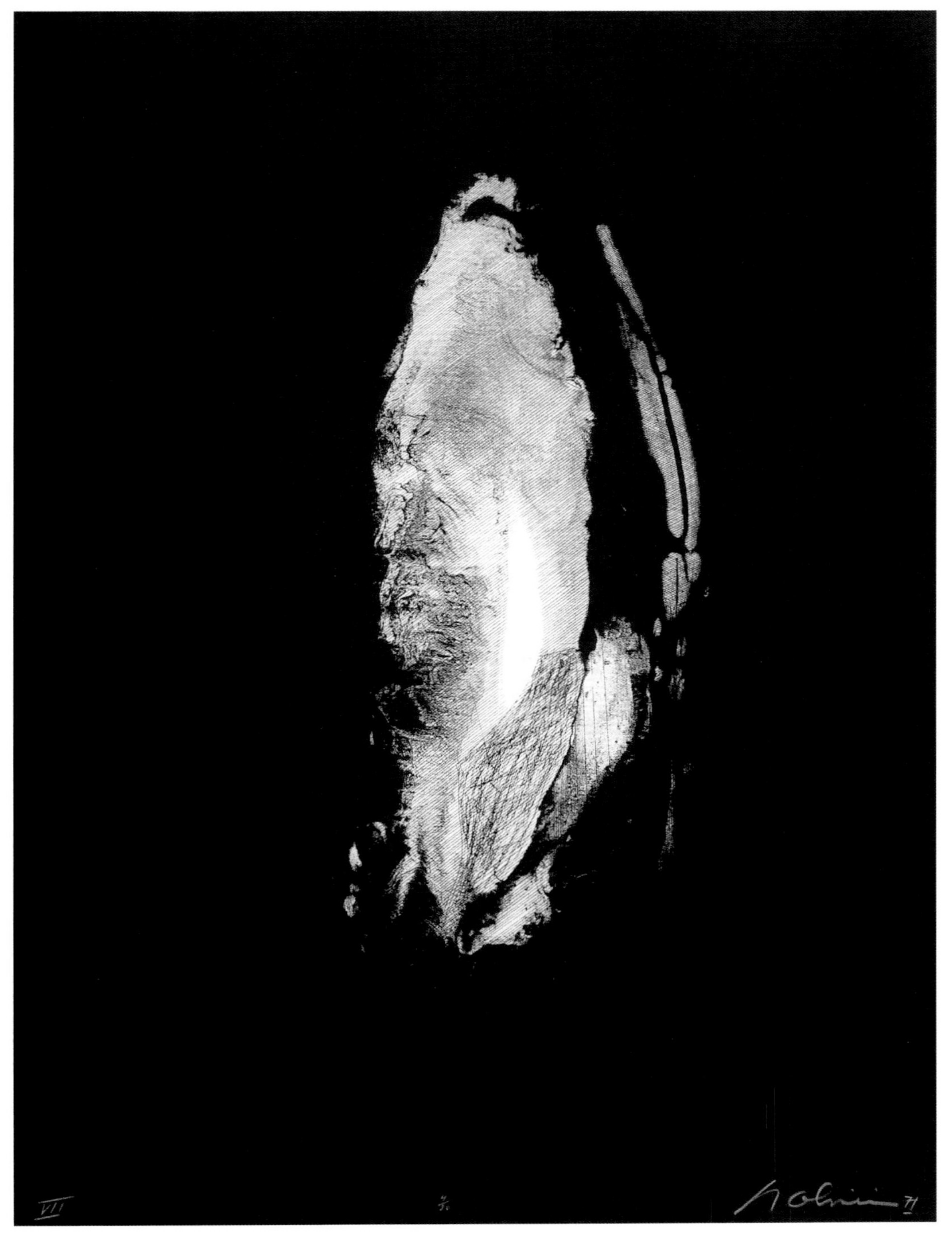

71

71
NATHAN OLIVEIRA
Untitled, pl. VII
from the portfolio
To Edgar Allan Poe, 1971
Lithograph
30 3/16 x 22 3/8 in. (sheet)

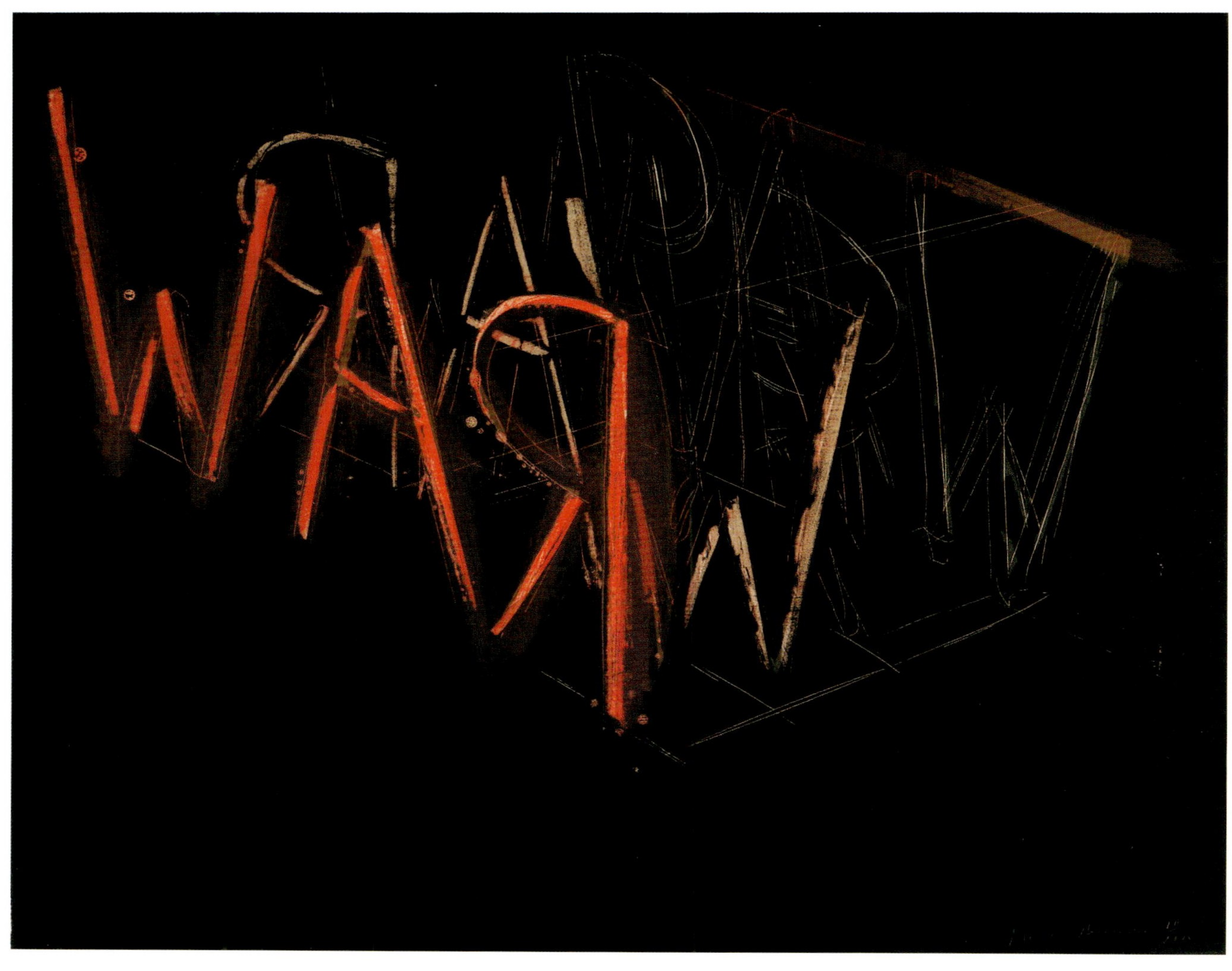

72

72
BRUCE NAUMAN
War, 1971
Color lithograph
22 1/2 x 28 1/4 in. (sheet)

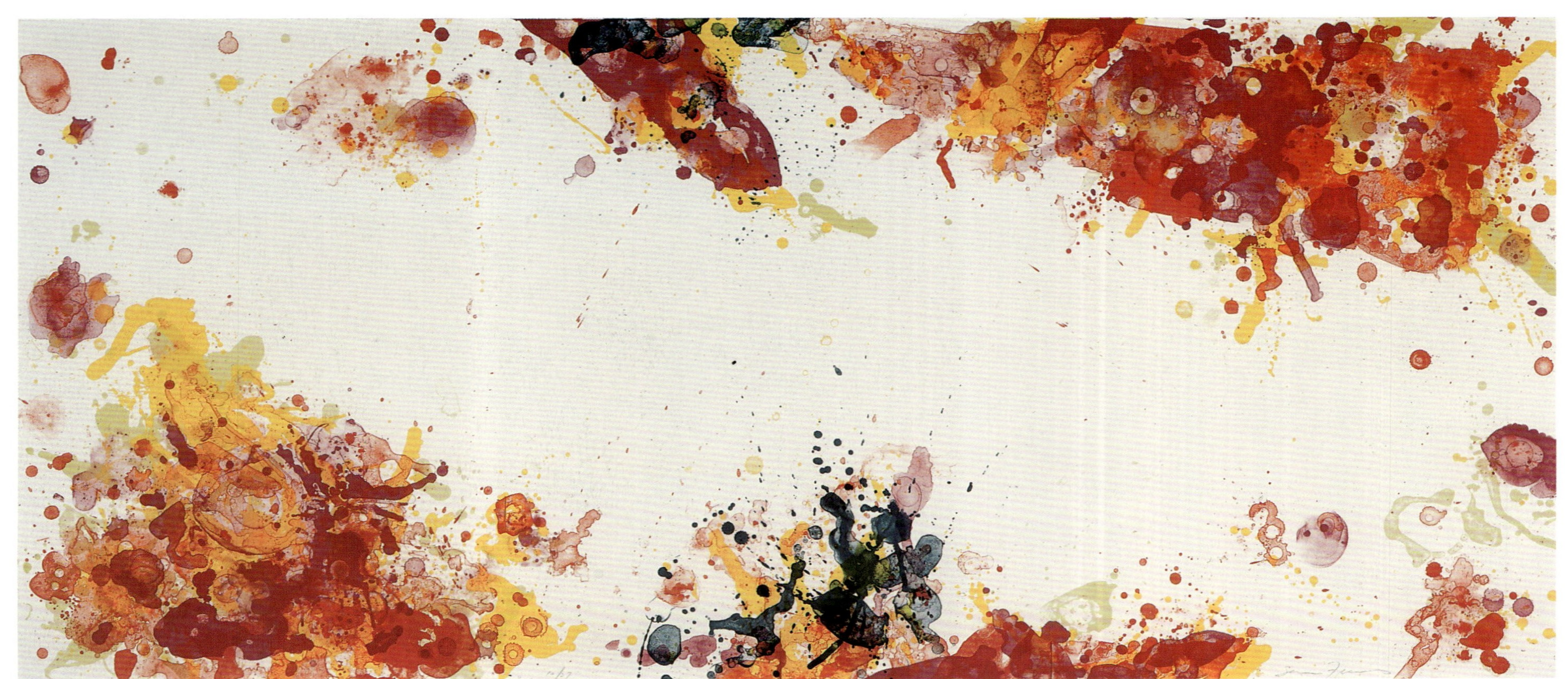

73

73
SAM FRANCIS
Spleen (Red), 1971
Color lithograph
35 x 78¾ in. (sheet)

74
ELLSWORTH KELLY
Mirrored Concorde, 1971
Chromed steel sculpture on oak base
22¾ x 26½ x 10 in. (overall sculpture),
28½ x 25¾ x 13½ in. (overall base)

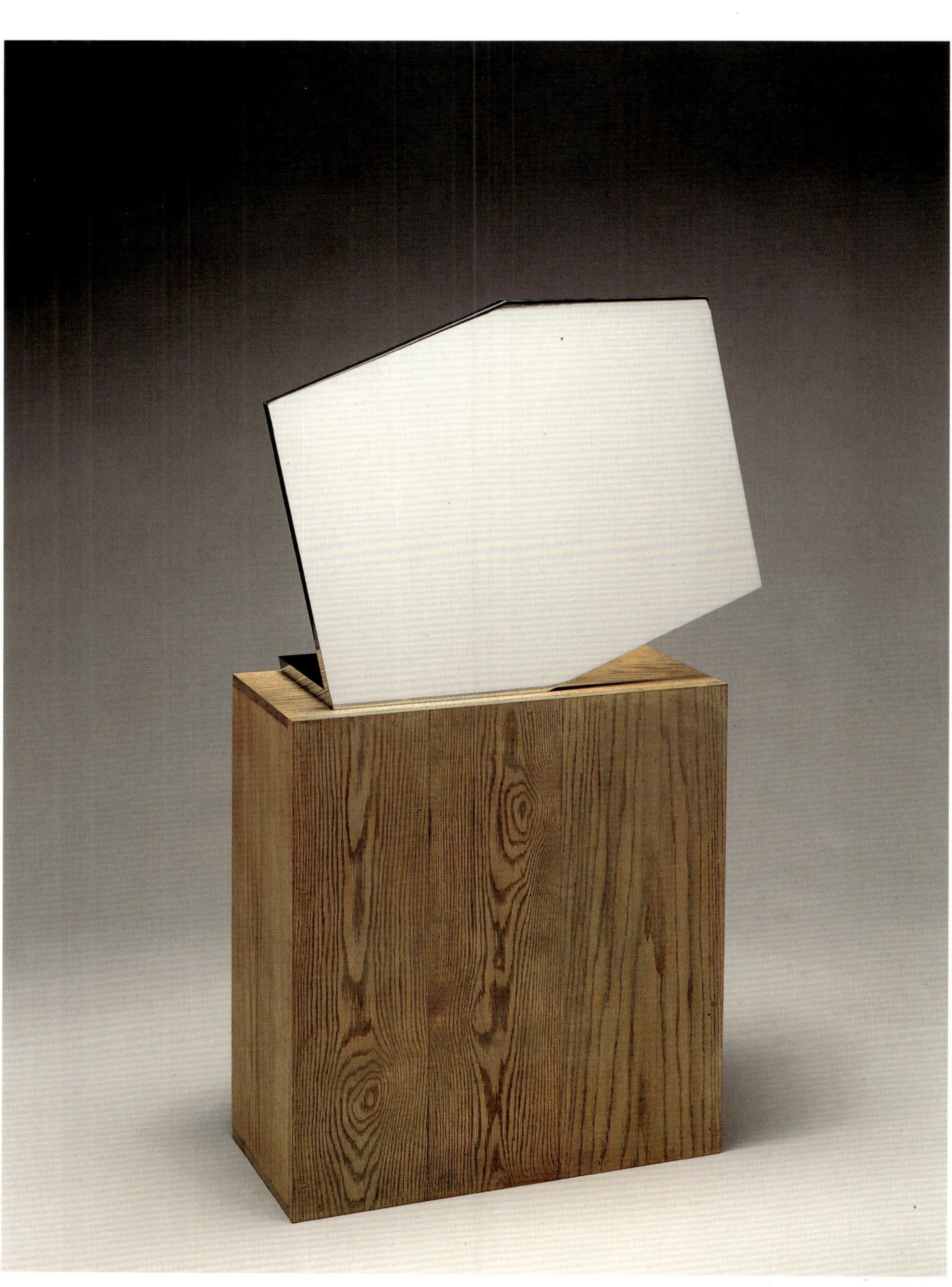

74

75

75
RICHARD SERRA
Du Common, 1972
Lithograph
51½ x 40½ in. (sheet)

76
ROBERT MOTHERWELL
Untitled ["Red/Rojo 8–11"], in the book *A la pintura/To Painting*, 1968–1972
Color aquatint, displayed in a white Formica-laminated box
25⁹⁄₁₆ x 37¹⁵⁄₁₆ in. (sheet), 28 x 40 x 6 in. (box)

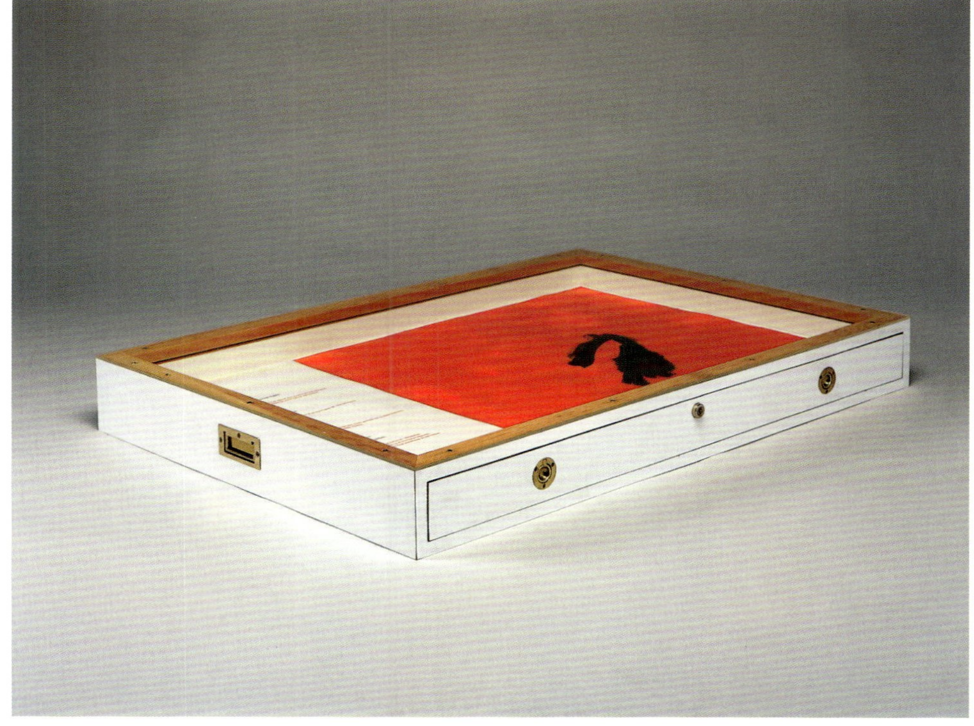

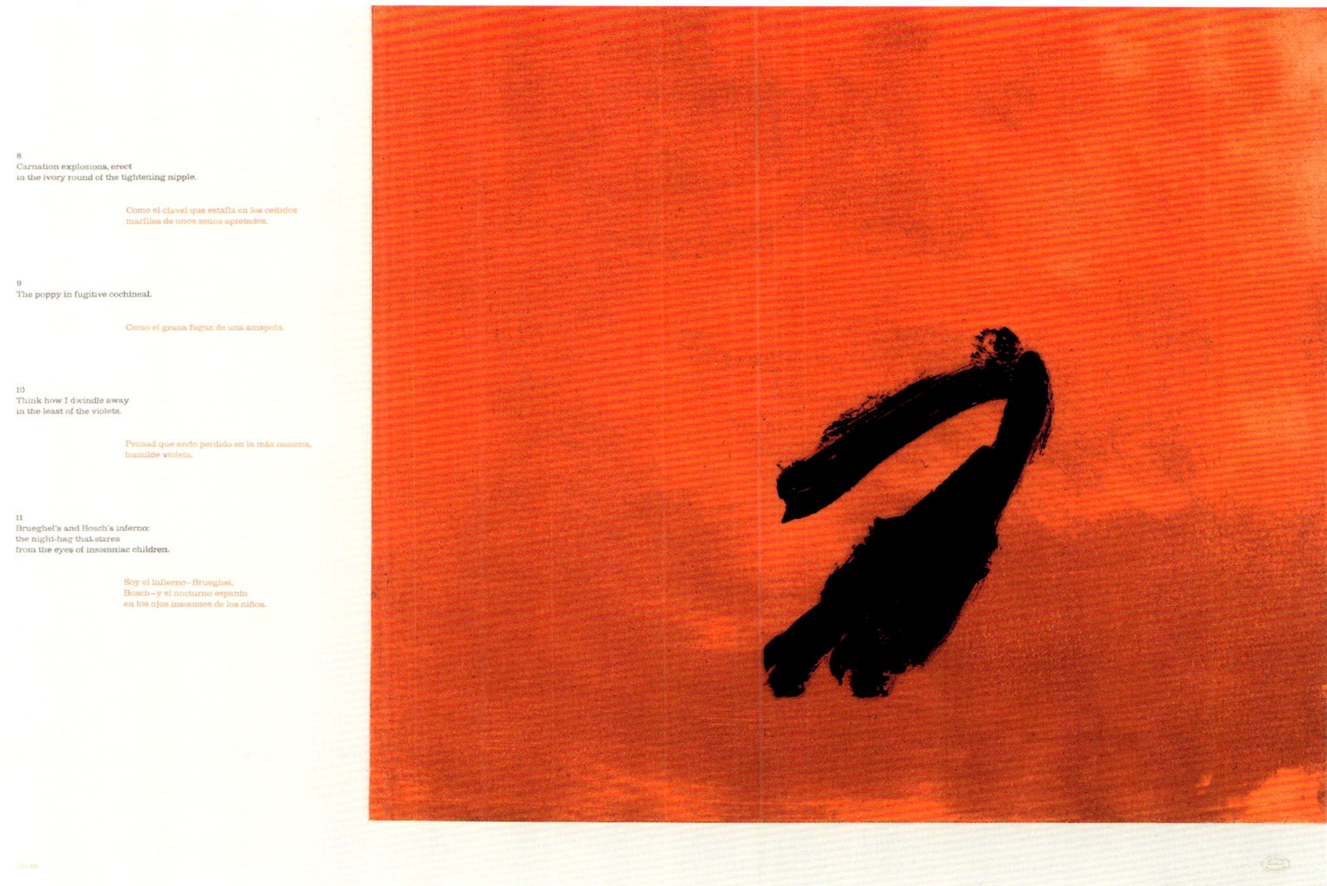

76

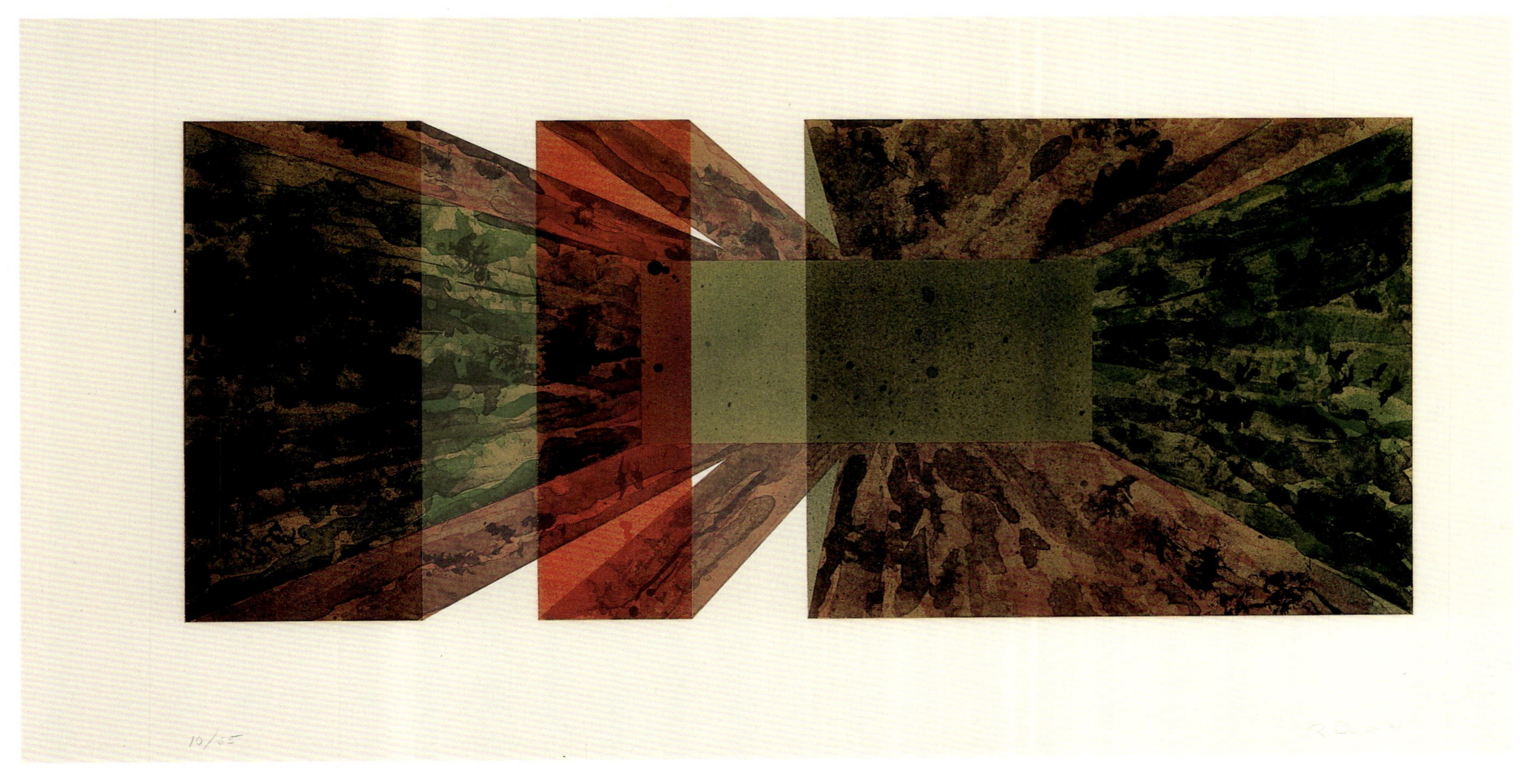

77

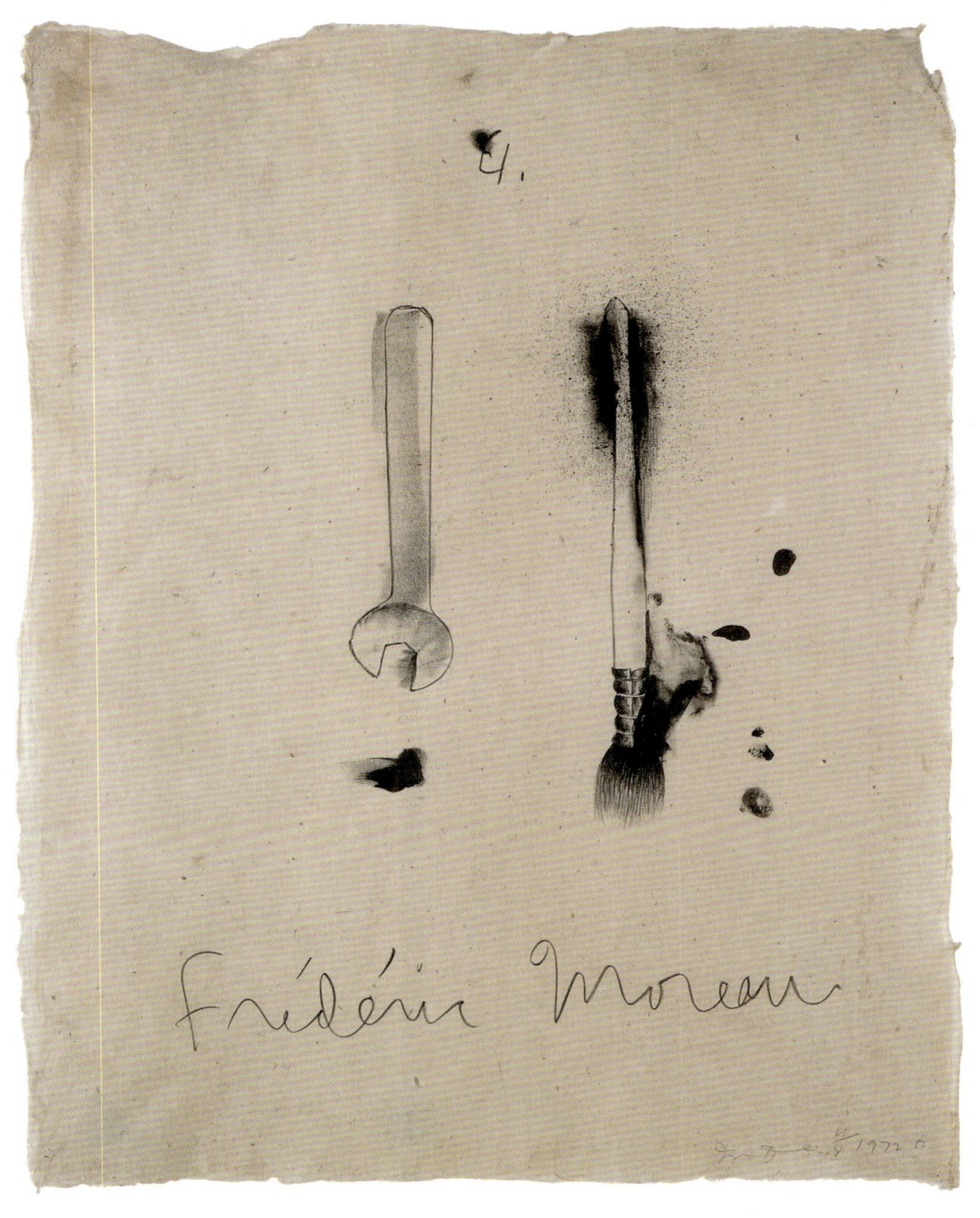

78

77
RON DAVIS
Double Slice, 1972
Inkless intaglio on color lithograph
20¼ x 39½ in. (sheet)

78★
JIM DINE
Frédéric Moreau,
from the series
Flaubert Favorites (Edition A), 1972
Lithograph on handmade Nepalese paper
24⅞ x 18⅞ in. (sheet)

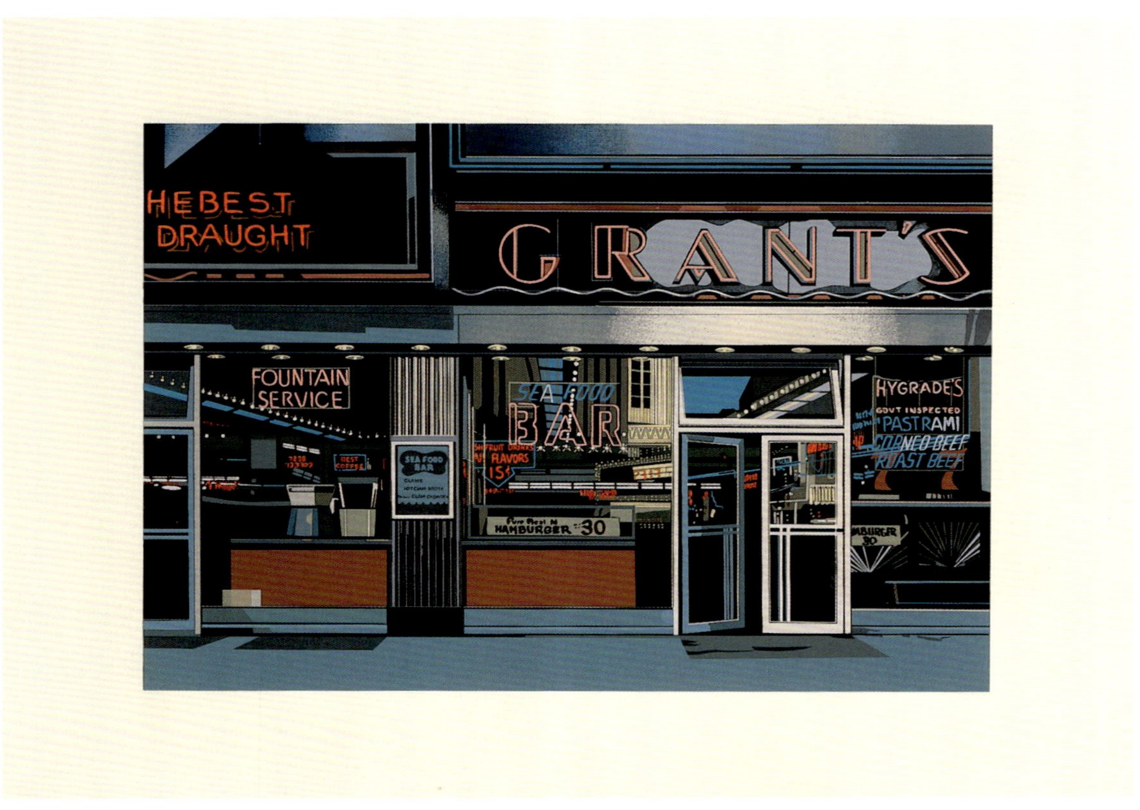

79

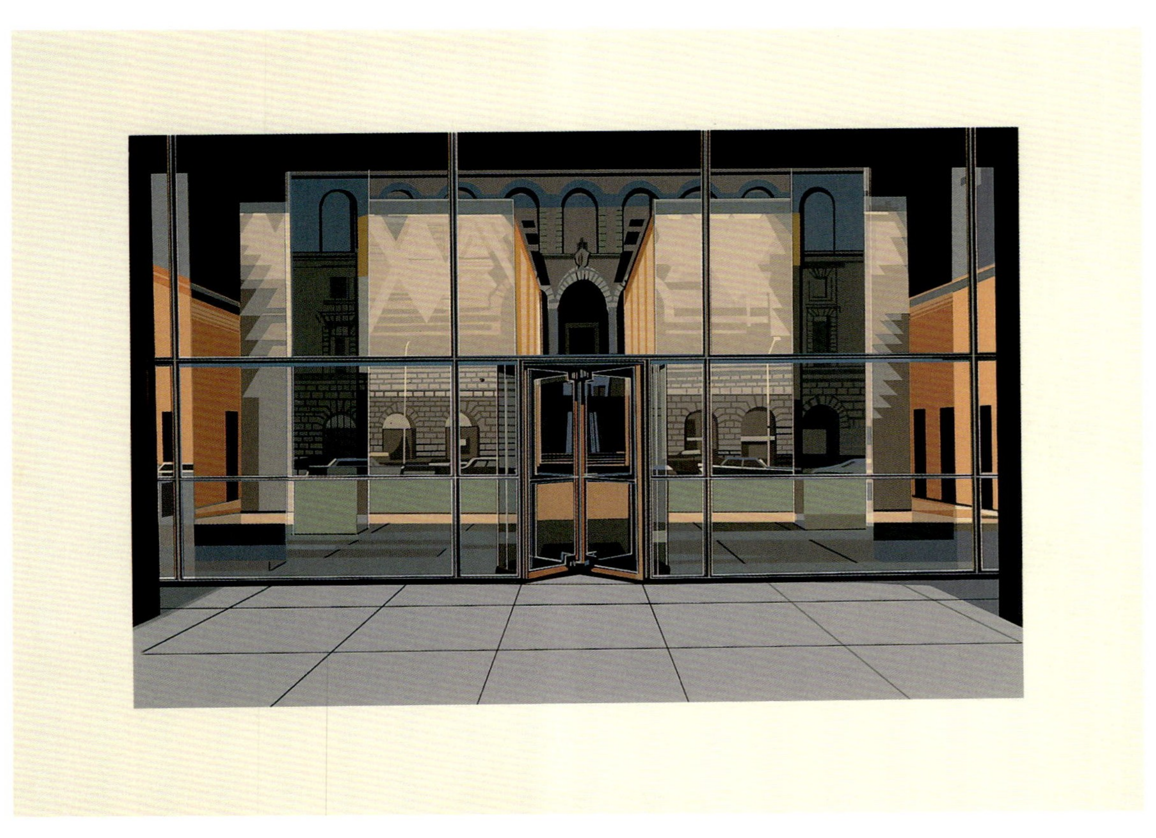

81

Plates 79–82

RICHARD ESTES

4 prints from the series of 8,

Urban Landscapes I, 1972

Color screenprints

$19\frac{1}{2}$ x $27\frac{1}{2}$ in. (each sheet)

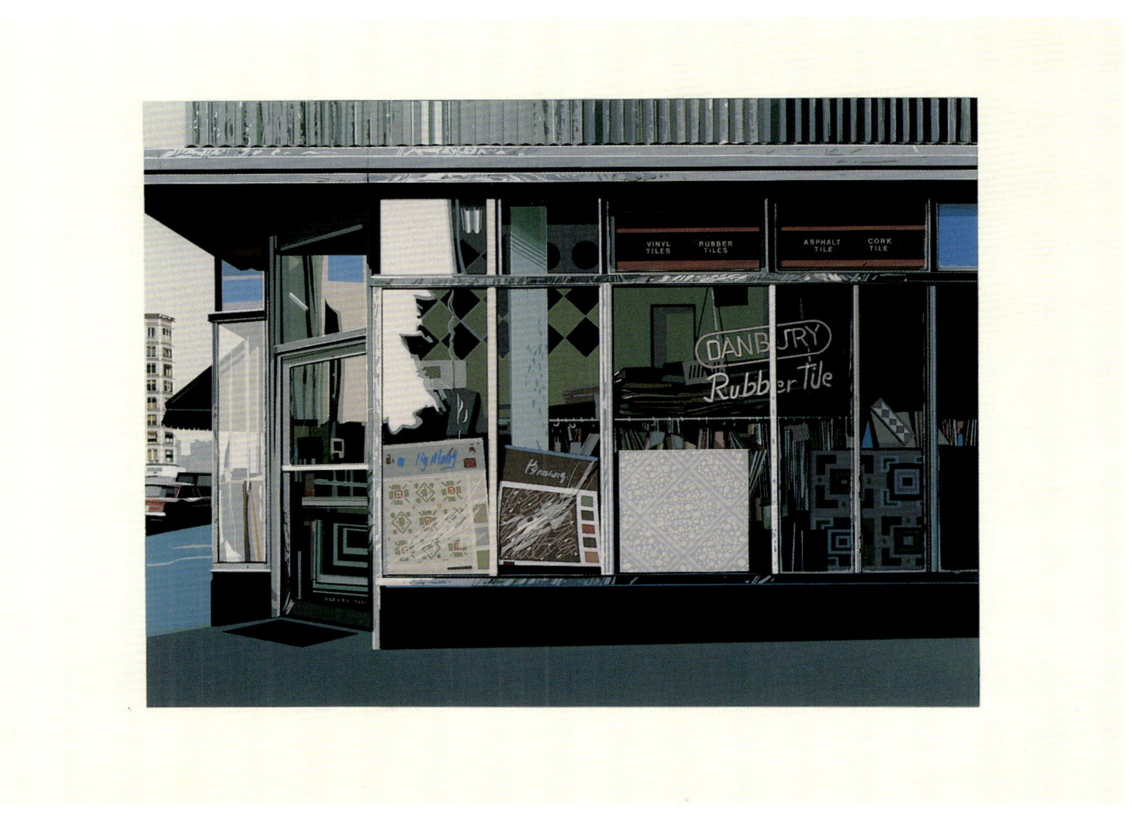

80

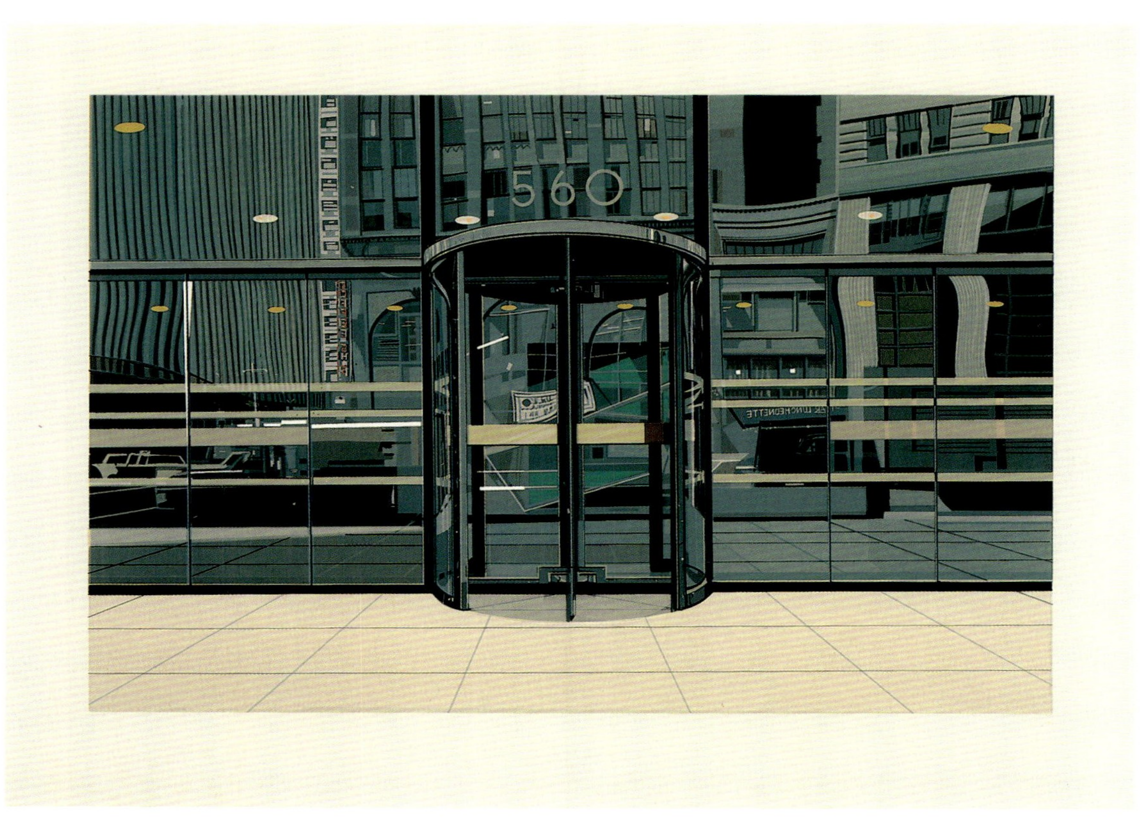

82

79 *Grant's*
80 *Danbury Tile*
81 *Seagram Building*
82 *560*

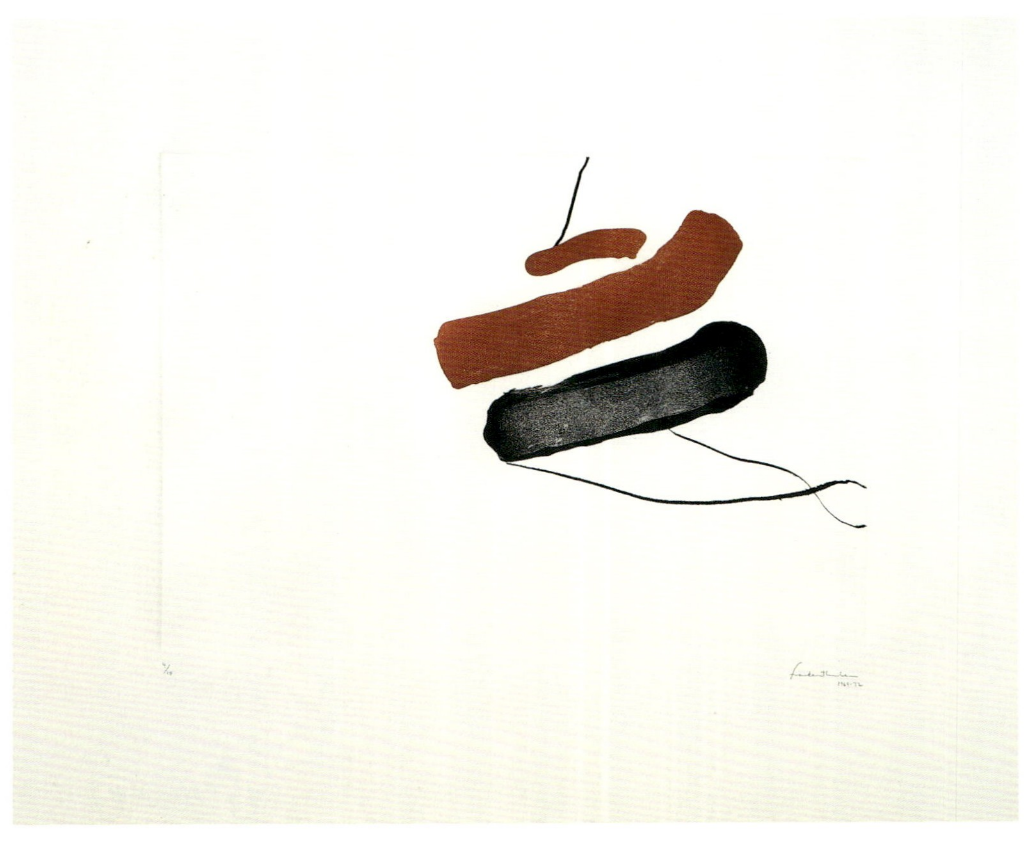

83

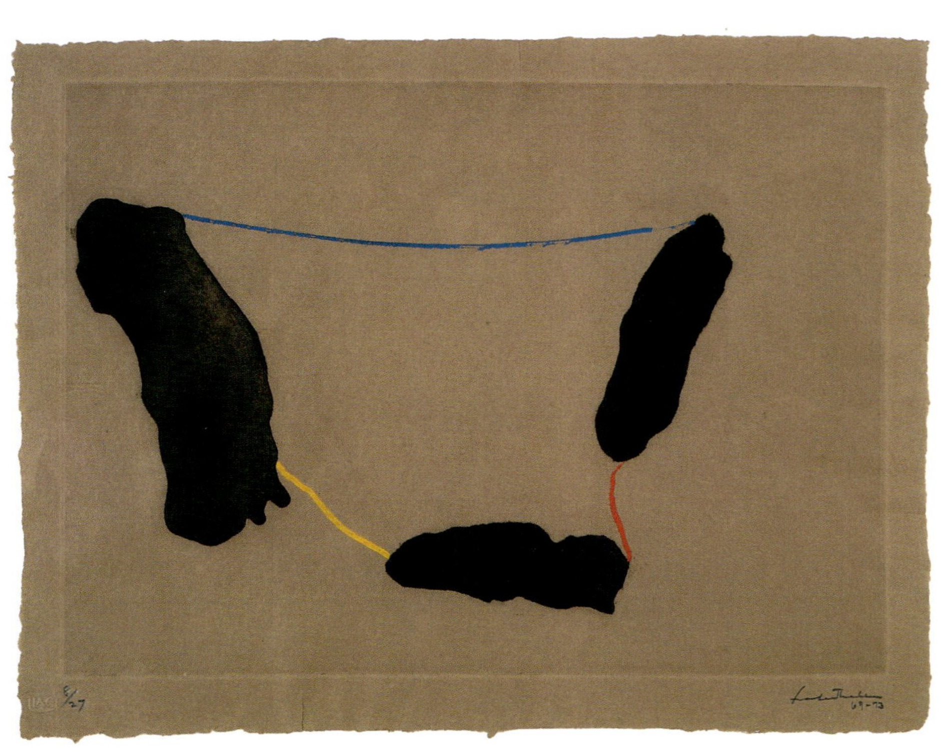

84

83
HELEN FRANKENTHALER
Crete, 1969–1972
Color etching and sugar-lift aquatint,
$22^{1}/_{2}$ x 27 in. (sheet)

84
HELEN FRANKENTHALER
Connected by Joy, 1969–1973
Color etching and sugar-lift aquatint on
Jeff Goodman handmade brown paper
$16^{1}/_{2}$ x 21 in. (sheet)

85
ED MOSES
Wedge Series: No. 5, 1973
Color lithograph on silk tissue
$24^{1}/_{4}$ x $18^{3}/_{8}$ in. (sheet)

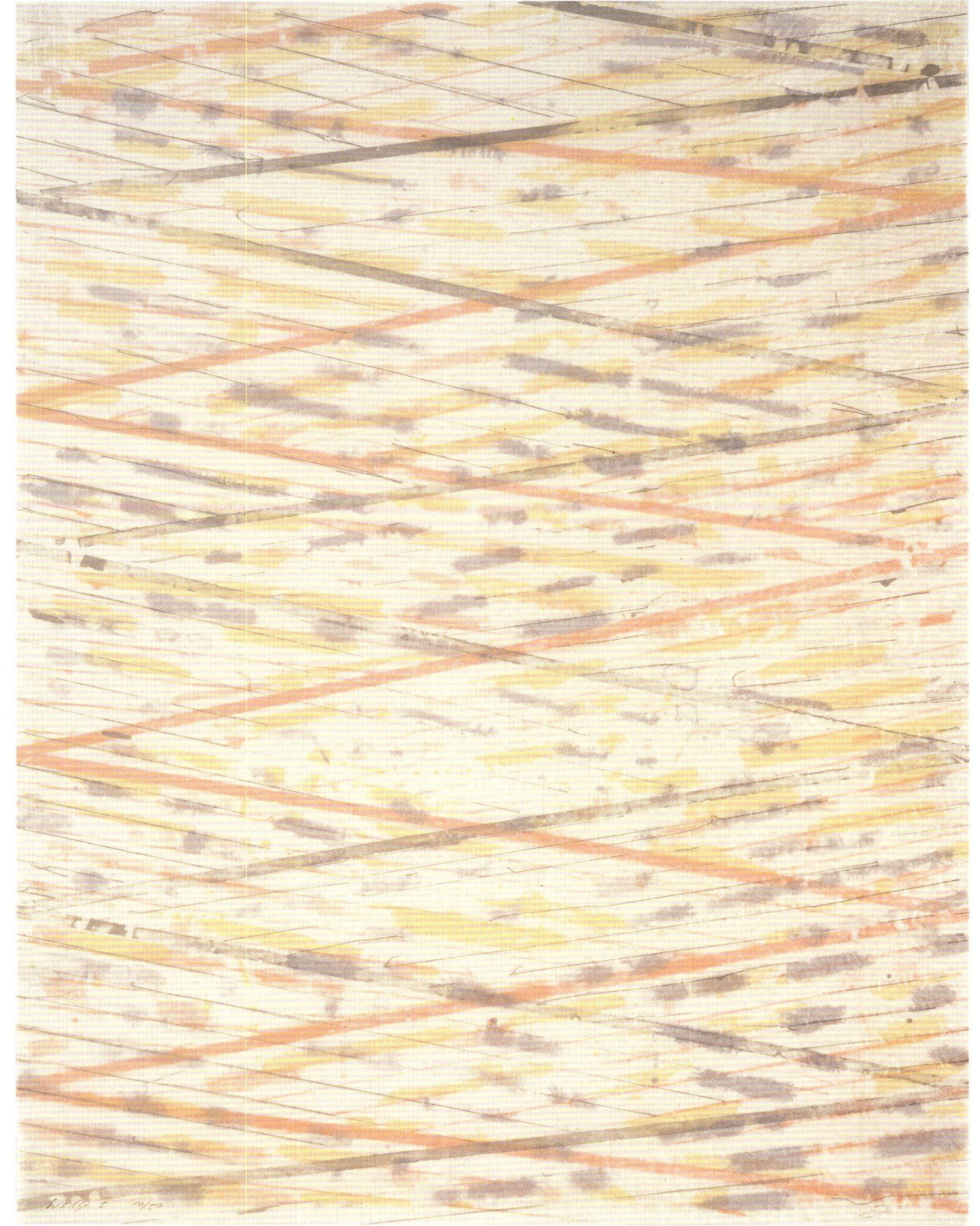

85

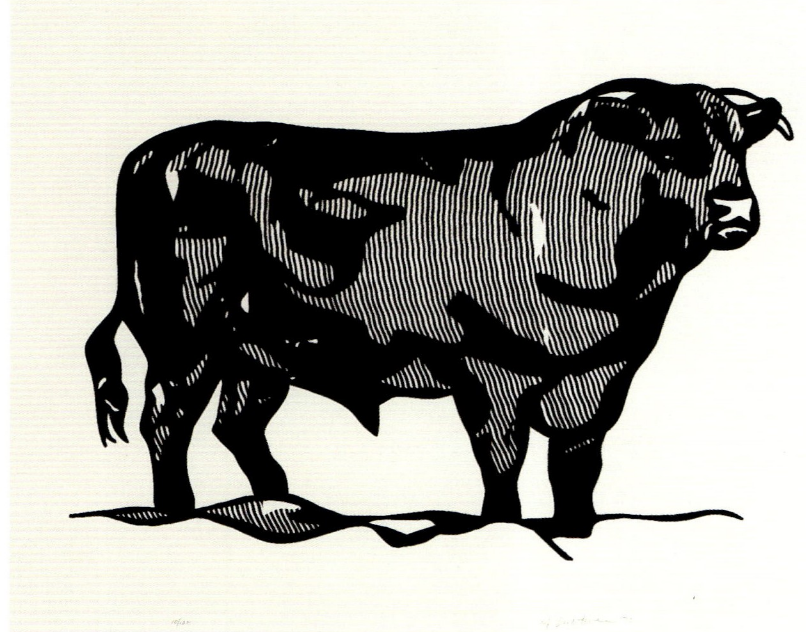

86

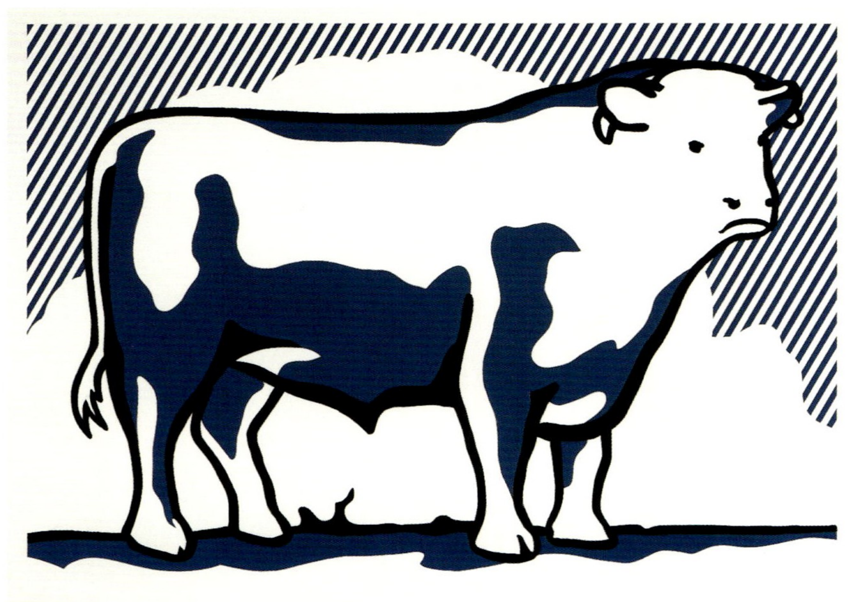

87

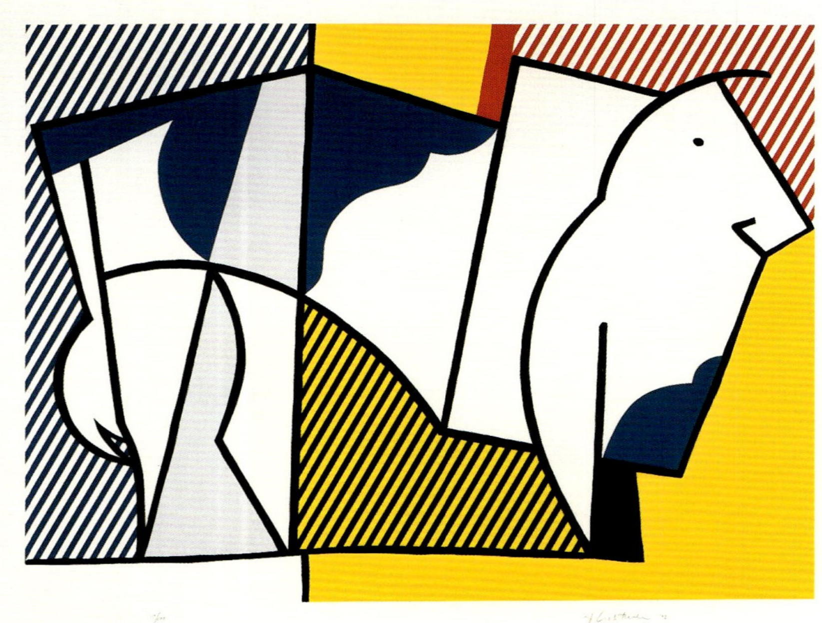

88

86
ROY LICHTENSTEIN
Bull I,
from the *Bull Profile Series,* 1973
Line-cut
27 x 35 in. (sheet)

87
ROY LICHTENSTEIN
Bull II,
from the *Bull Profile Series,* 1973
Color lithograph and line-cut
27 x 35 in. (sheet)

88
ROY LICHTENSTEIN
Bull III,
from the *Bull Profile Series,* 1973
Color lithograph, screenprint, and line-cut
27 x 35 1/16 in. (sheet)

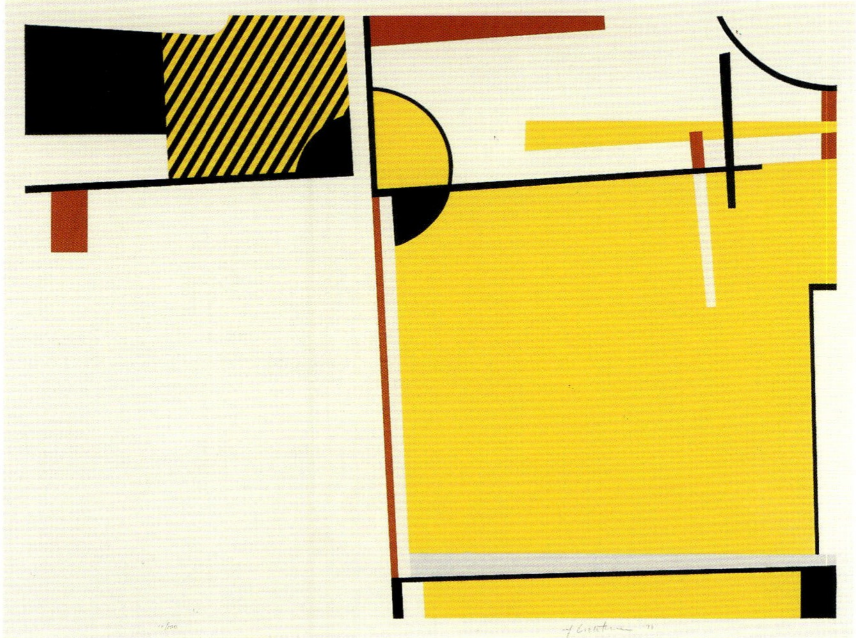

91

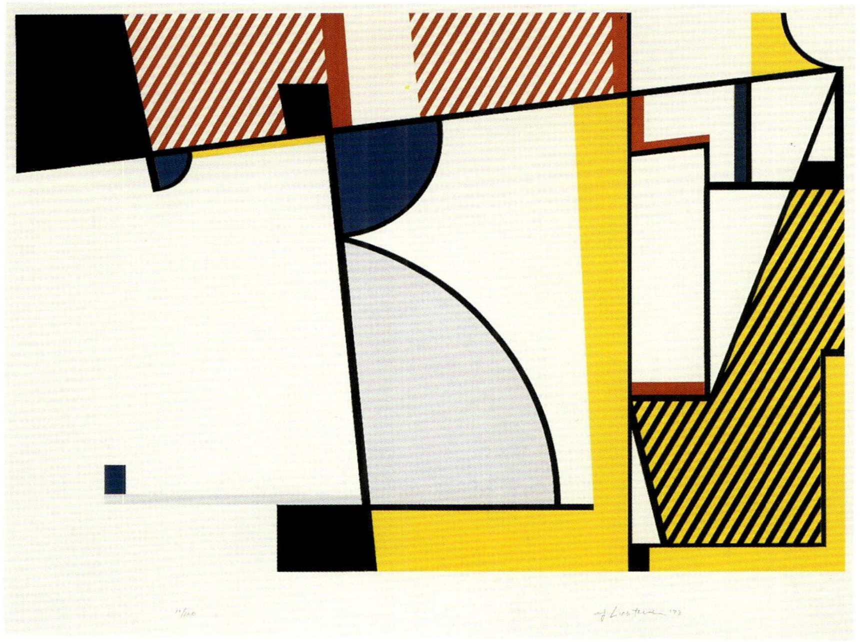

90

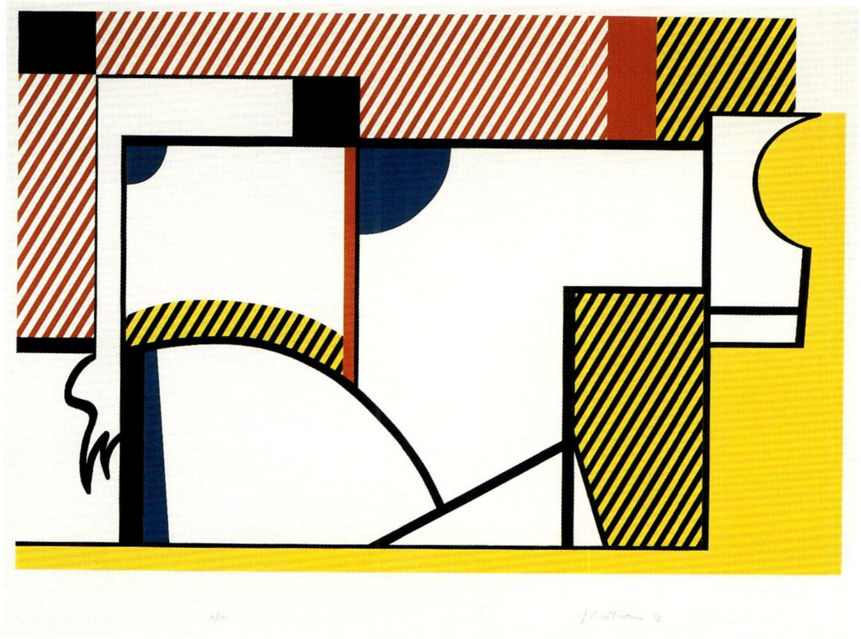

89

89
ROY LICHTENSTEIN
Bull IV,
from the *Bull Profile Series*, 1973
Color lithograph, screenprint, and line-cut
27 x 35 in. (sheet)

90
ROY LICHTENSTEIN
Bull V,
from the *Bull Profile Series*, 1973
Color lithograph, screenprint, and line-cut
$27\frac{1}{16}$ x $35\frac{1}{16}$ in. (sheet)

91
ROY LICHTENSTEIN
Bull VI,
from the *Bull Profile Series*, 1973
Color lithograph, screenprint, and line-cut
27 x 35 in. (sheet)

92
ELLSWORTH KELLY
Black Curve I (White Curve I), 1973
Lithograph with graphite
34 x 34 in. (sheet)

93★
ED RUSCHA
Evil, 1973
Color screenprint on woodgrain veneer
19⅞ x 29¹¹⁄₁₆ in. (sheet)

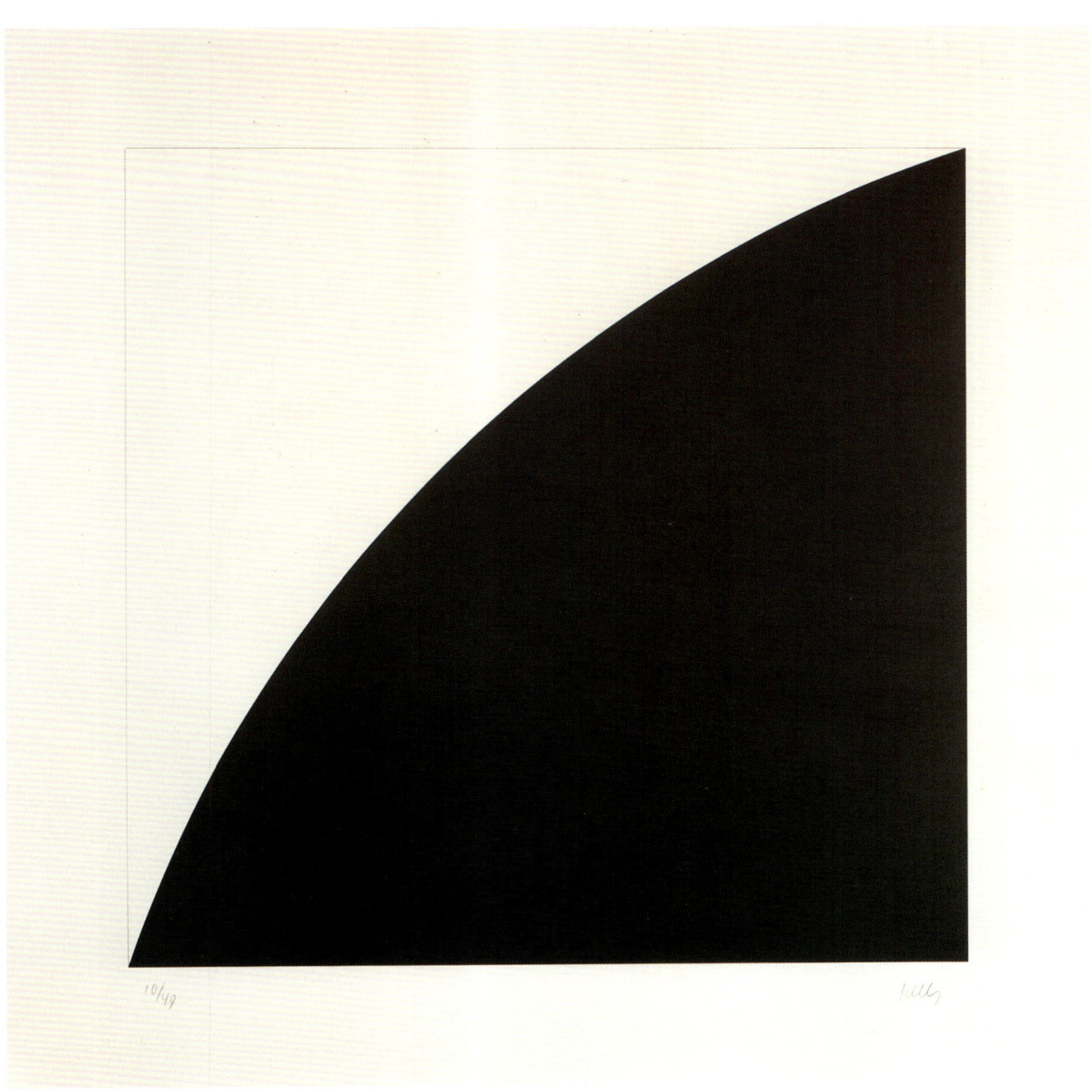

92

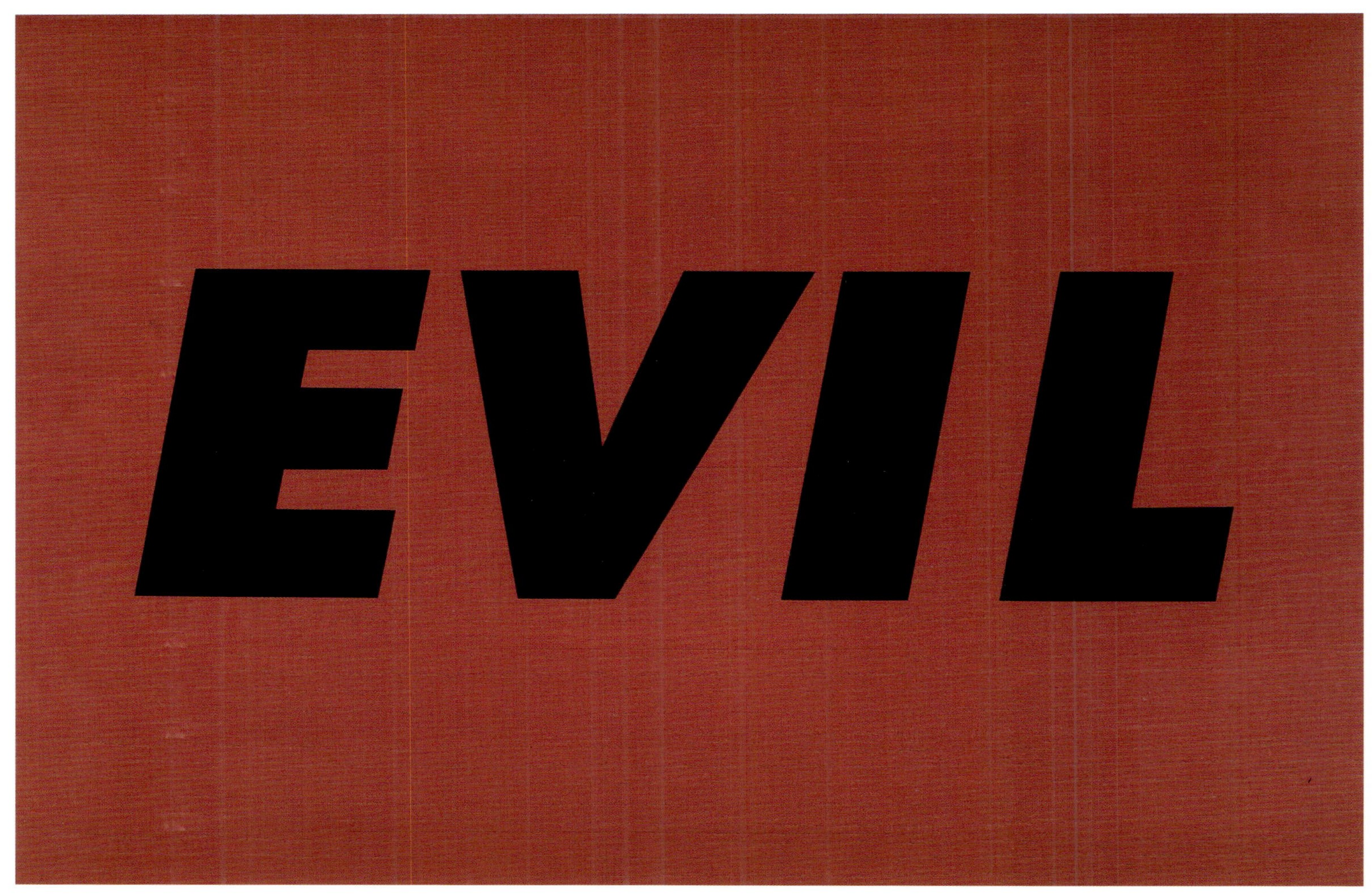

93

94
DAVID HOCKNEY
The Master Printer of Los Angeles, 1973
Color lithograph and screenprint
48 x 32 in. (sheet)

95
DAVID HOCKNEY
Celia,
8365 Melrose Ave., Hollywood, 1973
Lithograph
$47\frac{1}{2}$ x $31\frac{1}{2}$ in. (sheet)

96
JAMES ROSENQUIST
Off the Continental Divide, 1973–1974
Color lithograph
42 x 78 in. (sheet)

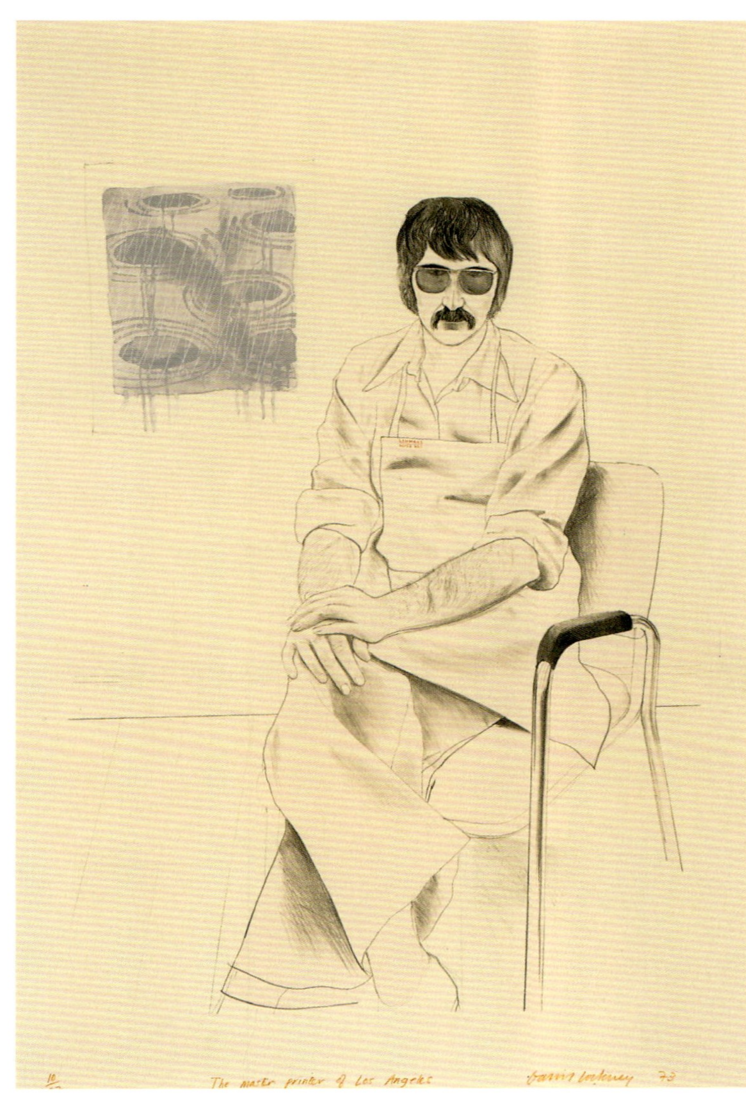

94

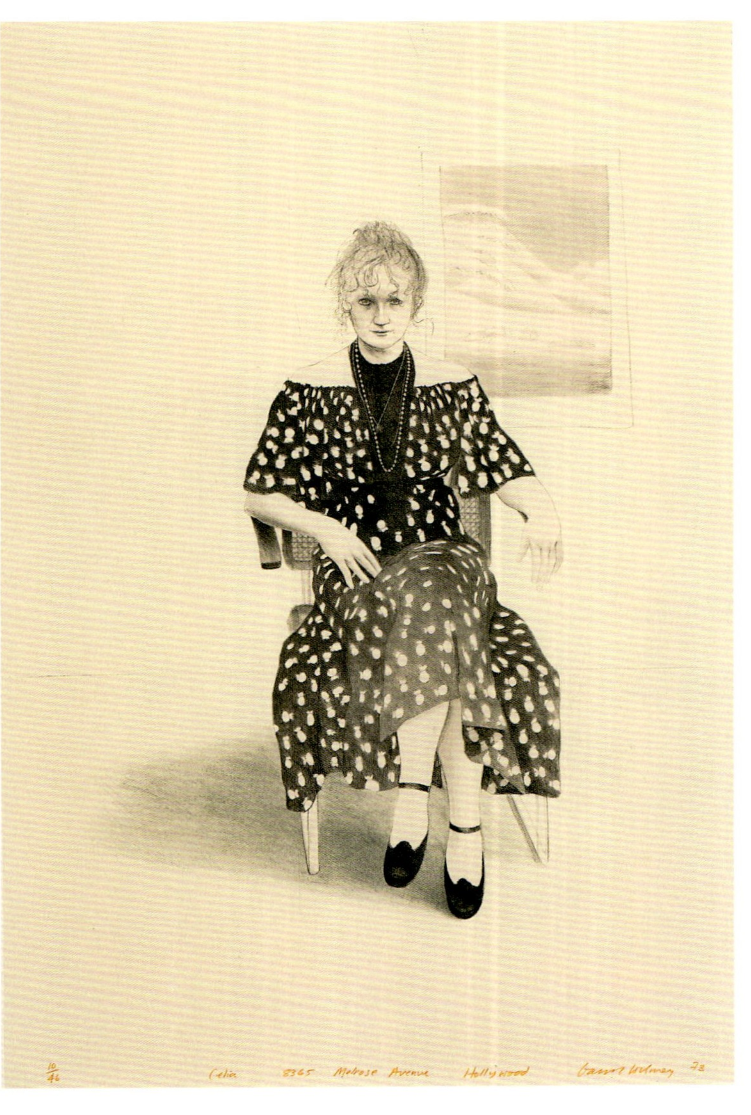

95

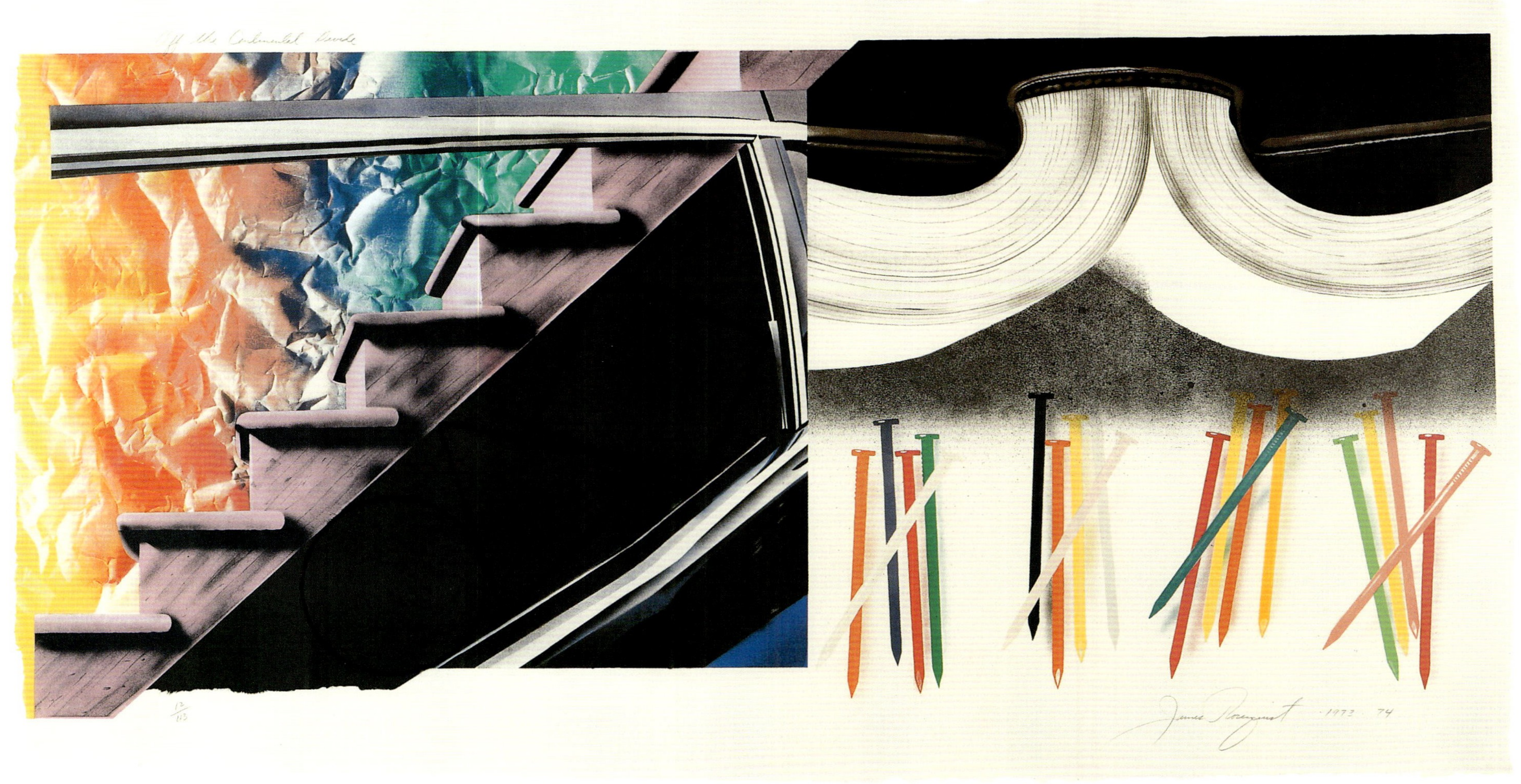

96

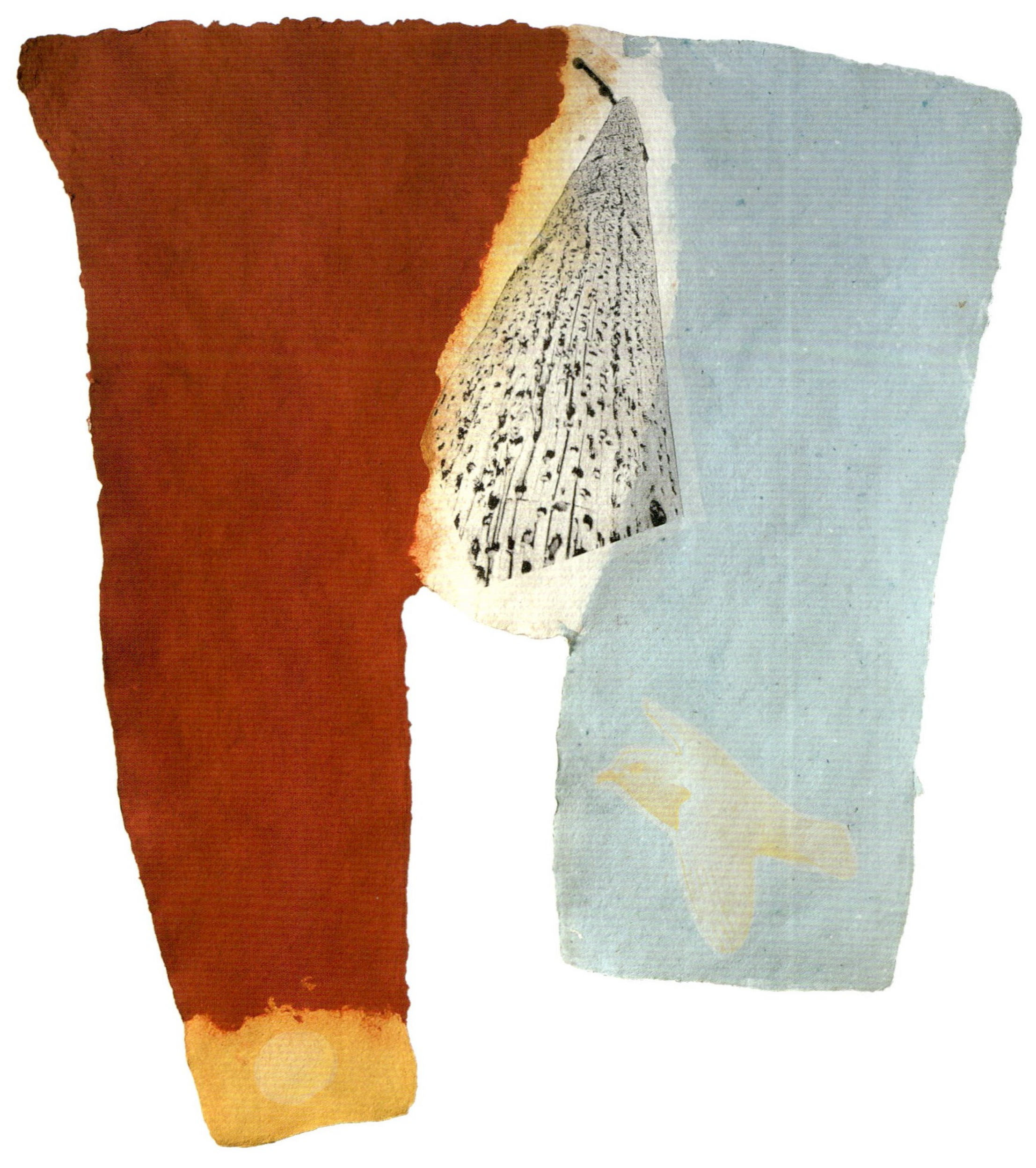

97

97★
ROBERT RAUSCHENBERG
Link, 1973–1974
Handmade paper, pigment, screenprint, tissue, and paper pulp
25 x 20 in. (overall)

98
ROBERT RAUSCHENBERG
Preview, from the *Hoarfrost Editions*, 1974
Photo-offset lithograph, newsprint and screenprint transfers, and collage, on silk chiffon and silk taffeta fabric
69 x 80½ in. (overall)

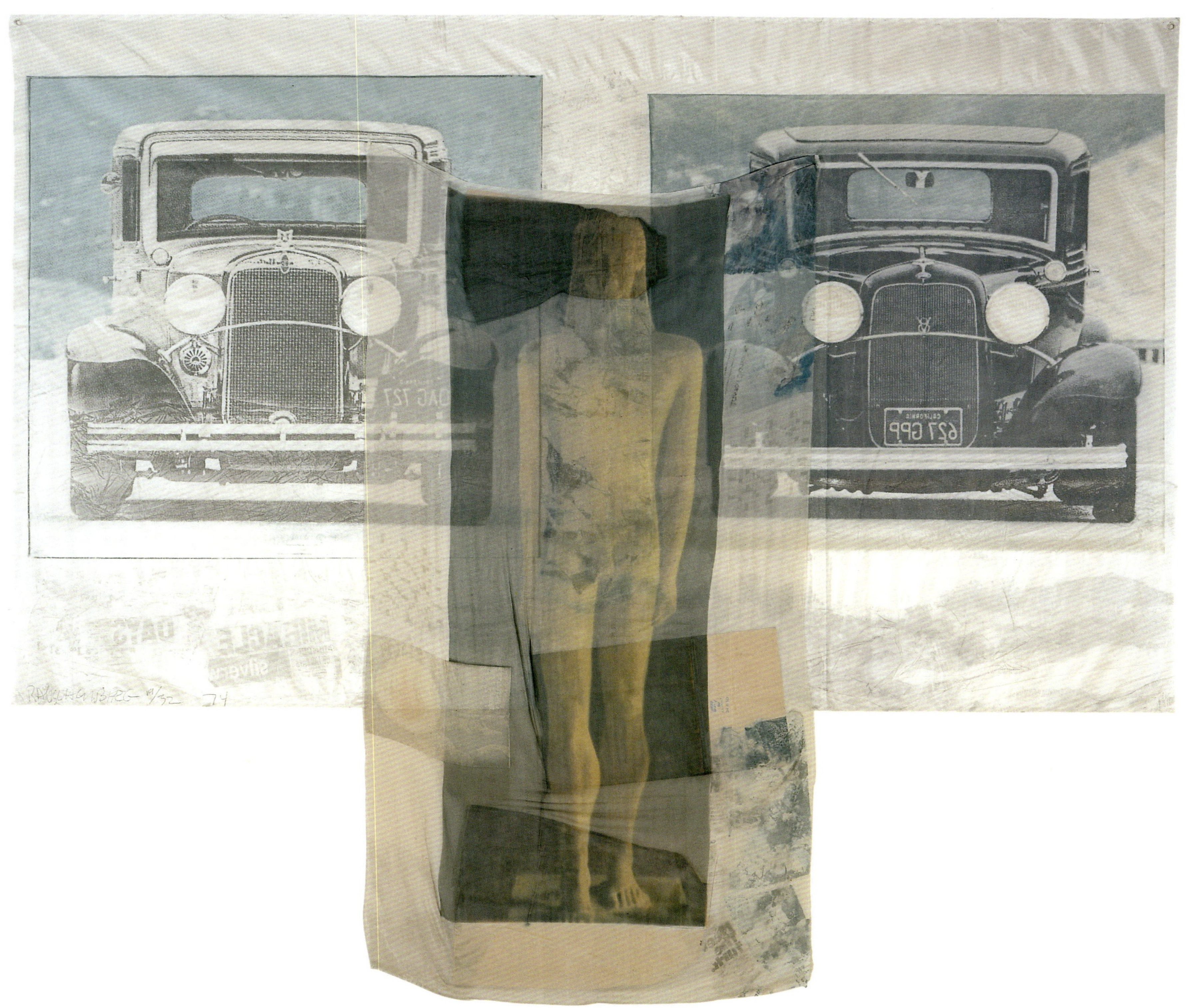

98

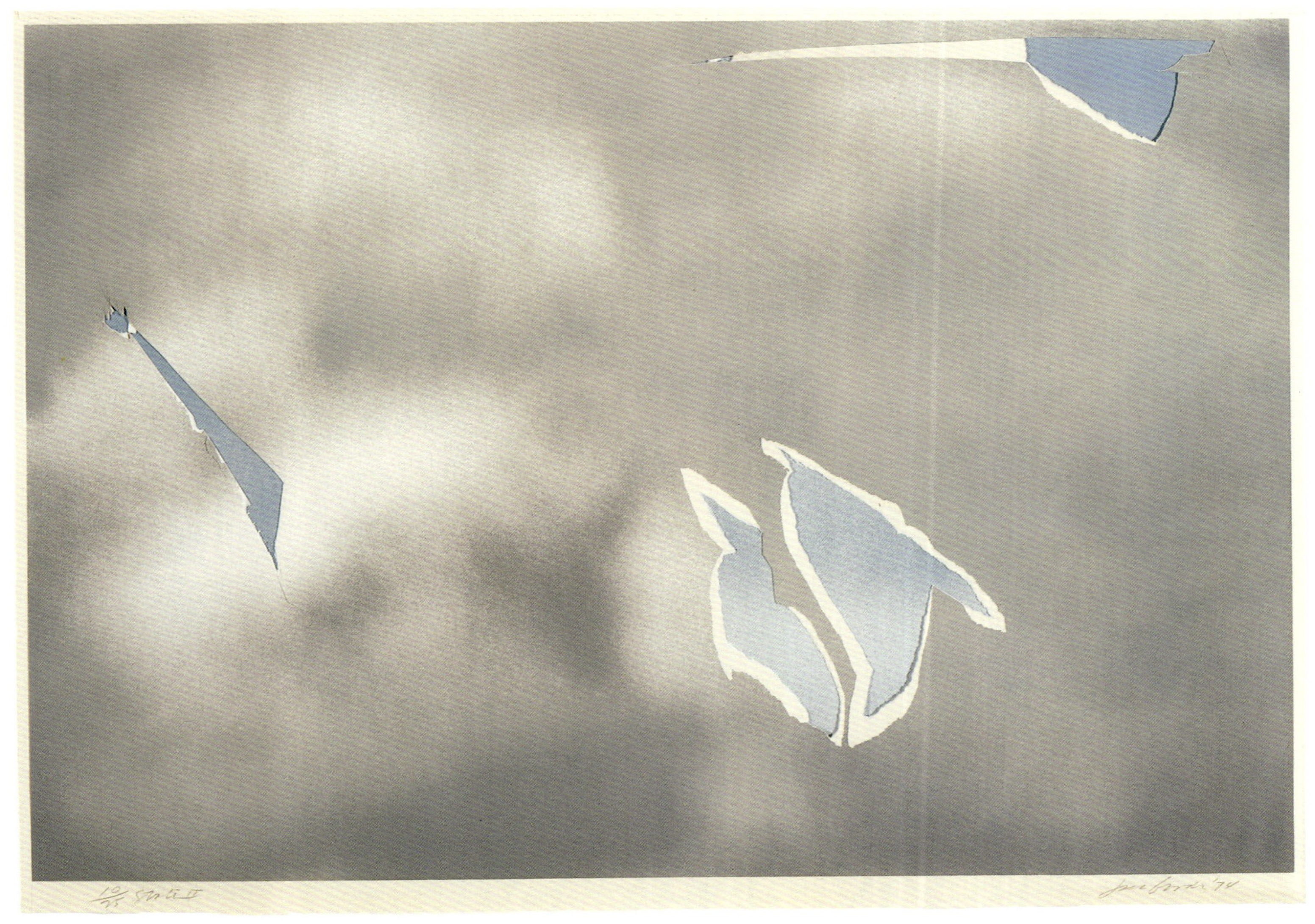

99

99
JOE GOODE
Untitled, State II, 1974
Color lithograph on two sheets of paper
30 x 41½ in. (sheet)

100
WILLIAM T. WILEY
Mr. Nobody, 1975
Color lithograph
42$\frac{5}{16}$ x 31$\frac{1}{16}$ in. (sheet)

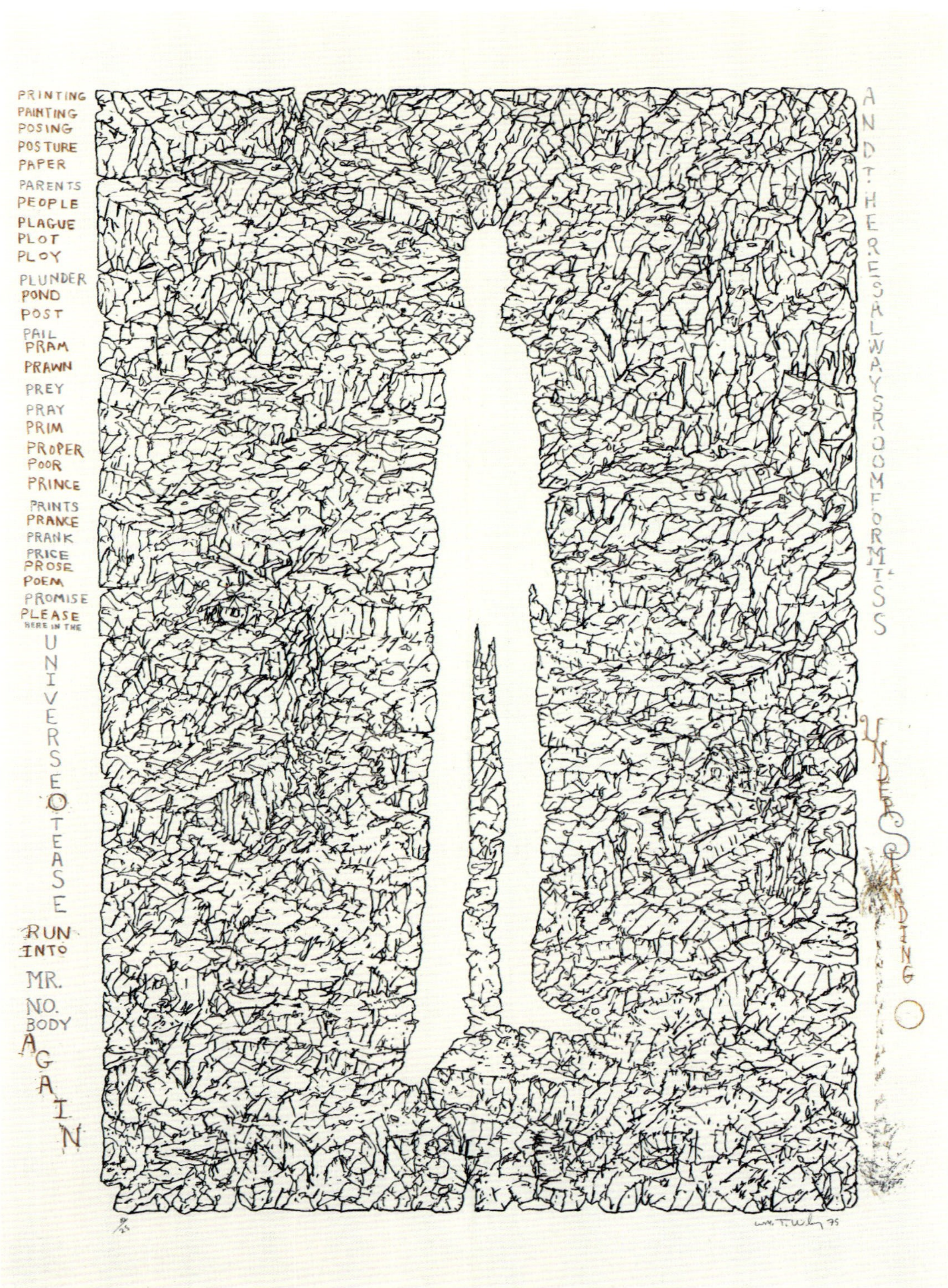

100

101
LOUISE NEVELSON
Dawnscape, 1975
Cast paper pulp
$27^{3}/_{4}$ x $30^{1}/_{2}$ in. (sheet)

102★
ELLSWORTH KELLY
Colored Paper Image V, 1976
Colored pressed paper pulp
$46^{1}/_{2}$ x $32^{1}/_{2}$ in. (sheet)

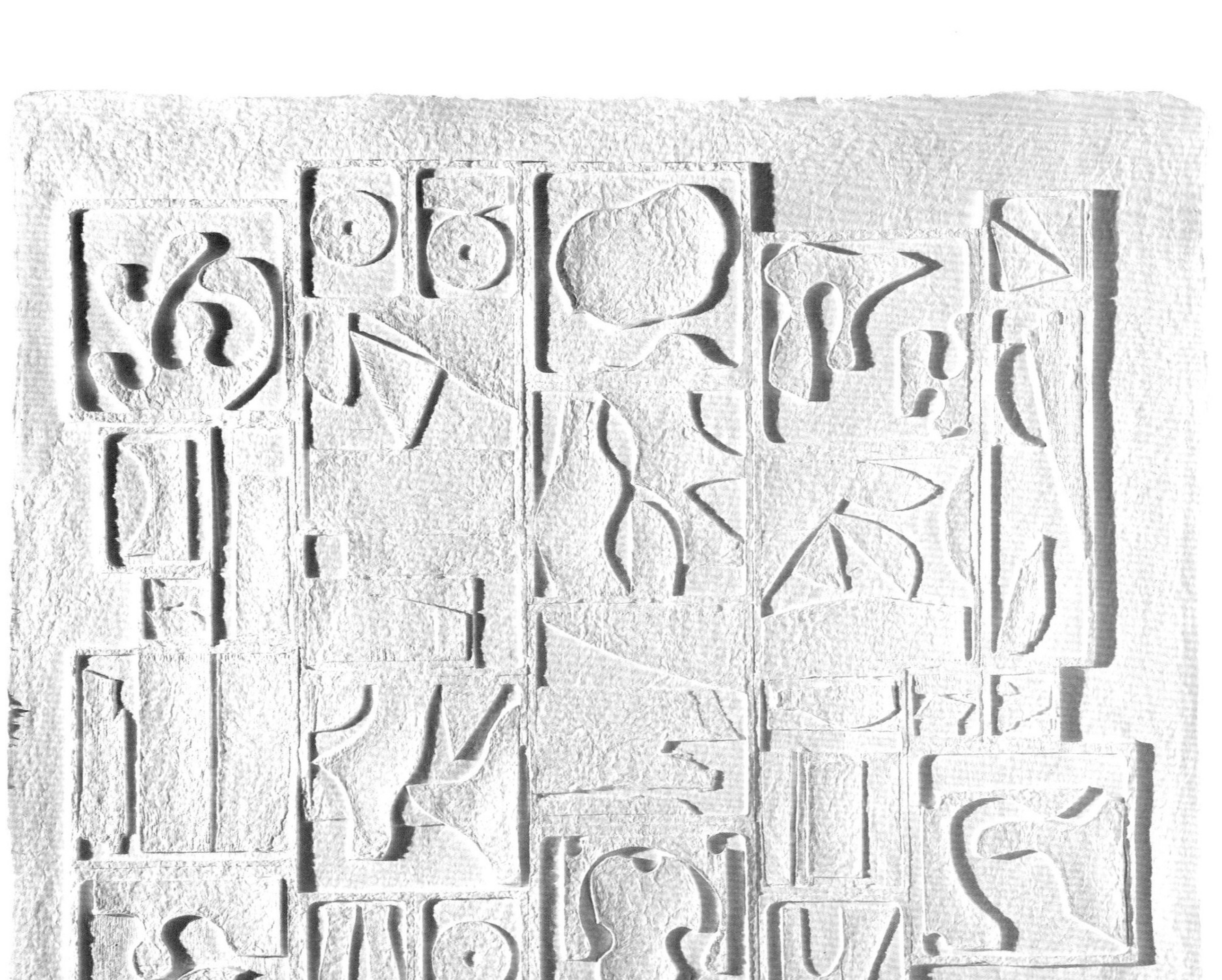

101

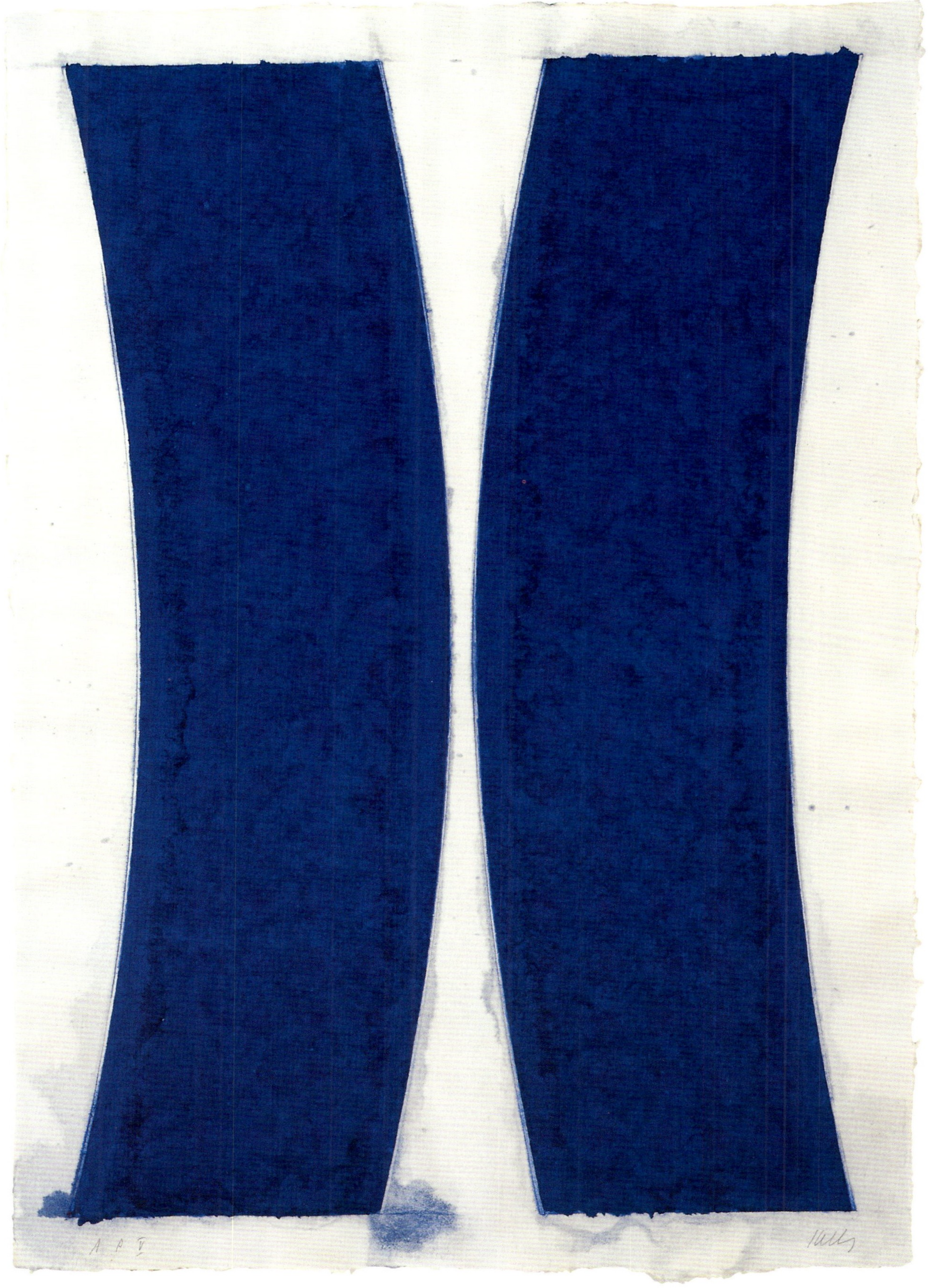

102

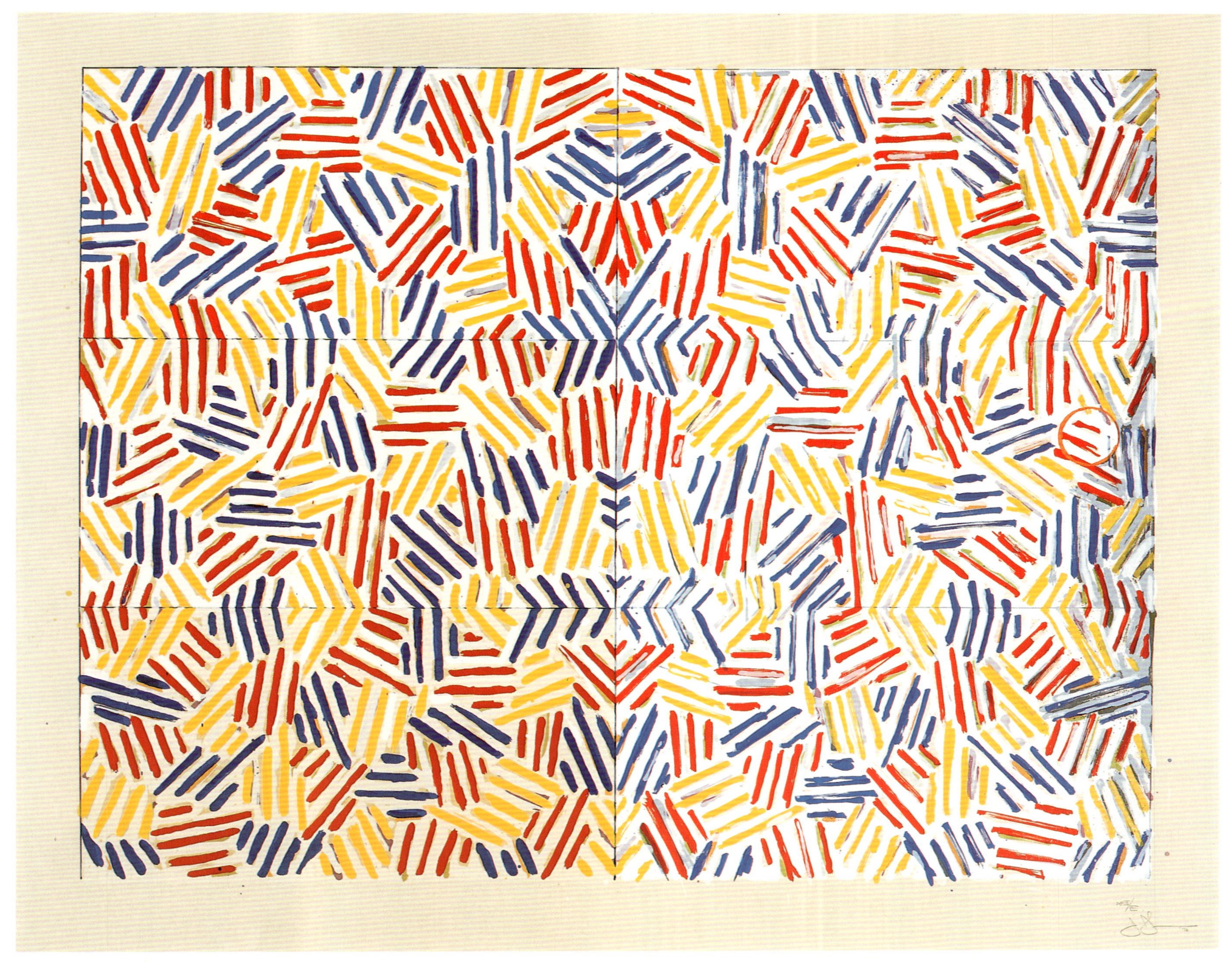

103

103★
JASPER JOHNS
Corpse and Mirror, 1976
Color screenprint
$42\frac{5}{8}$ x 53 in. (sheet)

104
FRANK STELLA
Sinjerli Variation IV,
from the *Sinjerli Variations Series,* 1977
Color lithograph
32 x $42\frac{1}{2}$ in. (sheet)

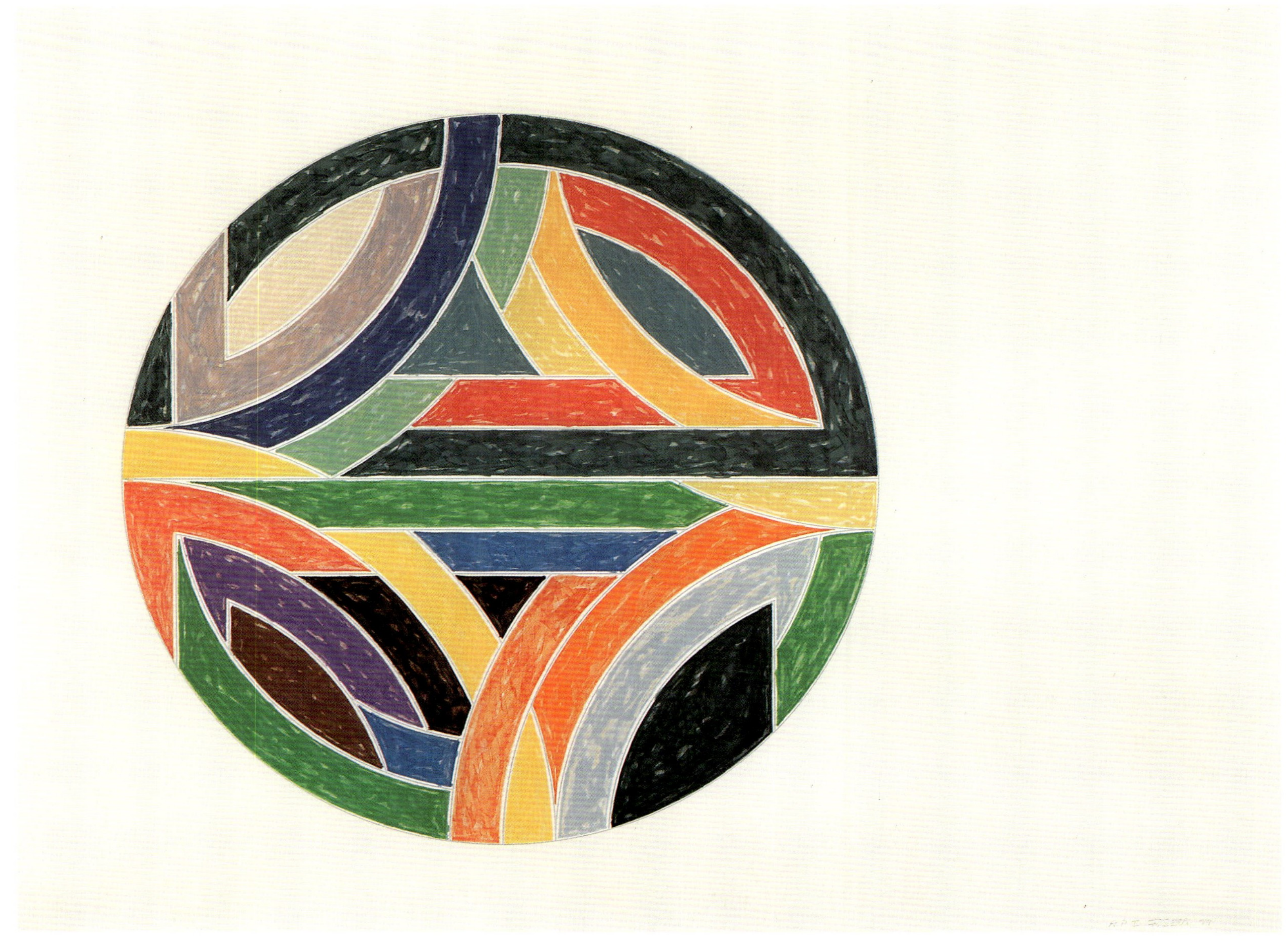

104

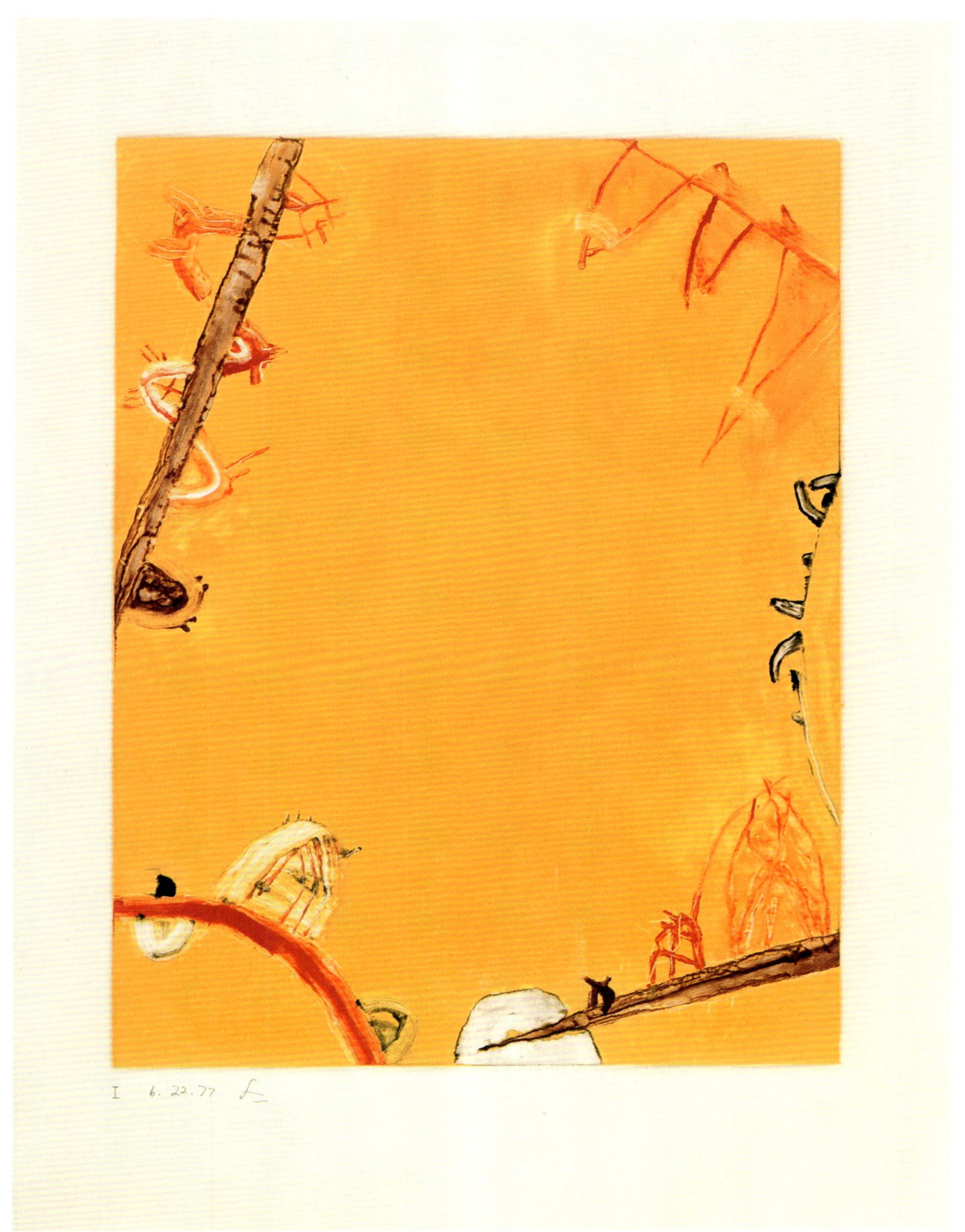

105

105
FRANK LOBDELL
6.22.77 I, 1977
Color monotype
29⅝ x 22¼ in. (sheet)

106
SAM FRANCIS
A Fixed Course of Changes #3, 1977
Color monotype
28½ x 22¼ in. (sheet)

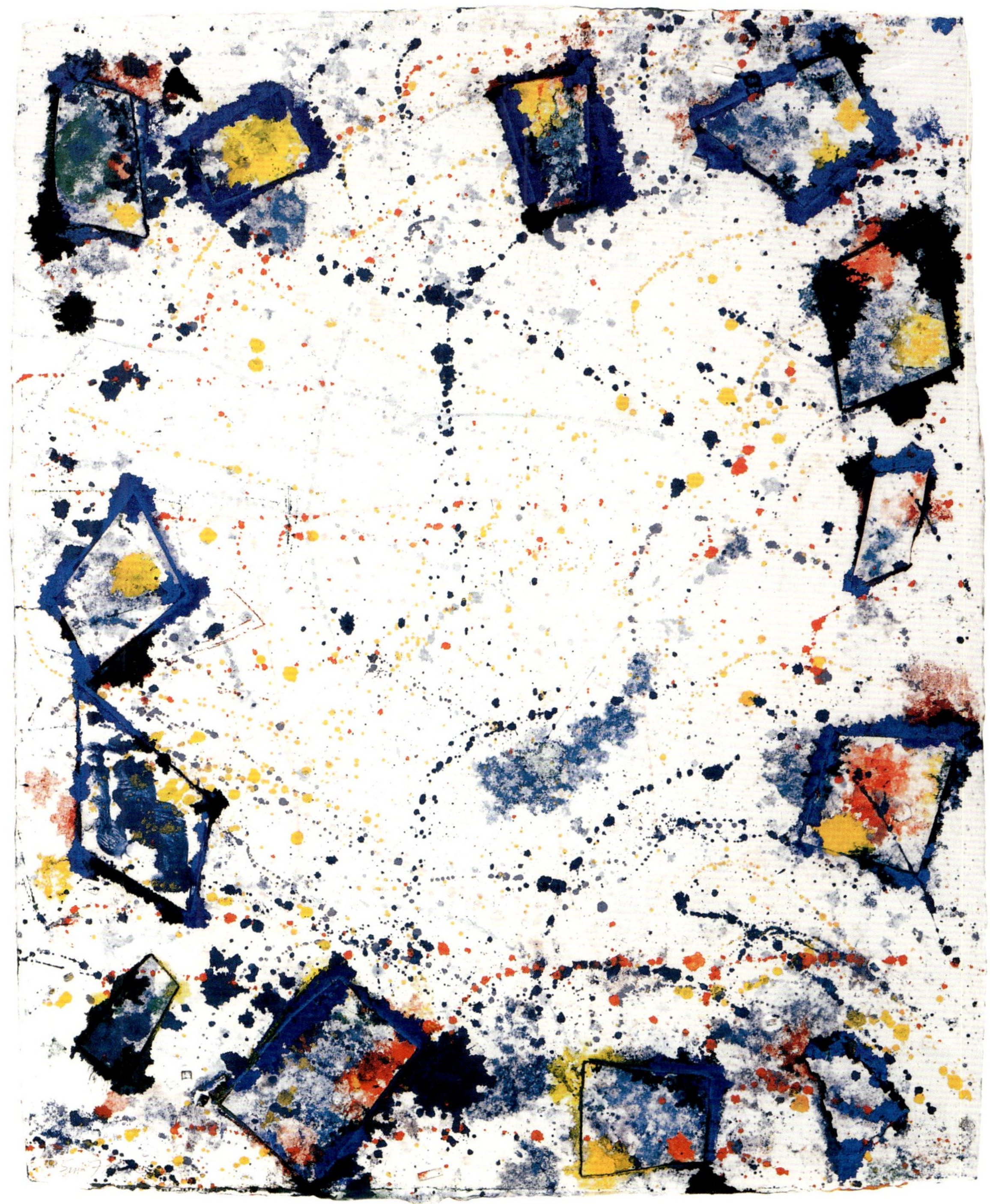

106

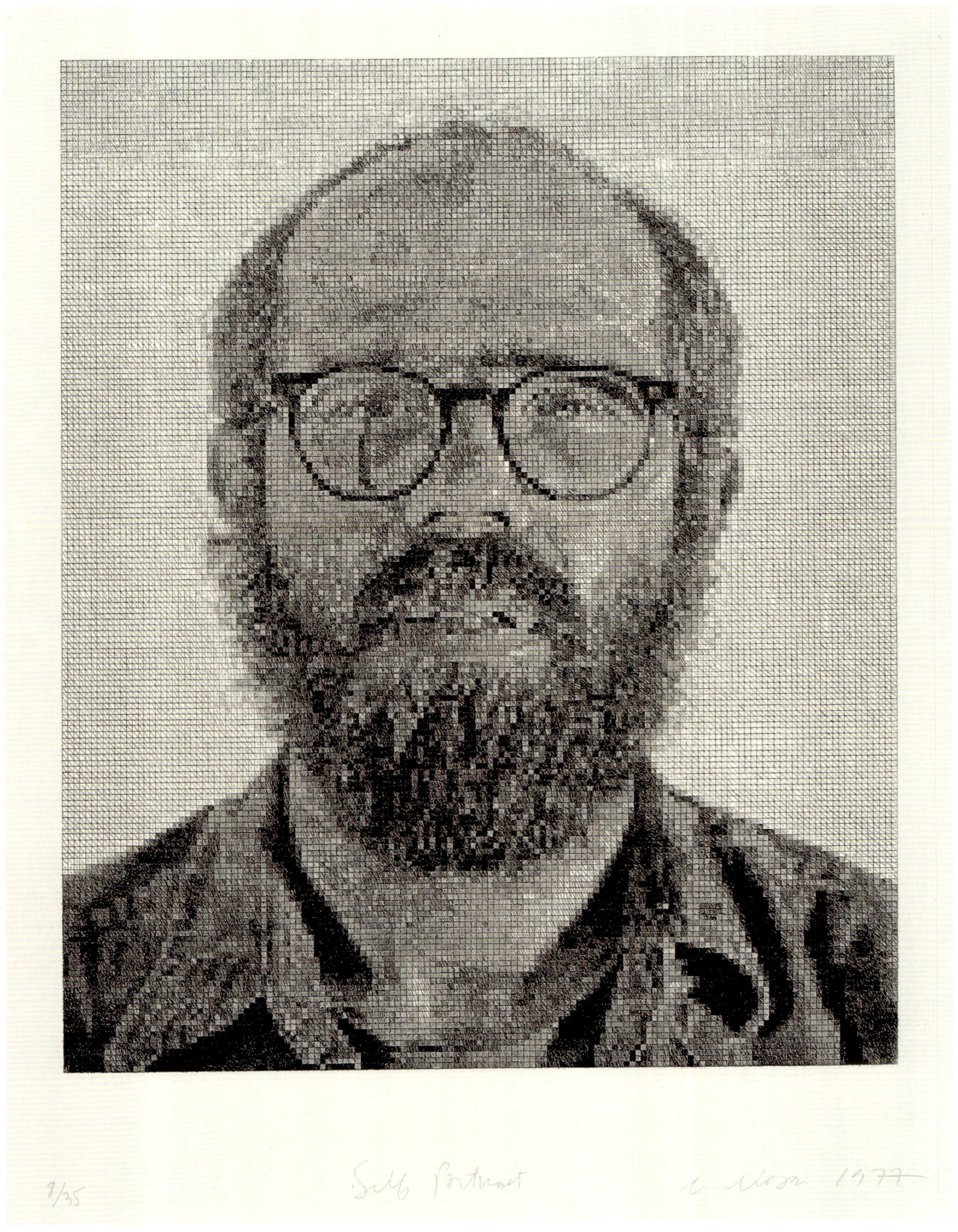

107

107
CHUCK CLOSE
Self-Portrait,
Black on White, 1977
Etching
54 1/8 x 40 3/4 in. (sheet)

108★
JASPER JOHNS
Savarin, 1977
Color lithograph
45 x 35 in. (sheet)

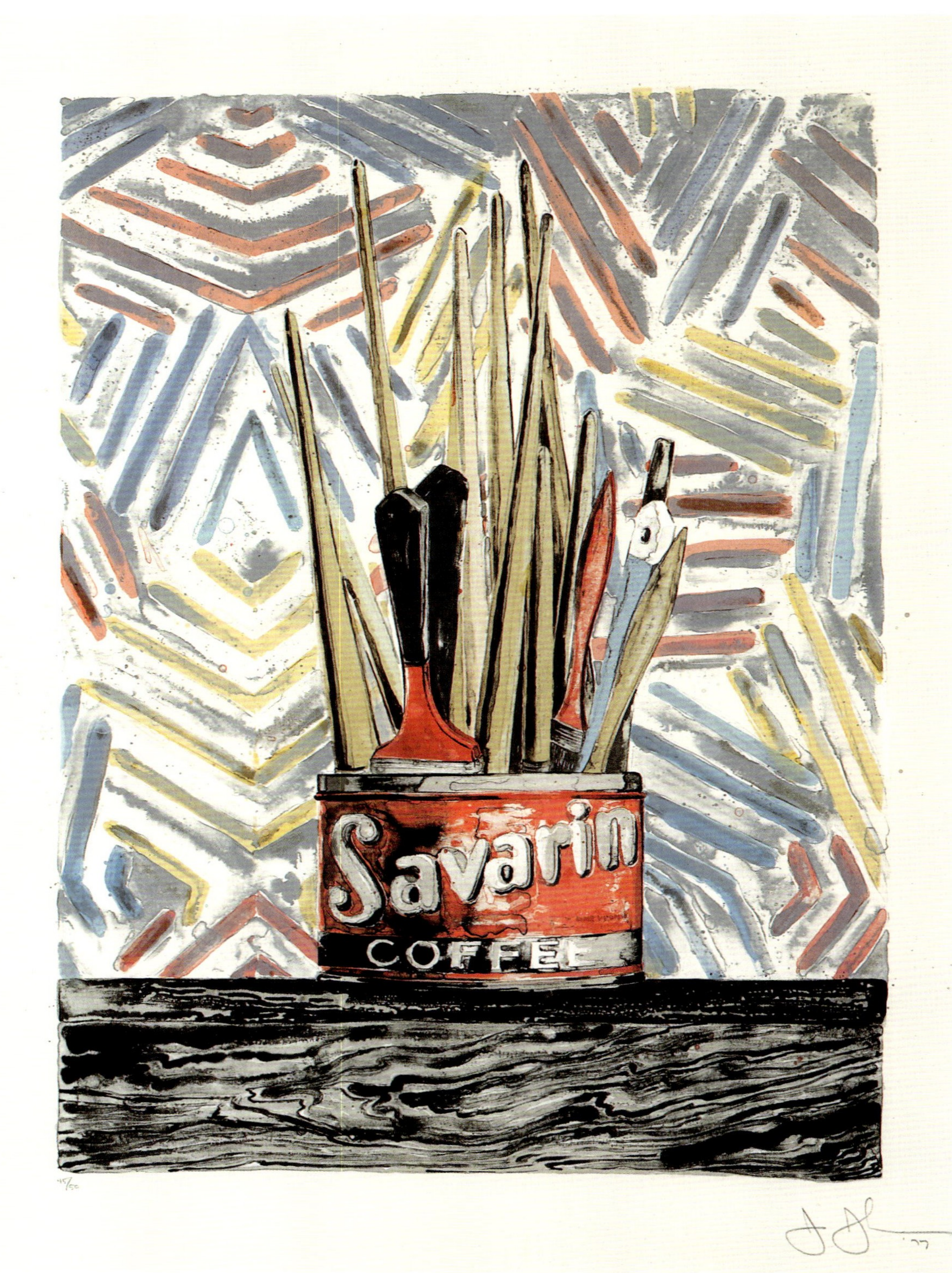

108

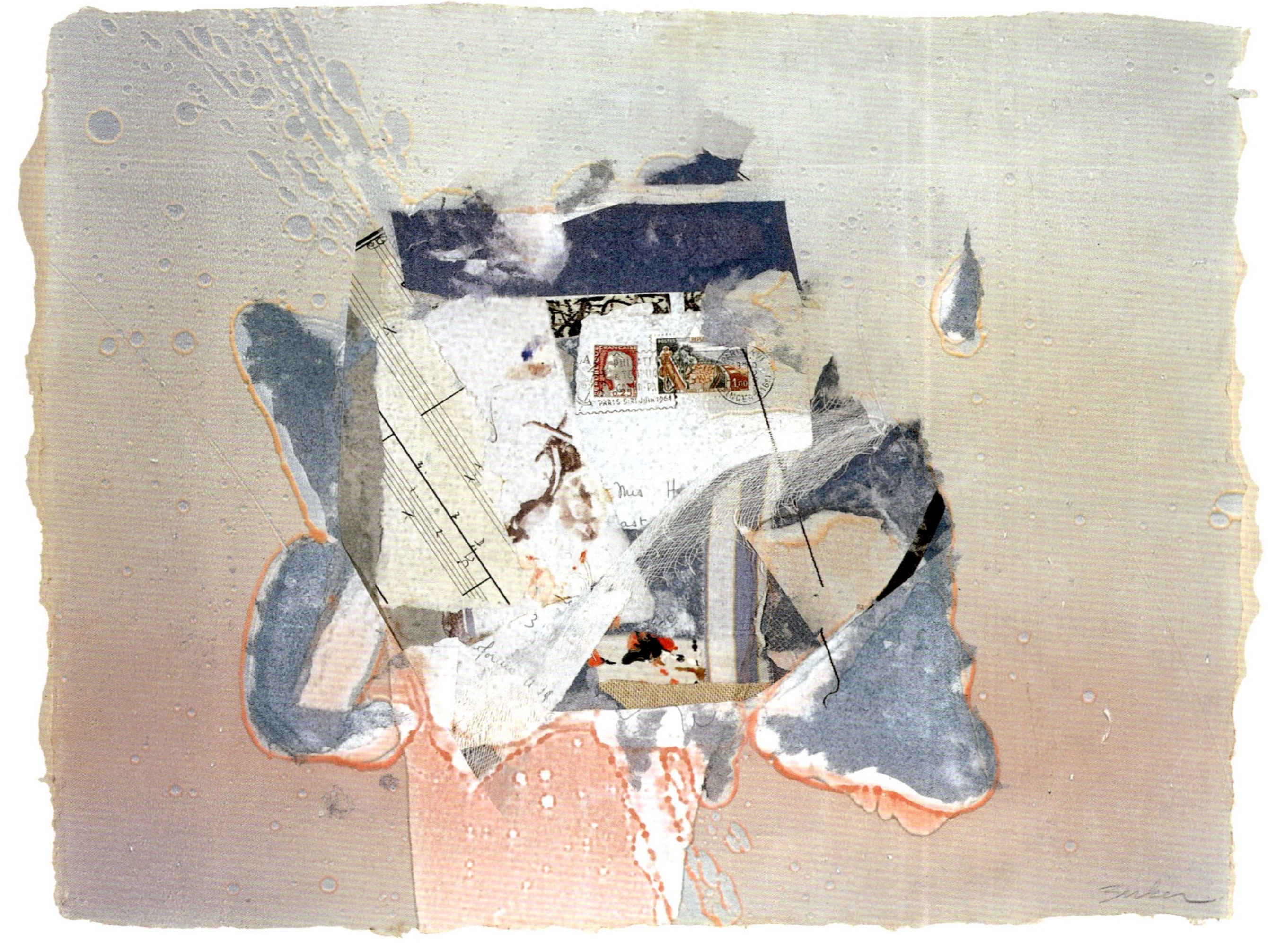

109

109
JOSEPH ZIRKER
Untitled, 1978
Color monotype
14 5/8 x 18 1/4 in. (sheet)

110
MATT PHILLIPS
Untitled, 1979
Color monotype
18 x 22 in. (sheet)

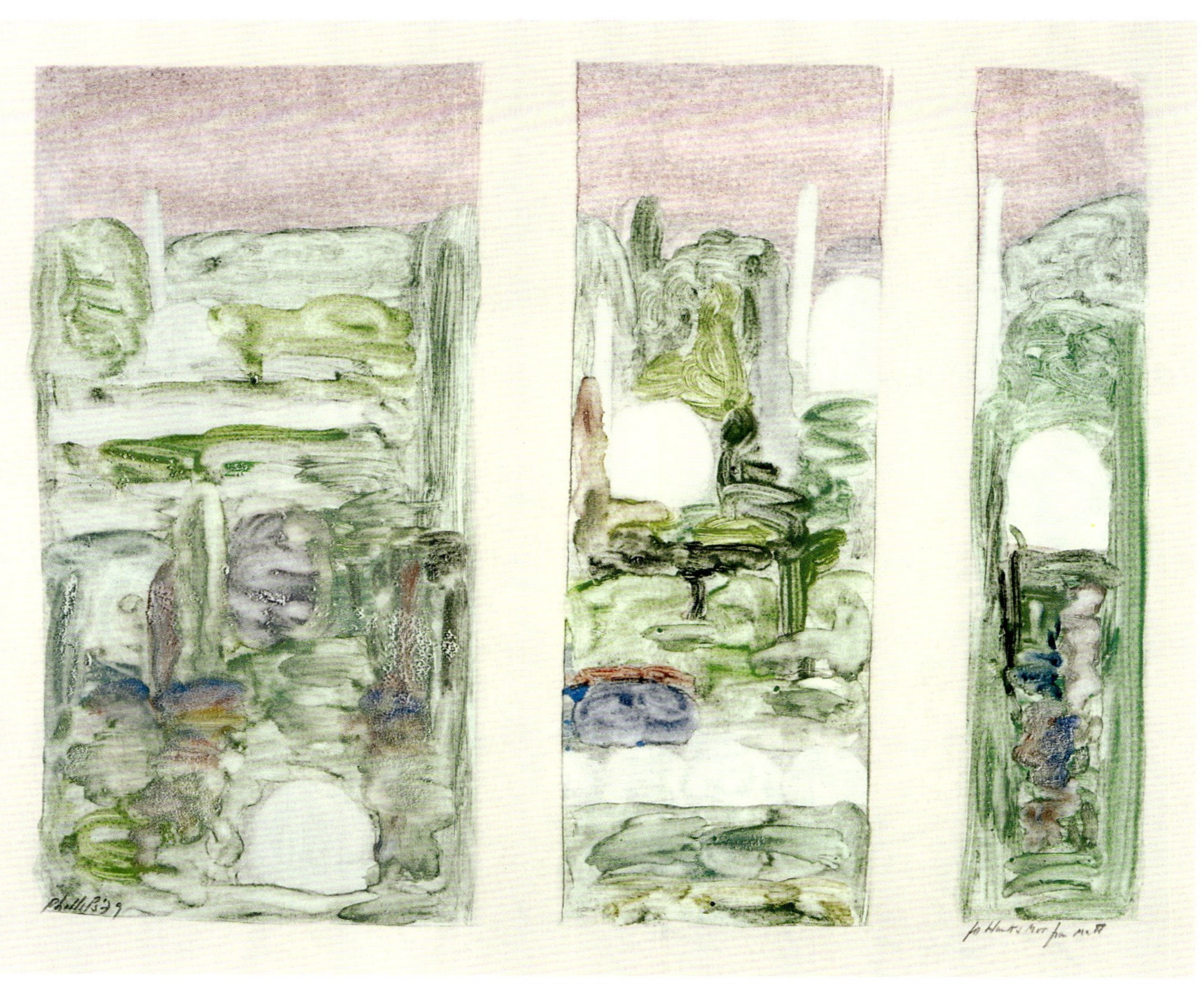

110

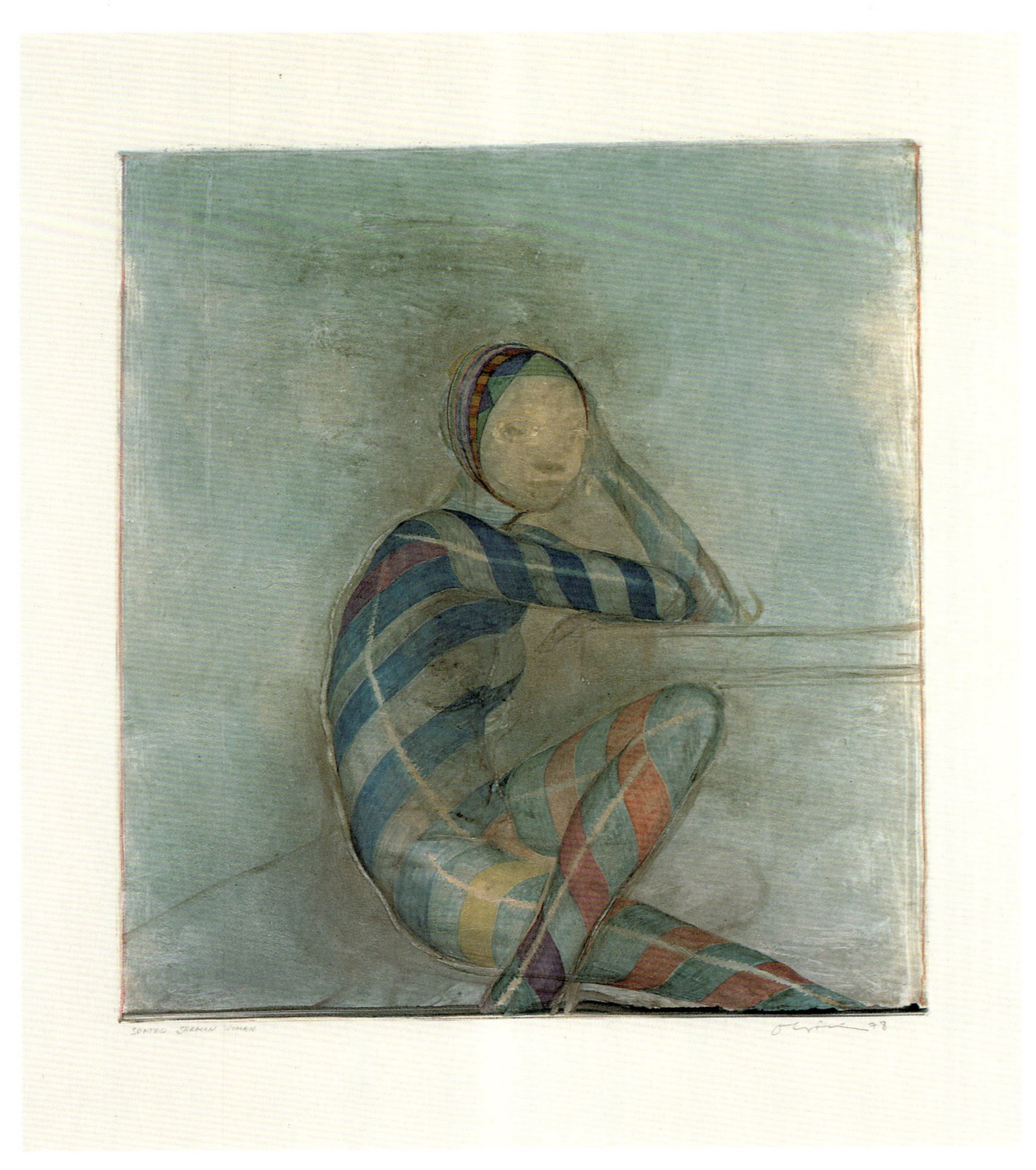

111

NATHAN OLIVEIRA

Seated Shaman Woman, 1978

Color monotype

26⅛ x 22¼ in. (sheet)

111

112

MARY FRANK

Untitled, 1978

Color monotype

31¾ x 35¼ in. (sheet)

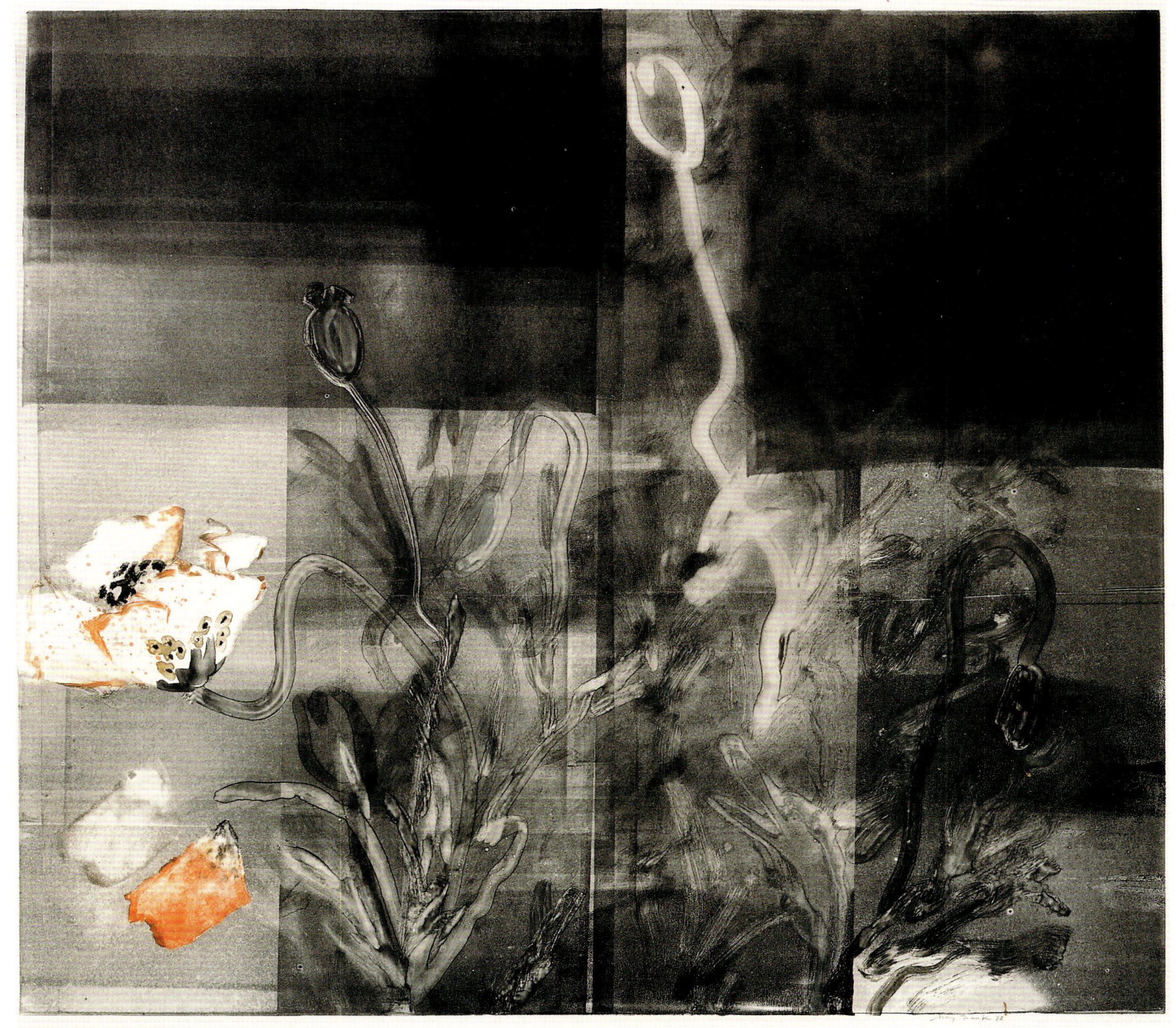

112

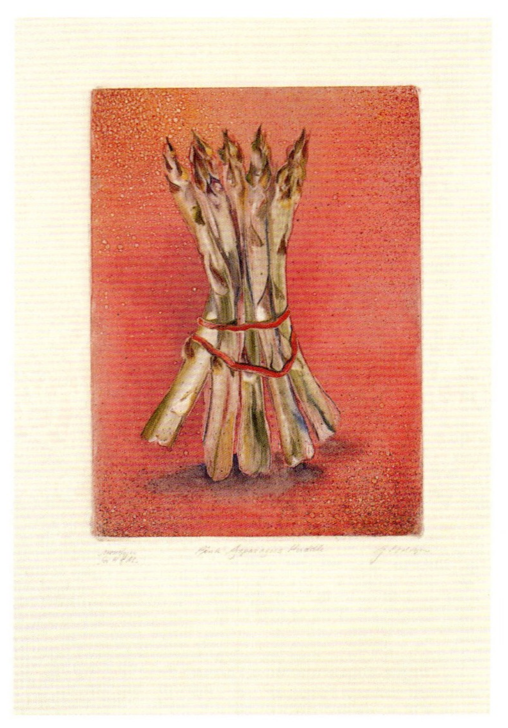

113

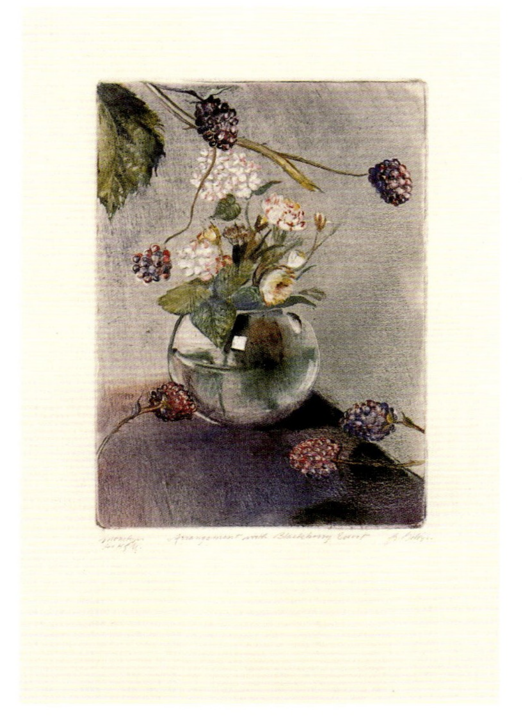

114

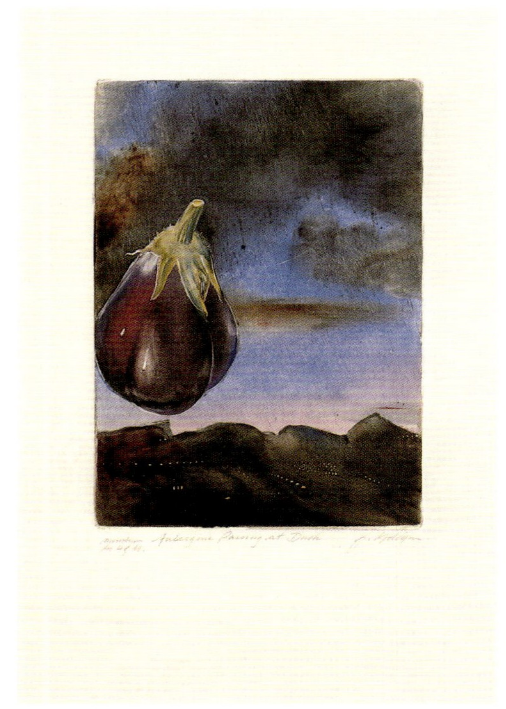

115

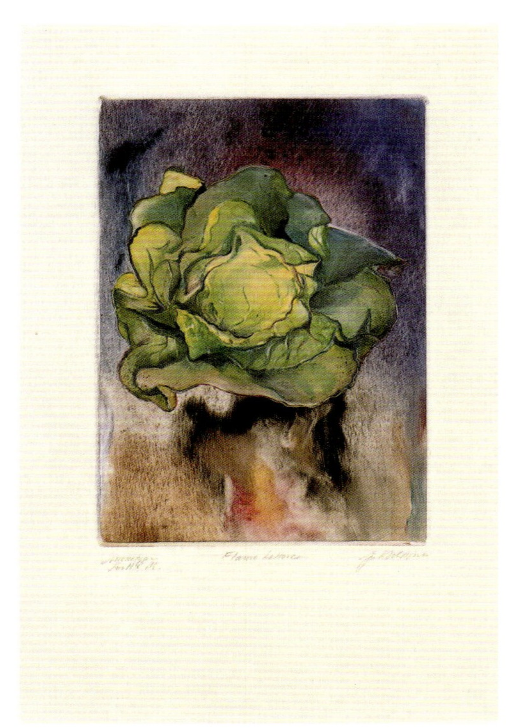

116

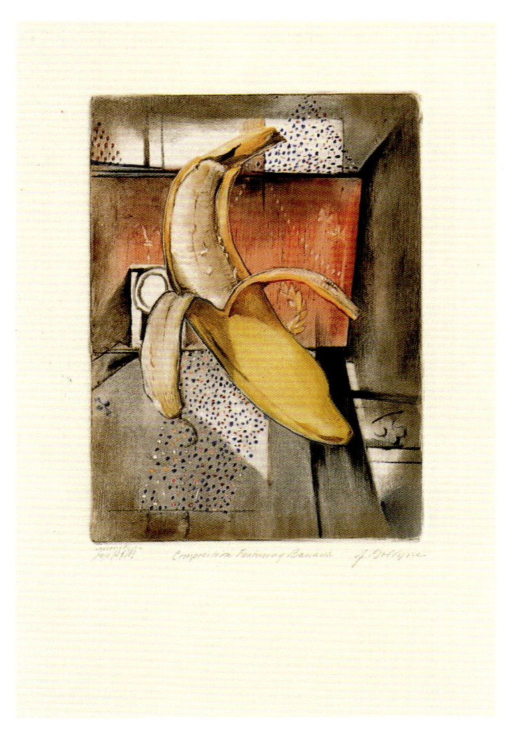

117

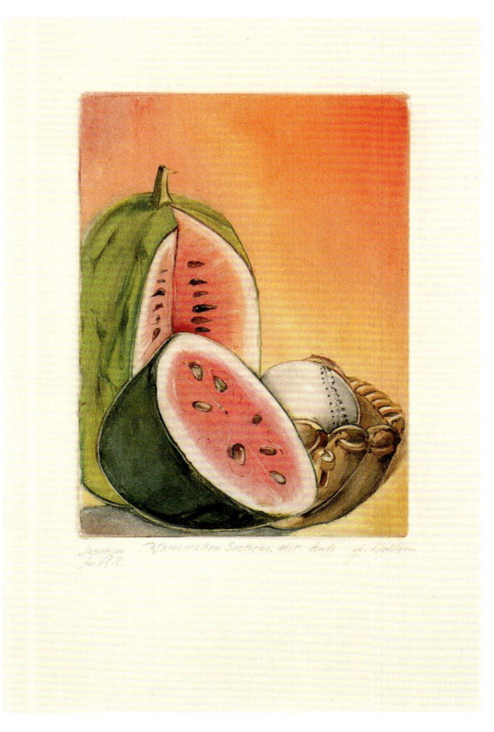

118

Plates 113–124★
JOSEPH GOLDYNE
Produce/A Portfolio of Twelve Monotypes, 1978
Color monotypes
11¼ x 15 in. (each folio sheet)

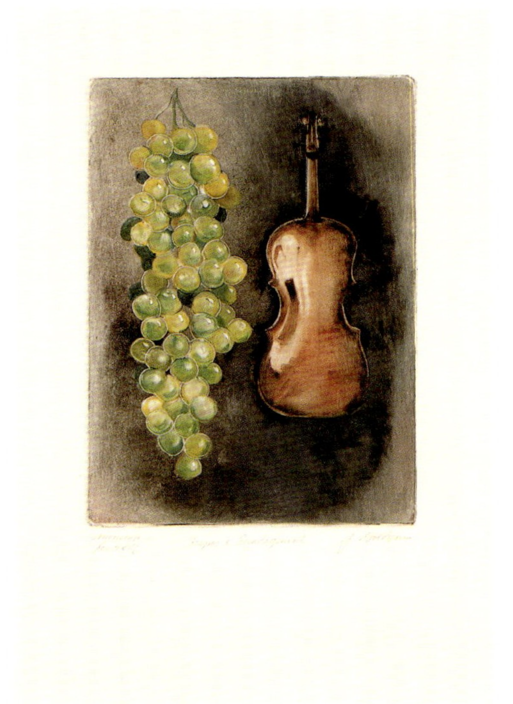

119

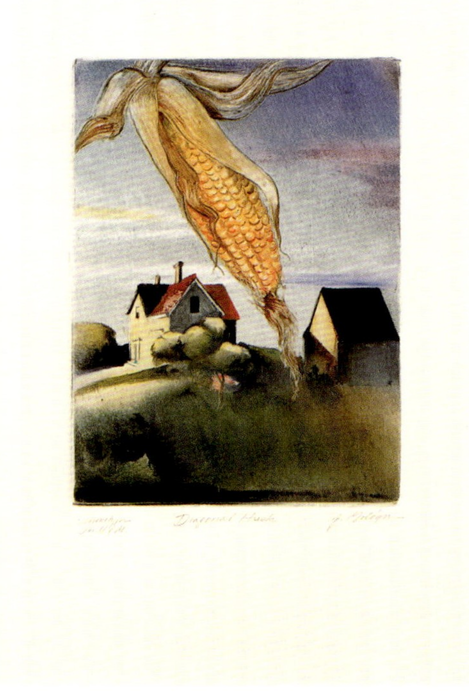

120

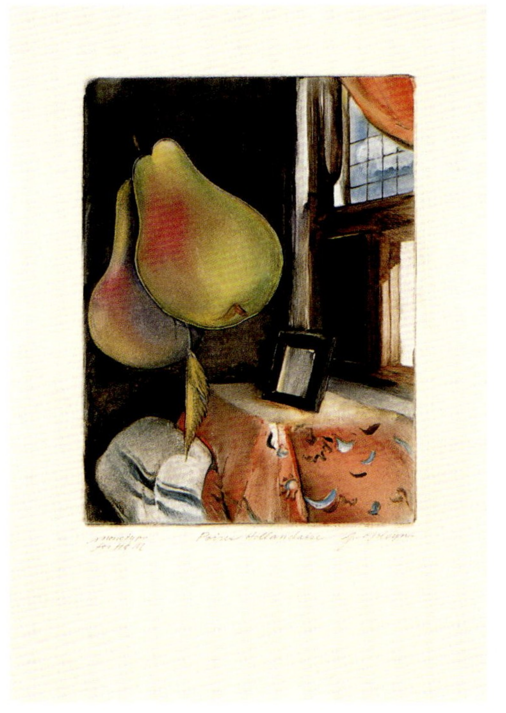

121

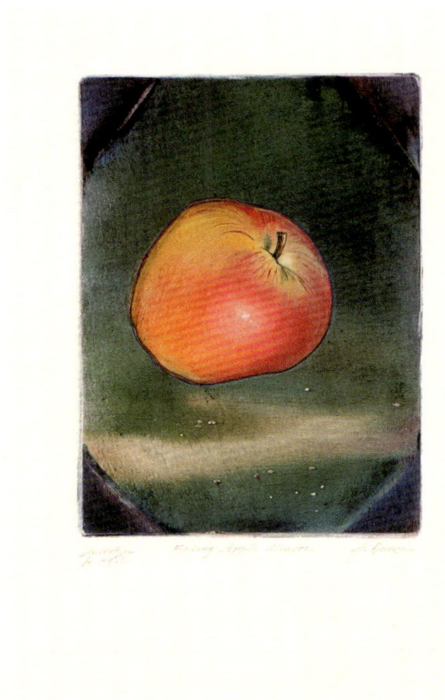

122

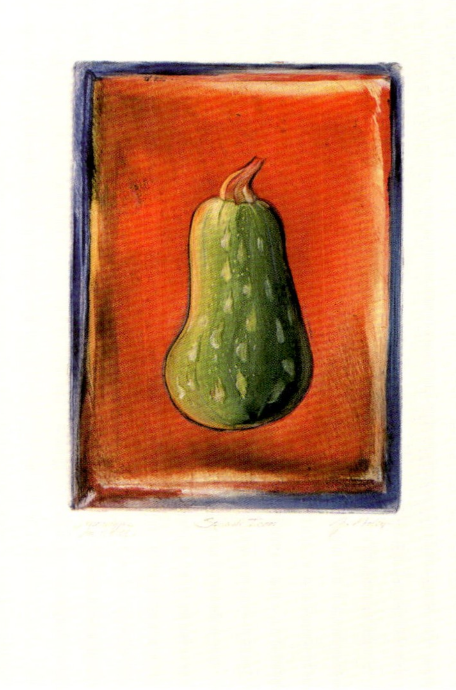

123

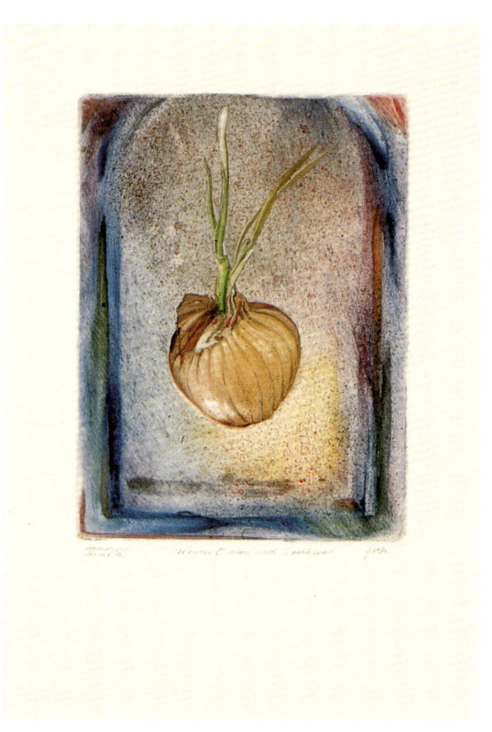

124

113 *Pink Asparagus Huddle*
114 *Arrangement with Blackberry*
115 *Aubergine Passing at Dusk*
116 *Flame Lettuce*
117 *Composition Featuring Banana*
118 *Watermelon Section, Mit, Ball*

119 *Grapes and Guadagnini*
120 *Diagonal Husk*
121 *Poires Hollandaise*
122 *Falling Apple Meadow*
123 *Squash Icon*
124 *Winter Onion* II

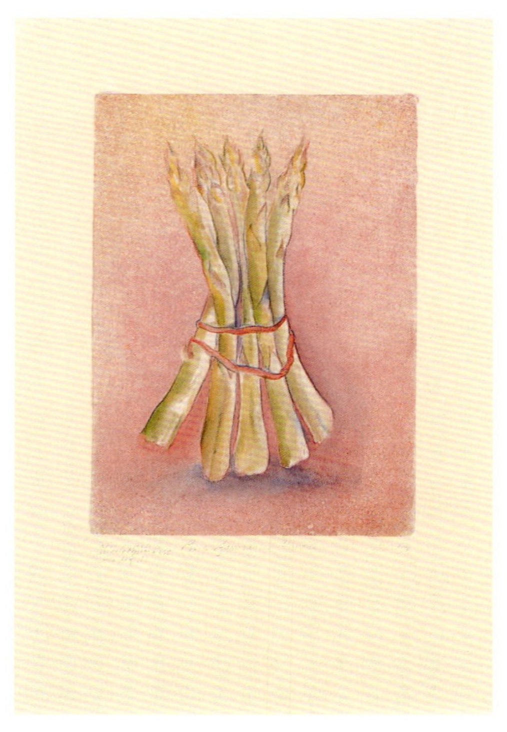

125

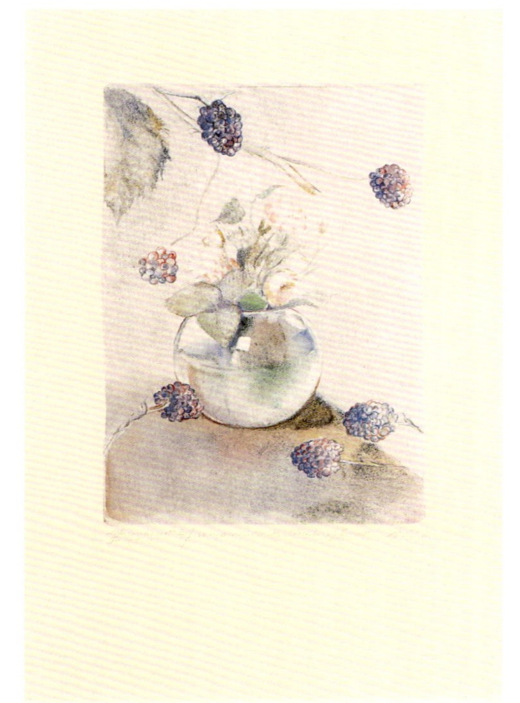

126

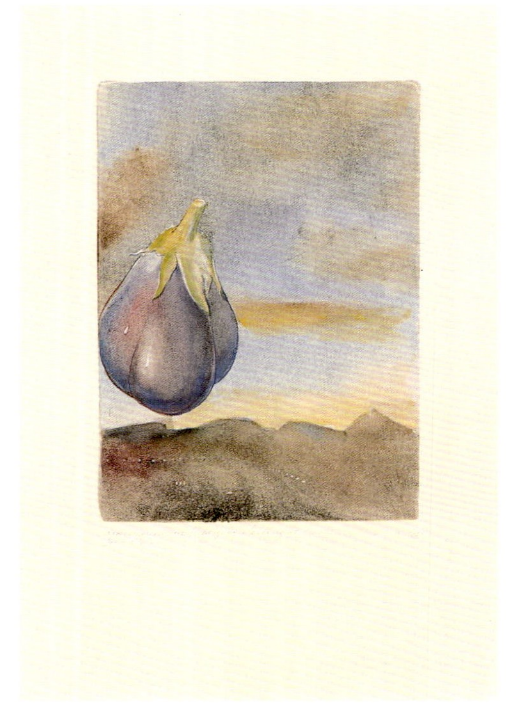

127

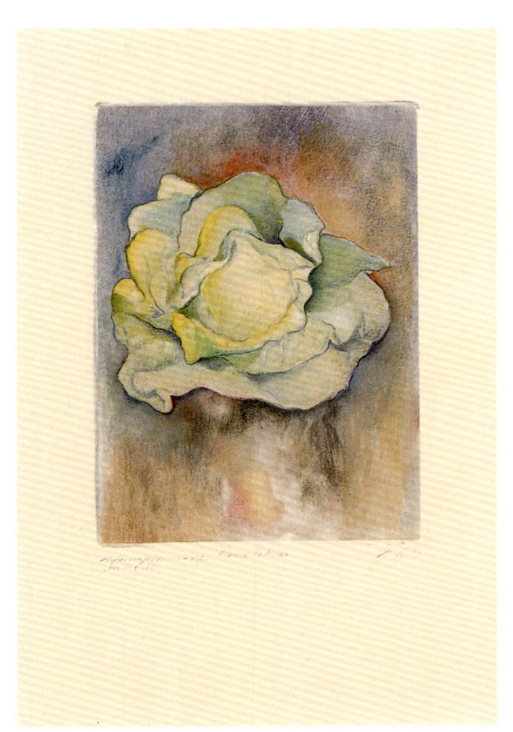

128

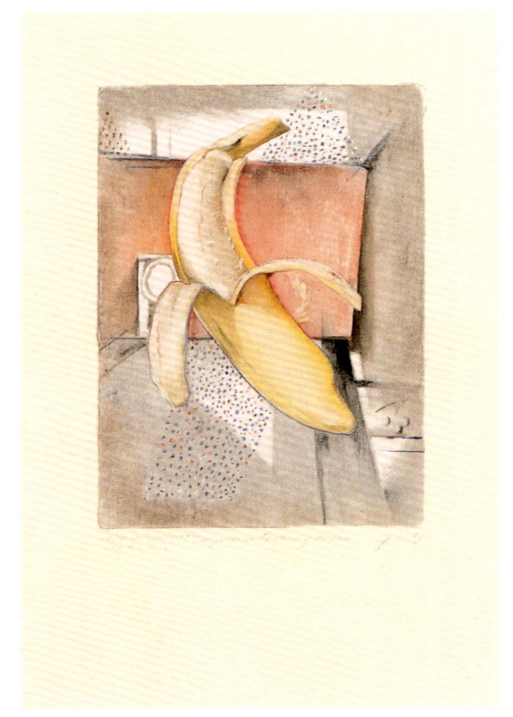

129

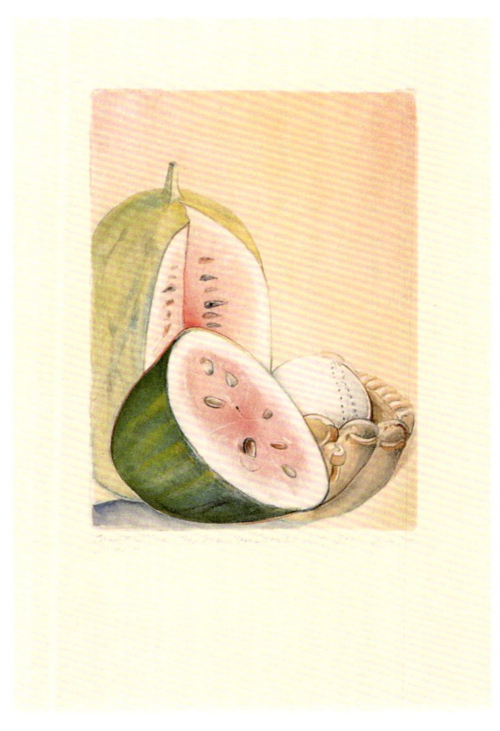

130

Plates 125–136★
JOSEPH GOLDYNE
Produce Series, 1978
Color monotypes (cognates) with watercolor
11 x 7½ in. (each sheet)

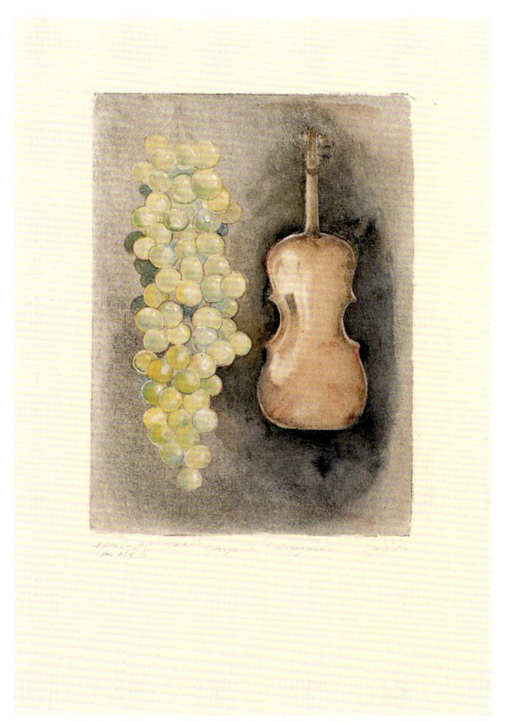

131

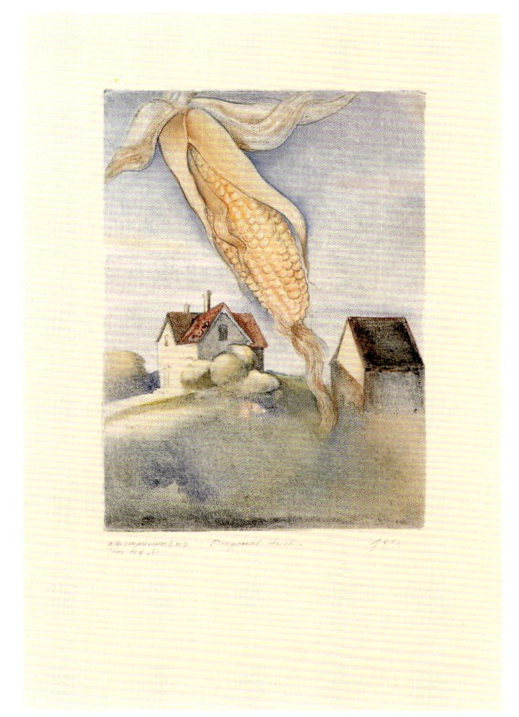

132

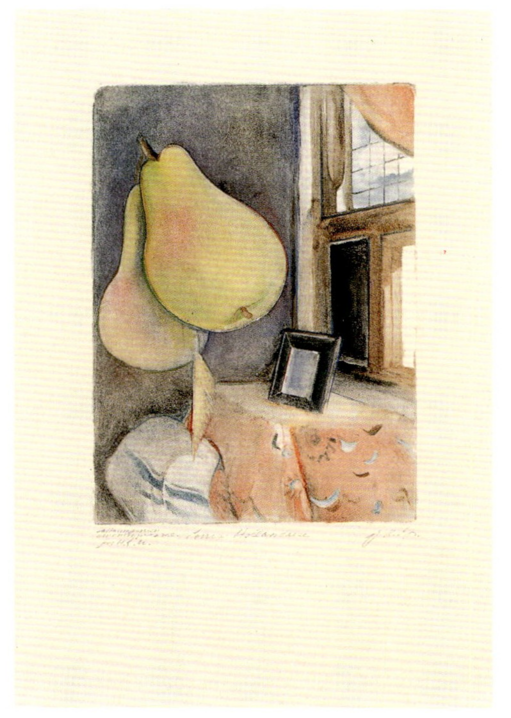

133

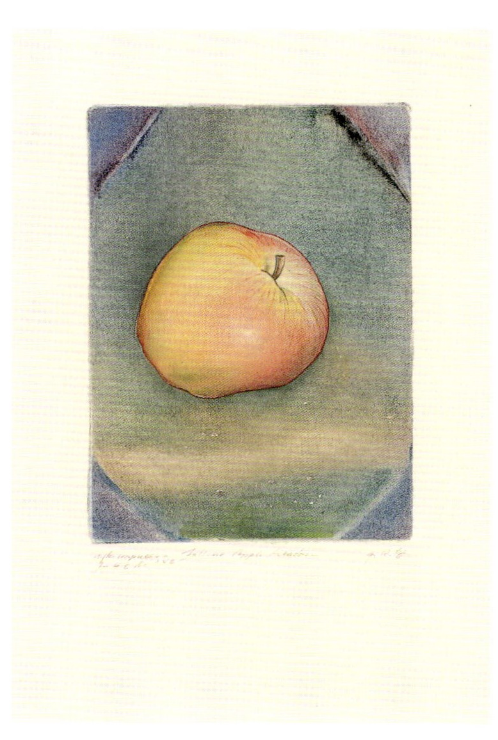

134

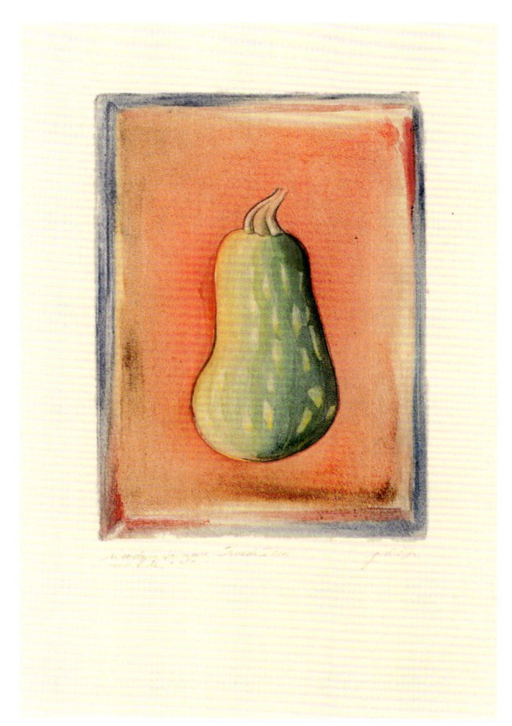

135

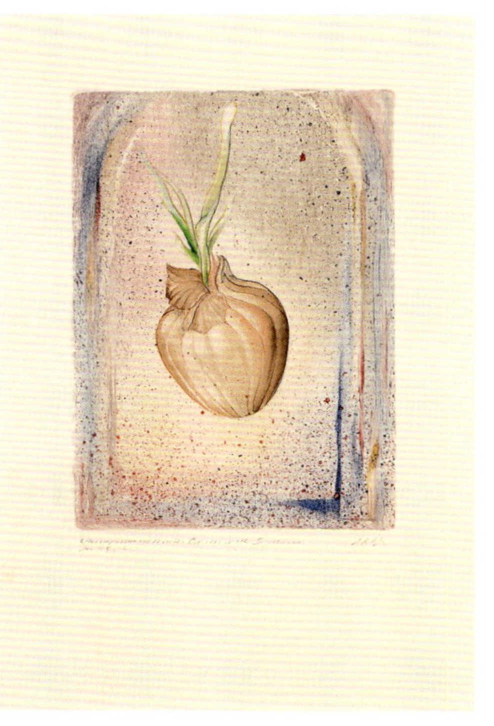

136

125 *Pink Asparagus Huddle*
126 *Arrangement with Blackberry*
127 *Aubergine Passing at Dusk*
128 *Flame Lettuce*
129 *Composition Featuring Banana*
130 *Watermelon Section, Mit, Ball*
131 *Grapes and Guadagnini*
132 *Diagonal Husk*
133 *Poires Hollandaise*
134 *Falling Apple Meadow*
135 *Squash Icon*
136 *Winter Onion II*

137
TOM HOLLAND
Eddy I, 1979
Color monotype on silk
24 x 20 in. (sheet)

138
JASPER JOHNS
Periscope I, 1979
Color lithograph
50 x 36 in. (sheet)

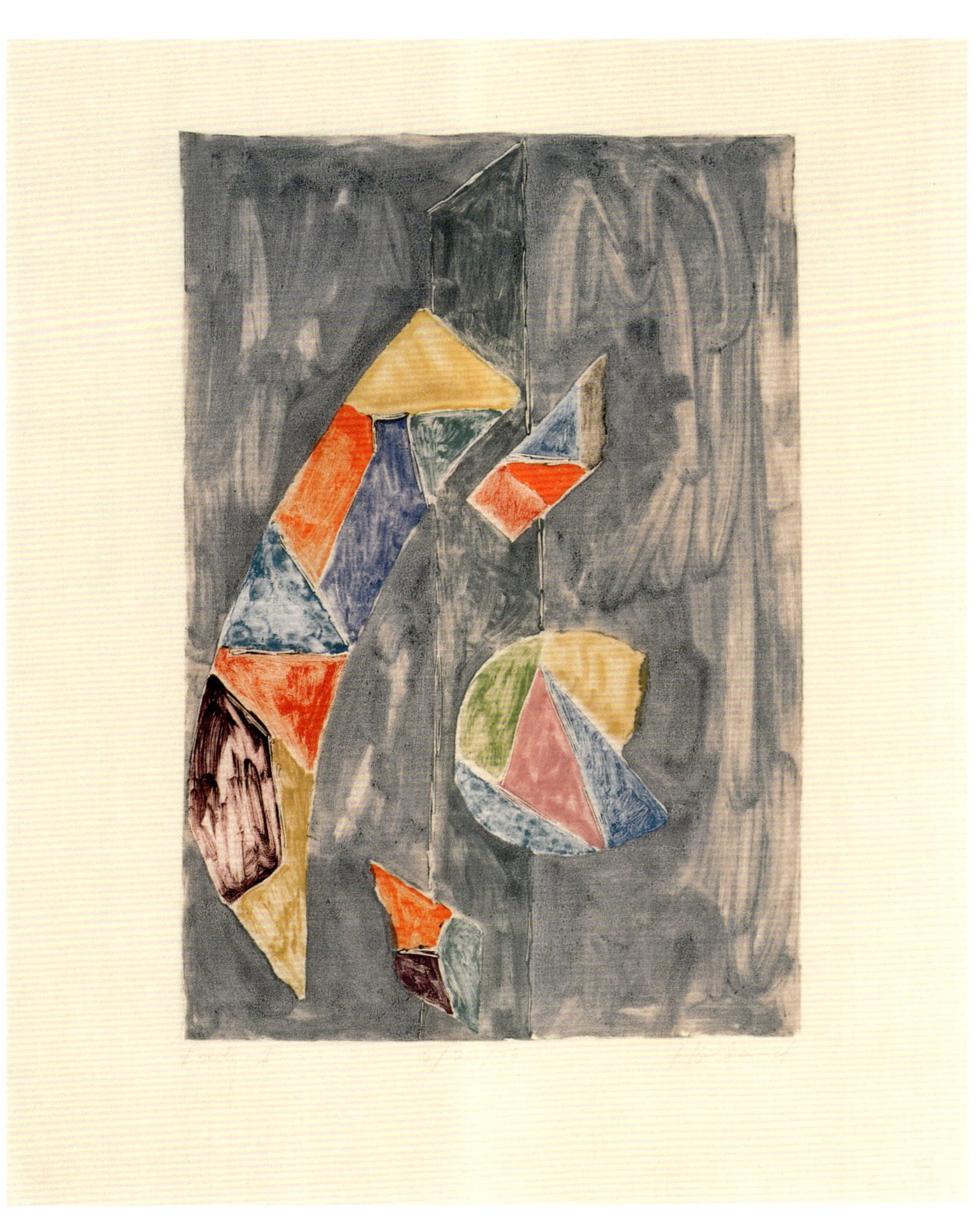

137

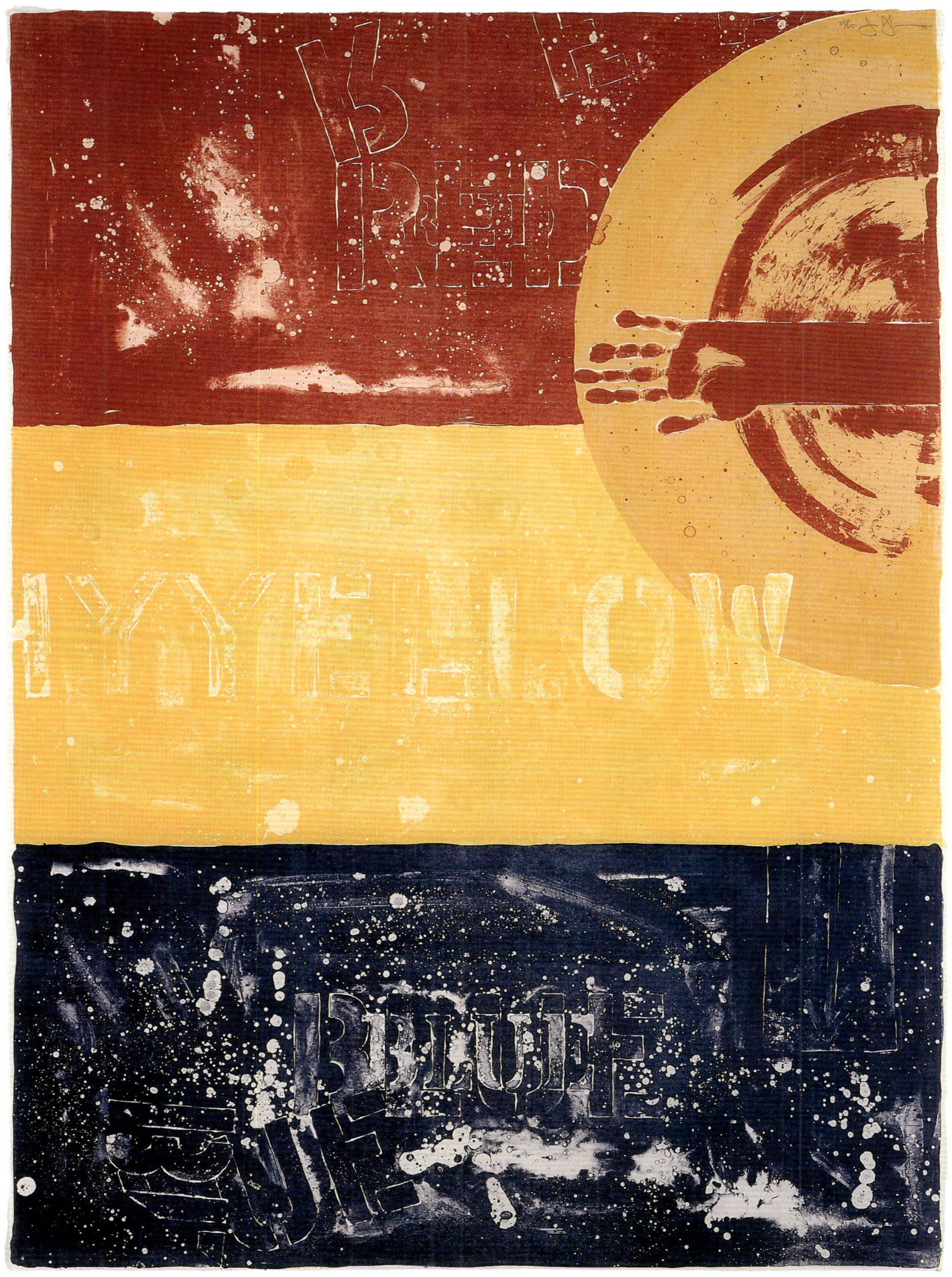

138

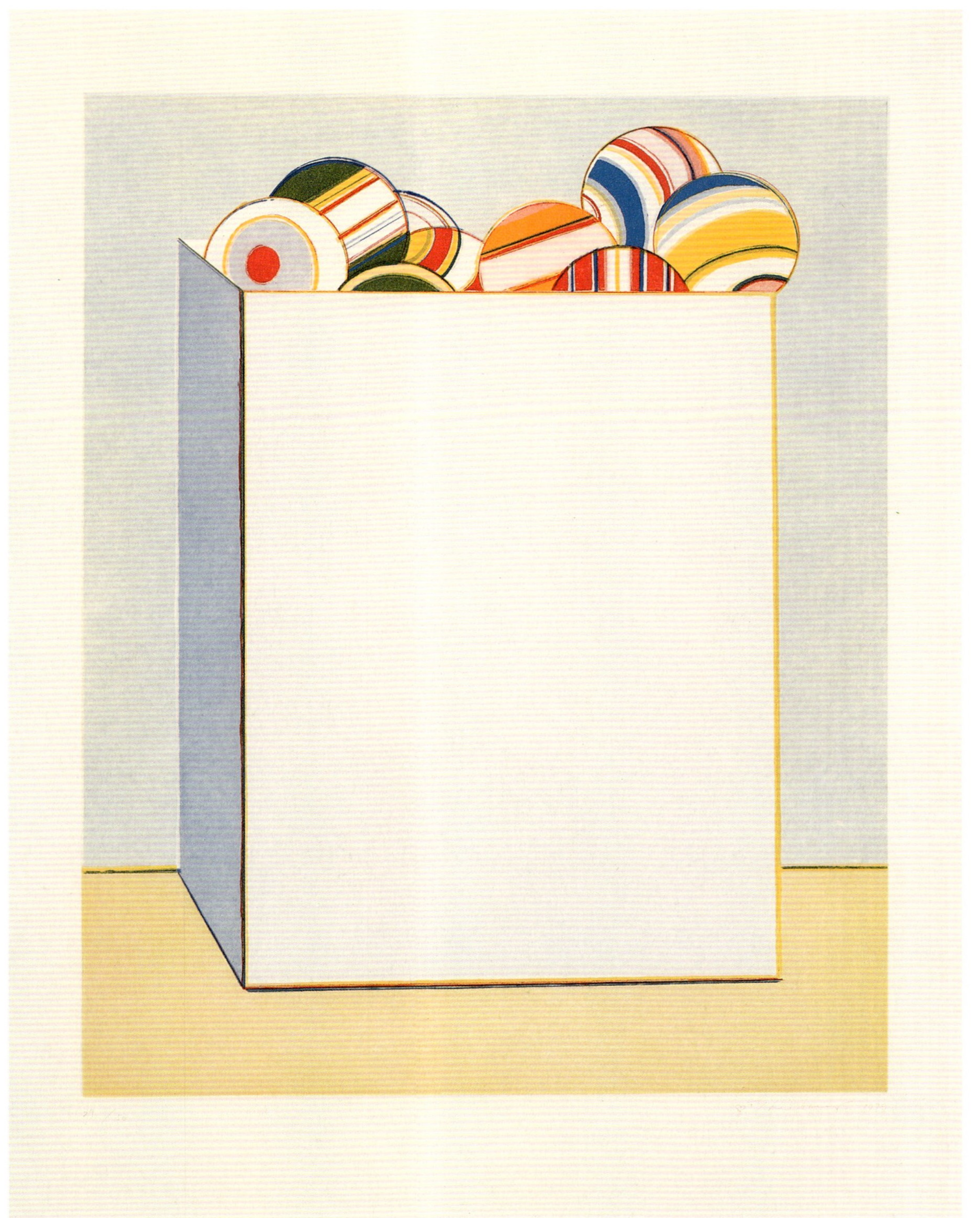

139

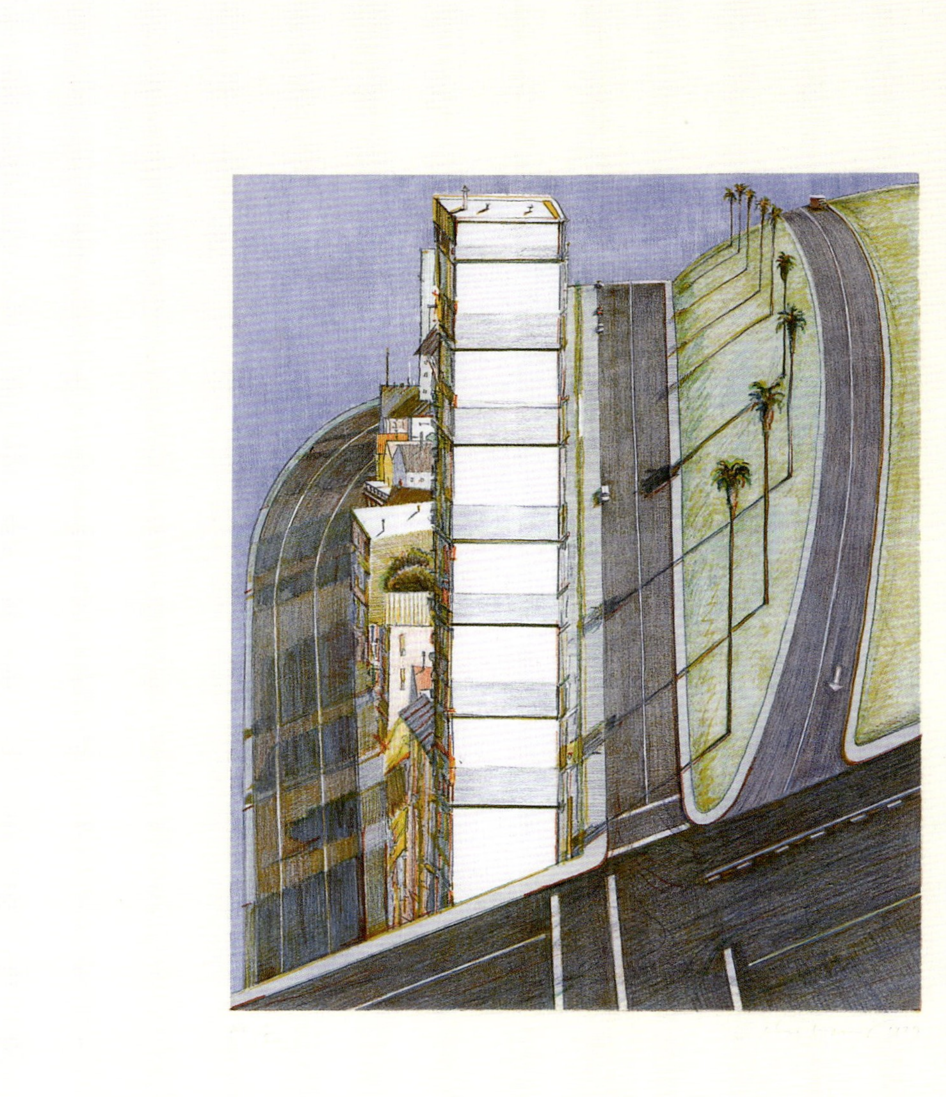

139
WAYNE THIEBAUD
Boxed Balls, pl. 6
from the portfolio *Recent Etchings I*, 1979
Color aquatint and drypoint
$29^{3}/_{4}$ x $22^{3}/_{4}$ in. (sheet)

140
WAYNE THIEBAUD
Palm Ridge, pl. 7
from the portfolio *Recent Etchings I*, 1979
Color aquatint and soft-ground etching
$29^{1}/_{2}$ x $22^{3}/_{4}$ in. (sheet)

140

The "expansionist 1970s" became the "excessive 1980s" in parlance describing the print market during the decade from 1980 to 1989. Intense interest in art broadened American markets that in turn demanded inventory, including prints. This phenomenon affected the print world at a time when many artists, already established in making prints, were regularly producing editions. They were encouraged to make many, and more. In addition, a younger generation of artists was also being encouraged to embrace the craft. With the widespread proliferation of workshops, there were more artists making prints than ever before. The result was an increased quantity of prints in the marketplace. One noticeable effect of this dynamic was the way prints looked.

The size of prints continued to increase in many print productions as American audiences became accustomed to large-scale pieces, whether in museums, corporate collections, or even domestic settings. Robert Rauschenberg's six-foot high *Booster*, remarkable for its size in 1967 when it was made, seemed more the norm among its 1980s counterparts, notably the six-and-a-half-foot-high *Fourteen Color Woodcut Bathrobe* by Jim Dine; the six-and-a-half-foot-high *View from the Window* by Roy Lichtenstein; and *Molecule Men*, an eight-foot-high screenprint by Jonathan Borofsky.

Booster was positively dwarfed by a handful of horizontal format prints made in the 1980s, including *Purple/Red/Gray/Orange* by Ellsworth Kelly at nineteen feet wide, David Hockney's *Caribbean Tea Time* at eleven feet wide, Jennifer Bartlett's *At Sea, Japan* at nine feet wide, and Judy Pfaff's *Manzanas y Naranjas* at six feet wide. Edition sizes on these prints were usually small, however (Pfaff's at fifteen, Borofsky's at twelve, Bartlett's at nine, and Kelly's at eighteen), when a common edition size was thirty-five or more. This perhaps indicated that although the prints made a strong statement by their size, they could realistically be accommodated only in oversized architectural spaces. Nevertheless they were taking over wall spaces that had formerly been occupied by paintings in many American venues.

Even monotypes, traditionally small in scale, grew larger in the 1980s with works such as Charles Arnoldi's untitled work at five feet high and Jim Dine's *Double Venus* at just over five feet high.

Like monotype, woodcut and screenprint enjoyed modest revivals in the 1970s. The two processes featured prominently in printed work of the 1980s but with a distinctive difference. Many woodcuts exhibited a strong physicality of surface, full of roughhewn marks and textures that indicated a coarsely cut block. Others involved complex compositions of many colors, thickly printed and often overlapping, which gave them the appearance of paintings. These ambitious undertakings with woodcut can be attributed, in part, to the fact that very few artists actually cut the entire block or blocks used to make the print. Instead, the strenuous and complicated work of cutting and printing was done by skilled technicians in the workshop. For example, Dine's *Fourteen Color Woodcut Bathrobe* and Robert Arneson's *Robert Arneson* were both cut at Experimental Workshop. Richard Diebenkorn's color woodcut *Blue with Red* was cut and printed by talented craftsmen in Kyoto, Japan, as part of Crown Point Press's program there. It exhibits surface sophistication but with a lyrical softness of form, as does Jennifer Bartlett's *At Sea, Japan*, which was also printed in the traditional Japanese woodcut method.

In *At Sea, Japan* Bartlett paired woodcut with screenprint, another process that underwent change in the 1980s. The six-panel print was made at Simca Print Artists, a workshop that produced screenprints of the highest quality, but which were new and different in appearance because they showed varied surface qualities. Led by the example of Jasper Johns, who created *Corpse and Mirror* at Simca in 1976 by painting on multiple screens to create transparent and opaque textures, artists in the 1980s began to make screenprints that exhibited a lively appearance, far from the flat, uninflected surfaces of screenprints from the 1960s.

Lithography and etching produced throughout the 1980s also revealed artistic concern with the vitality and richness of the printed surface. Artists such as Elizabeth Murray and Terry Winters created subtly colored lithographs with smudged layers. Multilayers of color aquatint were featured in a number of impressive prints by Pat Steir and Sean Scully at Crown Point Press during this period, none more eloquent in appearance than Richard Diebenkorn's *Spreading Spade* and *Large Bright Blue*.

In the subject matter for their prints of the 1980s, many artists diverged from the dialogue of figuration versus abstraction, which had dominated since the 1960s, by self-confidently looking at art history. David Hockney's *Caribbean Tea Time* was one of many of his vibrant reworkings of Picasso's late Cubism. Rauschenberg paid homage to fifteenth-century painting in his *Bellini* series and Jim Dine's *Double Venus* monotype is a reference to the Venus de Milo and other classical sculpture, a subject that had also figured prominently in his paintings and drawings. David Gilhooly acknowledged the artistic tradition of the memento mori in his *Selbstbildnis mit Tod*. Johns, of course, returned to the symbols of his early works with *The Seasons* in which the Mona Lisa, George Ohr pottery, and references to Marcel Duchamp's profile self-portrait are included as fragments. Roy Lichtenstein, who had continuously looked at artists and art movements in his paintings and prints, tackled specific artists in his *Landscape Series* prints, notably Henri Matisse in *View from the Window*.

Looking at Prints: The 1980s

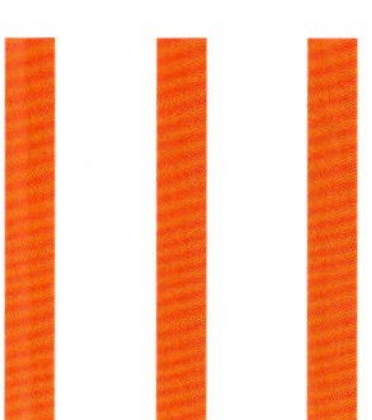

The 1980s

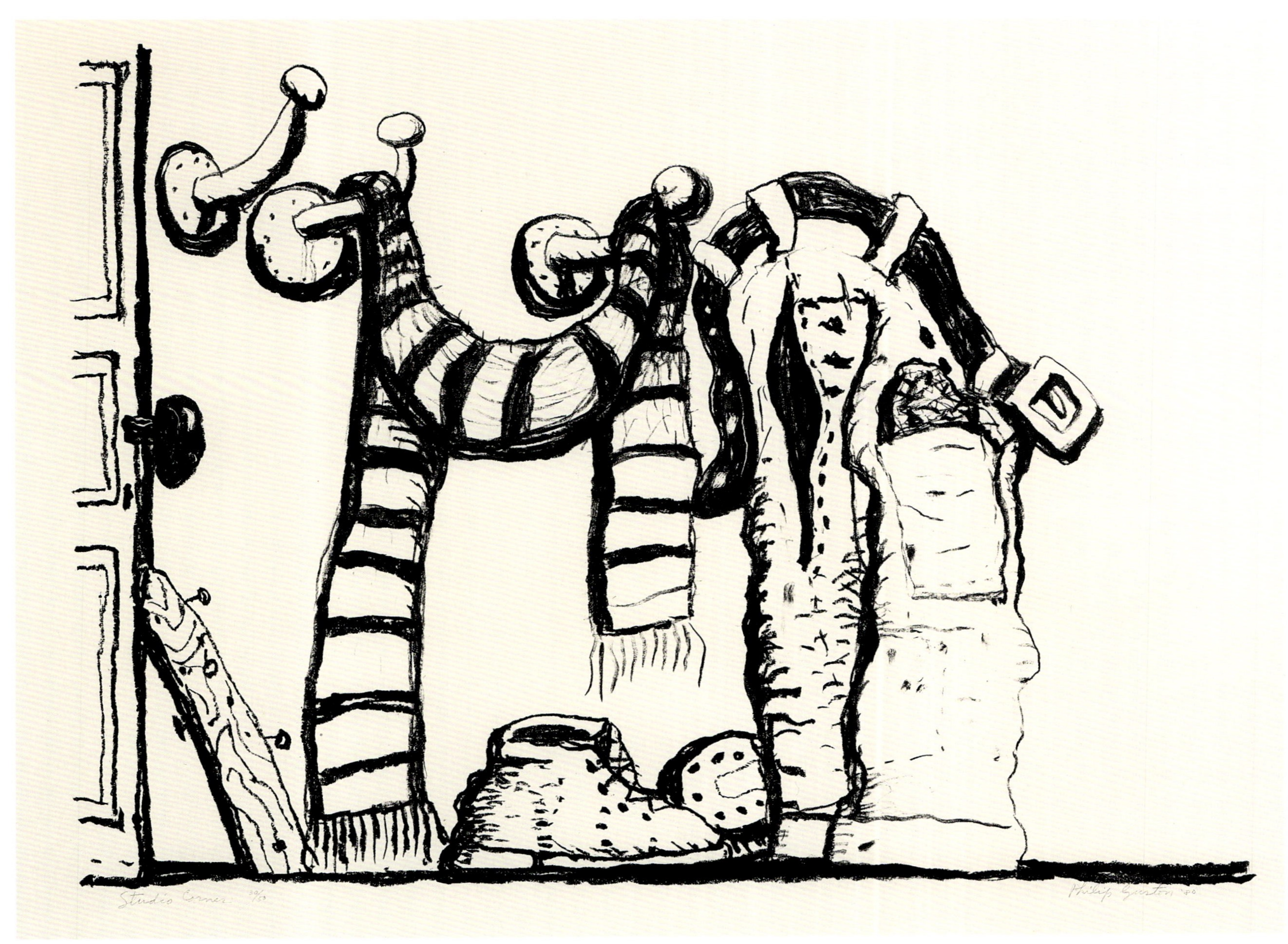

141

141
PHILIP GUSTON
Studio Corner, 1980
Lithograph
32 x 42½ in. (sheet)

14[illegible]
JENNIFER BARTLET[illegible]
At Sea, Japan, 198[illegible]
Color woodcut an[illegible]
screenprint on 6 sheet[illegible]
22½ x 104¼ in. (overall[illegible]

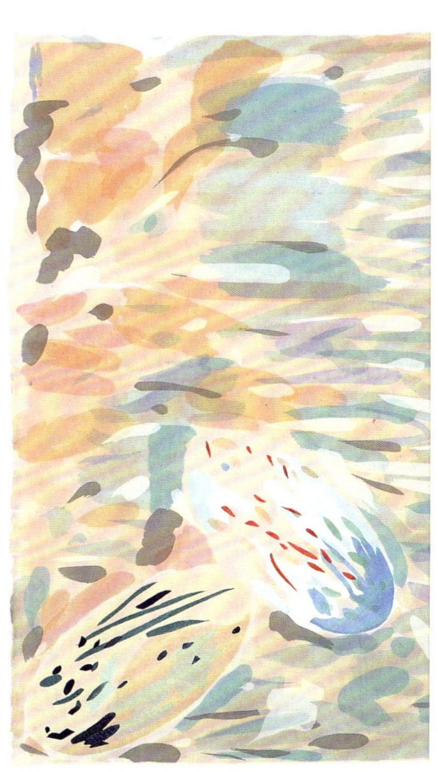

142

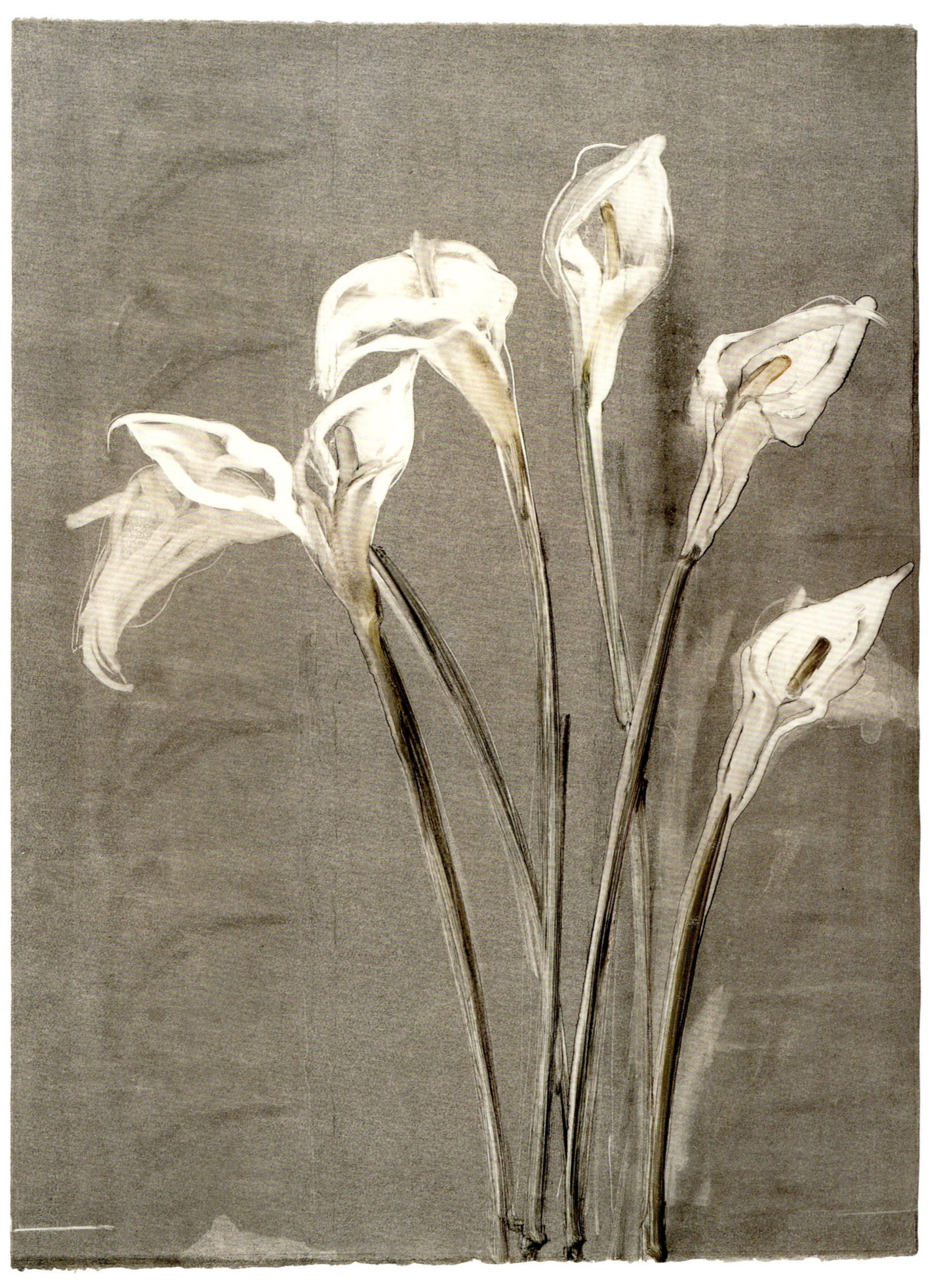

143

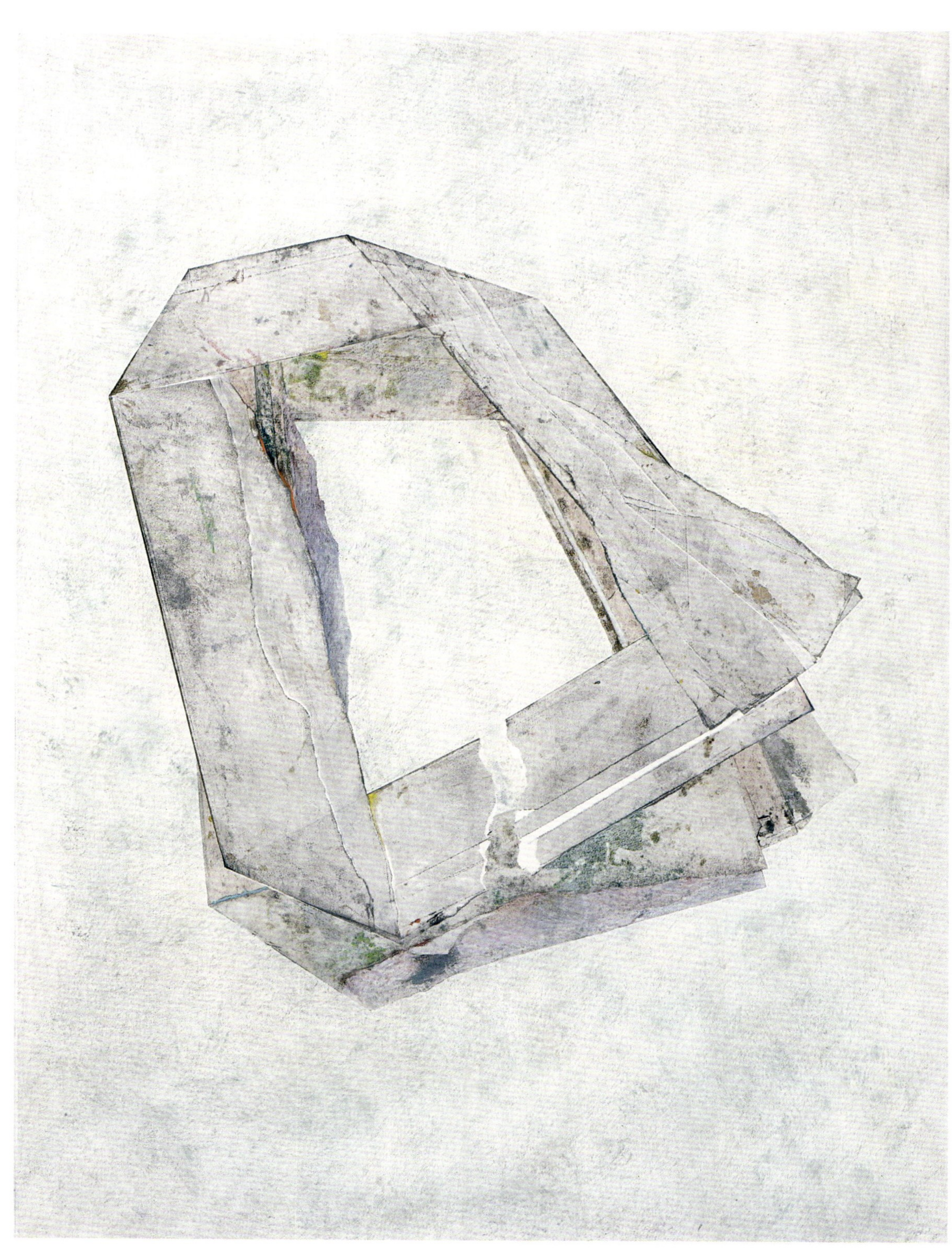

144

143
MICHAEL MAZUR
Calla Lily Diptych, 1980
Color monotype (cognate)
41 9/16 x 29 1/2 in. (sheet)

144
MIKLOS POGANY
Untitled, 1981
Color monotype
49 3/4 x 38 1/16 in. (sheet)

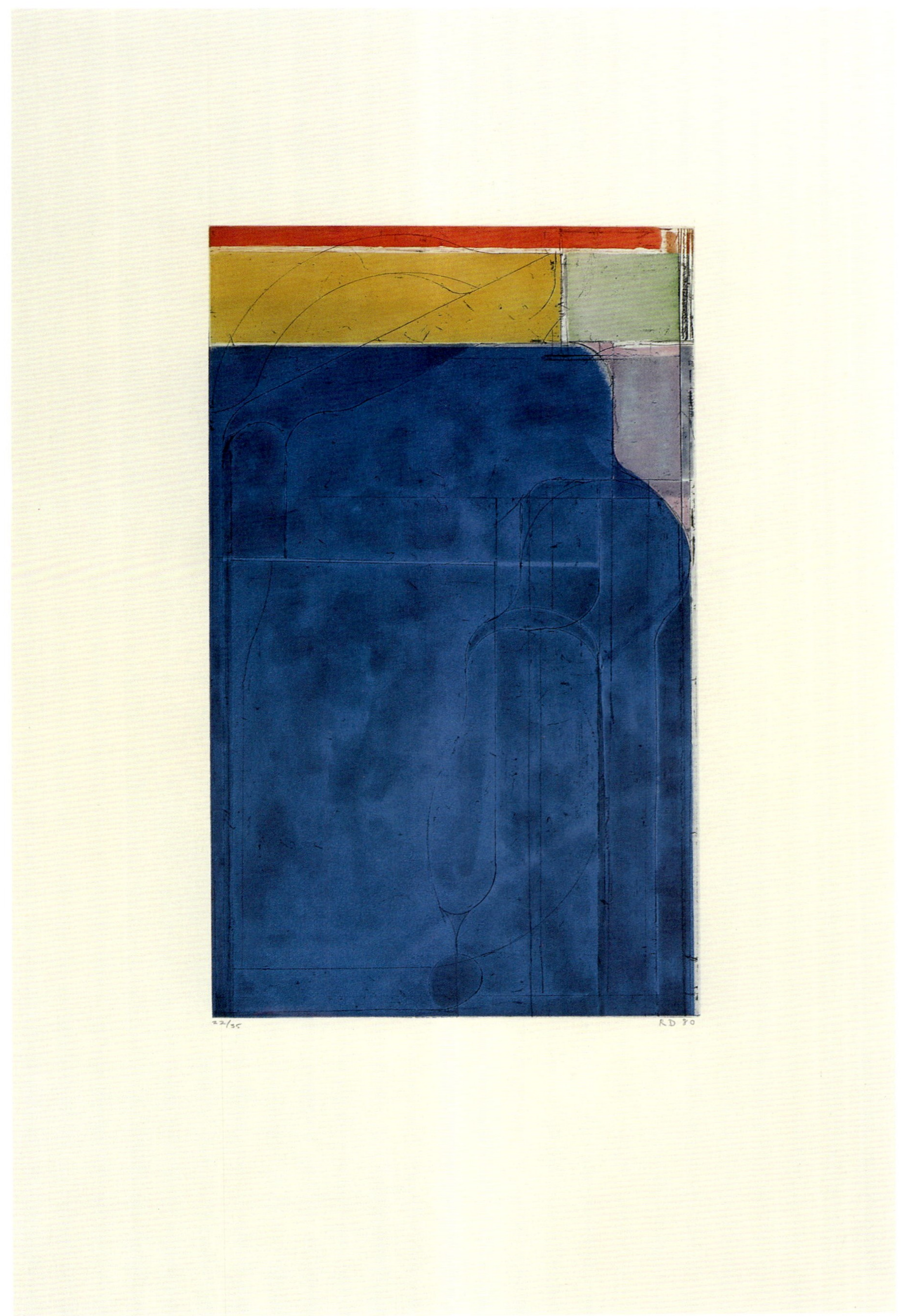

145

145★
RICHARD DIEBENKORN
Large Bright Blue, 1980
Color spit-bite aquatint and
soft-ground etching
40 x 26 in. (sheet)

146
RICHARD DIEBENKORN
Spreading Spade, 1981
Color aquatint, spit-bite aquatint,
and drypoint
36 3/8 x 30 7/8 in. (sheet)

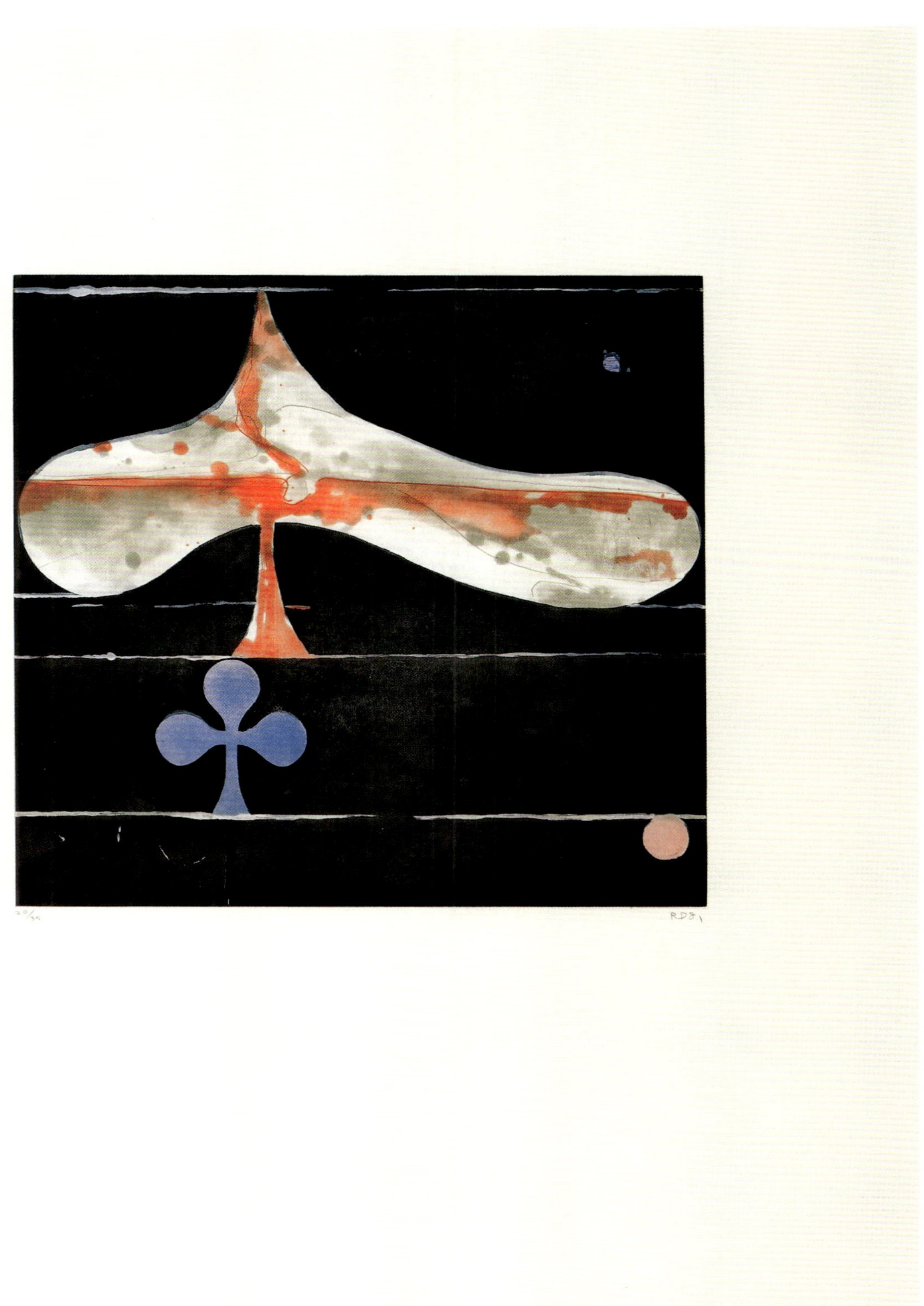

146

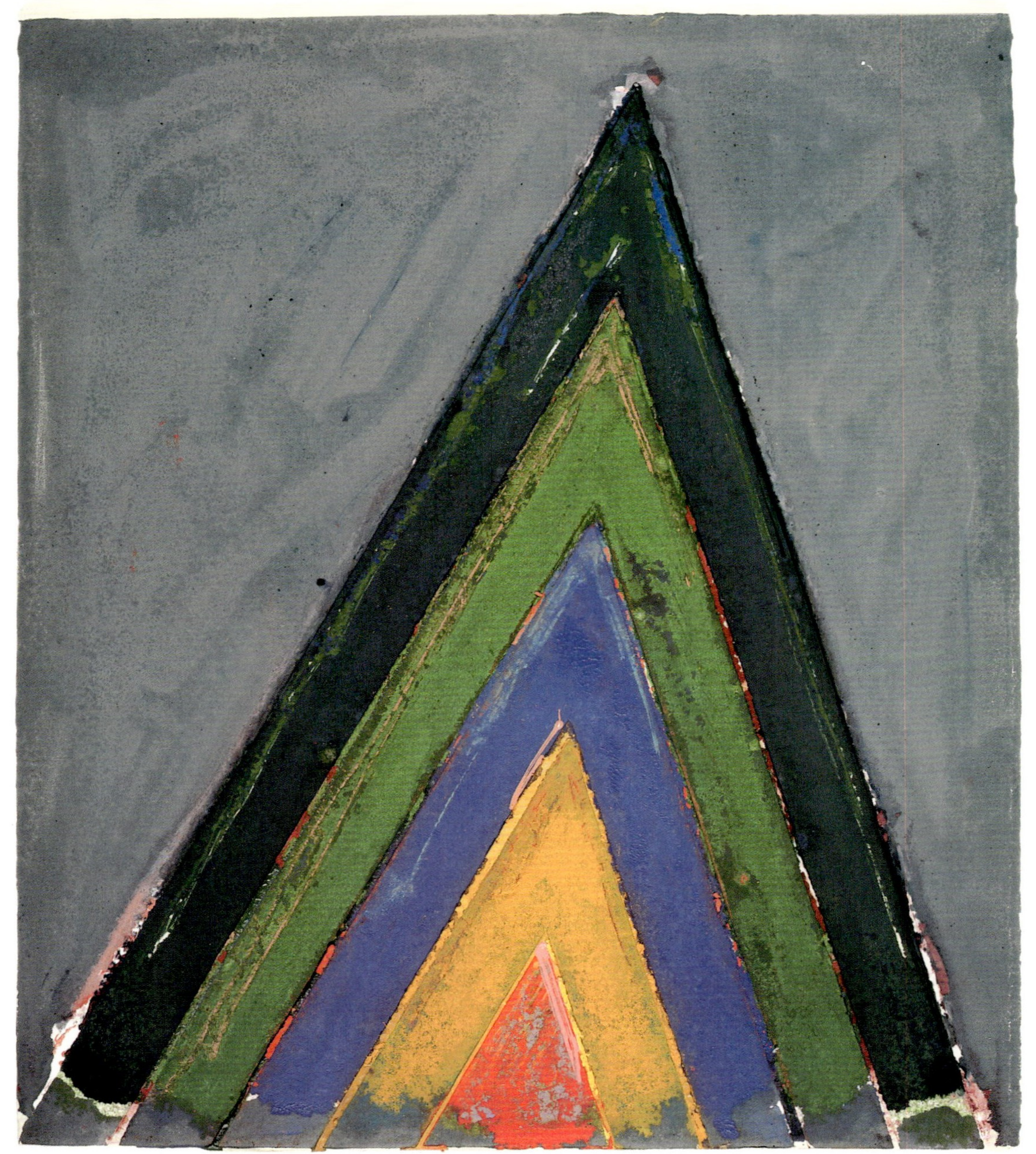

147

147
KENNETH NOLAND
Chevron, 1981
Color monotype
$29^{5}/_{8}$ x $25^{1}/_{8}$ in. (sheet)

148
VIJA CELMINS
Strata, 1982
Mezzotint
$29^{1}/_{2}$ x $35^{1}/_{4}$ in. (sheet)

148

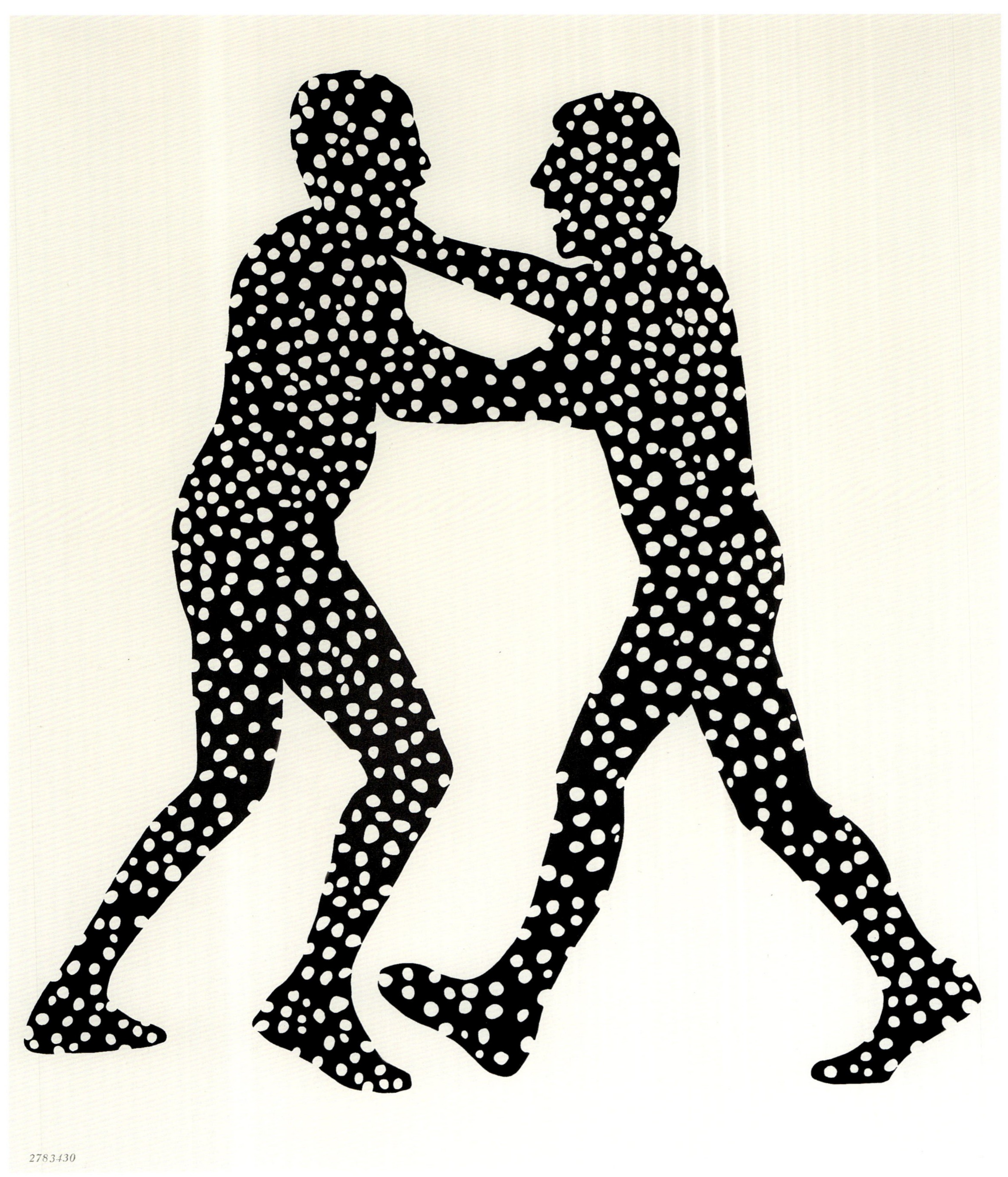

149

149
JONATHAN BOROFSKY
Molecule Men, 1982
Screenprint
96½ x 79¾ in. (sheet)

150
JIM DINE
Fourteen Color Woodcut Bathrobe, 1982
Color woodcut
77½ x 42 in. (sheet)

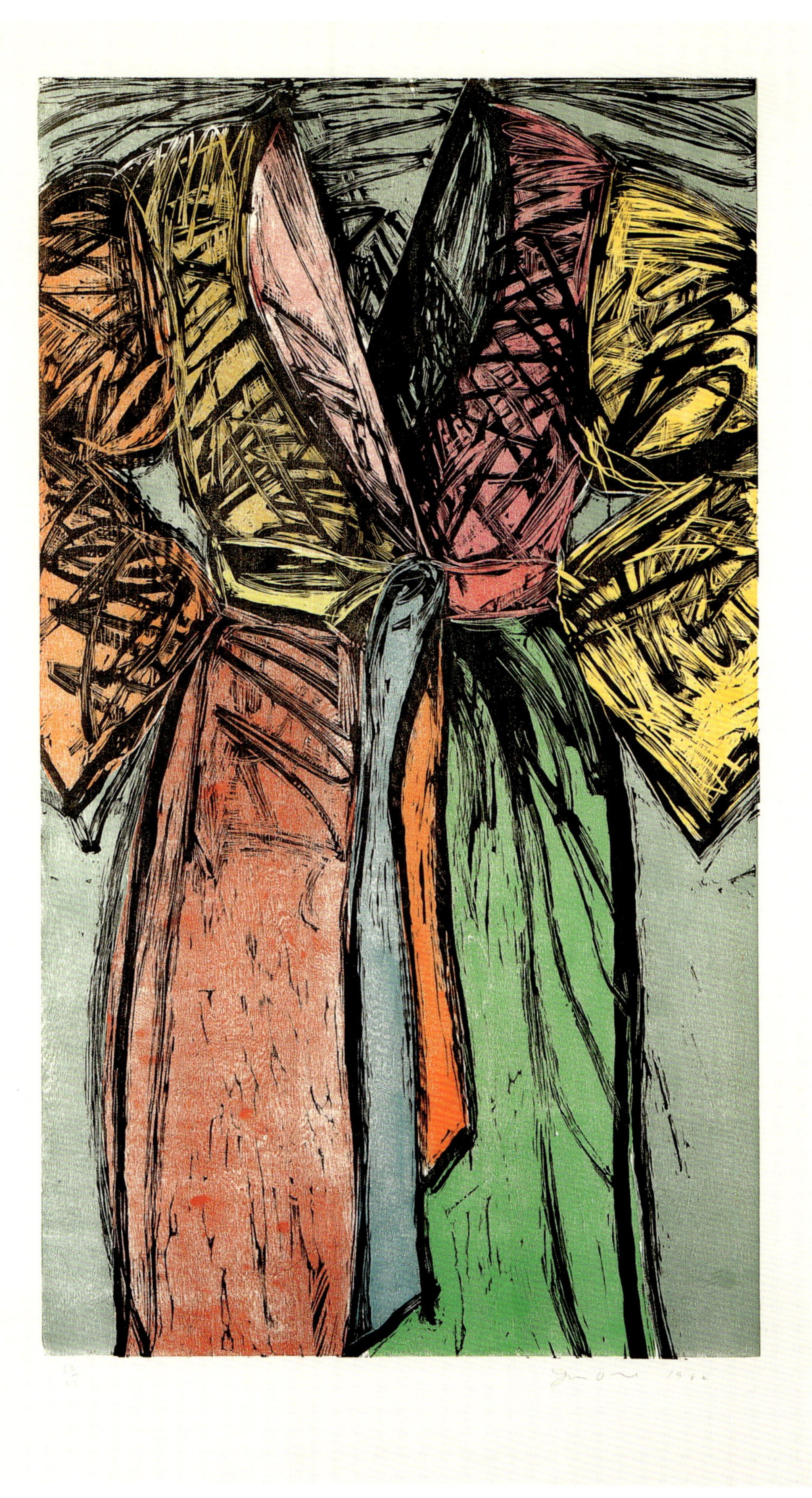

150

THE VOICE OF THE BRIDEGROOM AND OF THE BRIDE

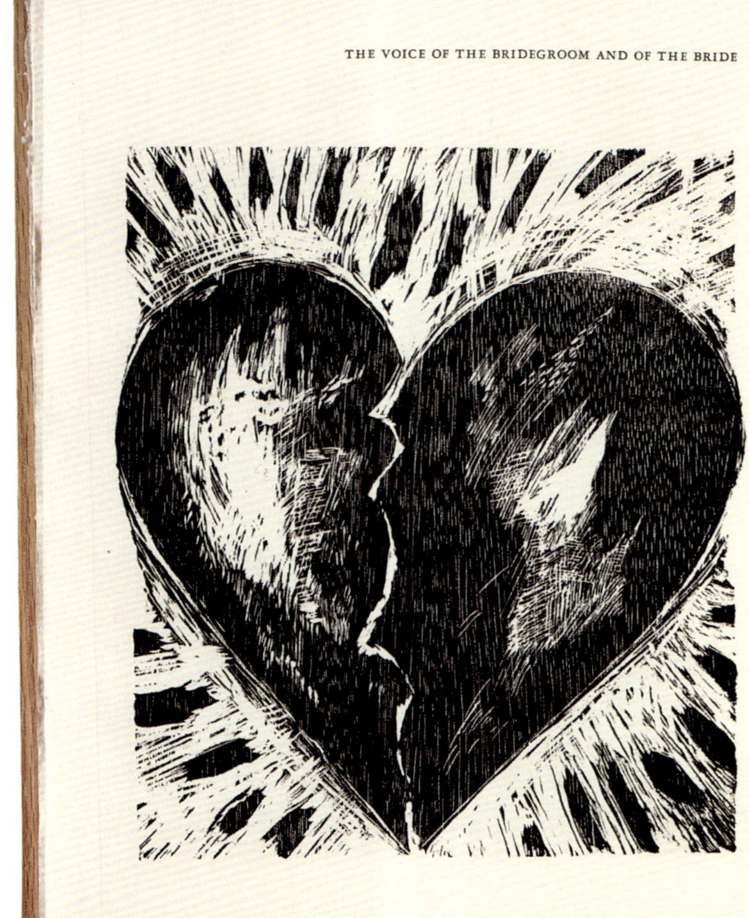

CHAPTER 18

19 And they cast dust on their heads, and cried, weeping and wailing, saying,
Alas, alas, that great city,
wherein were made rich all that had ships in the sea by reason of her costliness!
for in one hour is she made desolate.
20 Rejoice over her, thou heaven, and ye holy apostles and prophets;
for God hath avenged you on her.
21 ¶ And a mighty angel took up a stone like a great millstone, and cast it into the sea, saying,
Thus with violence shall that great city Babylon be thrown down,
and shall be found no more at all.
22 And the voice of harpers, and musicians, and of pipers, and trumpeters,
shall be heard no more at all in thee;
and no craftsman, of whatsoever craft he be, shall be found any more in thee;
and the sound of a millstone shall be heard no more at all in thee;
23 And the light of a candle shall shine no more at all in thee;
and the voice of the bridegroom and of the bride
shall be heard no more at all in thee:
for thy merchants were the great men of the earth;
for by thy sorceries were all nations deceived.
24 And in her was found the blood of prophets, and of saints,
and of all that were slain upon the earth.

CHAPTER 19

AND AFTER THESE THINGS I HEARD
a great voice of much people in heaven, saying,
Alleluia; Salvation, and glory, and honour, and power, unto the Lord our God:
02 For true and righteous are his judgments: for he hath judged the great whore,
which did corrupt the earth with her fornication,
and hath avenged the blood of his servants at her hand.
03 And again they said,
Alleluia. And her smoke rose up for ever and ever.
04 And the four and twenty elders and the four beasts fell down
and worshipped God that sat on the throne, saying,
Amen; Alleluia.
05 And a voice came out of the throne, saying,
Praise our God, all he his servants, and ye that fear him, both small and great.

151

151
JIM DINE
The Voice of the Bridegroom and of the Bride,
in the book *The Apocalypse/The Revelation of Saint John the Divine,* 1982
Woodcut
$14^{13}/_{16}$ x $11^{1}/_{8}$ in. (page)

152
JIM DINE
Double Venus, 1983
Color monotype
63 x 36 in. (sheet)

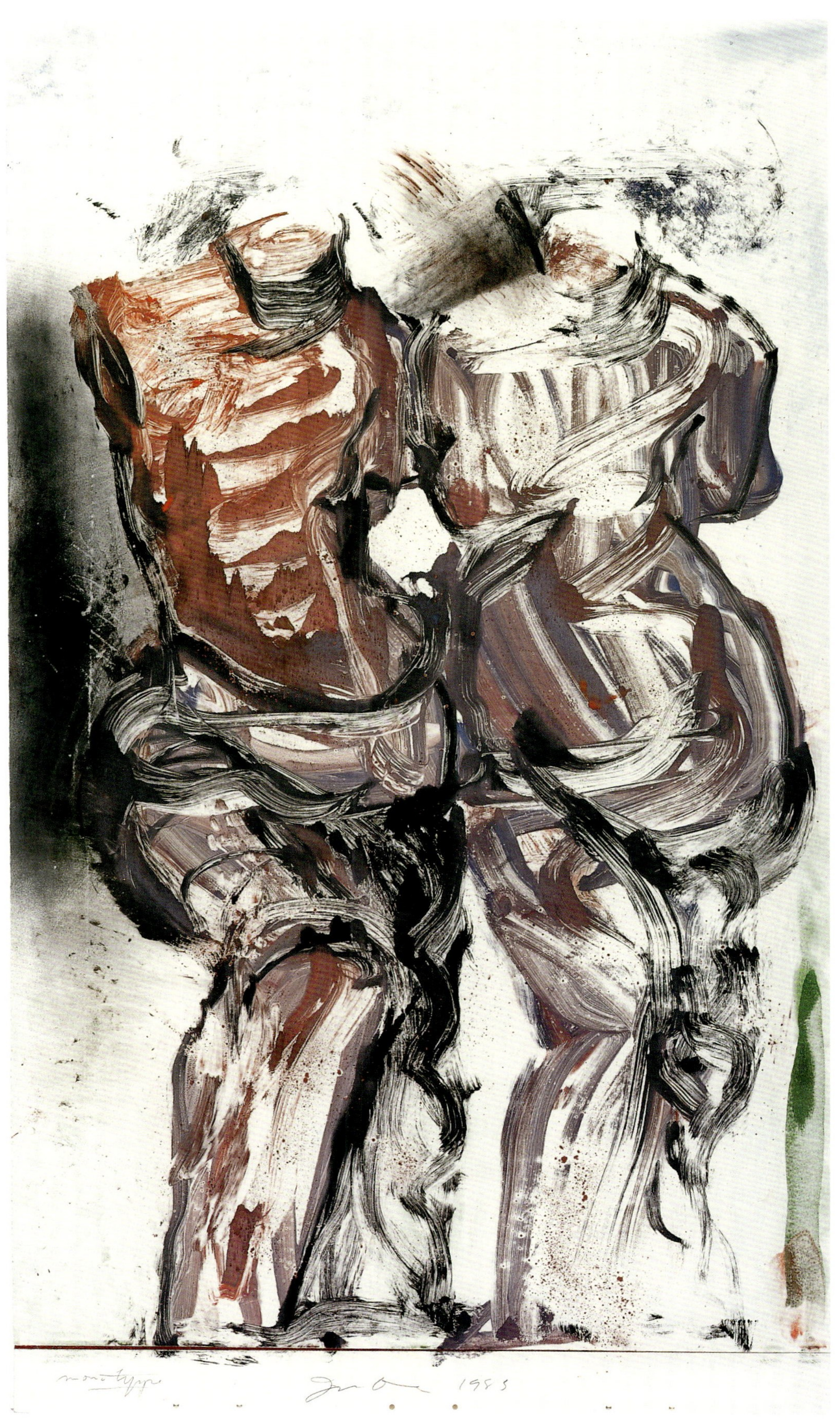

152

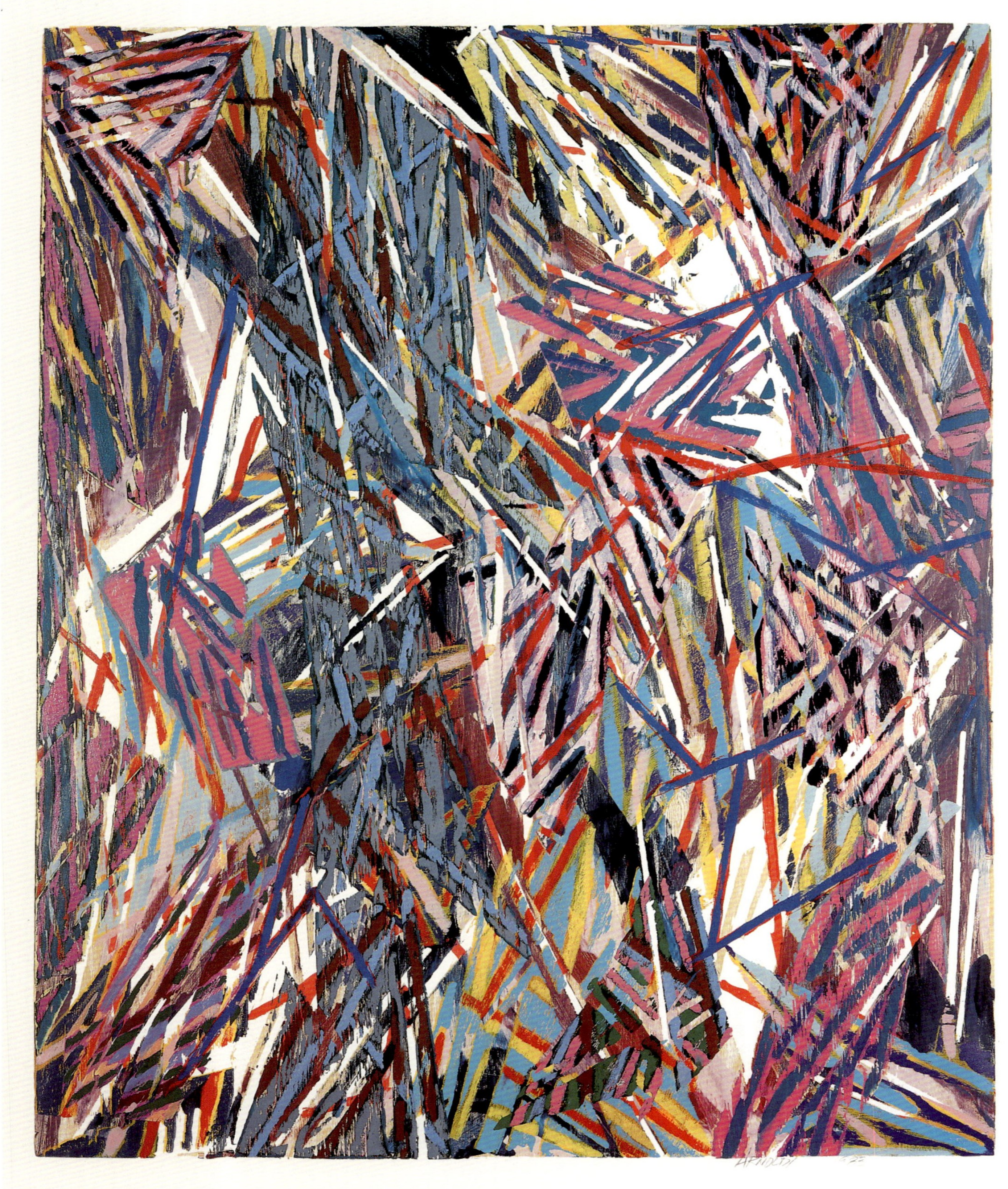

153

153
CHARLES ARNOLDI
Untitled, 1983
Color monoprint
59⅞ x 50 in. (sheet)

154★
LADDIE JOHN DILL
Untitled, 1985
Vacuum-cast paper relief,
hand painted by the artist
30 x 48 in. (overall)

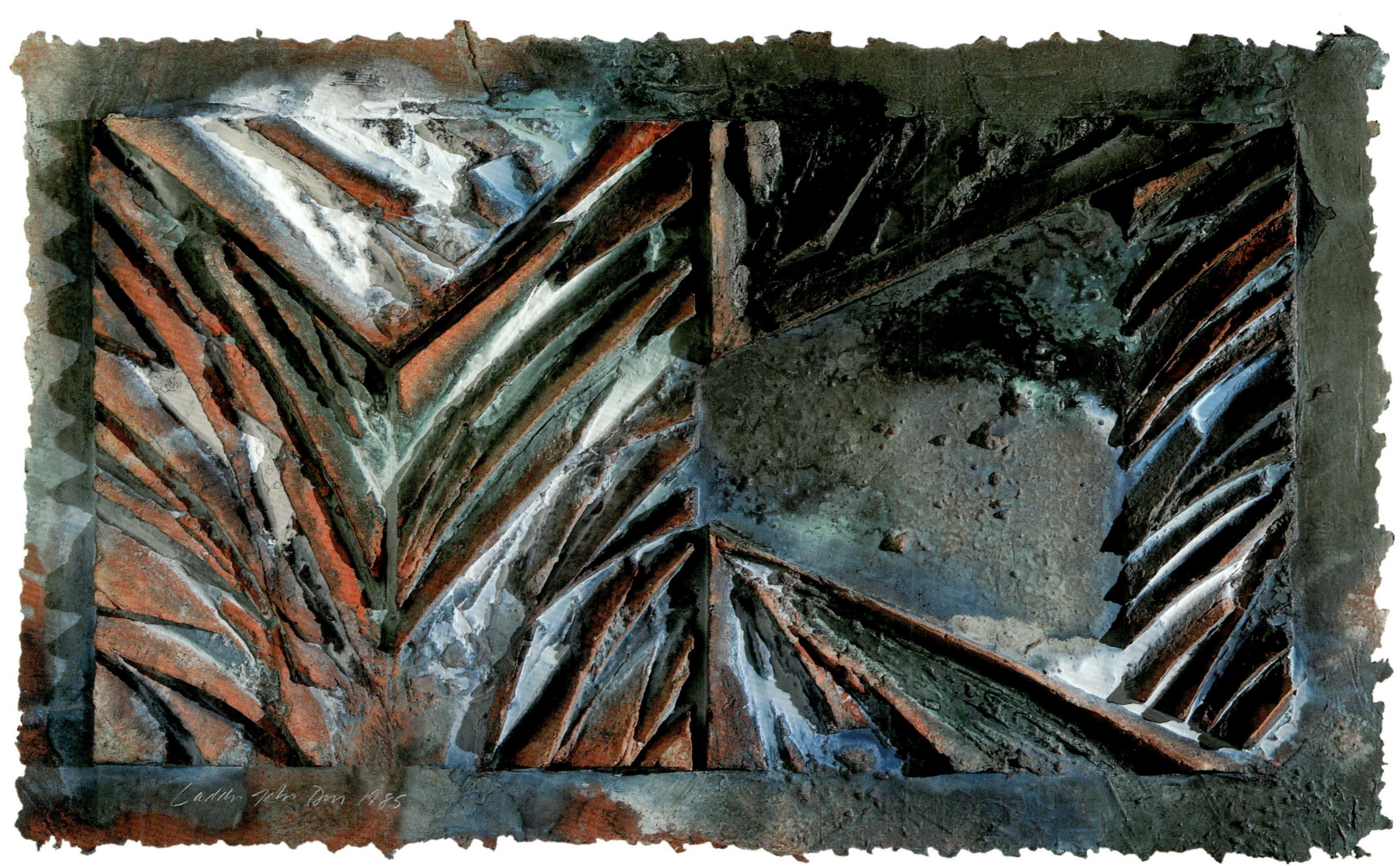

154

155
DAVID GILHOOLY
Selbstbildnis mit Tod,
from the series *3-A*, 1983
Monoprint etching
22 1/2 x 30 1/8 in. (sheet)

156
ROBERT ARNESON
Robert Arneson,
from the series *Five Guys*, 1983
Woodcut
31 5/16 x 24 13/16 in. (sheet)

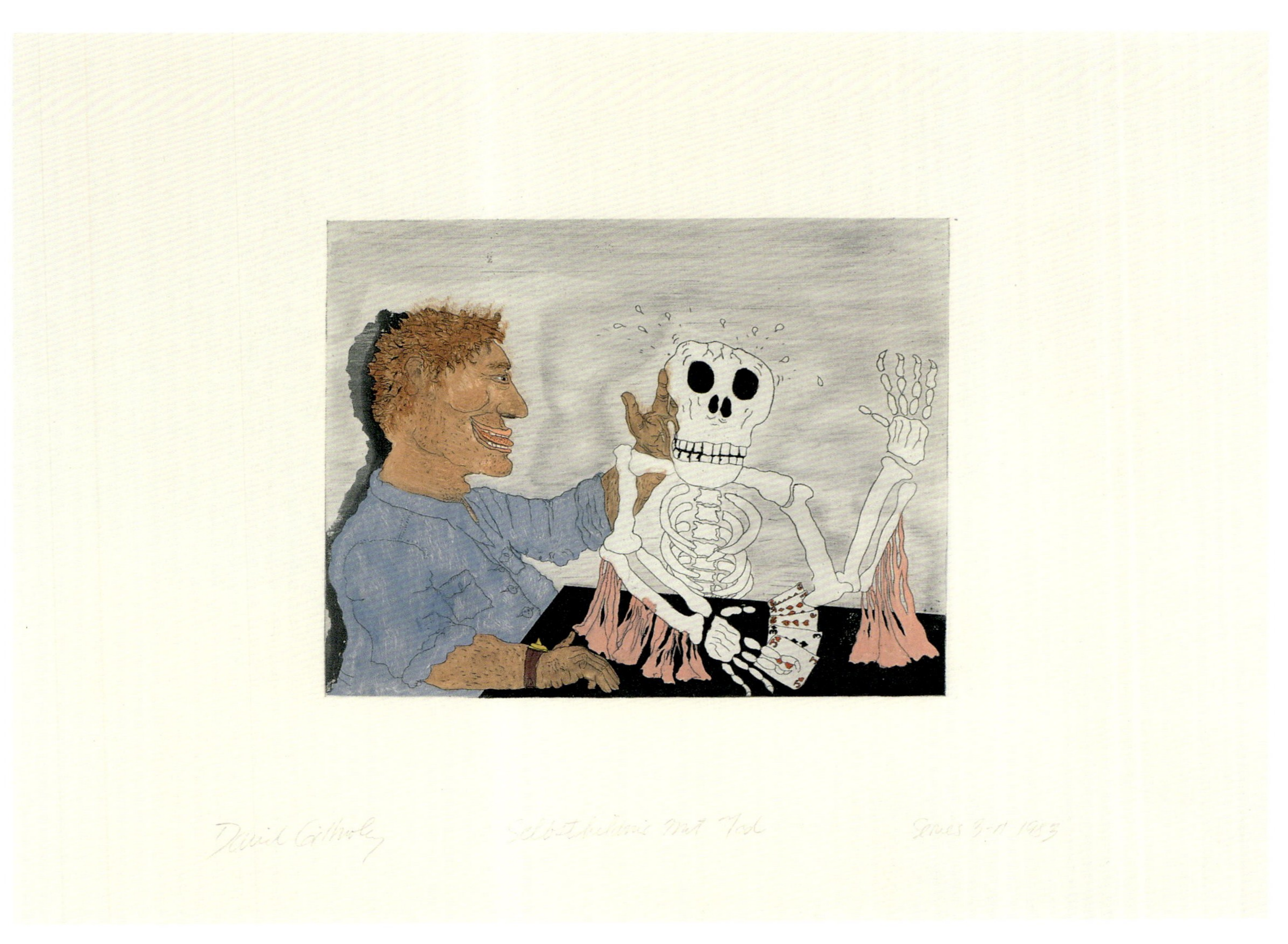

155

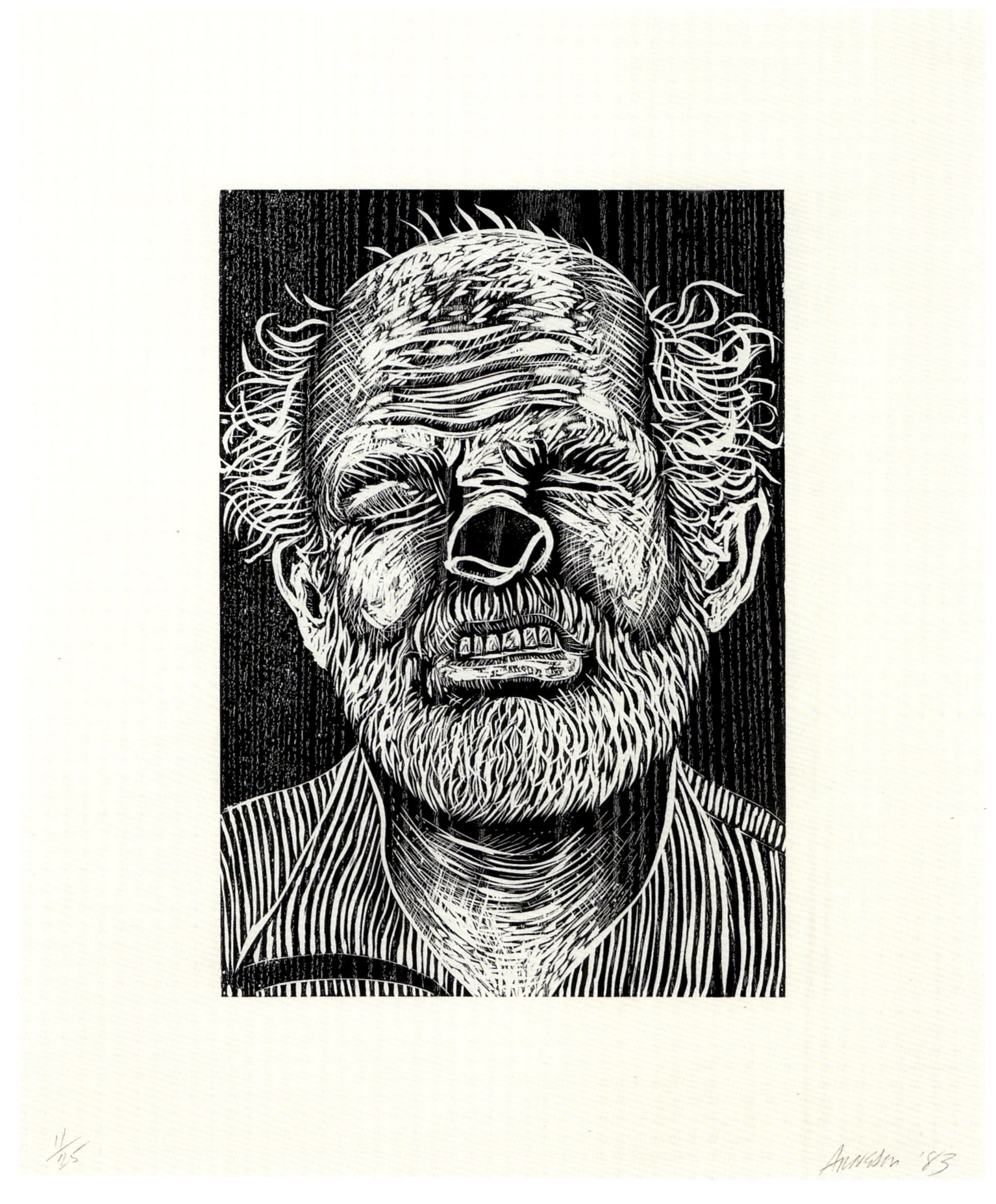

156

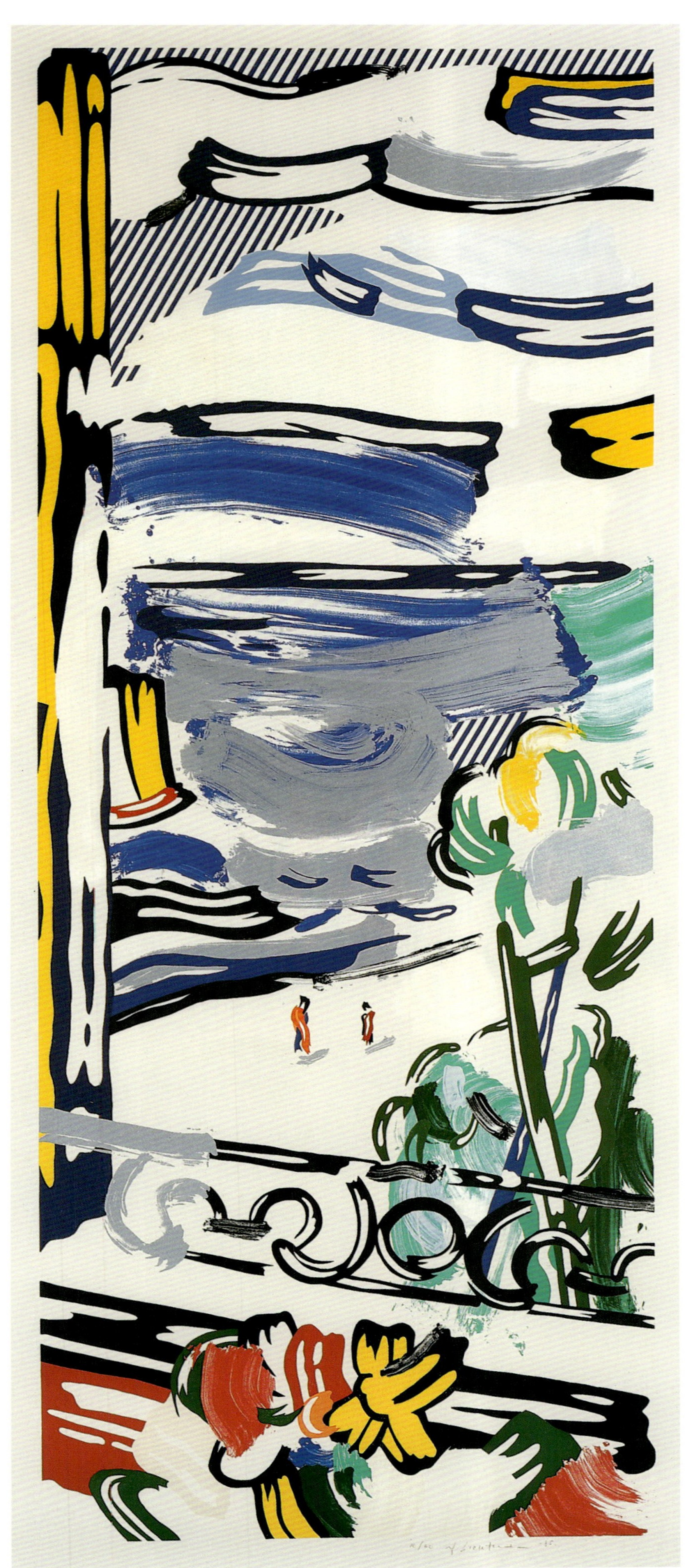

157

157
ROY LICHTENSTEIN
View from the Window,
from the *Landscape Series,* 1985
Color lithograph, woodcut, and screenprint
79 9/16 x 33 5/8 in. (sheet)

158
DAVID HOCKNEY
Caribbean Tea Time, 1985–1987
Double-sided four panel folding screen
84 5/8 x 134 1/2 in. (overall)

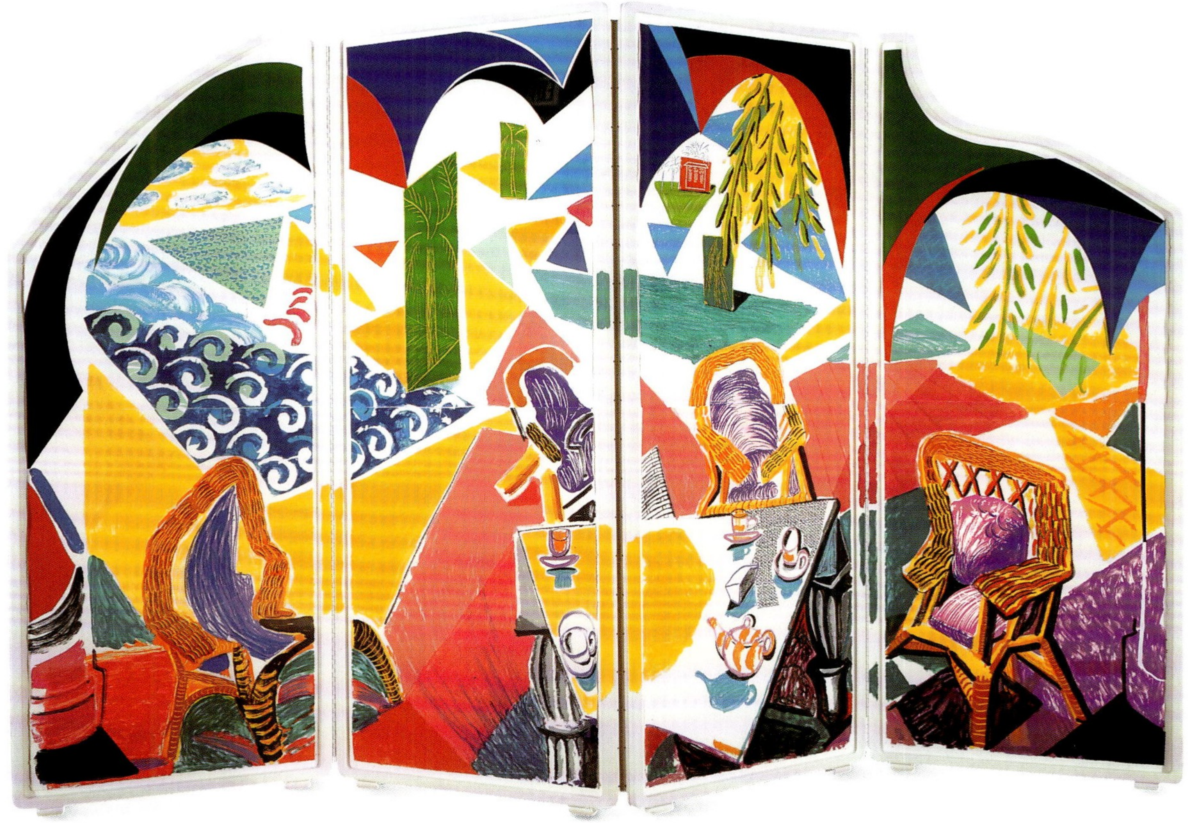

158

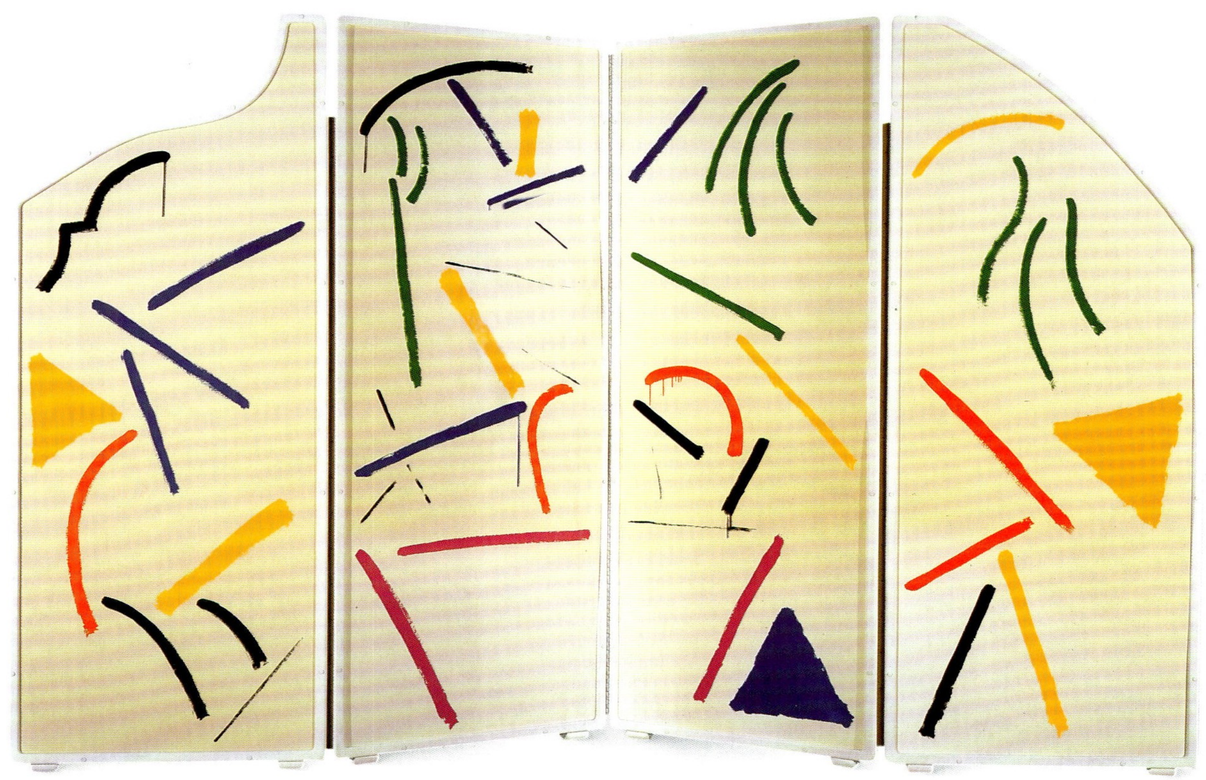

159★
SUSAN ROTHENBERG
Stumblebum, 1985–1986
Color lithograph
86½ x 42½ in. (sheet)

160
JUDY PFAFF
Manzanas y Naranjas, 1987
Color woodcut
56⅜ x 69½ in. (sheet)

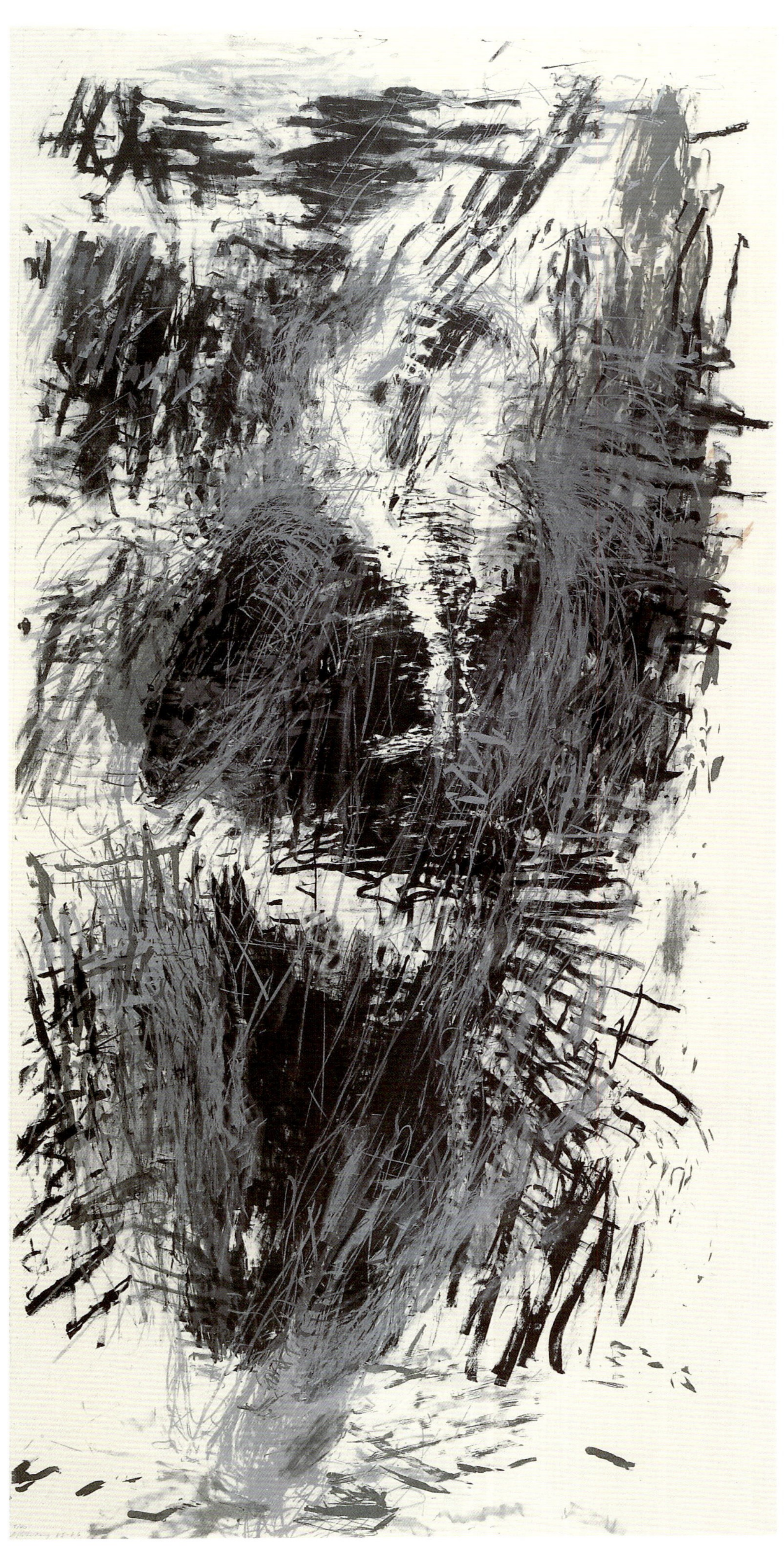

159

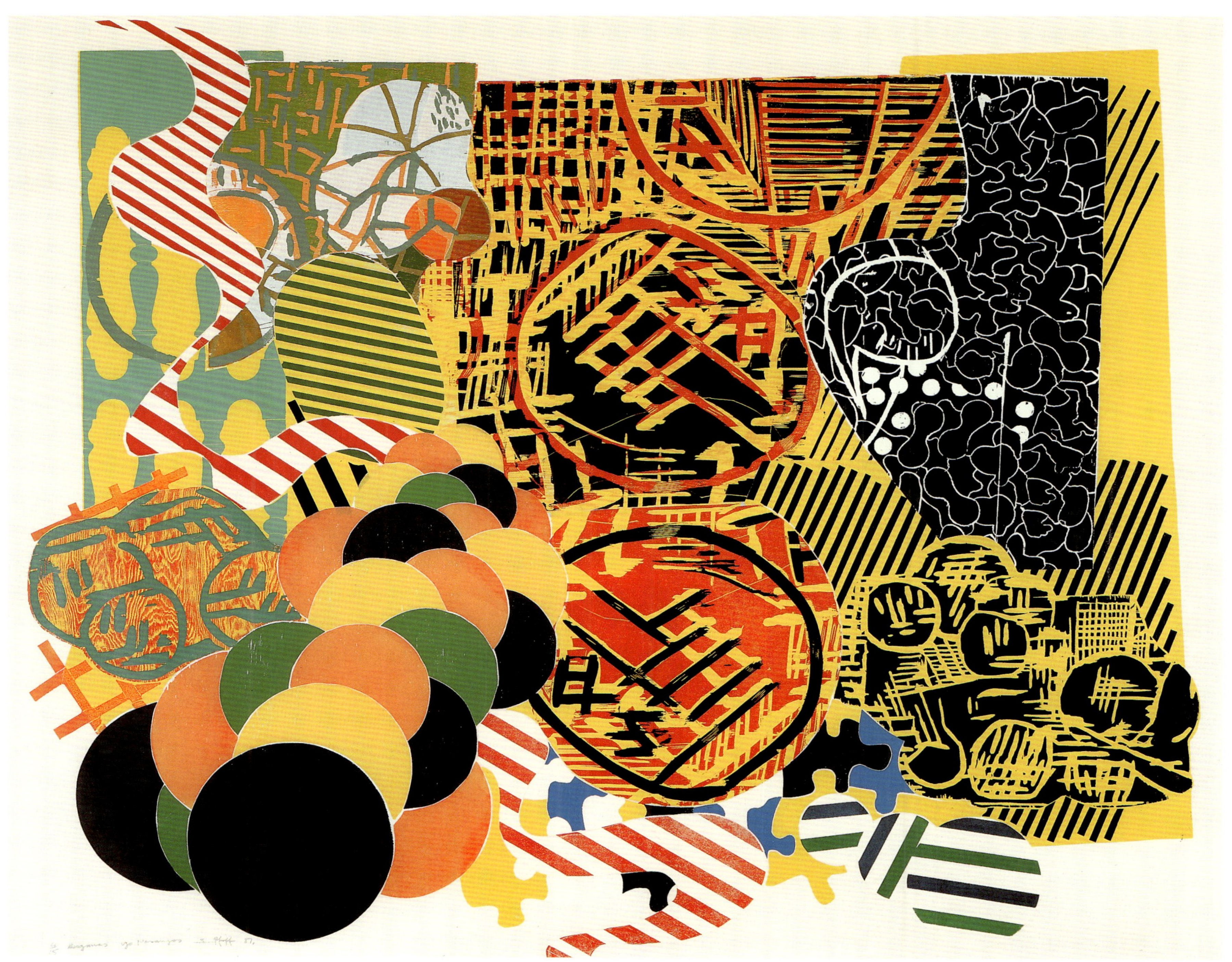

160

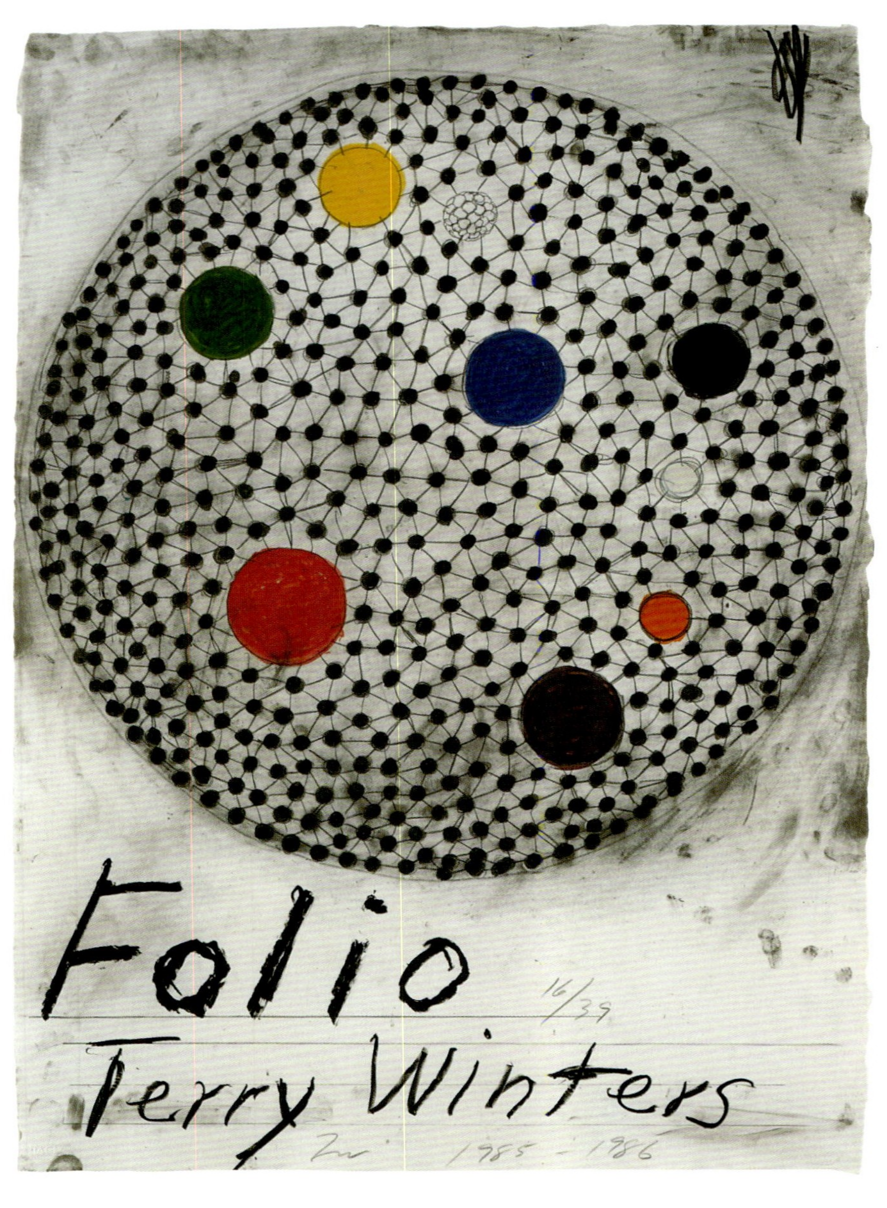

161

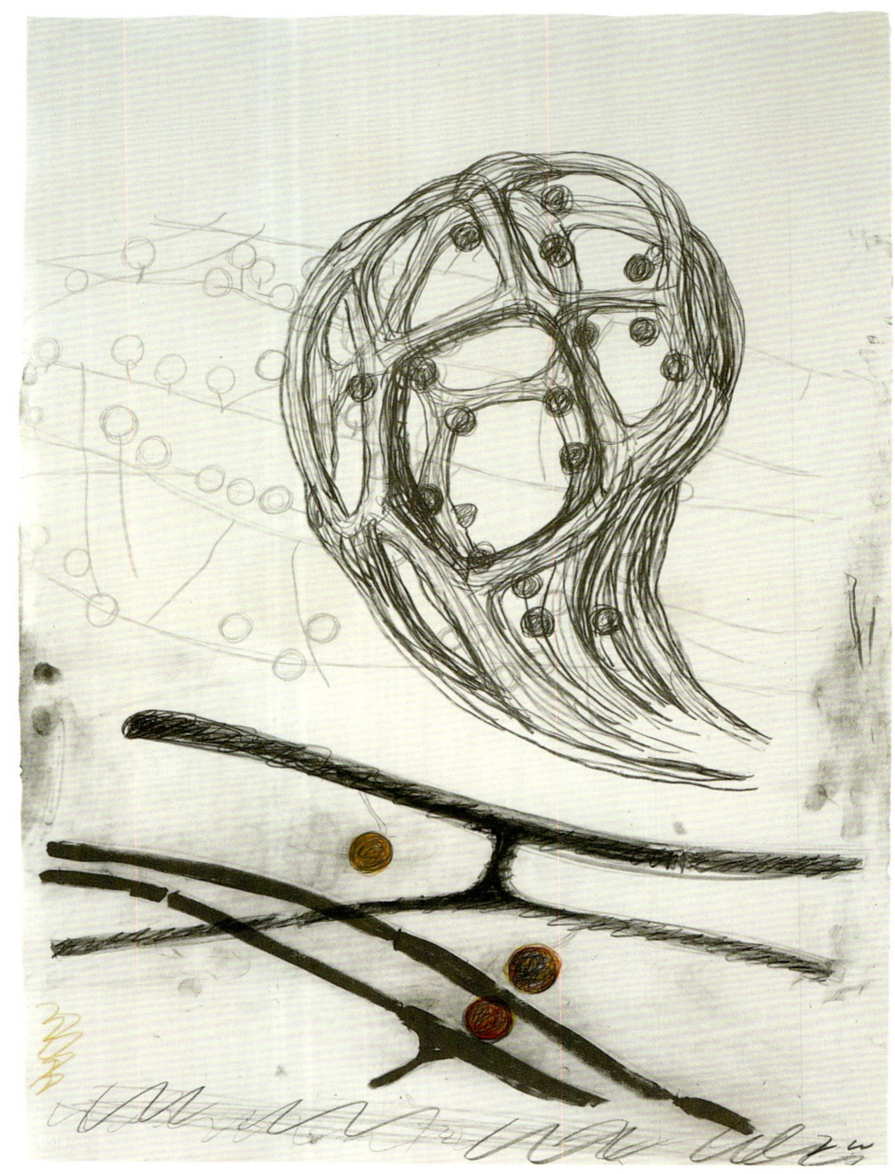

162

Plates 161–164★
TERRY WINTERS
4 prints from the portfolio
of 11, *Folio,* 1986
Color lithographs
31 x 22 in. (each sheet)

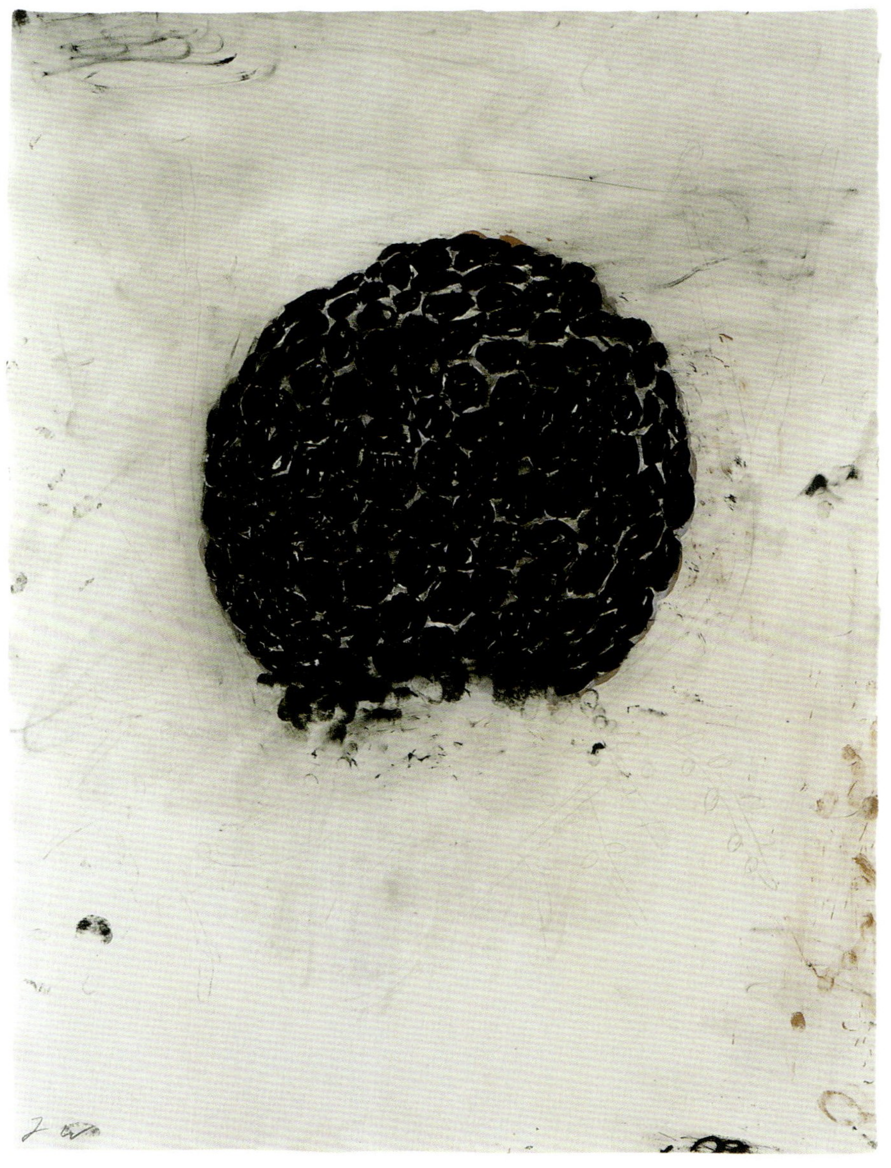

163

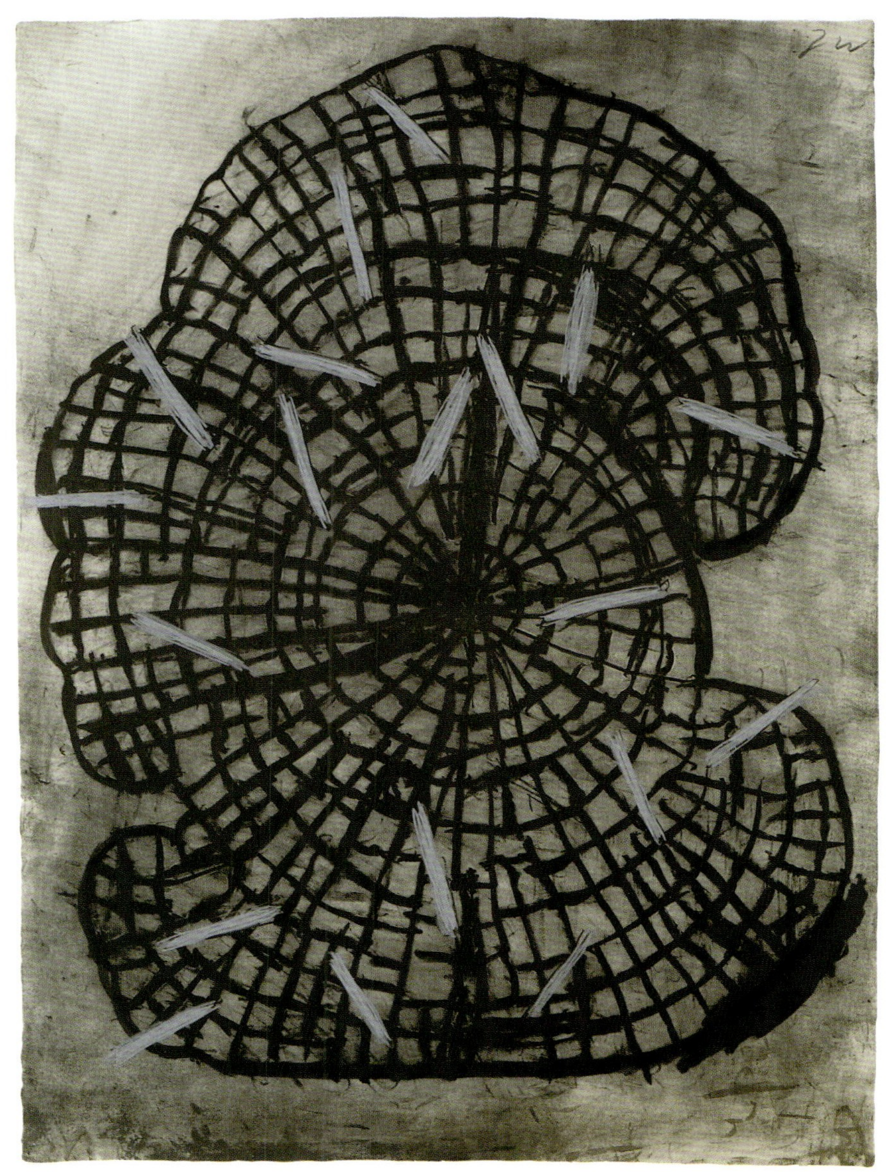

164

161 *Folio, Title Page*
162 *Folio One*
163 *Folio Two*
164 *Folio Three*

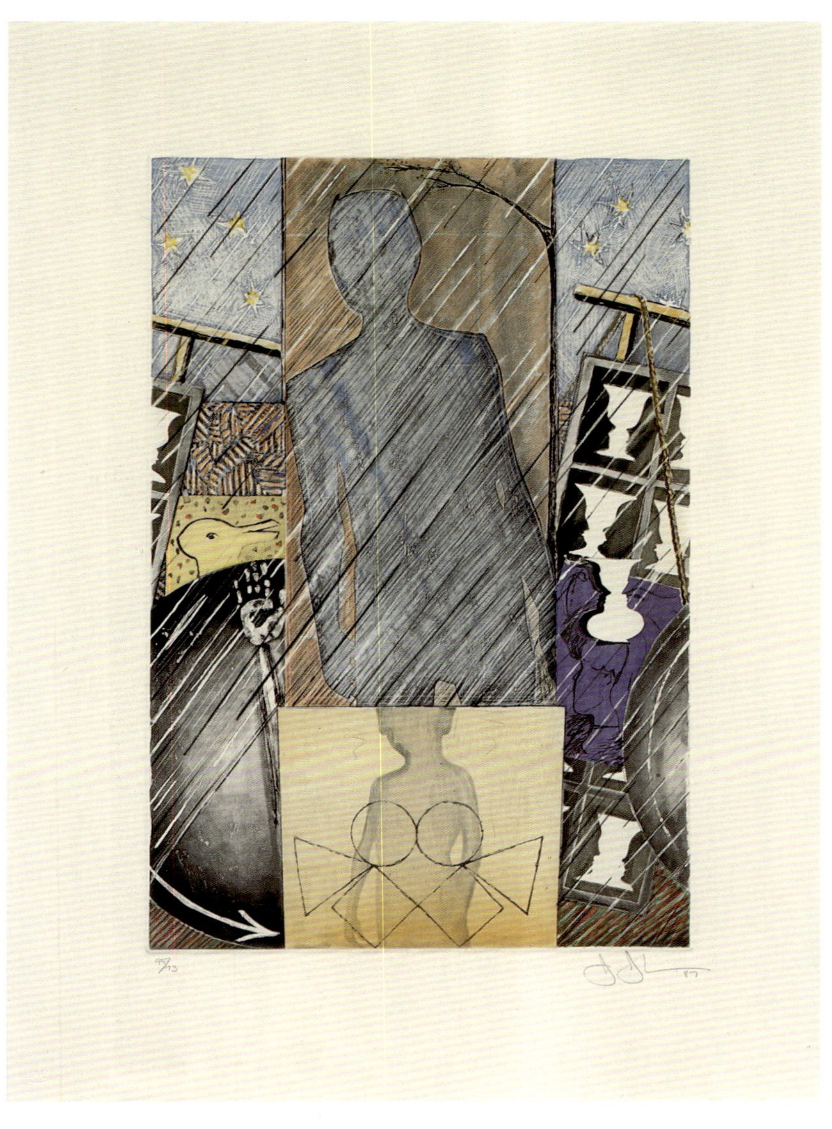

165

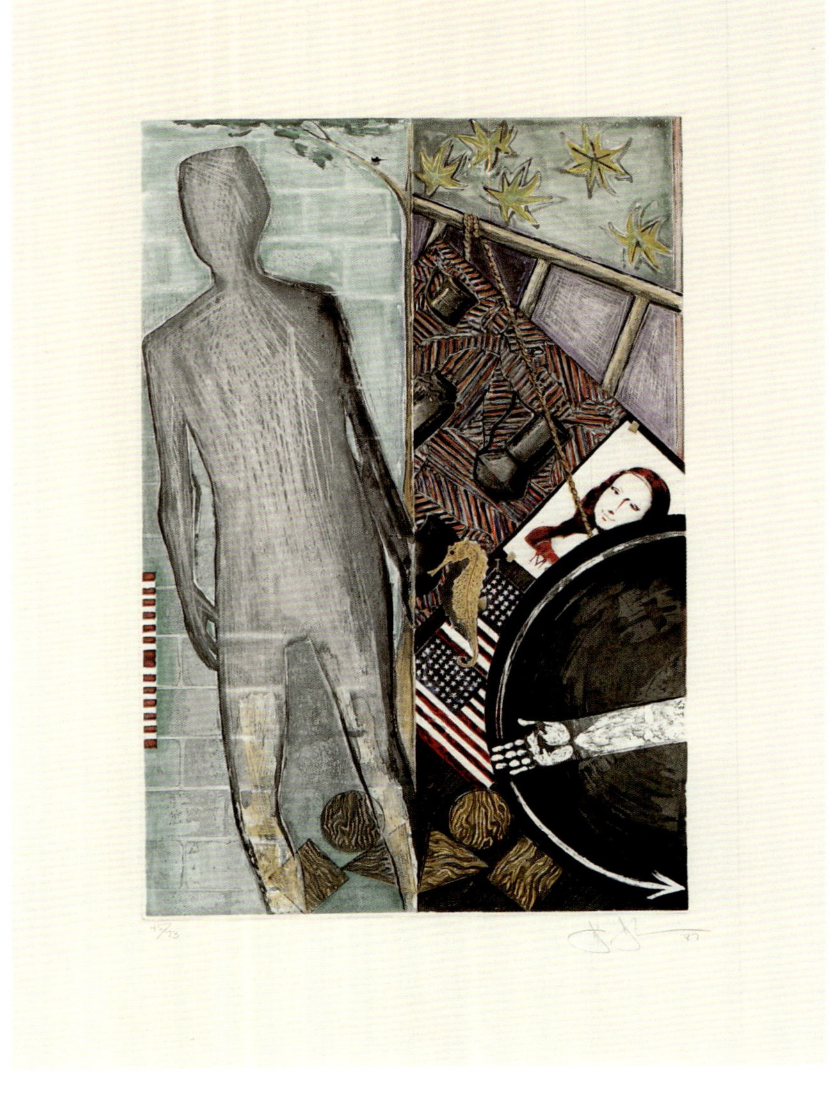

166

165★
JASPER JOHNS
The Seasons (Spring), 1987
Color sugar-lift aquatint,
spit-bite aquatint, drypoint, etching,
and scraping and burnishing
26 x 19 in. (sheet)

166★
JASPER JOHNS
The Seasons (Summer), 1987
Color sugar-lift aquatint,
spit-bite aquatint, drypoint, etching,
photogravure, and scraping and burnishing
26 x 19 in. (sheet)

167★
JASPER JOHNS
The Seasons (Fall), 1987
Color sugar-lift aquatint,
spit-bite aquatint, drypoint,
etching, and scraping and burnishing
26 x 19 in. (sheet)

168★
JASPER JOHNS
The Seasons (Winter), 1987
Color sugar-lift aquatint,
spit-bite aquatint, drypoint,
etching, and scraping and burnishing
26 x 19 in. (sheet)

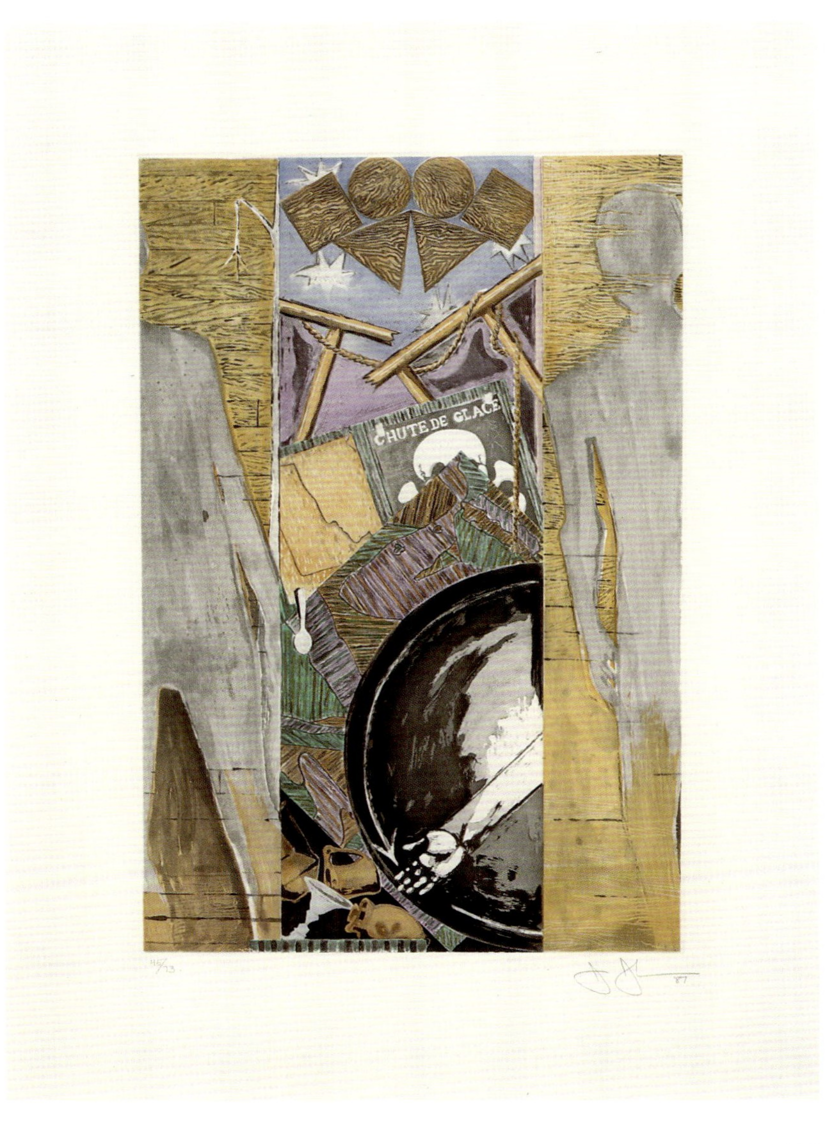

167

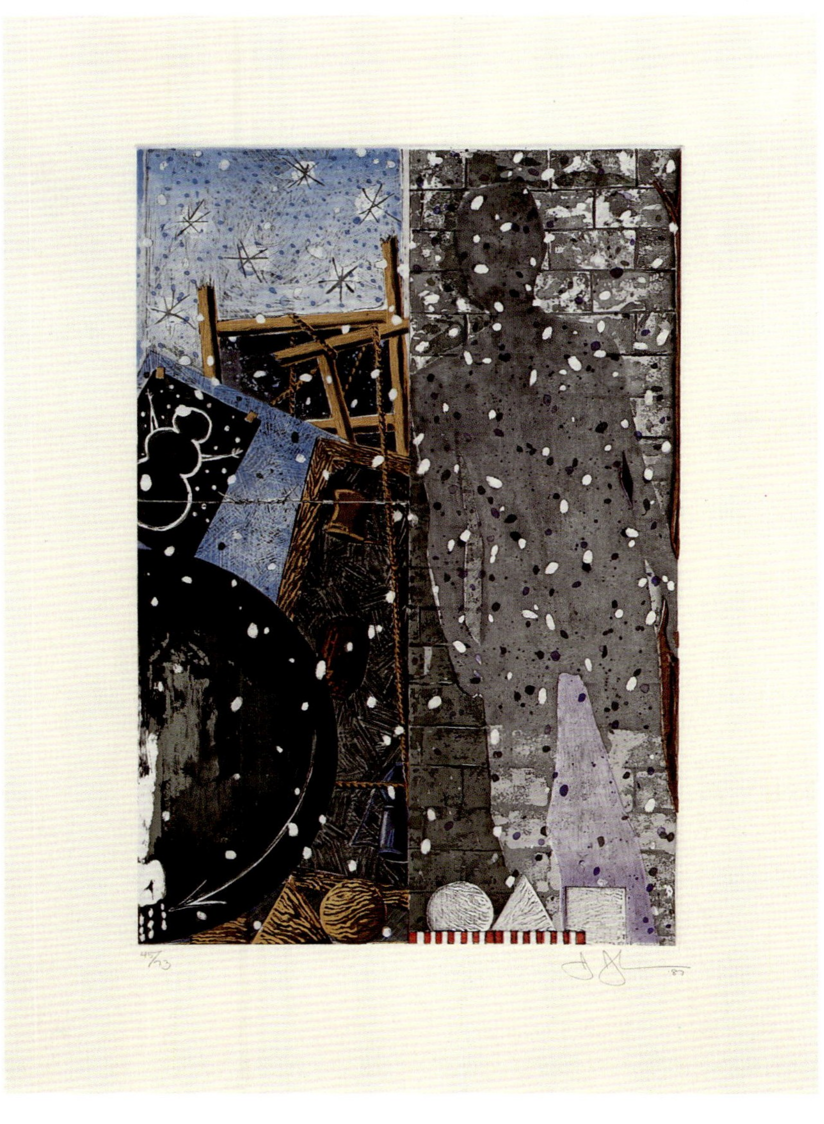

168

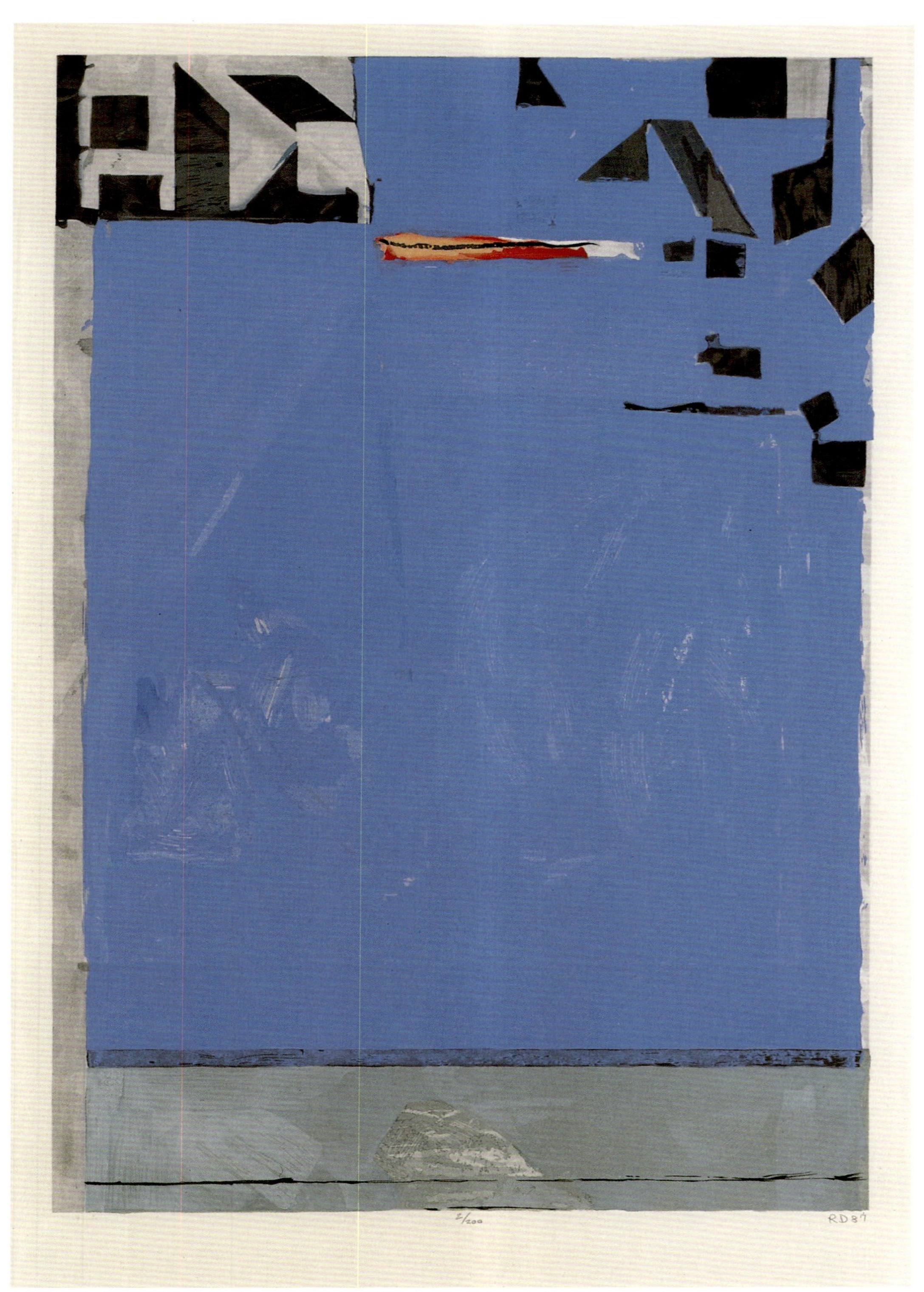

169

169
RICHARD DIEBENKORN
Blue with Red, 1987
Color woodcut
37¼ x 25½ in. (sheet)

170
ELIZABETH MURRAY
Up Dog, 1987–1988
Color lithograph
45½ x 46½ in. (overall, irregular)

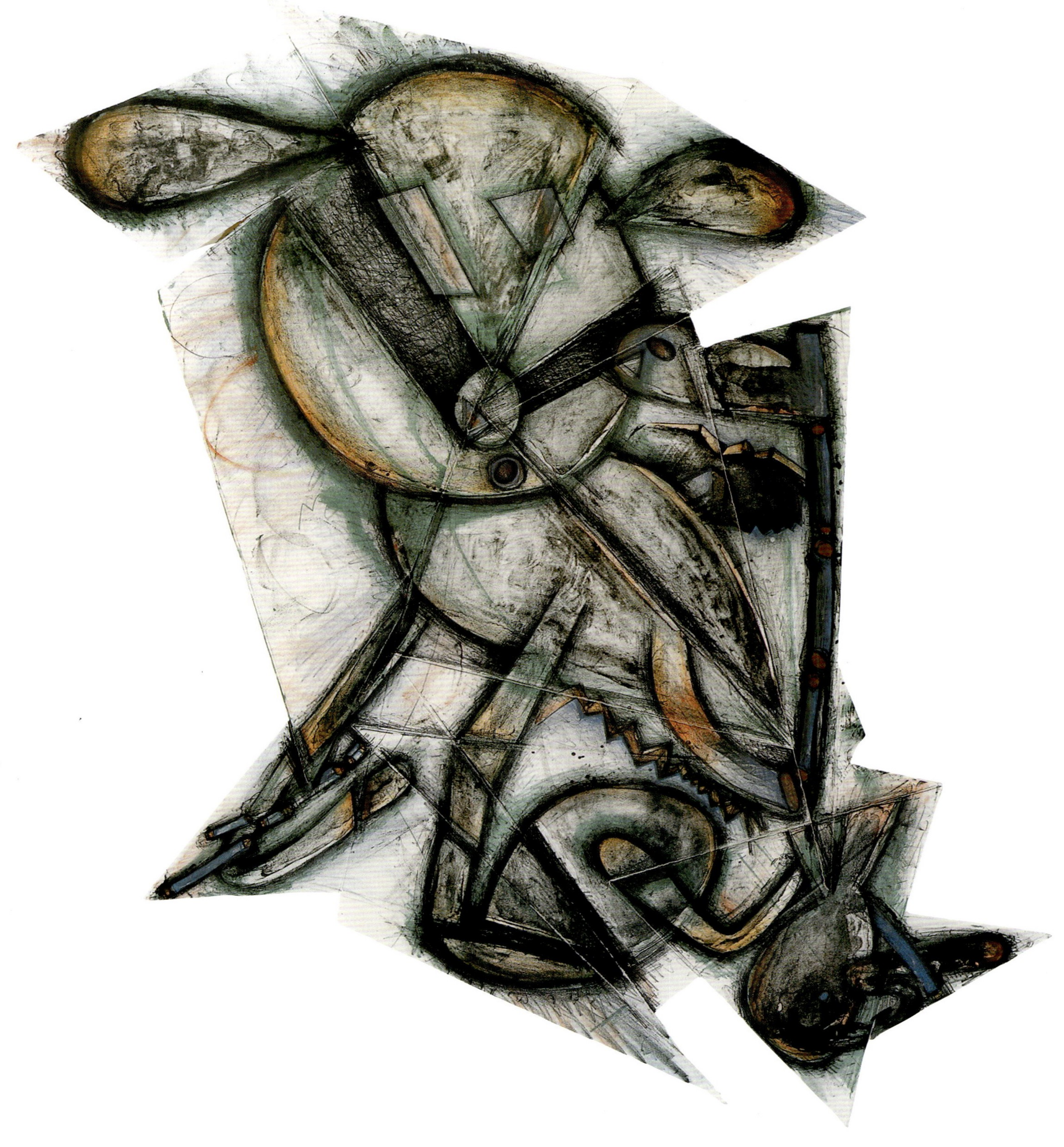

137 Looking at Prints: the 1980s

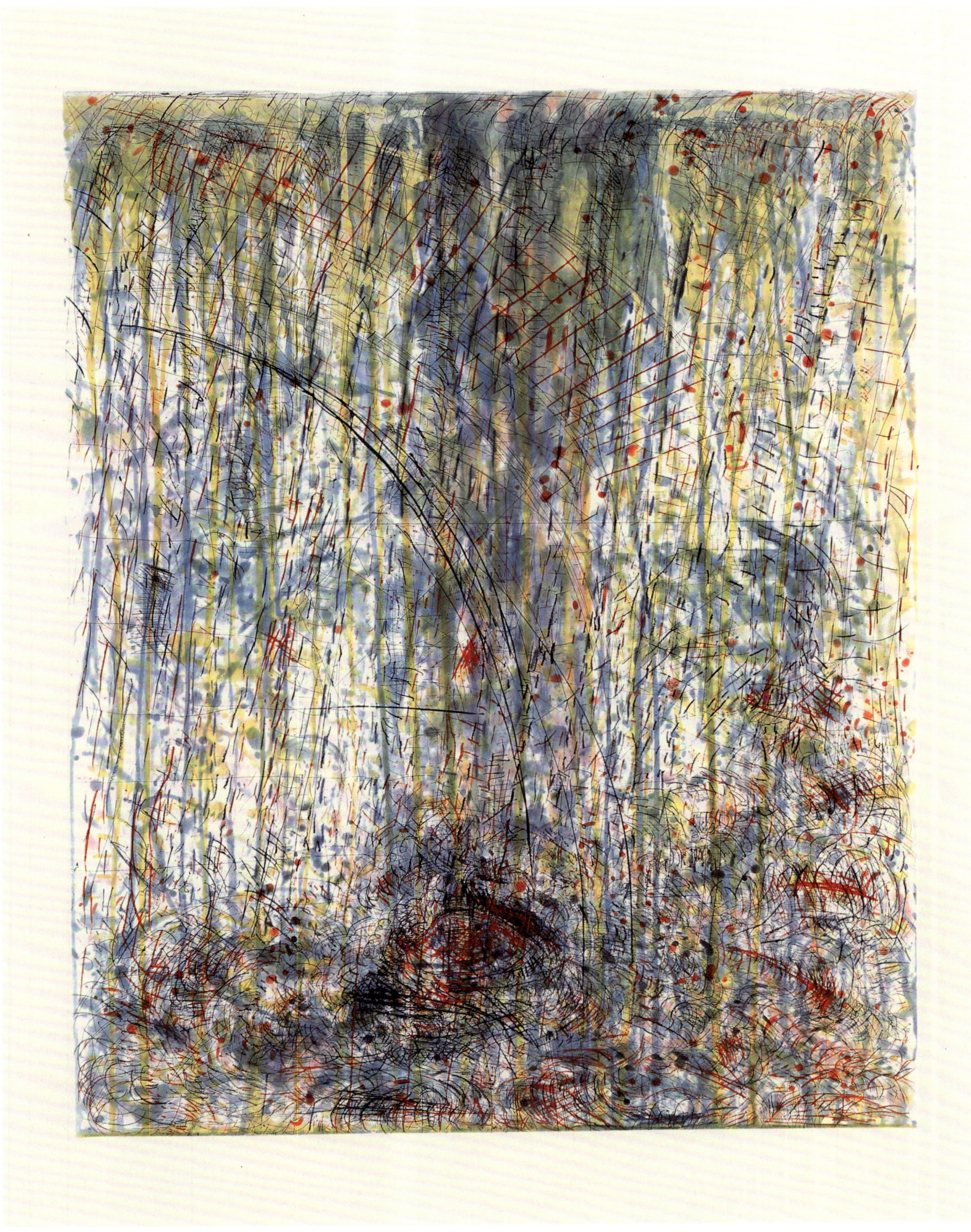

171
PAT STEIR
Waterfall, 1988
Color aquatint, spit-bite aquatint,
soft-ground etching, etching, and drypoint,
53 3/8 x 41 1/8 in. (sheet)

172
SEAN SCULLY
Sotto Voce, 1988
Color aquatint
41 1/4 x 51 3/4 in. (sheet)

171

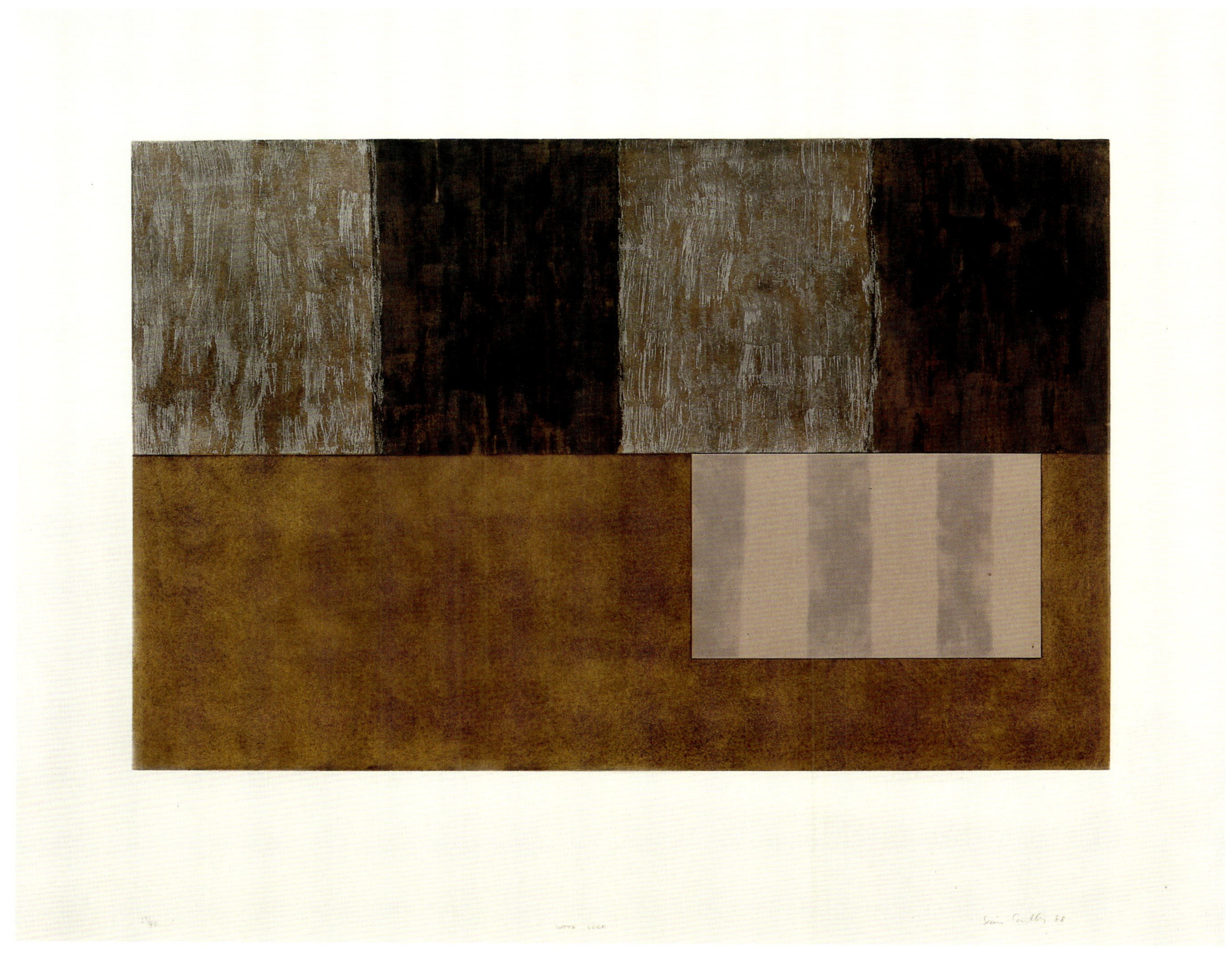

172

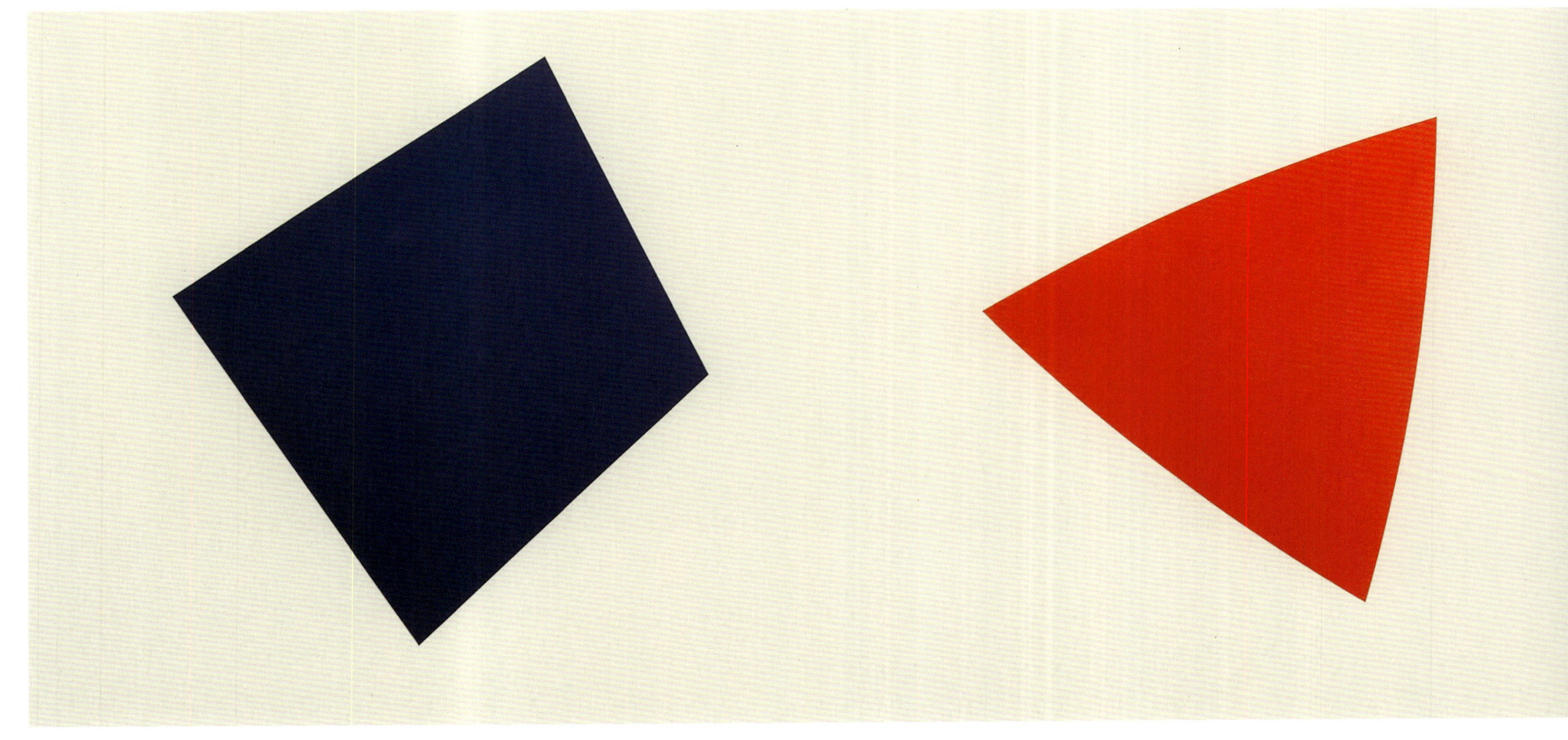

173
ELLSWORTH KELLY
Purple/Red/Gray/Orange, 1988
Color lithograph
51¾ x 225½ in. (sheet)

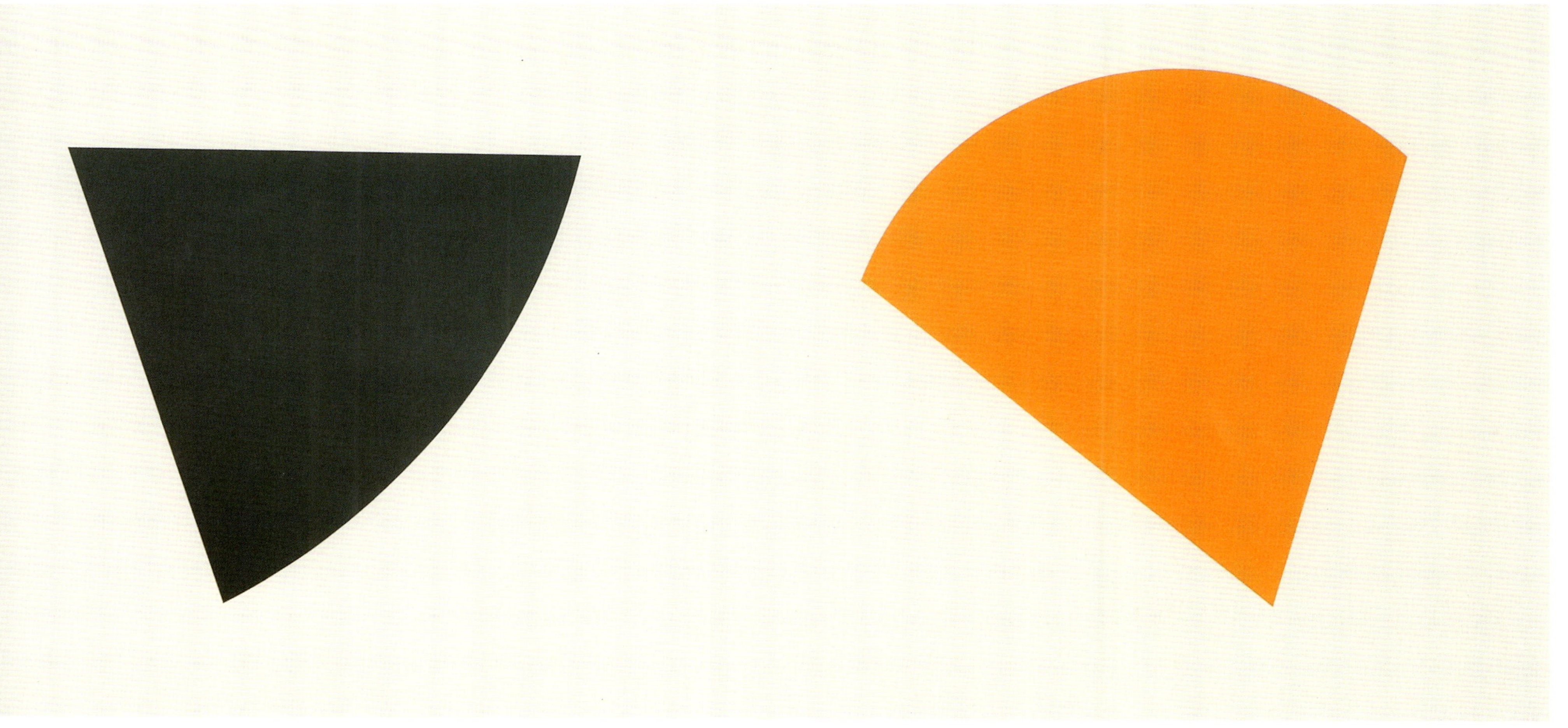

173

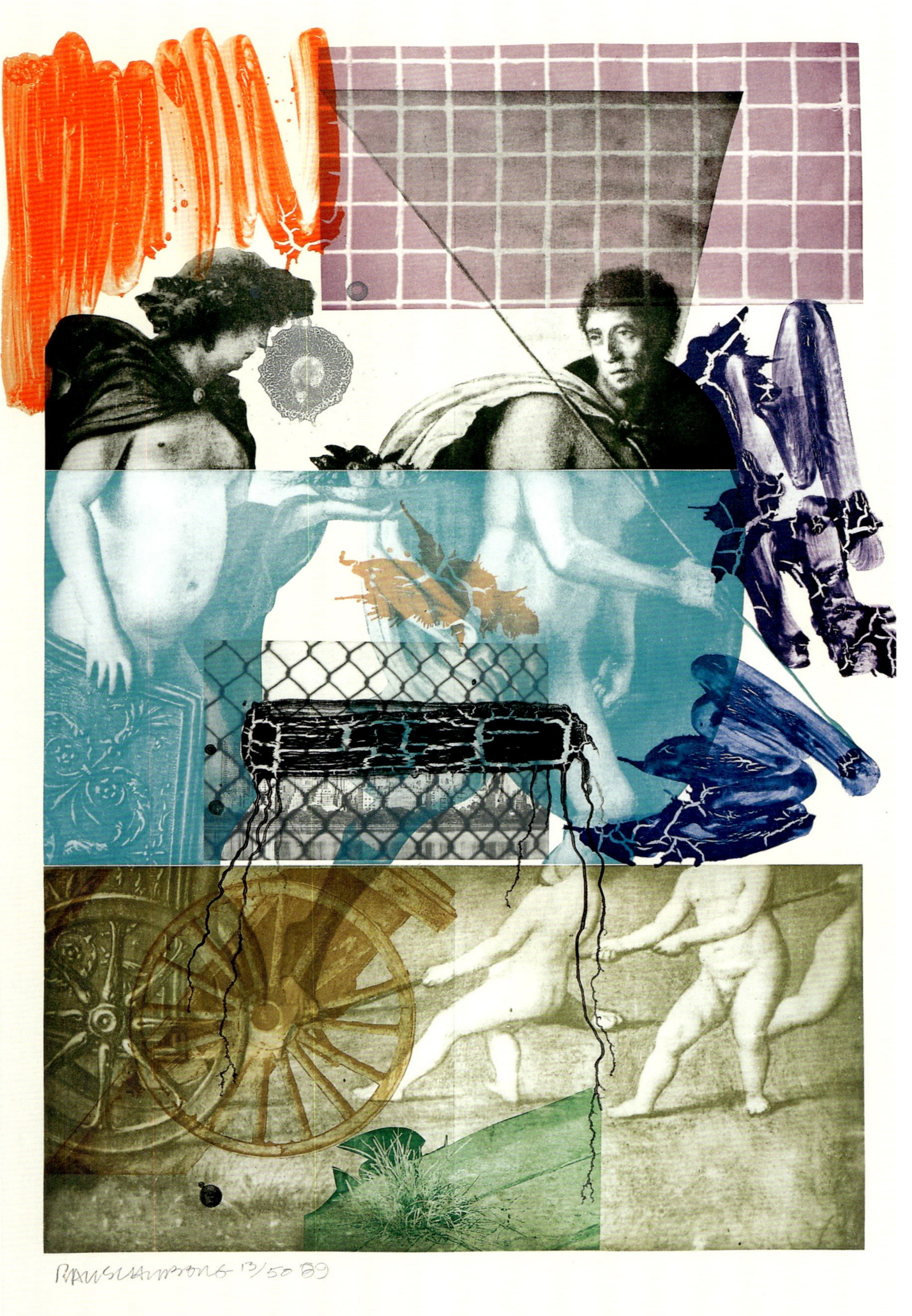

174

174
ROBERT RAUSCHENBERG
Bellini #5, 1989
Color photogravure
59 x 38¼ in. (sheet)

175★
JASPER JOHNS
Between the Clock and the Bed, 1989
Color lithograph
26¼ x 40¼ in. (sheet)

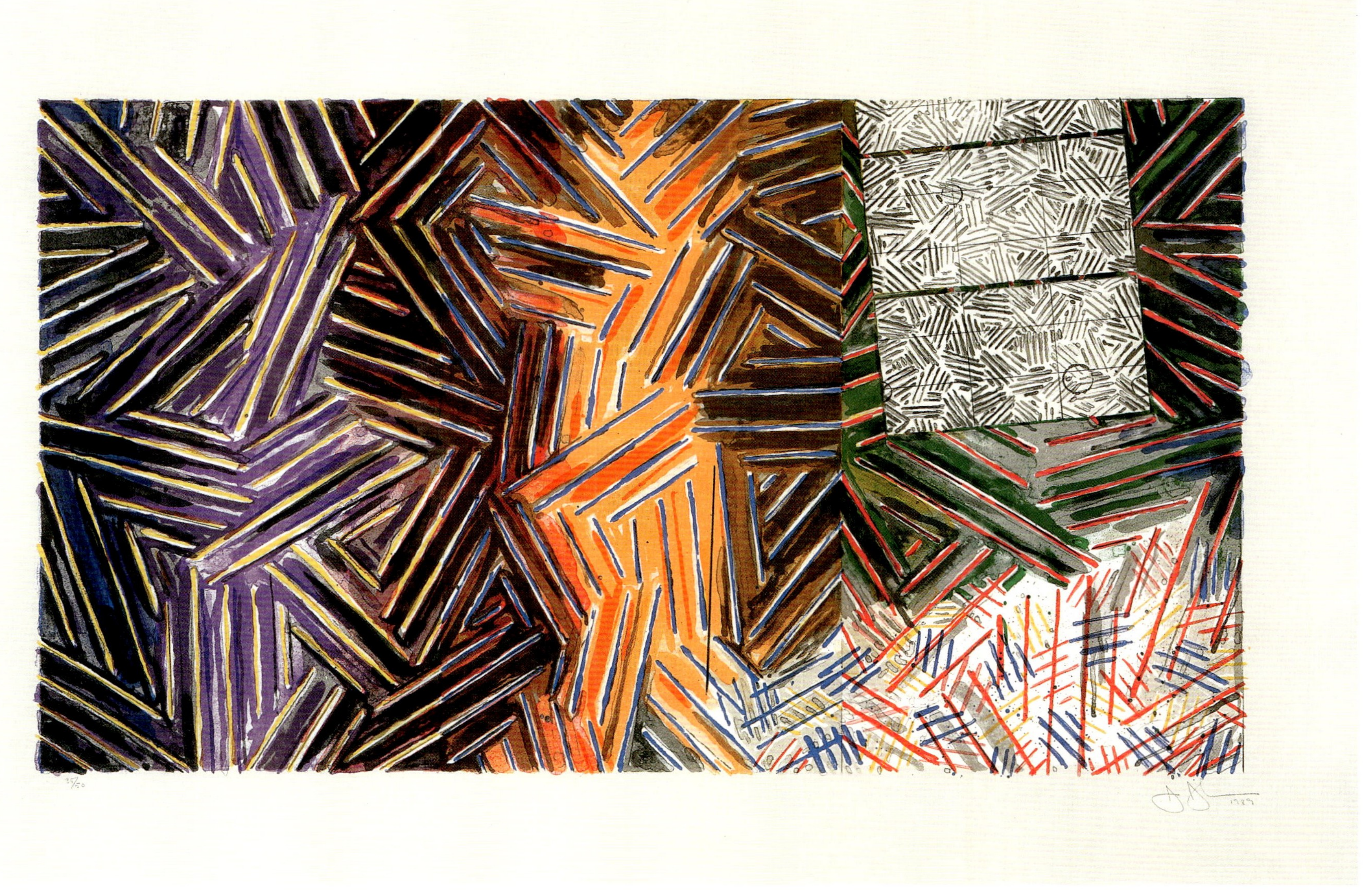

175

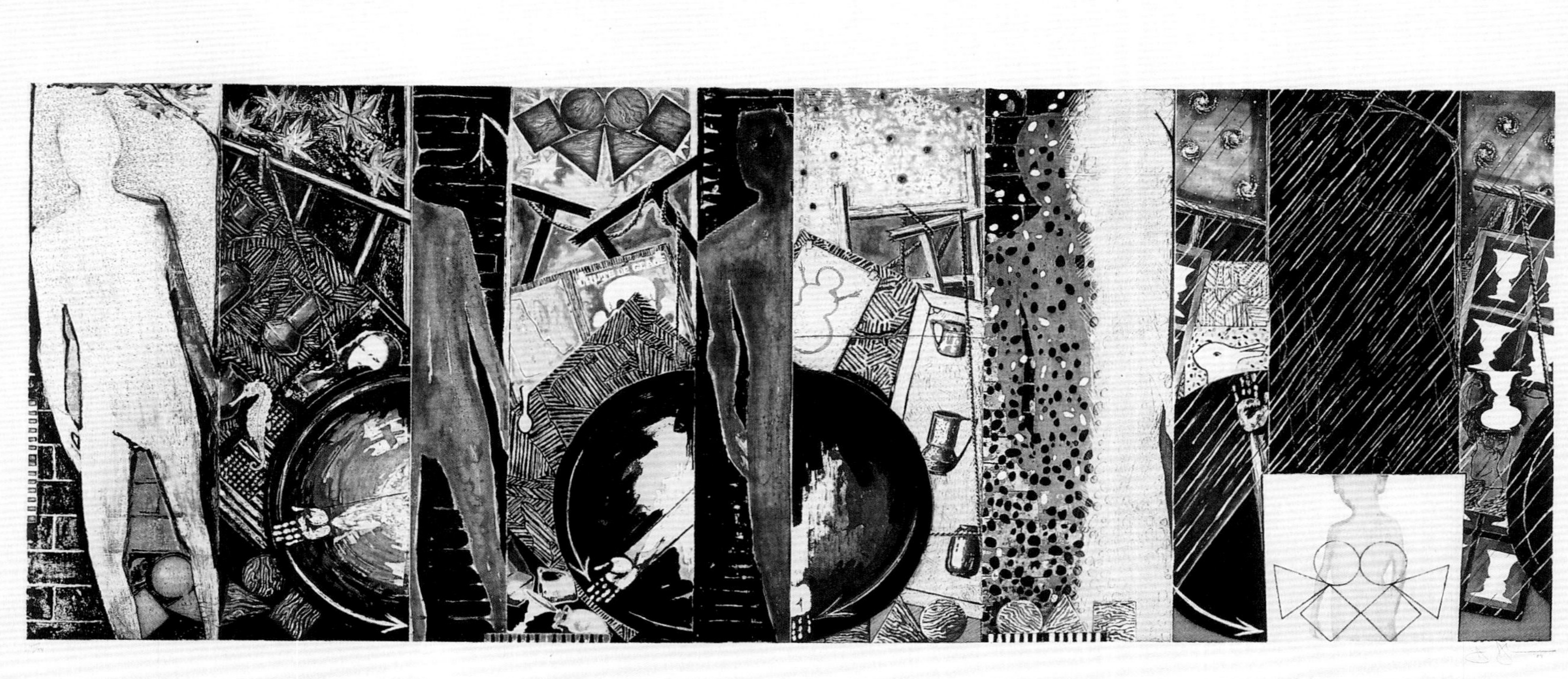

176

176★
JASPER JOHNS
The Seasons, 1989
Sugar-lift aquatint, spit-bite aquatint,
drypoint, etching, open-bite etching,
and scraping and burnishing
26¾ x 58¼ in. (sheet)

177★
JASPER JOHNS
The Seasons, 1989
Sugar-lift aquatint, spit-bite aquatint,
drypoint, etching, open-bite etching,
photogravure, and scraping and burnishing
46¾ x 32½ in. (sheet)

178★
JASPER JOHNS
The Seasons, 1990
Sugar-lift aquatint, spit-bite aquatint,
drypoint, etching, open-bite etching,
and scraping and burnishing on chine collé
50¼ x 44½ in. (sheet)

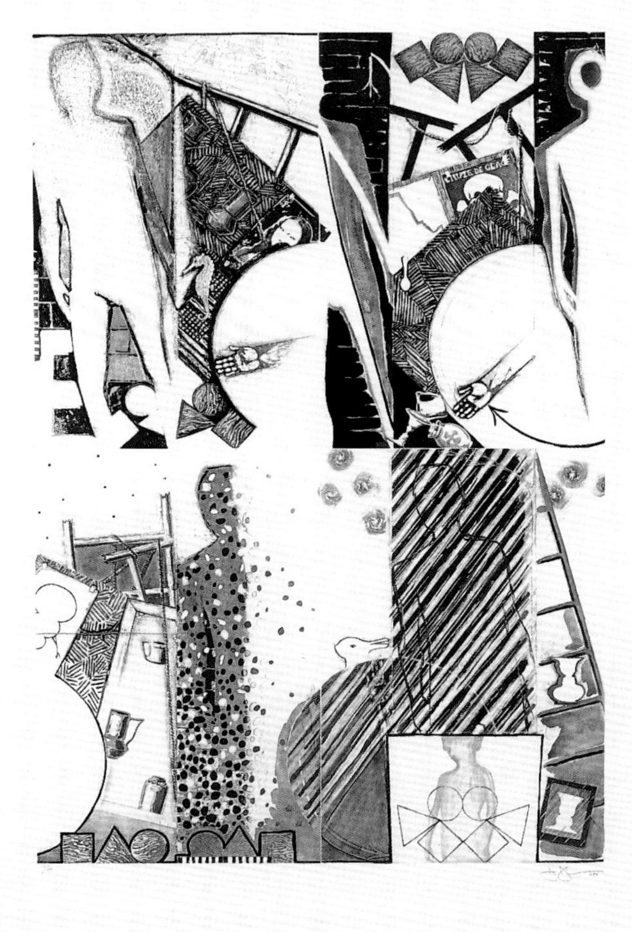

177

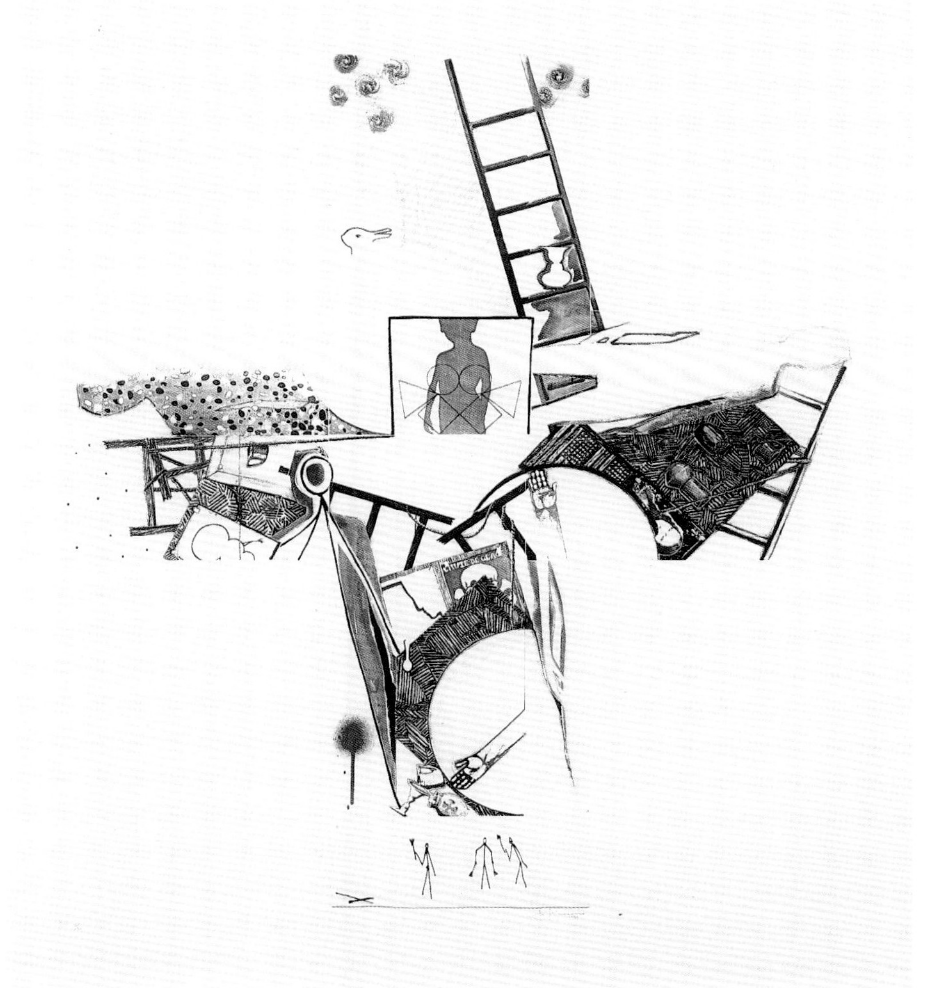

178

The Anderson Graphic Arts Collection at the Fine Arts Museums of San Francisco was formed almost entirely between 1968 and 1991. Consequently, the 1990s are represented in this exhibition largely by loans from the Andersons' private collection. These selections, representing their particular collecting focus, emphasize prints by artists whom the Andersons have followed since the 1960s, particularly Jasper Johns, as well as those artists considered heirs apparent to some of the artists and artistic traditions of previous decades.

Johns, whose works are represented significantly in this survey, has figured prominently in American printmaking since the 1960s. Revealing constant invention and experimentation, his prints have been hallmarks of each decade. Johns's work in the 1990s, notably the reworking of *The Seasons* prints and *Green Angel*, represent two explorations with etching techniques that differ considerably in style and appearance. While *The Seasons* are delicately colored in pastel hues and shades of gray, *Green Angel* contains deep, dark earth tones in layers of heavy aquatint. *Green Angel* is completely abstract, a kind of jigsaw puzzle composition, while any of *The Seasons* prints features readable arrangements and figurative drawing and pattern. Johns continues to make prints at the close of the decade that are fresh, elegant interpretations of earlier themes, yet unrelated in appearance to either *The Seasons* or *Green Angel*.

Roy Lichtenstein was another artist whose prints indicated a new direction in the 1990s. *Landscape with Poet* is an example with its softened, almost pastel, palette and its subject that reinterprets the art traditions of Asia, particularly Chinese landscape painting, with restrained energy. Intentionally missing are the exuberant brushstrokes and vibrant color combinations of his work from a decade earlier as he contemplated Zen concepts, and perhaps his own life.

A younger generation of artists who came to prominence in the 1990s through their paintings and sculpture found it easy to experiment with printmaking, some for the first time, at workshops that welcomed the challenges of their sometimes complex ideas. For the most part, these artists all used color, especially color aquatint, to remarkable effect in their prints. Many of them saw in printmaking opportunities for cross-fertilization with their painting. For Deborah Oropallo and Christopher Brown, printmaking suggested ways of working in color that could be directly applied to painting, and vice versa.

Brown, who had made prints intermittently since graduate school, favored etching techniques for his prints made in the 1990s at Crown Print Press. The print *Forty Flakes* reveals his delight in layering transparent and opaque aquatint. In making the print, he adapted techniques from painting by sanding the surface of the plate to modulate and activate color tonality.

Oropallo, who first approached printmaking cautiously with monotypes in the 1980s, had by the 1990s experimented with almost every technique available. Her prints often combine several processes, such as woodcut and etching, that move in and out of visual prominence from the foreground to the background.

Even Terry Winters, whose first monochromatic efforts in lithography found admiring audiences in the 1980s, achieved expressive effects using color etching and aquatint in the 1990s. In *Multiple Visualization Technique*, his signature black form is obscured by contrasting red and yellow forms in a complex web of thick lines, revealing the power of color in his art.

Emphasis on the unexpected use of color is reflected in the title of Kiki Smith's self-portrait print, *My Blue Lake*. Smith, acknowledged by ULAE as the legatee of Robert Rauschenberg because of her extensive and creative use of photography in printmaking, used a startling blue lithograph as a kind of wash over the skin of her flattened body image.

Jennifer Bartlett is an artist whose printmaking identified her in the 1980s as the successor to Jasper Johns, especially the screenprints made at Simca Print Artists in the 1990s. Bartlett followed in Johns's footsteps at Simca with her painterly handling of screenprint in prints from the late 1980s and 1990s. Her series *The Four Seasons* uses pattern and personal symbols in a kind of jumbled iconography, perhaps in homage to Johns's own *Seasons* prints created a few years before. No less complex than the Johns prints, next to his Bartlett's seasons are almost aggressively colorful, featuring bold primary colors and bright plaid patterns. The inclusion of the two in the Anderson Collection can be considered symbolic both of a personal collecting direction and American printmaking in general in the 1990s that took the best from the past, but always moved forward in new and different ways.

Looking at Prints: The 1990s

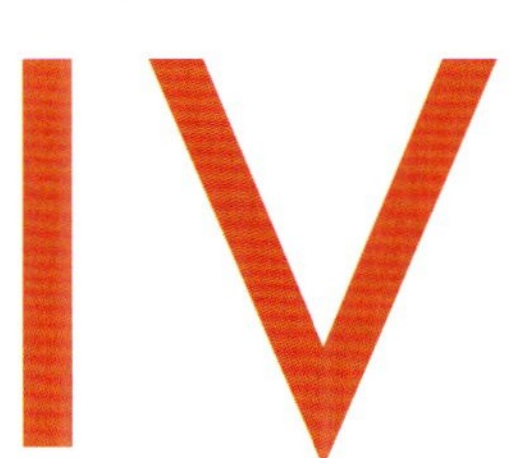

The 1990s

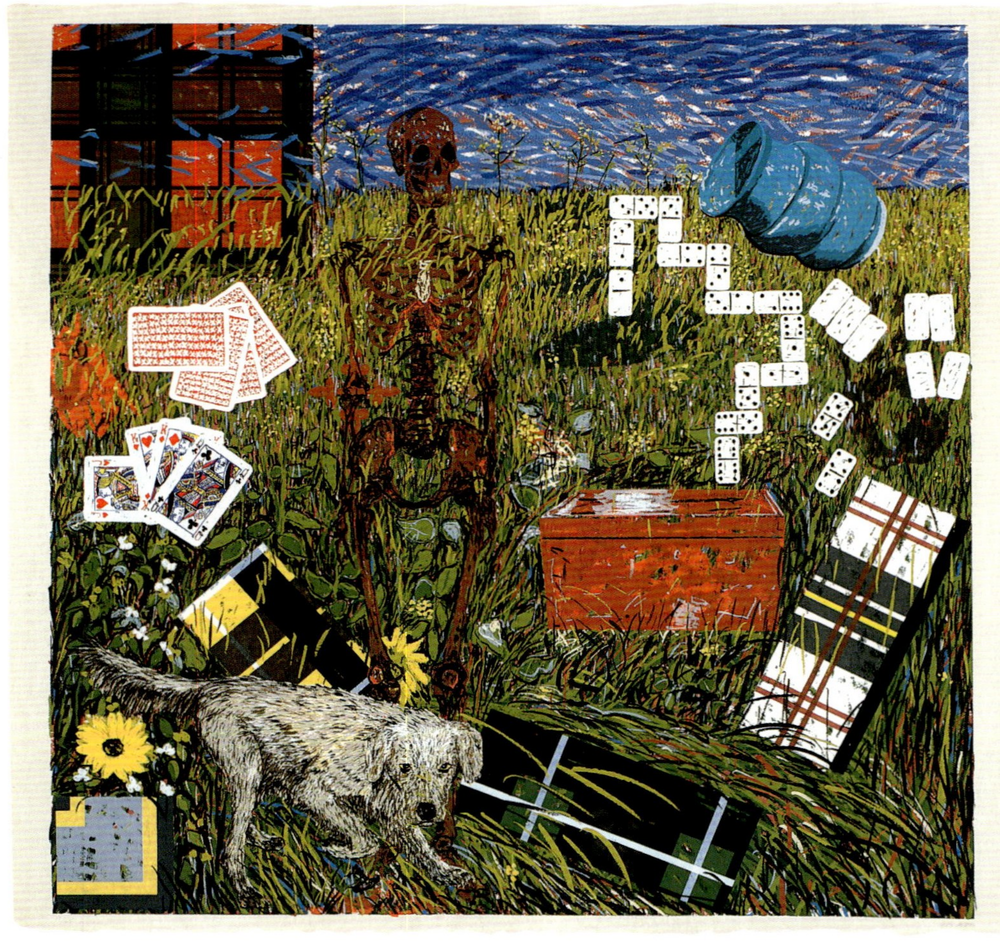

179

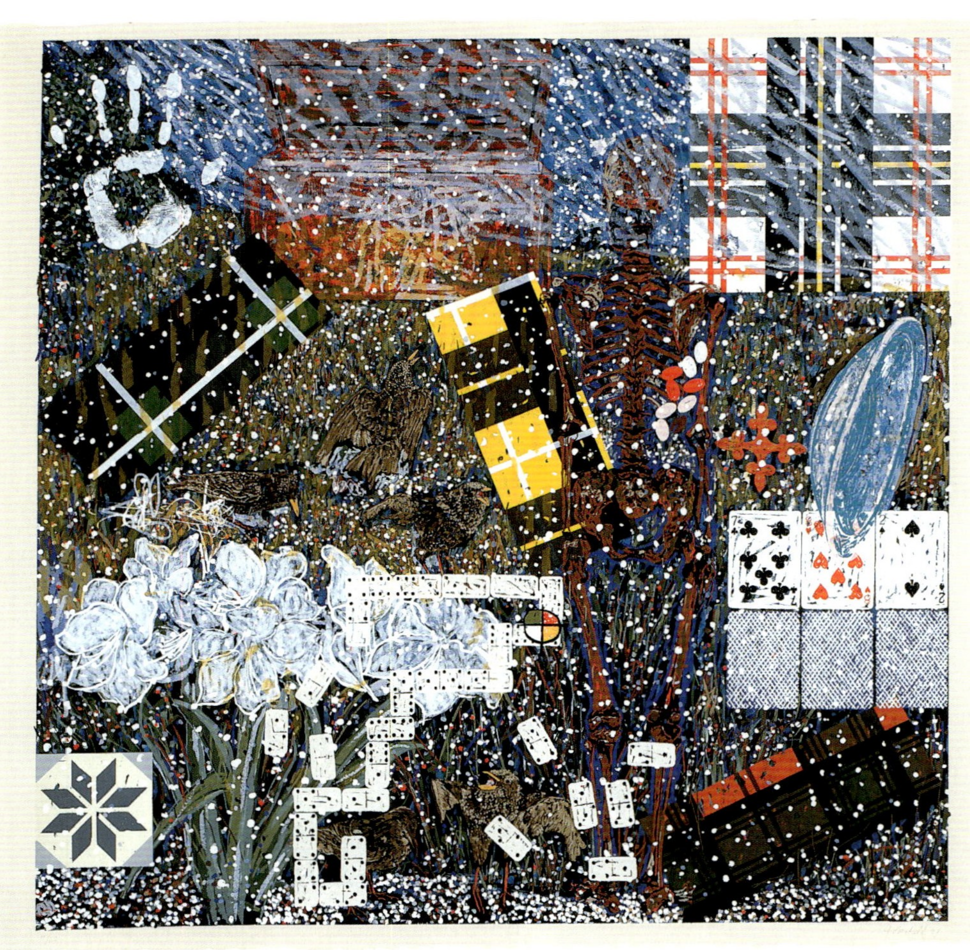

180

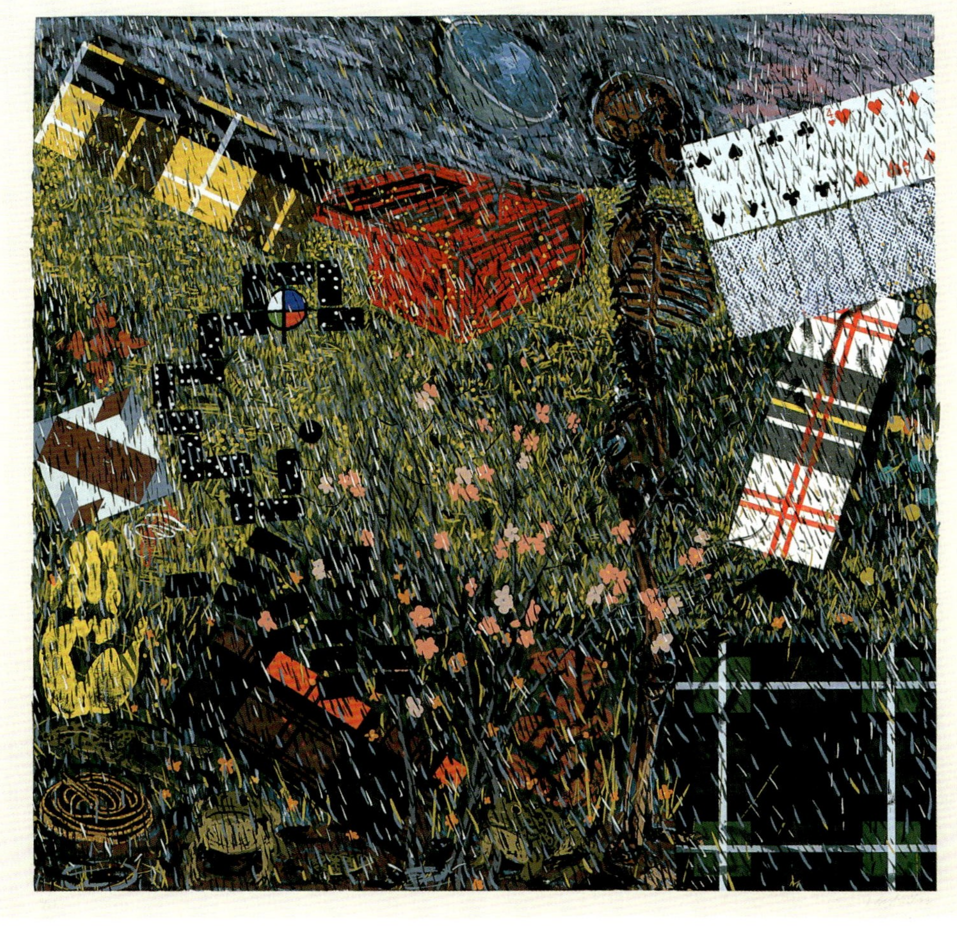

181

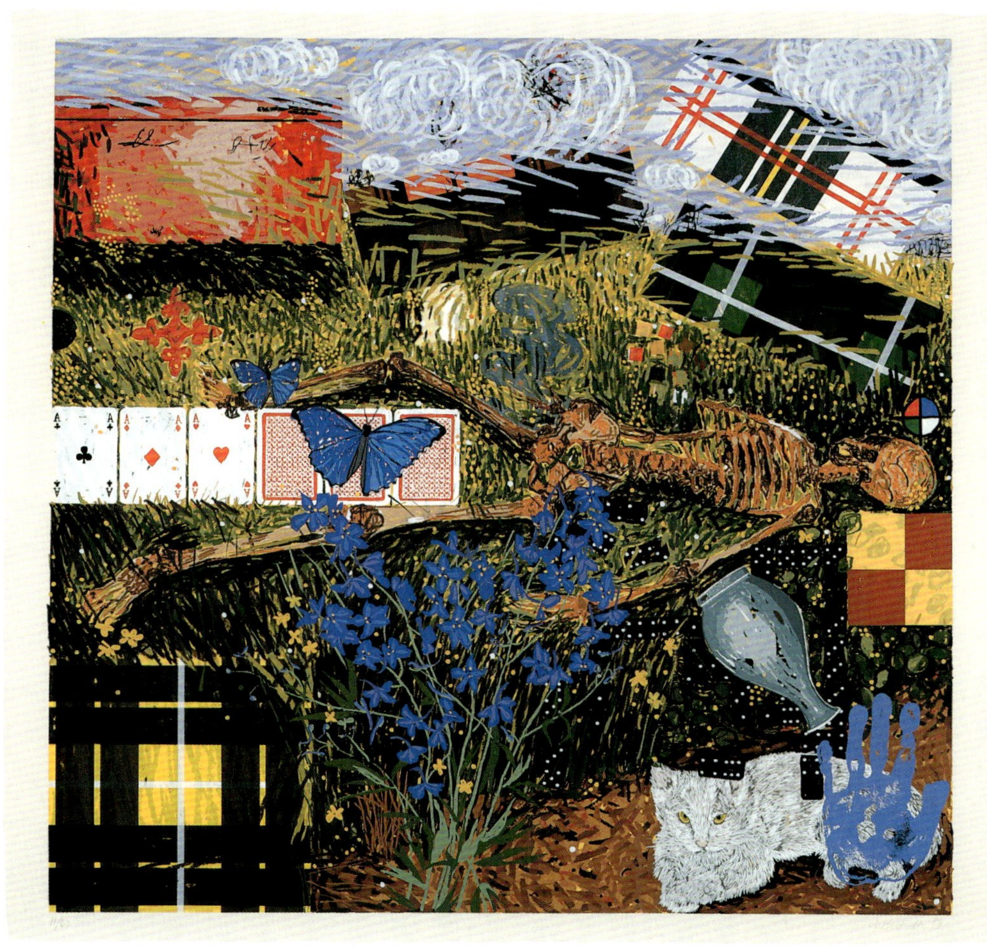

182

179
JENNIFER BARTLETT
The Four Seasons: Autumn, 1990
Color screenprint
33 x $34^{3}/_{4}$ in. (sheet)

180
JENNIFER BARTLETT
The Four Seasons: Winter, 1991
Color screenprint
33 x $34^{3}/_{4}$ in. (sheet)

181★
JENNIFER BARTLETT
The Four Seasons: Spring, 1992
Color screenprint
33 x $34^{3}/_{4}$ in. (sheet)

182★
JENNIFER BARTLETT
The Four Seasons: Summer, 1993
Color screenprint
33 x $34^{3}/_{4}$ in. (sheet)

183★
BILL JENSEN
For Alice, 1990–1991
Color spit-bite aquatint, sugar-lift aquatint, and scraping and burnishing
$22\frac{1}{2} \times 21\frac{3}{4}$ in. (sheet)

184★
CHRISTOPHER BROWN
Forty Flakes, 1991
Color aquatint and soft-ground etching
42 x 41 in. (sheet)

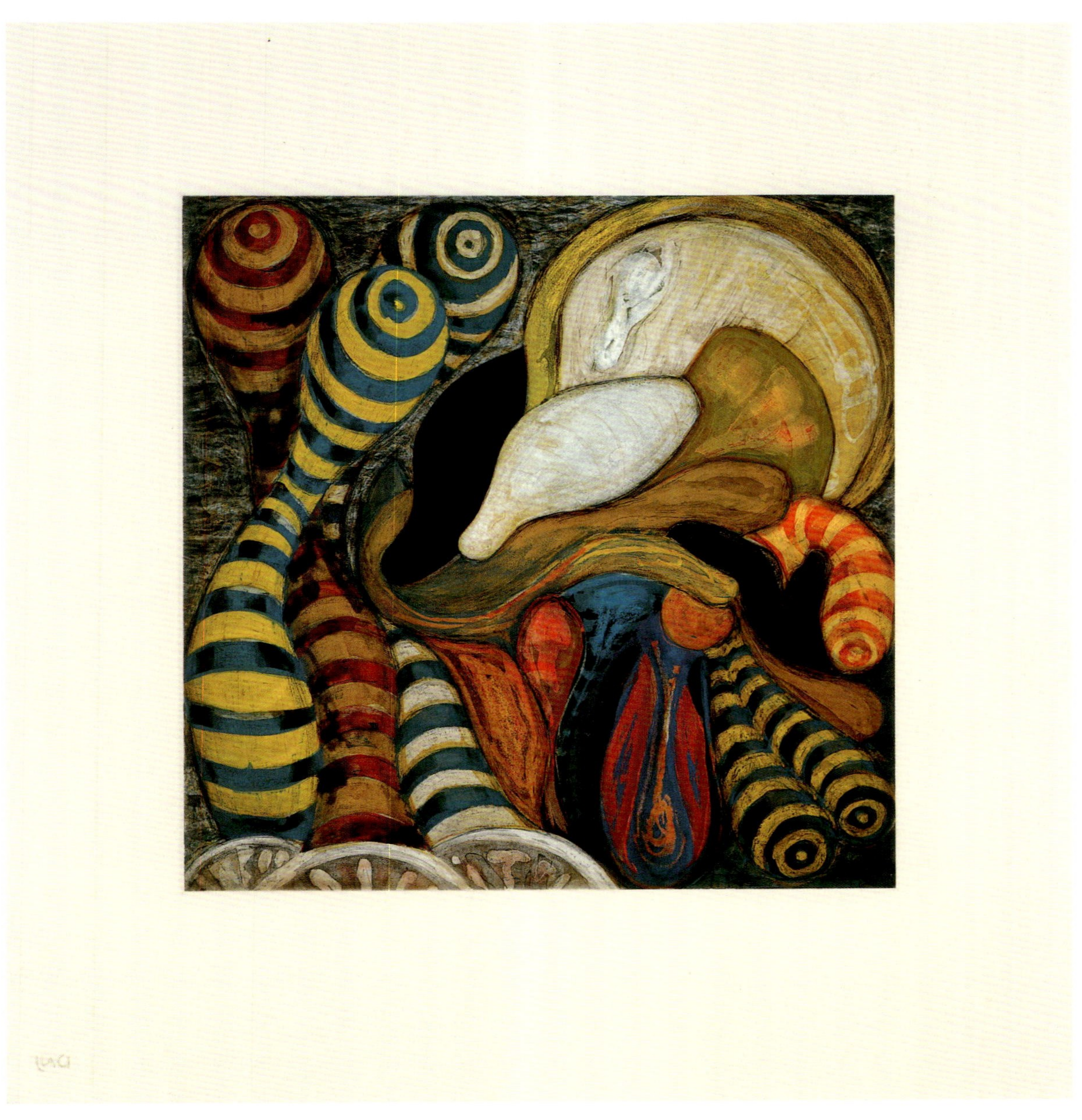

183

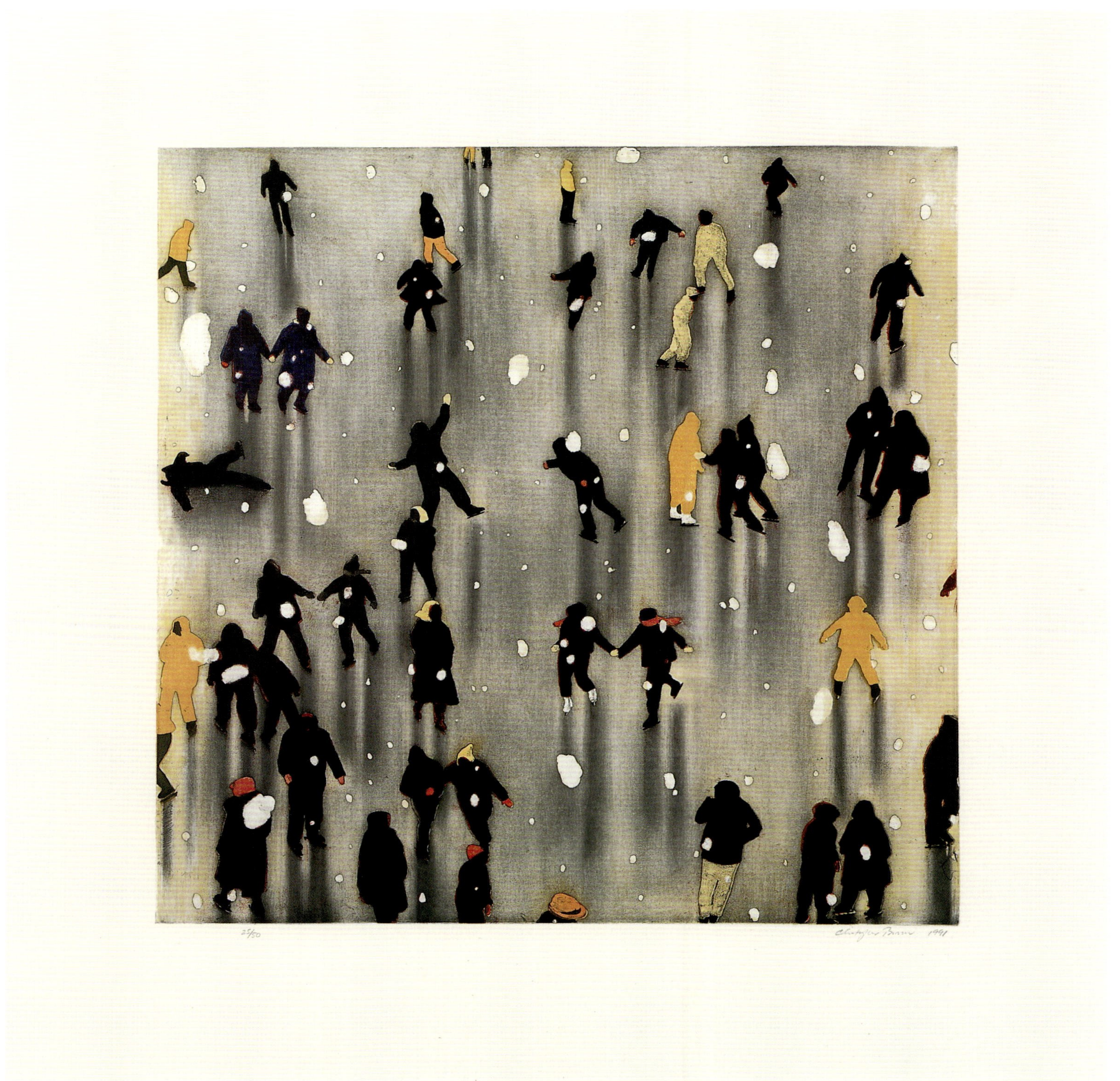

184

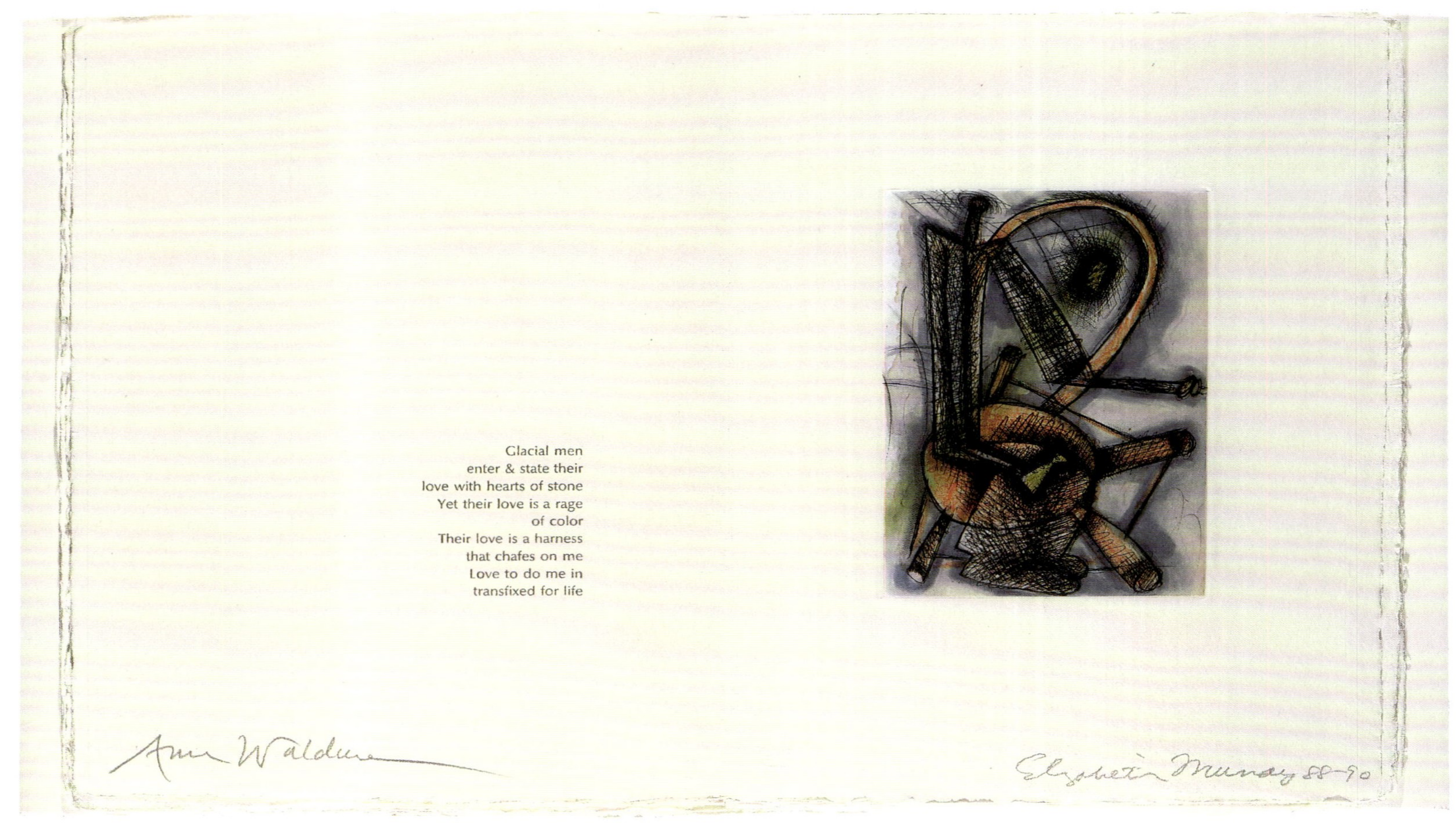

Glacial men
enter & state their
love with hearts of stone
Yet their love is a rage
of color
Their love is a harness
that chafes on me
Love to do me in
transfixed for life

185

185★
ELIZABETH MURRAY
Pl. 11 in the book *Her Story*, by Anne Waldman, 1988–1990
Color lithograph and etching
11³⁄₈ x 17³⁄₄ in. (page)

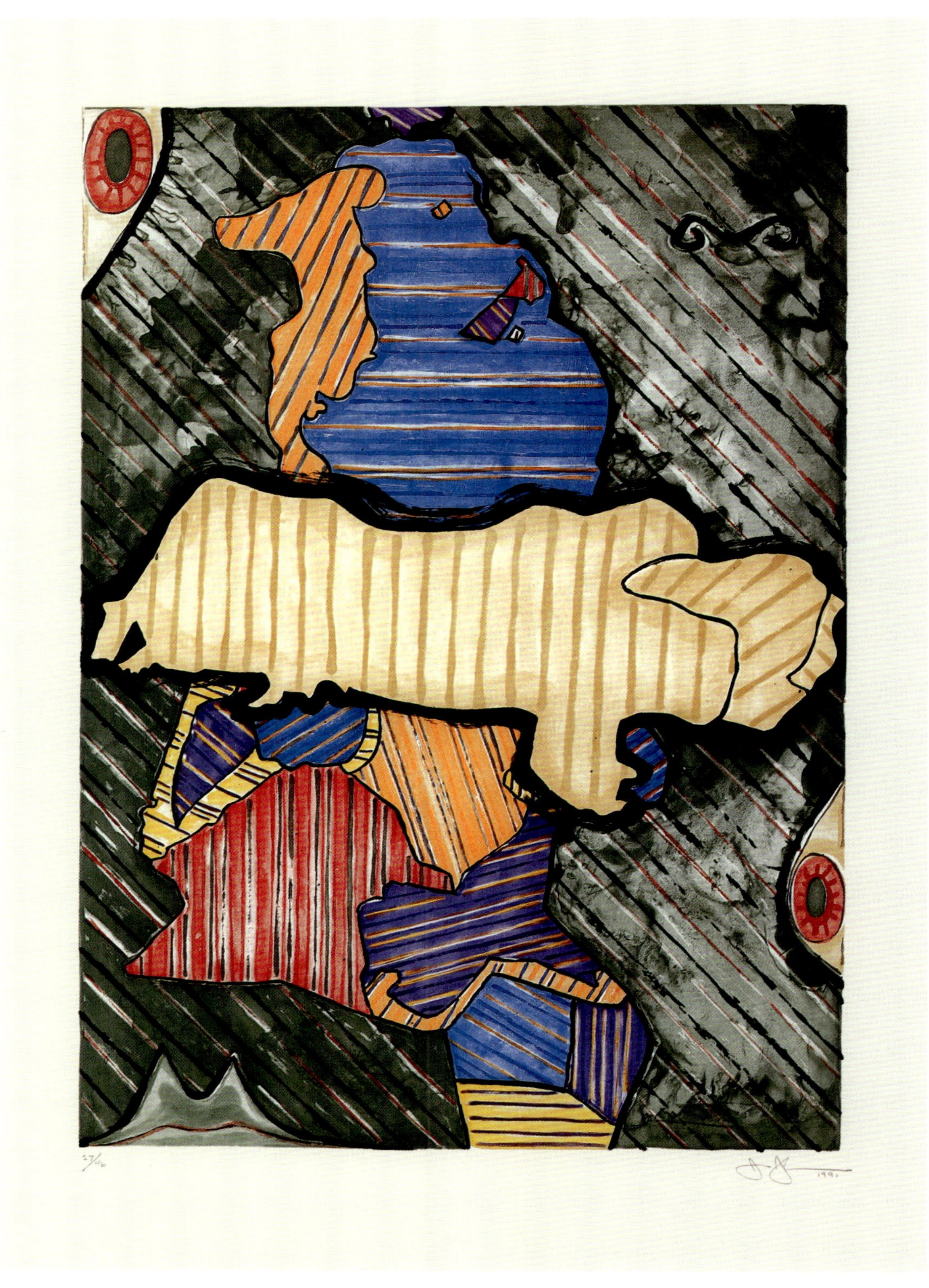

186

186★
JASPER JOHNS
Green Angel, 1991
Color spit-bite aquatint and sugar-lift aquatint on Barcham Green paper
31 x 22¹⁄₂ in. (sheet)

187★
ROBERT THERRIEN
Untitled [hangman], 1993
Color aquatint
26½ x 20 in. (sheet)

188★
ROBERT THERRIEN
Untitled [red chapel], 1993
Color aquatint
26½ x 20 in. (sheet)

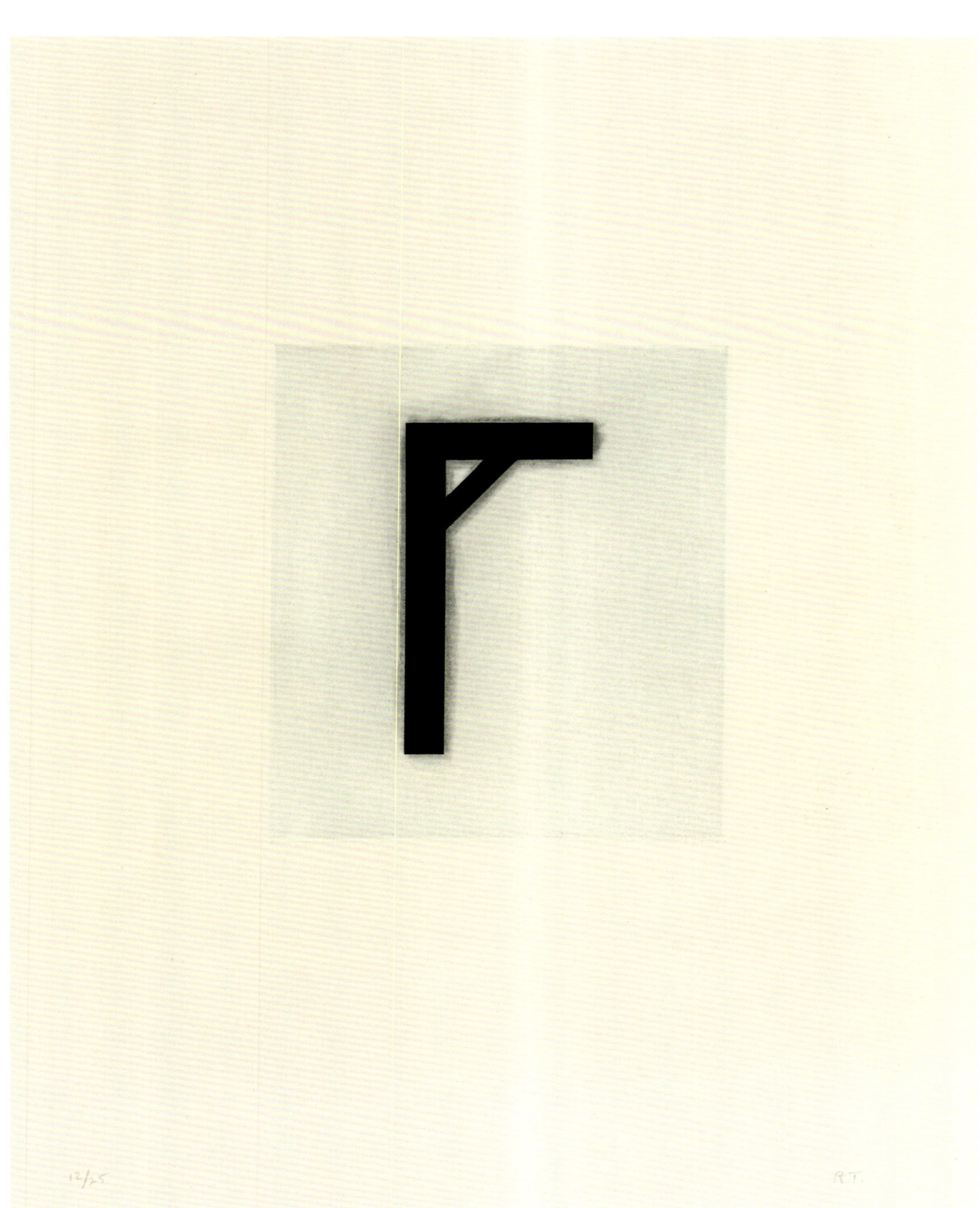

187

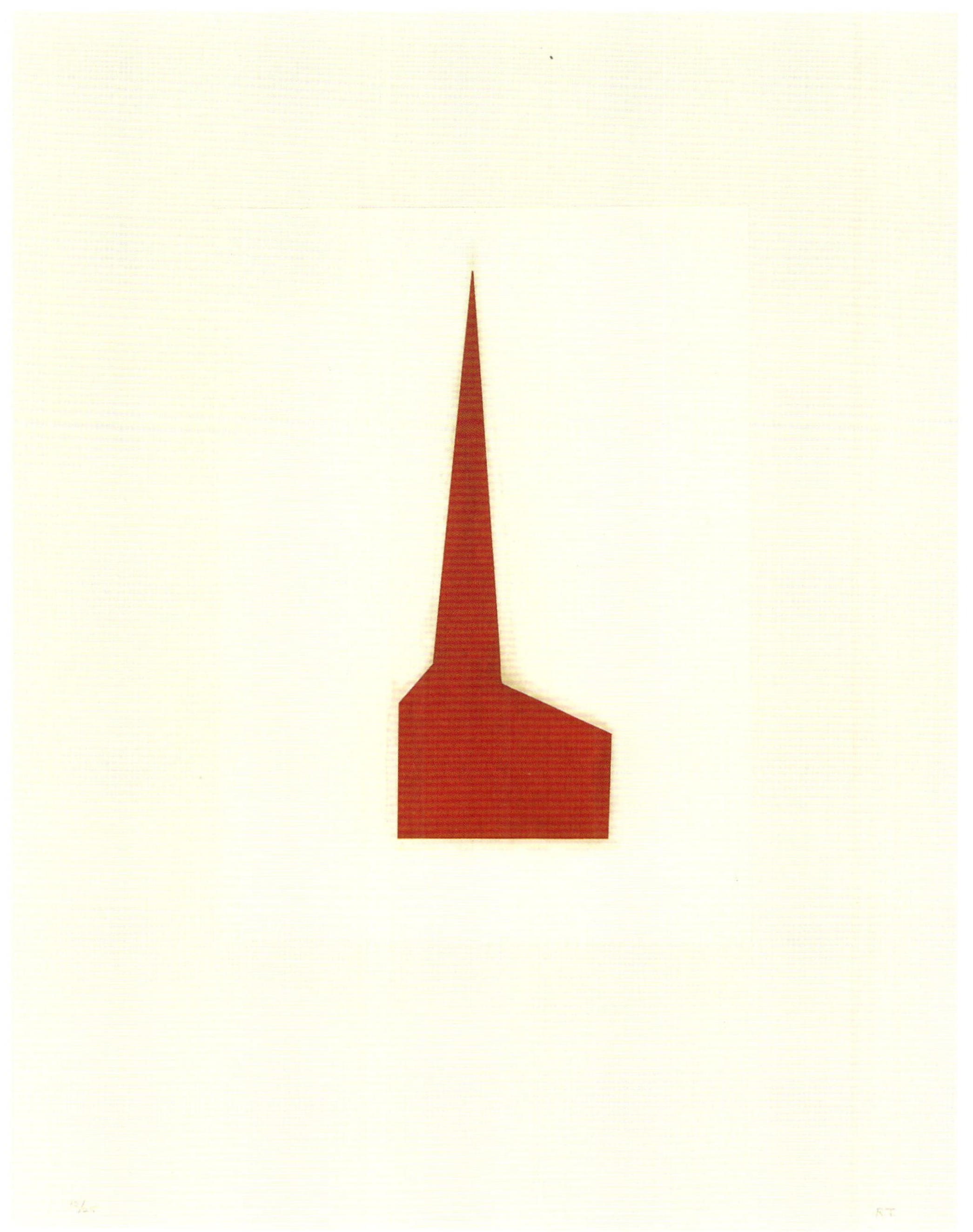

188

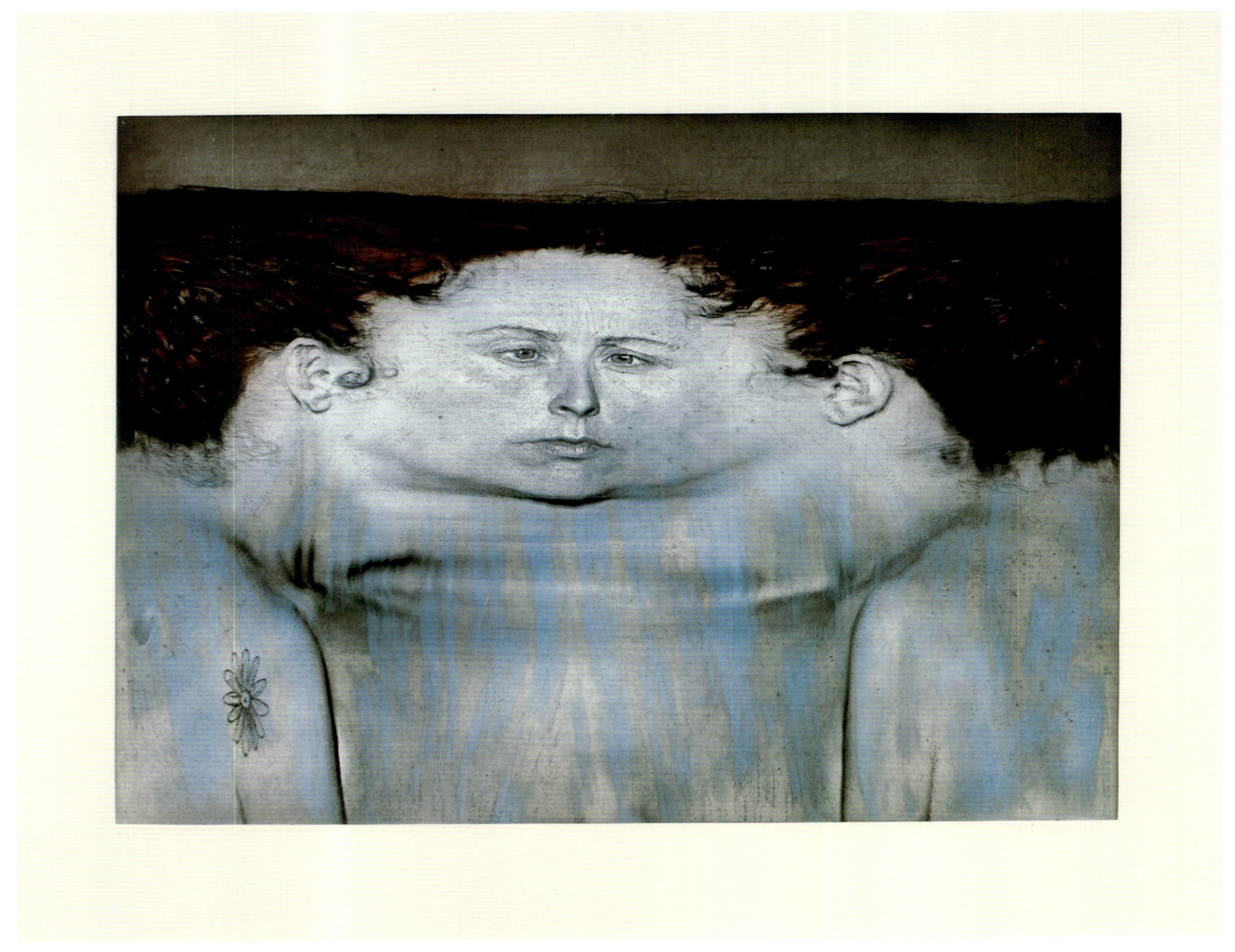

189

189
KIKI SMITH
My Blue Lake, 1995
Color lithograph and photogravure
$43\frac{1}{2}$ x $54\frac{3}{4}$ in. (sheet)

190
ROY LICHTENSTEIN
Landscape with Poet, 1996
Color lithograph and screenprint
$90\frac{1}{2}$ x $36\frac{1}{8}$ in. (sheet)

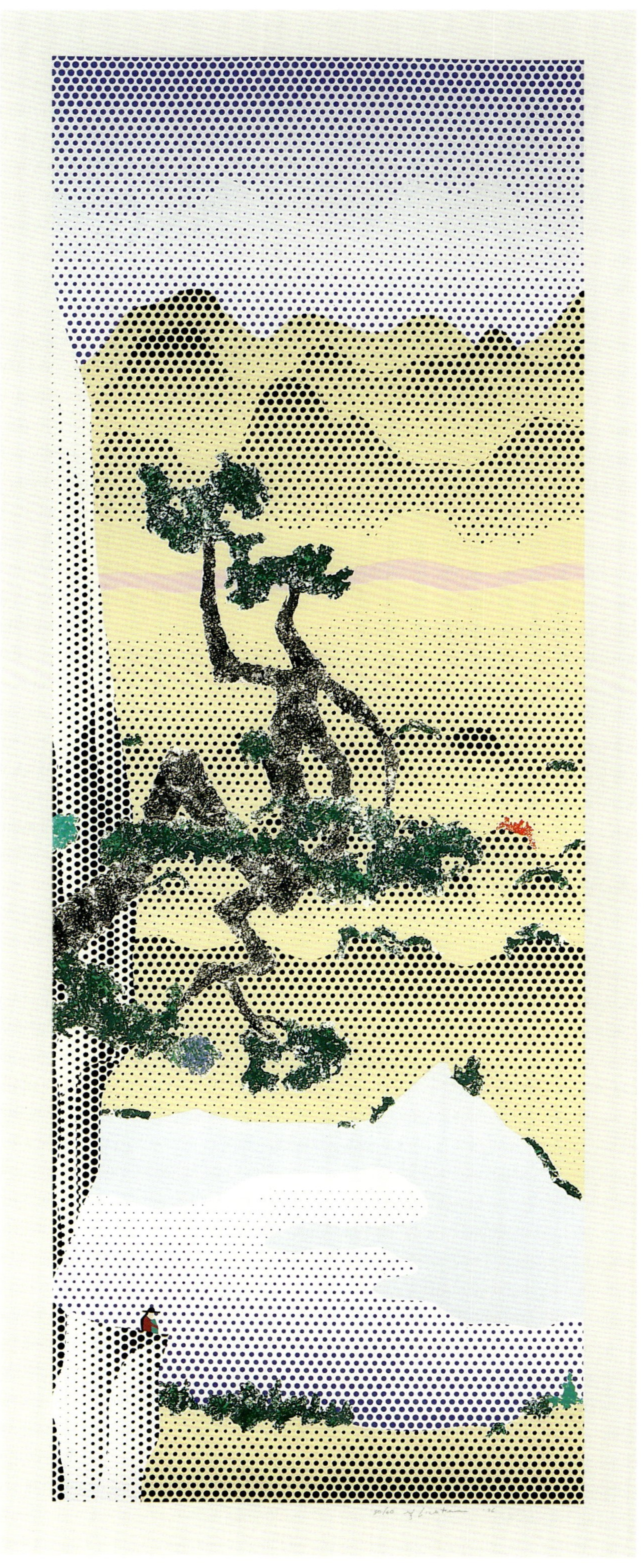

190

191★
DEBORAH OROPALLO
Rails, 1996
Color woodcut and etching
30 x 28 in. (sheet)

192★
TERRY WINTERS
Multiple Visualization Technique, 1998
Color sugar-lift aquatint,
spit-bite aquatint, and open-bite etching
53 x 42 in. (sheet)

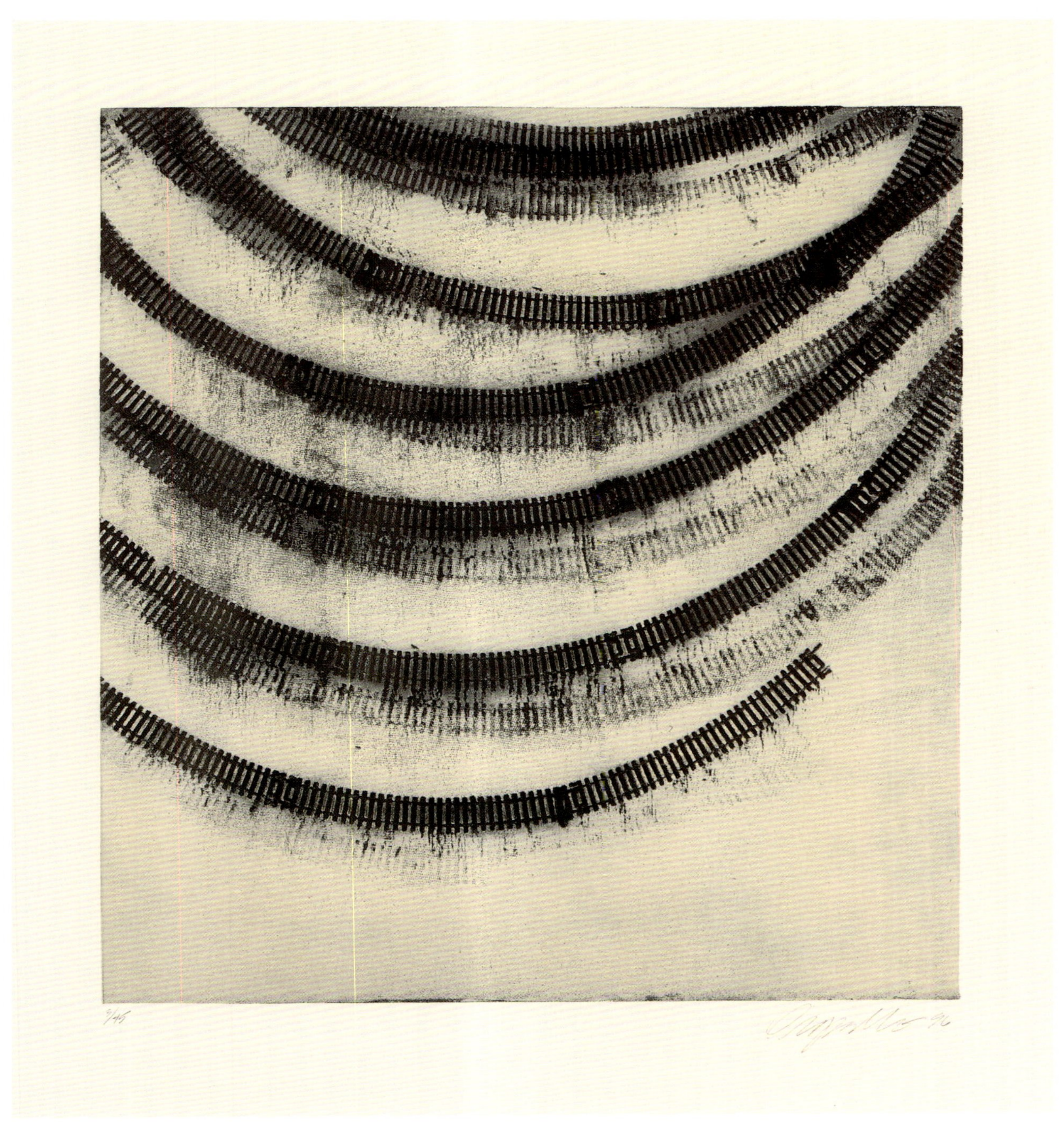

191

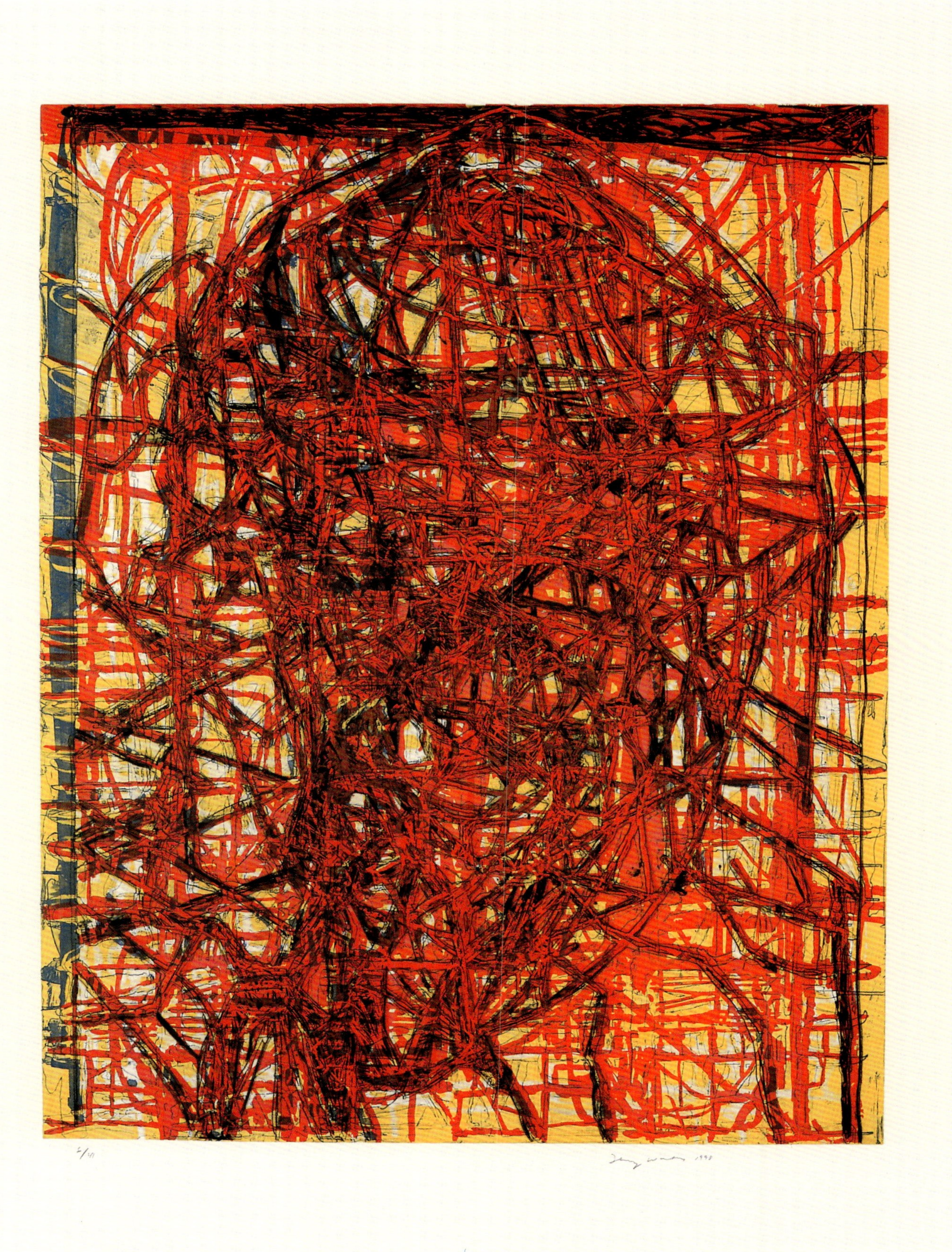

192

A Chronology of Printmaking in America

1940–2000

Many sources have been consulted for the timeline. Among the most helpful were: James Watrous, *A Century of American Printmaking 1880–1980* (Madison: The University of Wisconsin Press, 1984); Riva Castleman, *American Impressions: Prints since Pollock* (New York: Alfred A. Knopf, 1985); Trudy Hansen et. al., *Printmaking in America: Collaborative Prints and Presses, 1960–1990* (New York: Harry N. Abrams, Inc. in association with the Mary and Leigh Block Gallery, Northwestern University, 1985); *The Print Collector's Newsletter,* 1970 to 1996; and *Art on Paper,* 1996 to the present.

The 1940s

1940 Stanley William Hayter arrives in New York from Paris, where he has closed his Atelier 17 printmaking workshop. He joins the staff at the New School for Social Research, teaching innovative methods of intaglio printing in a printmaking course.

Carl Zigrosser, director of the Weyhe Gallery in New York, organizes the first museum show devoted to silkscreen prints (screenprints) at the Springfield Museum of Fine Arts, Massachusetts. In the catalogue of the exhibition, he introduces the term "serigraph."

1941 The Library of Congress, Washington, D.C., presents the first of its *National Exhibition of Prints,* featuring the work of a broad cross section of American printmakers.

1942 Harry Sternberg, a printmaking instructor at the Art Students League, New York, writes *Silk Screen Color Printing* (New York: McGraw Hill), a technical manual on screenprint production that will influence the development of the medium.

1944 The National Serigraph Society is formed to promote the screenprint as a fine arts medium.

Hayter and Studio 17, an exhibition at the Museum of Modern Art, New York, features prints produced by sixty of Hayter's New York Atelier 17 artists. After its New York showing, the exhibition travels throughout the United States and Latin America.

1945 With the end of World War II, Lynton Kistler resumes printing lithographs in Los Angeles for artists living in southern California such as Jean Charlot, Man Ray, and Eugene Berman.

Hayter establishes Atelier 17 as an independent intaglio workshop in New York at 41 East 8th Street.

Mauricio Lasansky, who attended Atelier 17 in 1944, is invited to direct the printmaking program at the University of Iowa, Iowa City. Under his leadership, the program advances intaglio printmaking in new directions.

1946 Alfred Sessler initiates a sophisticated printmaking program at the University of Wisconsin, Madison, with courses in lithography, intaglio, woodcut, and, later, screenprinting. The Wisconsin program represents the rise of university programs and workshops throughout the

fig. 1

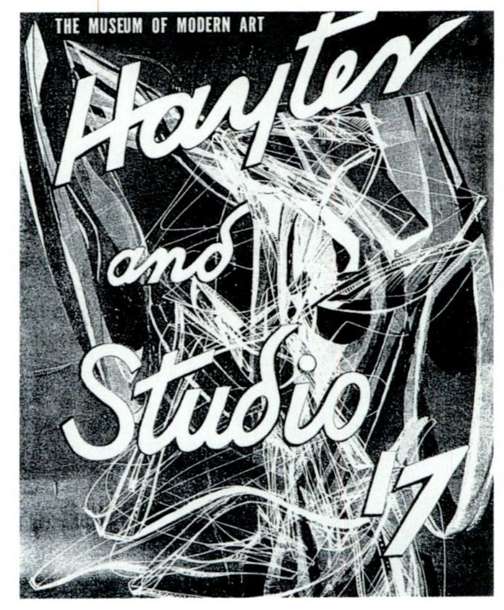

United States, particularly in the midwest, offering varied programs in all aspects of printmaking.

1947 *The First National Print Exhibition* is organized by curator Una Johnson at the Brooklyn Museum, New York. It begins a long succession of annual and biennial exhibitions at the museum to introduce and encourage new talent in printmaking.

Irwin Haas's monthly column "The Print Collector" is first featured in the May issue of *ARTnews*. It will run for ten years before it is dropped as a monthly feature in 1957.

Chris Ritter, director of the Laurel Gallery in New York, issues the portfolio *Laurels Number One,* which contains prints by Joan Miró, Stanley Hayter, Reginald Marsh, Anne Ryan, George Constant, and Will Barnet. Ritter will offer three more *Laurels* portfolios in 1947 and 1948, presenting contemporary American artists to a wider public.

1948 Lithographer and printer Robert Blackburn establishes the Bob Blackburn Workshop in New York (later changed in 1955 to the Creative Graphics Workshop and in 1959 to the Printmaking Workshop).

Artists Clinton Adams and June Wayne join Lynton Kistler at his Los Angeles lithographic workshop and continue to work there into the 1950s.

1949 Stanley Hayter, having provided instruction in intaglio methods to countless artists at Atelier 17 in New York, the California School of Fine Arts, the Philadelphia Print Club, the Art Institute of Chicago, and Brooklyn College, publishes *New Ways of Gravure* (New York: Pantheon Books), which becomes one of the most influential handbooks on intaglio printmaking.

In its exhibition *A New Direction in Intaglio*, the Walker Art Center, Minneapolis, exhibits prints by Lasansky and his students at the Iowa University workshop, including Lee Chesney, John Paul Jones, Ernest Freed, Glen Alps, Donn Steward, and others who will influence American printmaking in the 1950s and 1960s.

The Abby Aldrich Rockefeller Print Room is established at the Museum of Modern Art, New York, to celebrate the 1940 gift by Mrs. Rockefeller of over 1,500 prints. William S. Lieberman is named associate curator in charge and begins an ambitious exhibition program featuring contemporary prints.

The exhibition *Technical Processes in Contemporary Printmaking* and a related panel discussion is organized by the University of Minnesota Gallery for the annual meeting of the Midwest College Art Conference (later the Mid-America College Art Association).

The trend toward large-scale prints is initiated with Louis Schanker's six-foot long woodcut *Dance Macabre,* followed in 1952 by Leonard Baskin's six-foot high woodcut *Man of Peace*.

The 1950s

1950 Gustave von Groschwitz at the Cincinnati Art Museum organizes the first biennial exhibition of color lithography, including an international group of contemporary artists.The exhibitions continue through 1958.

1951 The Brooklyn Society of Etchers, which had reorganized and expanded in 1947, changes its name to the Society of American Graphic Artists (SAGA) in recognition of the range of techniques now included as fine art printmaking processes.

The International Graphic Arts Society (IGAS) is established as a nonprofit membership organization for the creation and distribution of international contemporary works of graphic art. In 1952 IGAS initiates a publication program by subscription by which members commit to purchase no fewer than three prints annually. Artists represented in the publishing program are among the most progressive of the day, including Stanley Hayter, Adolph Dehn, Louis Schanker, Seong Moy, Margaret Lowengrund, Boris Margo, Federico Castellon, Adja Yunkers, Armin Landeck, and Gabor Peterdi.

Carl Zigrosser, curator at the Philadelphia Museum of Art, contributes his article "American Prints since 1926: A Complete Revolution" to the November *Art Digest*.

In New York, the lithographer Margaret Lowengrund establishes her gallery and print workshop, the Contemporaries, which encourages original printmaking through exhibitions of contemporary American prints.

fig. 2

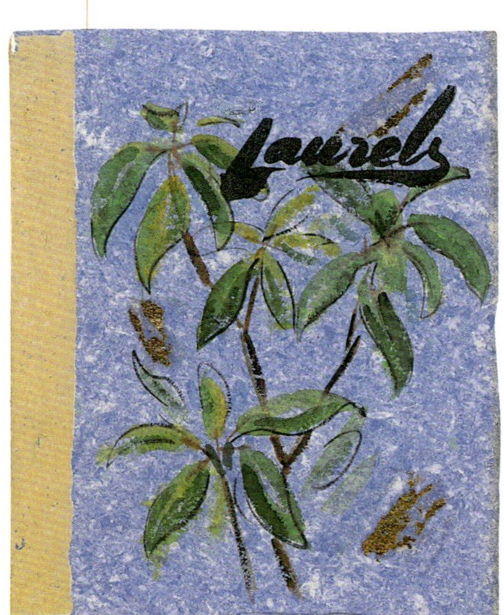

fig. 1 Cover of the Museum of Modern Art *Bulletin* (August 1944) that served as the catalogue for the *Hayter and Studio 17* exhibition at the museum.

fig. 2 Cover of *Laurels Number One* (May 1947), designed by Chris Ritter on Douglass Howell handmade paper.

1952 *New Expressions in Fine Printmaking: Ideas, Methods, and Materials* is an exhibition organized by Una Johnson at the Brooklyn Museum that emphasizes technical advancements in printmaking.

The Philadelphia Museum of Art presents the exhibition *A Decade of American Printmaking,* featuring a number of color lithographs and ambitious color woodcuts by younger artists.

Rio Grande Graphics, established by woodcut artist Adja Yunkers as part of his short-lived Rio Grande Workshop in New Mexico, issues three print portfolios, published by Ted Gotthelf in New York. The portfolios, one each with works by Yunkers, Gabor Peterdi, and Seong Moy, are accompanied by introductory essays from museum curators John Palmer Leeper, William Lieberman, and Una Johnson.

1953 *Young American Printmakers under 35* is presented at the Museum of Modern Art, New York.

June Wayne is one of the jurors at the Second National Print Exhibition sponsored by the University of Southern California, Los Angeles.

1954 Atelier 17 adds instruction in color woodcut to its program.

1955 *14 Painter-Printmakers,* an exhibition at the Brooklyn Museum, features the work of the members of the loose alliance "14 Painter-Printmakers," which included some of the current most progressive contemporary artists, such as Will Barnet, Werner Drewes, Sue Fuller, Boris Margo, Seong Moy, Louis Schanker, Kurt Seligmann, Minna Citron, Worden Day, Perle Fine, Jan Gelb, Alice Trumbull Mason, Karl Schrag, John von Wicht, and Gabor Peterdi.

Atelier 17 in New York closes, Stanley Hayter having reestablished Atelier 17 in Paris in 1950. Over 135 artists—*émigrés,* American printmakers, and young art students—worked at the New York atelier from 1940 to 1955, including Willem de Kooning, Robert Motherwell, Louise Nevelson, Mark Rothko, and Alexander Calder.

1956 Pratt-Contemporaries Graphic Arts Center is established in New York City with the aid of a $50,000 grant from the Rockefeller Foundation. It merges Margaret Lowengrund's Contemporaries gallery/workshop with its own program. The new program offers not only professional training in printmaking but print exhibitions and (later) a publication, *Artist's Proof,* on the historical and technical aspects of printmaking. In 1957 the program will be renamed the Pratt Graphic Arts Center.

The Print Council of America is incorporated as a national membership group of curators, collectors, art historians, and art enthusiasts dedicated to the promotion of historical and contemporary printmaking. In 1959 the

fig. 3 The birthplace of Universal Limited Art Editions at 5 Skidmore Place, West Islip, Long Island.

fig. 4 Lessing Rosenwald, artist Misch Kohn, June Wayne, and master printer Bohuslav Horak at the Tamarind Lithography Workshop, Los Angeles, 1961.

group will organize *American Prints Today/1959*, an exhibition and catalogue that will travel across the United States to sixteen major museums.

Curator Una Johnson organizes the exhibition *Ten Years of American Prints 1947–1956* at the Brooklyn Museum, its catalogue including an essay on the major achievements and changes in printmaking in the decade, and also an expanded version of her 1952 essay, "New Expressions in Fine Printmaking."

1957 Universal Limited Art Editions (ULAE), first founded in 1955 by Maurice and Tatyana Grosman as a reproductive screenprinting enterprise (Limited Art Editions), is established to publish fine art prints and books in West Islip, New York. Their first project, a collaboration between artist Larry Rivers and poet Frank O'Hara, is printed on Bavarian lithographic stones found discarded in the Grosmans' front yard.

1958 Jules Heller, professor at the University of Southern California, writes *Printmaking Today* (New York: Henry Holt and Company), a book that includes instructions on making various kinds of prints, sources for graphic art supplies, formulas and recipes, and chapter sections on new directions in various printmaking media.

1959 George Lockwood founds Impressions Workshop in Boston as a facility primarily devoted to lithography, but also featuring intaglio, and, later, screenprinting, relief, and letterpress printing. Peter Milton, Michael Mazur, Saul Steinberg, and Adja Yunkers will work there.

Artist Sam Francis begins his first lithographs at ULAE, although they are not printed until 1968. In 1960 he will complete his first series of lithographs in Zurich, Switzerland.

Gabor Peterdi, who had had established graphic art workshops at the Brooklyn Museum Art School and Hunter College, writes *Printmaking: Methods Old and New* (New York: The Macmillan Company), a technical handbook for artists. Peterdi's book describes some of the experimentation in printmaking that occurred during the decade, including collagraphy (a technique of printing from cardboard), Edmond Casarella's "paper cut" prints made from cut-paper collage matrices, metal relief printing by Michel Ponce de León, and printmaking using new acrylic materials by Boris Margo and Arthur Deshaies.

The 1960s

1960 Tamarind Lithography Workshop is founded by June Wayne in Los Angeles with an initial grant of $135,000 awarded in 1959 by the Ford Foundation. The workshop is formed to stimulate development of lithography in the United States through programs of artist-fellowships and technical training for printers. Clinton Adams is associate director and Garo Antreasian is master printer.

Willem de Kooning, a guest artist at the University of California, Berkeley, makes two lithographs that are editioned by Nathan Oliveira and George Miyasaki. He uses a floor mop to draw on the stones.

Sheila Marbain opens Maurel Studios, a screenprinting workshop that will produce prints, posters, and three-dimensional editions in the 1960s for artists such as Claes Oldenburg, Robert Rauschenberg, Robert Motherwell, and Roy Lichtenstein.

1961 Pratt Graphics Center begins publishing *Artist's Proof*, a periodical devoted to the specialist printmaker, which will run for ten years. Artist and printmaker Fritz Eichenberg is the first editor.

The Print Council of America publishes *What Is an Original Print?* a pamphlet edited by Joshua Binyon Cahn that provides criteria for originality in fine art printmaking. There will be revised editions in 1964 and 1967.

William Lieberman, curator of prints and illustrated books at the Museum of Modern Art, arranges with a series of grants from the Celeste and Armand Bartos Foundation to purchase for the museum's collection the first impression from every edition published by ULAE. By this time Mrs. Grosman has published works by Jasper Johns and Larry Rivers.

1962 Crown Point Press is founded by Kathan Brown as an etching workshop in Point Richmond, California. The press later moves to Berkeley in 1963 where Brown publishes prints by Richard Diebenkorn and Wayne Thiebaud in 1965, then relocates to Oakland where the press is active from 1971 to 1986, when it moves to San Francisco.

fig. 3

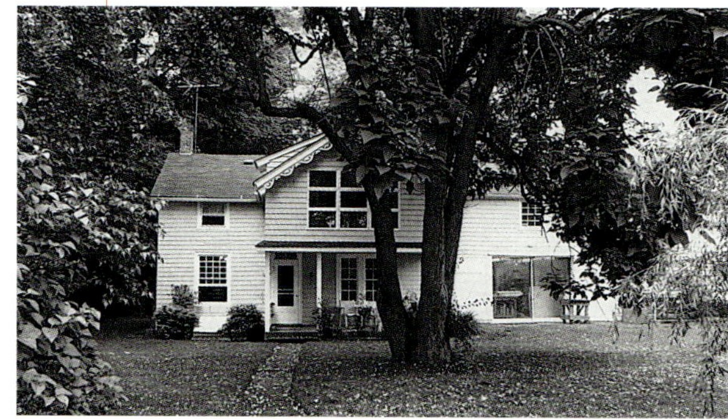

fig. 4

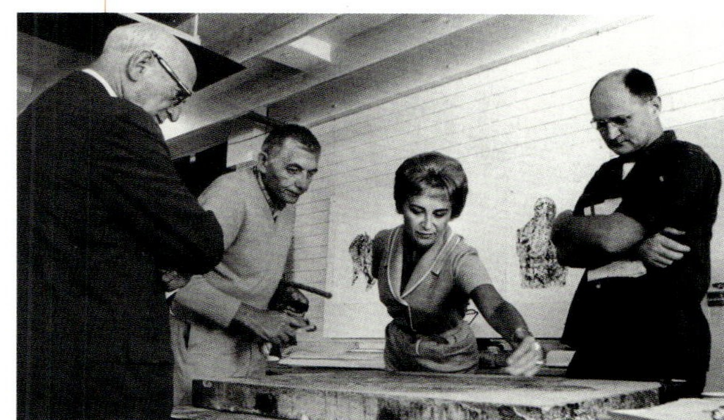

Robert Rauschenberg makes the statement—"I began lithography reluctantly, thinking that the second half of the 20th century was no time to start writing on rocks"—in "Work Notes–1962," a written response to a museum's inquiry about his lithograph project *Urban* at ULAE. First published in Edward A. Foster's introduction to the exhibition catalogue *Robert Rauschenberg Prints 1948–1970* (Minneapolis: Minneapolis Institute of Arts, 1970), the quote is considered representative of the ambivalent feelings harbored by many young New York artists on being invited to make lithographs at ULAE by Mrs. Grosman.

The Print Council of America produces the second of its *American Prints Today* exhibitions, accompanied by a catalogue, that will travel throughout the United States to major museums.

1963 *Accident*, a print made by Robert Rauschenberg at ULAE with a fractured lithographic stone, is considered an example of the new disregard for traditional printmaking standards and wins the Grand Prix of the International Print Exhibition at Ljubljana, Yugoslavia.

1964 Irwin Hollander, a Tamarind graduate, establishes Hollanders' Workshop in New York. He will print and publish works by several Abstract Expressionist artists, including Robert Motherwell and Willem de Kooning, before closing in 1972.

Art collectors John and Kimiko Powers help Tatyana Grosman establish a kind of subscription fund through which contributors are offered prints as they are published by ULAE.

American Painters as New Lithographers is the exhibition that opens the newly renovated galleries at the Museum of Modern Art. All of the prints in the exhibition, with the exception of three by Sam Francis, were made at ULAE.

The well-known, 76 year-old painter Josef Albers produces a suite of eight lithographs, *Midnight and Noon/ Homage to the Square,* as an artist-fellow at Tamarind.

Ten Works by Ten Painters, a portfolio of screenprints, is published by the Wadsworth Atheneum, Hartford, Connecticut, in an edition of 500. The artists are George Ortman, Frank Stella, Ellsworth Kelly, Robert Motherwell, Andy Warhol, Stuart Davis, Roy Lichtenstein, Larry Poons, Robert Indiana, and Ad Reinhardt. None of the artists are directly involved in the production of the prints, most having supplied drawings that are translated into stencils for printing.

1965 Carl Zigrosser and Christa M. Gaehde are co-authors of the book *A Guide to the Collecting and Care of Original Prints* (New York: Crown Publishers) that includes chapters on "The Artist and the Print Market" and "The Dealer and the Print Market."

Tamarind-trained master printer Joseph Zirker establishes Original Press in San Francisco to work with Deborah Remington, Frank Lobdell, and Richard Diebenkorn. In 1967, Original Press is succeeded by

fig.5

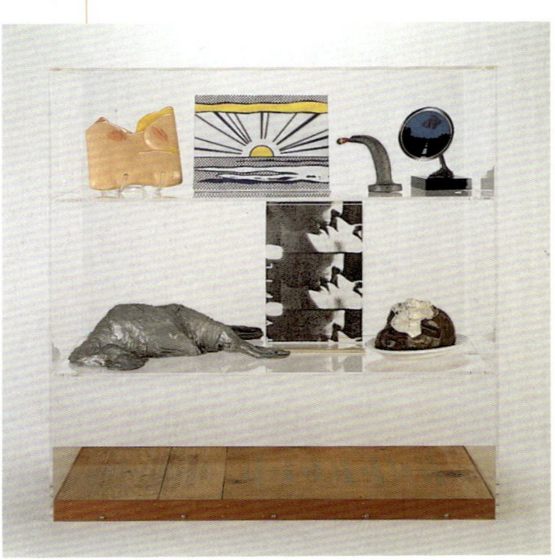

fig.6

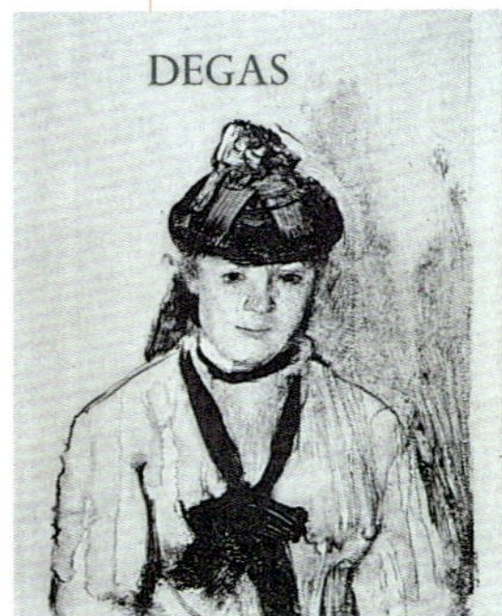

fig.5 *Seven Objects in a Box* (1966) a collection of Pop Art multiples by Allan d'Arcangelo, Jim Dine, Roy Lichtenstein, Claes Oldenburg, George Segal, Andy Warhol, and Tom Wesselmann, published by Tanglewood Press.

fig.6 Cover of the 1968 exhibition catalogue *Degas Monotypes*.

fig.7 Claes Oldenburg working at Gemini G.E.L. on the wood relief model used to create the molds for *Profile Airflow*, 1968.

fig.8 Josef Albers inspecting proofs of his *Embossed Linear Constuctions* with Ken Tyler of Gemini G.E.L., 1969.

fig.9 Robert Rauschenberg cutting mylar for his *Stoned Moon* project at Gemini G.E.L., 1969.

Collector's Press with printer Ernest de Soto who continues to work with California artists such as Nathan Oliveira, Roy de Forest, and Bruce Conner.

Three volumes of *11 Pop Artists* are published by Original Editions. Each volume contains 11 screenprints, one each by artists who are among the most prominent in America—Allen d'Arcangelo, Jim Dine, Allen Jones, Roy Lichtenstein, Mel Ramos, James Rosenquist, Andy Warhol, and Tom Wesselmann. The project is organized by Rosa Esman, a gallery owner who promotes contemporary American art and who will produce other print portfolios, some with three-dimensional multiples, through her Tanglewood Press, including *New York Ten* (1965), *Seven Objects in a Box* (1966), and *Ten from Leo Castelli* (1967).

1966 Gemini Graphic Editions Limited (Gemini G.E.L.) is established in Los Angeles as a print publishing workshop by Kenneth Tyler, Sidney B. Felsen, and Stanley Grinstein. Tyler, a Tamarind-trained master printer, had previously operated his own printing firm, Gemini Ltd., as a contract shop beginning in 1965. Josef Albers is the first artist invited to do a lithographic project at the workshop.

After almost ten years of producing only lithographs, an NEA grant allows ULAE to expand its workshop to include intaglio processes. Donn Steward, already on staff and trained as an intaglio printer, becomes ULAE's first master printer for intaglio. He will work with Cy Twombly and Robert Motherwell on ULAE's first intaglio projects in 1967 and 1968.

1967 Andy Warhol, an artist who uses screenprint extensively in his paintings, produces the ten-screenprint portfolio *Marilyn Monroe*. The images are printed purposefully off-register and in a wide range of colors from black to day-glo green.

Booster, Robert Rauschenberg's first project at Gemini G.E.L., is published. At six feet in height, the print is credited as immediately redefining the possibilities of size and scale in contemporary prints.

Artist Frank Stella makes his first prints, the *Star of Persia Series*, at Gemini.

1968 Eugenia Parry Janis's exhibition *Degas Monotypes* at the Fogg Art Museum stimulates the interest of artists in the monotype. Enthusiastic response to the medium prompts many printers and publishers to add monotype to their production repertoire.

Art in America initiates a print publishing program, binding a Larry Rivers color lithograph into the July–August issue, in an edition of 46,000.

Vogue magazine publishes the article "The Print Revival," by Barbara Rose, in its September issue.

American Graphic Workshops: 1968, an exhibition at the Cincinnati Art Museum curated by Mary Welsh Baskett, includes independent workshops such as Hollanders Workshop, Tamarind, ULAE, and also six workshops affiliated with art schools including Pratt Graphics Center, Tyler School of Art at Temple University, and the universities of Indiana, Iowa, Wisconsin, and Yale.

Andy Warhol produces the first of his two screenprint portfolios, *Campbell's Soup I*, with ten versions of the soup cans used as the subject of his 1962 painting. The second portfolio, *Campbell's Soup II*, will be published the following year.

Donald Saff establishes the Institute for Research in Art/Graphicstudio at the University of South Florida, Tampa, with a program that provides educational instruction for students and also a print publishing program that attracts such well-known artists as Phiip Pearlstein in 1969 and James Rosenquist in 1971.

Mixografia, a new process that allows prints to be made in high relief, is developed by Luis Remba in Mexico City for the artist Rufino Tamayo. In 1984 the Mixografia workshop will move to Los Angeles, where American artists are introduced to the process.

Gemini G.E.L. initiates a print subscription program in which a subscriber commits to a one-year contract to buy at a discounted price one print from each edition published that year.

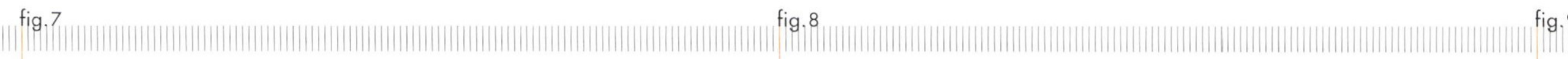

fig.7

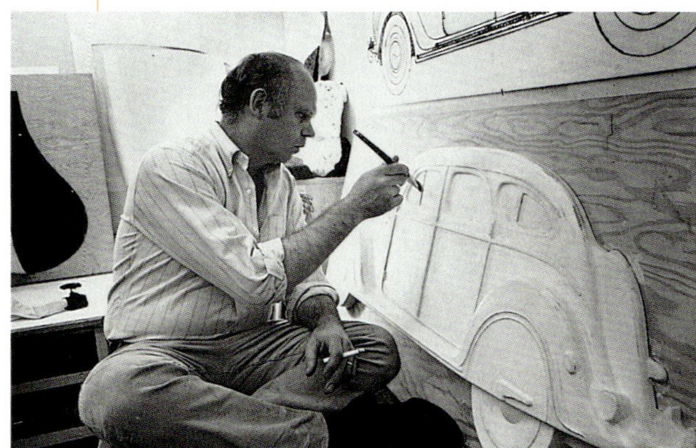

fig.8

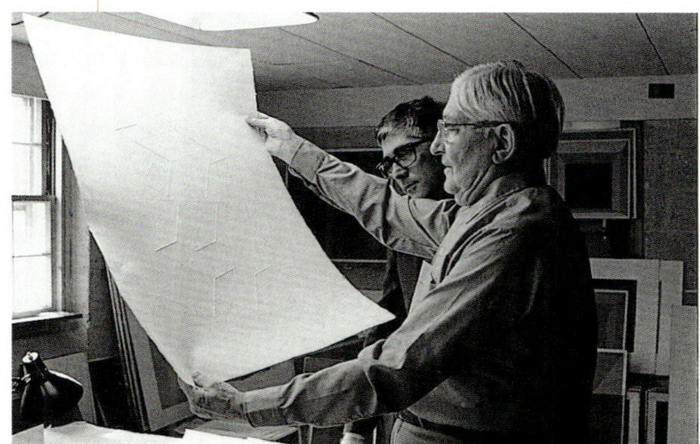

fig.9

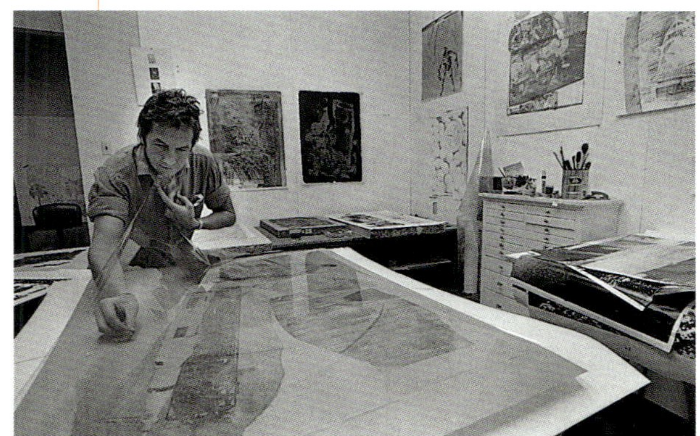

Brooke Alexander founds Brooke Alexander Inc. in New York City, to specialize in prints as a dealer and independent publisher (without a production workshop). His first editions will be works by Josef Albers, Alex Katz, and Philip Pearlstein. In 1974 he will become Robert Motherwell's print distributor.

1969 In response to Claes Oldenburg's interest in producing *Profile Airflow* (1969), a hybrid print combining lithography and bas-relief sculpture, Gemini G.E.L. adds small-scale sculpture projects (multiples) to its publishing program: Lichtenstein's *Untitled Heads I* and *II* (1970), Oldenburg's *Geometric Mouse—Scale C* and *Ice Bag—Scale B* (1971), and John Chamberlain's *Le Molé* (1971).

The 1970s

1970 "Original Art, Hot off the Presses," an article in *Life* magazine is published in the 23 January issue, giving mainstream attention to the burgeoning industry of fine art print publishing.

The *Print Collector's Newsletter* debuts as a bimonthly publication, featuring an international review of auctions, book reviews, a list of new prints published, news of the print world, and articles on special topics by well-known authorities on graphic art. The publication will run with much the same format for twenty-six years, until its closure in 1996.

The newsletter's first issue (March–April 1970) includes the column "Multiples and Objects Published" with the explanation that "We use the term multiples to refer to 3-dimensional art objects, other than lithographs, screenprints, etchings, and relief prints, that are made in signed and numbered limited editions." Among the eight multiples listed are works by Richard Artschwager, Ernest Trova, and Victor Vasarely.

Jean Milant, a Tamarind-trained master printer, opens Cirrus Editions, a workshop in Los Angeles for lithography and screenprinting. Tamarind Lithography Workshop sends out a press release announcing the opening.

Landfall Press opens in Chicago under the direction of Jack Lemon, also a Tamarind-trained master printer.

Artist Sam Francis opens the Litho Shop, Inc., in Santa Monica, California, to produce his own editions.

Tamarind Lithography Workshop closes in Los Angeles, and the equipment and archives move to the University of New Mexico where the Tamarind Institute is established as an educational center with Clinton Adams as director, Garo Antreasian as technical director, and June Wayne as advisor.

fig. 10

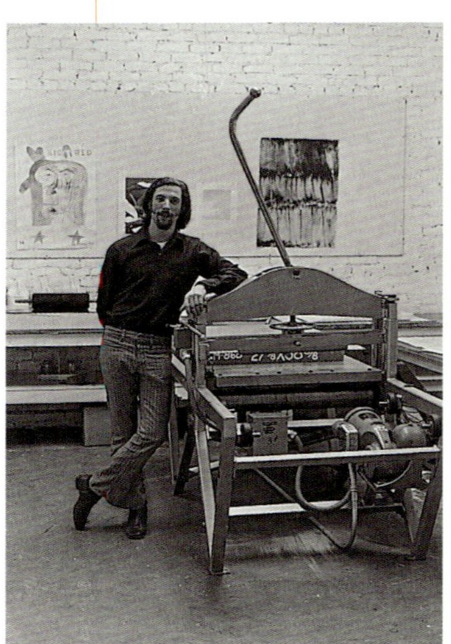

The first extensive catalogue of Jasper Johns's prints, *Jasper Johns: Prints 1960–1970* by Richard Field, is published in conjunction with an exhibition at the Philadelphia Museum of Art. In all, 128 prints, mostly lithographs, are documented as having been made by Johns since his first print at ULAE in 1960. The catalogue will serve as a catalogue raisonné of the prints until 1994.

Robert Rauschenberg produces a print, *Earth Day*, and a poster in celebration of the first Earth Day as a contribution to the American Environmental Foundation. The print, published by Gemini G.E.L., is one of many that Rauschenberg and other artists and presses will produce for various social and political causes during the 1970s and into the 1980s.

1971 Contemporary printmaking continues to receive coverage in the American mainstream press in January, with a 5 January article by Elizabeth Stevens, "The Great Graphic Boom of the '50s and '60s" in the *Wall Street Journal*, and in *Time* magazine's article on print publishing at Gemini G.E.L. that appears in the 18 January issue.

The Tamarind Book of Lithography: Art and Techniques (New York: Harry N. Abrams, Inc.) is published, by Clinton Adams and Garo Antreasian, with a foreword by June Wayne. The book is lauded as a landmark publication in the history of American lithography.

Tamarind Institute announces an exhibition of seventy-six lithographs, *Tamarind: A Renaissance of Lithography*, which will circulate through the International Exhibitions Foundation.

Rauschenberg establishes the Untitled Press near his home on Captiva Island, Florida, to print and publish his own work and that of other artist-friends.

At the Museum of Modern Art, curator Riva Castleman organizes the exhibition *Technics and Creativity: Gemini G.E.L.*, a review of five years of prints and multiples produced at the workshop. The accompanying publication includes an essay by Castleman, a catalogue raisonné of the 285 Gemini publications issued by that date, and is encased in a white plastic box with a two-color offset lithograph/collage, *Target* (1970), by Jasper Johns.

Gemini publishes a print by Roy Lichtenstein to benefit the Museum of Modern Art and the opening of its new building. The Walker Art Center publishes Robert Rauschenberg's print *General Delivery* to commemorate its new building.

The exhibition *Silkscreen: History of a Medium* is organized by Richard Field at the Philadelphia Museum of Art, with sections on the contemporary screenprint up to 1970.

The Whitney Museum of American Art in New York presents the exhibition *Oversize Prints*, curated by Elke M. Solomon.

Johns's print *Decoy* is made at ULAE on a hand press and a hand-fed offset proofing press, starting a trend for the use of offset lithography by many artists that would continue through the decade. For Johns, *Decoy* is the first print that he will use as the basis for a painting of the same name. In 1972 the landmark print will be the sole subject of the exhibition *Jasper Johns's Decoy: The Print and the Painting* at Hofstra University, Hempsted, Long Island.

The 6 December auction at Sotheby Parke Bernet Los Angeles is the first exclusively contemporary print sale to be held. Included in the auction are 125 prints and multiples by fifty-two artists from a 1959 Vasarely to three prints published in 1971. The first exclusively contemporary print auction in New York will be at Sotheby Parke Bernet in 1975.

1972 *The Complete Printmaker* by John Ross and Clare Romano (New York: Free Press) is published as a resource for artists and teachers and those interested in the technical aspects of printmaking processes.

The World Print Council is founded in San Francisco as a nonprofit organization serving the international community of artists/printmakers, providing exhibition opportunities that will increase the public understanding and appreciation of prints.

fig. 11

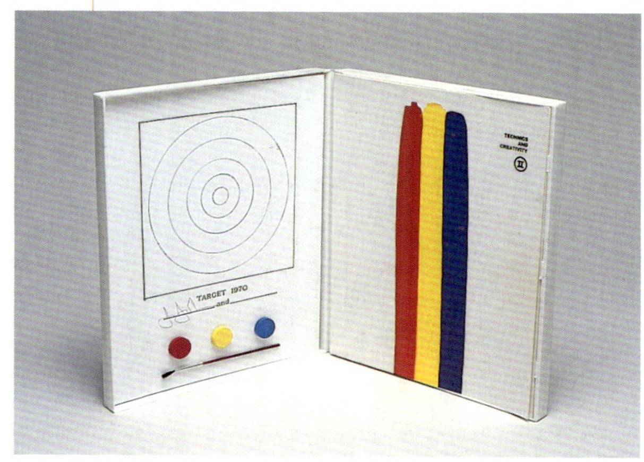

fig. 10 Jean Milant at his newly opened workshop, Cirrus Editions, in Los Angeles, 1970.

fig. 11 The catalogue for the exhibition *Technics and Creativity: Gemini G.E.L.* with *Target* (1970) by Jasper Johns, 1972.

ULAE announces the publication of Robert Motherwell's *A la pintura*, a book of twenty-one intaglio prints that was over four years in the making. The book is immediately hailed as one of the most important artist's books of the twentieth century and is featured in the exhibition *Robert Motherwell's A la pintura: The Genesis of a Book,* curated by John McKendry at the Metropolitan Museum of Art, New York, that same year.

Keith, Chuck Close's first print, measuring 46 by 35 inches, is the largest mezzotint ever produced. It takes over three months to complete at Crown Point Press and is published by Parasol Press.

Simca Print Artists, founded by Hiroshi Kawanshi, invites Jasper Johns to collaborate in making screenprints. *Flags I* (1973), one of their first copublications, is printed from thirty-one screens and is lauded for its complex layered surface.

1973 The International Institute of Experimental Printmaking is established by Garner Tullis in Santa Cruz, California, emphasizing the exploration of paper as an artistic medium.

Helen Frankenthaler works on the woodcuts *East and Beyond* (1973) and *Savage Breeze* (1974) at ULAE. Both prints are considered precursors to the woodcut revival that will occur in the United States later in the decade.

The periodical *Art in America* publishes two articles on the newly elevated status of prints in the world of contemporary art in its July–August issue: Judith Goldman's "The Print Establishment" and Diane Kelder's "The Graphic Revival" (in her regular column).

Robert Rauschenberg's *Link,* made with Marius Peraudeau and staff at his Moulin à Papier Richard de Bas in Ambert, France, marks the beginning of Gemini G.E.L.'s international collaborations with Rauschenberg. Later collaborations will take place in India and China.

New trends in paper making and experimentation with paper in prints are among the topics discussed in the May–June issue of the *Print Collector's Newsletter,* which is entirely devoted to the topic of paper.

Petersburg Press of London sets up a print workshop in Frank Stella's New York home so that he can more easily be involved in the printing process.

1974 Kenneth Tyler leaves Gemini G.E.L. to found his own workshop, Tyler Graphics Ltd., in Bedford Village, New York. The shop will move to Mt. Kisco in the late 1980s.

The March issue of *ARTnews* is designated a "Special Prints Issue," its cover featuring Robert Rauschenberg's lithograph *Tanya*, a portrait of ULAE's Tatyana Grosman. In addition to articles on historical prints, it features one on ULAE, "Quality in Edition Prints" by Jacob Kainen, and an announcement of new print editions.

fig. 12

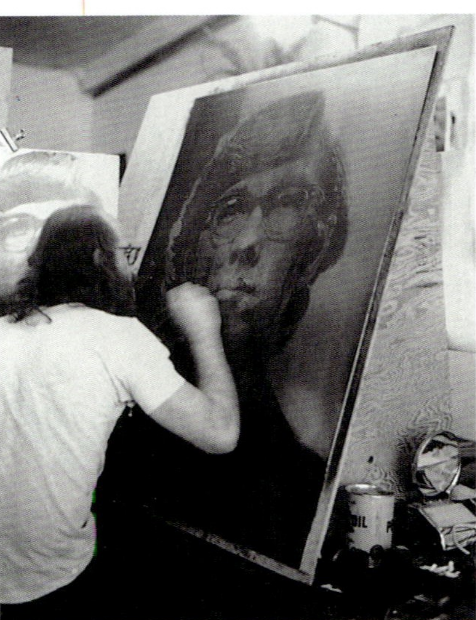

fig. 12 Chuck Close working on *Keith* at Crown Point Press, Oakland, 1972.

fig. 13 David Hockney applying colored pulp to newly made sheets of wet paper for *Paper Pool 18: Le Plongeur* at Tyler Graphics, Bedford Village, New York, 1978.

The first issue of the *Tamarind Technical Papers*, an illustrated technical journal, is published by the Tamarind Institute. In 1978 the name is shortened to the *Tamarind Papers* when the journal expands to include critical and historical studies on the art of lithography.

1975 Tamarind celebrates its fifteenth anniversary with an invitation to fifteen artists to create four lithographs each, which are published in 1977 as *Tamarind Suite Fifteen*. Among the artists are Elaine de Kooning, Fritz Scholder, Edward Ruscha, and Nathan Oliveira.

For the *National Experimental Printmaking Show*, held at Tusculum College in Greeneville, Tennessee, the juried competition is open to artists working in any media that pushes prints in new directions. With this restriction, the organizers diverge from the rules of most competitions that allow only traditional techniques. They hope to encourage more flexible policies of eligibility in print competitions.

The Print Council of America forms a committee to propose a new Print Council definition of the original print. Its current definition, dating back to 1967, proves too restrictive and is criticized as geared to the market and the consumer but not responsive to artists and new techniques.

Landfall Press, which had previously included only lithography in the repertoire of processes it offered, publishes a portfolio of six etchings by six artists, *Landfall Press Etchings*, to celebrate the inauguration of its new etching workshop.

Recent American Etchings, an exhibition curated by Richard Field, is seen at the Davison Art Center, Wesleyan University, and organized for travel in 1976 by the National Collection of Fine Arts, Smithsonian Institution. Among the twenty artists in the exhibition are several who are identified with Minimalist art, including Sol LeWitt, Robert Mangold, Brice Marden, and Robert Ryman. In the catalogue accompanying the exhibition Field acknowledges ULAE and Crown Point Press as the two most prominent etching workshops.

1976 At the annual meeting of the College Art Association, Alan Shestack, director of the Yale University Art Gallery, chairs a session entitled "The Production and Marketing of Fine Prints."

In the 7 June issue of the *New Yorker* magazine, Calvin Tomkins contributes a profile of ULAE founder Tatyana Grosman.

1977 The World Print Competition 1977, supported by a grant from the National Endowment for the Arts and sponsored by the California College of Arts and Crafts and the San Francisco Museum of Modern Art, announces twenty-six awards in three categories from among 4,088 print entries.

The Chicago Museum of Contemporary Art presents the exhibition *Landfall Press: A Survey of Prints 1970–1977*.

Xerox/Xerox/Xerox, an exhibition with a catalogue at the Department of Art, University of Colorado, includes xerographic or photocopy prints made by sixty-eight artists.

"The Romance of Learning a New Medium for an Artist," by Helen Frankenthaler, appears in the *Print Collector's Newsletter* for July–August. The article is an edited transcription of Frankenthaler's lecture to the Drawing and Print Club/Founders Society at the Detroit Institute on 3 May. Frankenthaler discusses her recent work in woodcut with Tyler Graphics.

The Metropolitan Museum of Art, New York, initiates an art publications department to publish posters and limited edition prints by contemporary artists. The publications will be offered for sale in a shop at the museum, later called the Mezzanine Gallery.

1978 A 5 February article in the *New York Times* describes the phenomenon of publishing prints as tax shelters. In a tax shelter print scheme, a taxpayer purchases a master plate, a limited edition of prints produced from that plate, and the copyright to the master image. The taxpayer then claims an investment tax credit and depreciation in the amount of the purchase price. The practice is identified as being marginally legal and the *Print Collector's Newsletter* begins a series of updates on its popularity and legality that continues for the next two years. Eventually the practice disappears after 1980 when the U.S. Treasury approves the establishment of a print advisory panel to review the fair market value of such print publishing ventures.

fig. 13

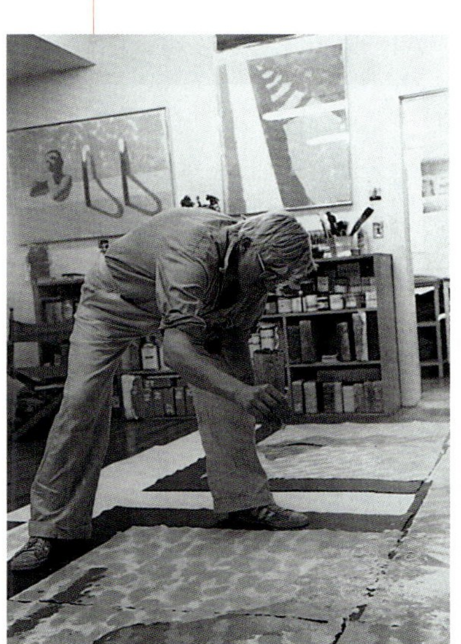

Beginning in April, Point Publications of Crown Point Press publishes *View*, a periodical that extensively interviews its published artists. Among those included in the first issue, edited by Robin White, are John Cage, Pat Steir, Robert Barry, Robert Mangold, Chris Burden, and Tom Marioni. Cage had just made his first etchings at Crown Point, a portfolio of seven prints entitled *Seven Day Diary: Not Knowing*.

A three-day conference, *Paper–Art & Technology*, takes place at the San Francisco Museum of Modern Art, sponsored by the World Print Council. Participants include artists, printers, and print curators, including Kenneth Noland, Garo Antreasian, Garner Tullis, Kenneth Tyler, Michel Joly, Yasuichi Kubota, Riva Castleman, Andrew Robison, and Robert Flynn Johnson.

Jane Farmer curates the exhibition *New American Monotypes* for the Smithsonian Institution, Washington, D.C. In her catalogue she attributes current artistic interest in monotypes as reaction against the machine-crafted prints of the 1960s. The exhibition will tour the United States for over a year under the auspices of the Smithsonian Institution Traveling Exhibition Services (SITES).

The *Print Collector's Newsletter* of November–December is devoted to special articles on the monotype.

David Hockney completes his *Paper Pools* project at Tyler Graphics. The pieces, some of which consist of multi-panels, are composed of colored paper pulp formed in molds.

1979 *Paper as Medium*, a traveling exhibition accompanied by a catalogue, is organized by curator Jane Farmer for SITES and includes works by fifty-one artists who are using paper in different ways as the sole medium for their art. The *Print Collector's Newsletter* of July–August is devoted to articles addressing the phenomenon of paper making as a medium used by more and more artists; a corresponding boom occurs in the production of handmade papers by mills and graphic workshops.

The 1980s

1980 In this year, significant museum exhibitions focus on the subject of contemporary prints and printmakers, including:

- Walker Art Center's *Collaborations on Paper: Six American Printshops,* an exhibition that looks at the creative relationships between artists and printers/publishers from the workshops Crown Point Press, Gemini G.E.L., Landfall Press, Tyler Graphics, Ltd., Universal Limited Art Editions (ULAE), and Vermillion Editions;

fig. 14

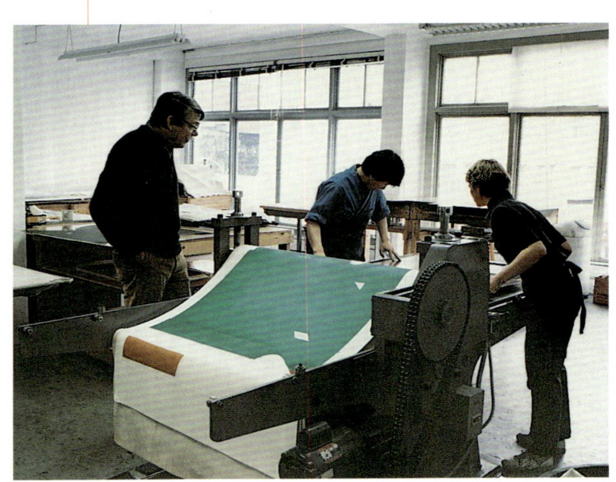

- Los Angeles County Museum of Art's *Sam Francis: Monotypes*, an exhibition of fifty-two monotypes that chronicles the artist's work from 1977 to 1979 with Garner Tullis at the Institute of Experimental Printmaking;
- Sterling and Francine Clark Institute's *Helen Frankenthaler Prints 1961–1979: A Retrospective* in Williamstown, Massachusetts;
- and Museum of Modern Art's *Printed Art: A View of Two Decades*, an exhibition organized by Riva Castleman that features more than 175 works by artists from the United States and abroad.

The prints in Richard Diebenkorn's *Eight Color Prints* series, published by Crown Point Press, are his first color intaglios and his first color prints since 1969. The prints will be included in the catalogue raisonné of his graphic work to 1980, *Richard Diebenkorn: Etchings and Drypoints 1949–1980* (Houston: Houston Fine Art Press) that will be published in 1981.

1981 The National Gallery of Art, Washington, D.C., establishes the Gemini G.E.L. archive with an initial gift from Gemini G.E.L. and its published artists that includes over 250 prints and sculpture editions and also proofs, drawings, and other preparatory materials.

Hanafuda: Jasper Johns, a film by Katrina Martin featuring Johns at work on screenprints at Simca Print Artists in New York, premieres at the Collective for Living Cinema.

1982 Gemini G.E.L. publishes a portfolio of eight lithographs by eight artists—Sam Francis, Philip Guston, David Hockney, Jasper Johns, Ellsworth Kelly, Bruce Nauman, Robert Rauschenberg, and Richard Serra—to benefit the Foundation for Contemporary Performance Arts, Inc. The portfolio is one of many equally ambitious portfolio projects that will be produced during the decade by other presses and publishers to benefit nonprofit causes. Notable are the 1983 portfolios *New York, New York* published by the New York Graphic Society to benefit the New York Cultural Council Foundation and *Eight by Eight* published by the Los Angeles Museum of Contemporary Art as a fund-raising effort.

Frank Stella: Prints 1967–1982, the first retrospective of his prints, opens at the University of Michigan, Ann Arbor. It is organized by Richard Axsom, who compiles the catalogue raisonné of Stella's prints that is published in 1983.

The Institute of Experimental Printmaking in San Francisco changes its name to Experimental Workshop.

Crown Point Press initiates its color woodcut program in Japan. Working with Tadashi Toda, a master printer, artists Pat Steir, William T. Wiley, and Francisco Clemente create color woodcuts in Kyoto during the first year of the project.

Tatyana Grosman dies at the age of 78. The ULAE workshop will continue under Bill Goldston, the workshop's director and a long-time master printer at the press.

The Art Institute of Chicago acquires Mrs. Grosman's personal collection of ULAEs entire production through purchase and Mrs. Grosman's gift of over 4,200 drawings, proofs, and other archival materials.

The Rutgers Archives for Printmaking Studios is created at the Jane Voorhees Zimmerli Art Museum, Rutgers University, as a repository for the prints, proofs, and other materials relating to the history and production of a group of printmaking workshops including Derrière L'Etoile, Magnolia Editions, made in California, Pelavin Editions, Solo Press, and Teaberry Press.

The Archives offers subscriptions to the *Rutgers Archives for Printmaking Studios Portfolio* to help support the work of member presses whose prints are documented at Rutgers.

1983 *The Print Collector's Newsletter* in its January–February issue provides a list compiled by Lisa Peters of 163 print workshops that are active in the United States. The list shows that New York has the most (38) workshops of any city. Further, the list shows that printmaking is a thriving enterprise with 97 workshops founded in the 1970s still operating, and that at this point in the 1980s 49 workshops were founded.

fig. 15

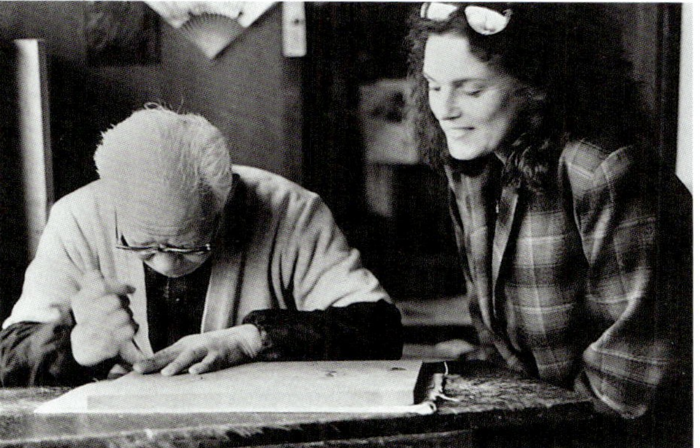

fig. 14 Richard Diebenkorn with printers Hidekatsu Takada and Marcia Bartholme working on *Green*, his largest and most sought-after print, at Crown Point Press, Oakland, 1986.

fig. 15 Artist Pat Steir with woodcarver Reizo Monjyu, who is cutting a block for Steir's *Kyoto Chrysanthemum*, in Kyoto, Japan, 1982.

The American Artist as Printmaker is the title of the 23rd Brooklyn Print National, curated by Barry Walker.

1984 Garner Tullis leaves Experimental Workshop in San Francisco to establish Garner Tullis Workshop in Santa Barbara, which specializes in monotypes. Experimental Workshop continues under the direction of Ann McLaughlin.

The National Gallery of Art publishes *Gemini G.E.L.: Art and Collaboration*, the catalogue by curator Ruth E. Fine that accompanies the exhibition she has organized to celebrate the founding of the Gemini archive at the Gallery in 1981.

In *A Century of American Printmaking: 1880–1980* (Madison: University of Wisconsin) James Watrous surveys the period 1940 to 1980 in five chapters, including the last, entitled "Controversial Practices and Continuing Innovations."

The Walker Art Center acquires the archive of Tyler Graphics Ltd. through gift and purchase that includes an archive print of each editioned image already produced and twelve hundred proofs, prints, and working sketches, as well as unique works. Archive proofs are promised from all future editions issued by Tyler Graphics.

Gemini G.E.L. at Joni Moisant Weyl is established as the New York gallery exhibiting and representing the publications of Los Angeles-based Gemini G.E.L. The gallery will show new editions as they are published and also mount historical exhibitions.

1985 Crown Point Press, which had opened a gallery at its workshop in Oakland in 1981, will open a New York gallery with Karen McCready as director.

In September, the Museum of Modern Art dedicates its contemporary print gallery as the Tatyana Grosman Gallery in honor of the legendary founder of ULAE who died in 1982. Mrs. Grosman's personal collection of prints is auctioned at Christie's in a nostalgic sale earlier in the year.

Riva Castleman, director of the department of prints and illustrated books at the Museum of Modern Art, writes *American Impressions: Prints since Pollock* (New York: Alfred A. Knopf), an illustrated survey of forty-five years from 1940 to 1985.

Joe Wilfer moves to New York to cofound the Spring Street Workshop with Richard Solomon of Pace Editions. The workshop, affiliated with Pace Prints gallery, will produce memorable editions by Chuck Close, Jim Dine, and others over the next decade.

1986 *Contemporary Print Symposium II* is held at the Los Angeles County Museum of Art with panel discussions and sessions on "Contemporary Print Publishing," "Status of the Contemporary Print Gallery," and "Collaboration Between Artist and Printer."

fig. 16

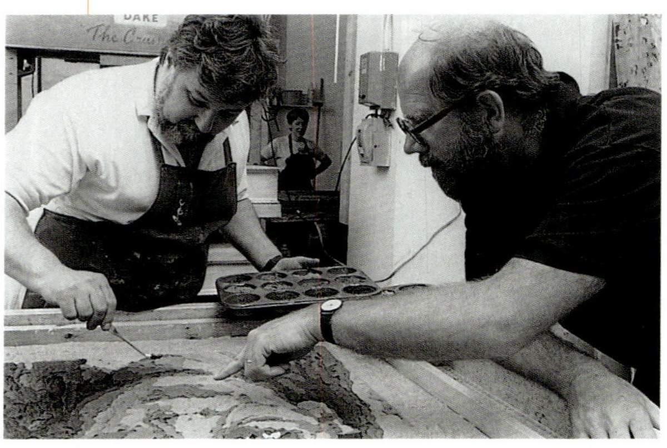

The archive of Cirrus Editions is acquired by the Los Angeles County Art Museum through purchase and gifts from Cirrus. Prints will be added to the Archive as they are published. Work on a catalogue raisonné by curator Bruce Davis begins and is included in the 1995 publication *Made in L.A.: The Prints of Cirrus Editions* (Los Angeles: Los Angeles County Museum of Art) that accompanies a major exhibition.

The Graphicstudio Archive is established at the National Gallery of Art and includes preparatory drawings, sculpture maquettes, trial proofs, and single edition prints. Materials will continue to be added to the archive as future editions are published. Graphicstudio was founded in 1968, closed in 1975 owing to funding problems, and then reopened in 1981. The archive will be celebrated with an exhibition organized by Ruth E. Fine and Mary Lee Corlett at the Gallery in 1991, accompanied by an extensive catalogue.

Ken Tyler, Master Printer and the American Print Renaissance, by Pat Gilmour, is published (New York: Hudson Hills Press in association with the Australian National Gallery).

Cliff Ackley, curator at the Boston Museum of Fine Arts, organizes *70s into 80s: Printmaking Now,* a survey of American and European printmaking efforts over a decade. Topics discussed in the accompanying catalogue essay are monotype inking in edition prints, the popularity of the unique variant, and the black-and-white print revival. Ackley also notes the significance of contemporary European printmaking, especially woodcut, and its effect on American style and practice.

Jane Glaubinger, curator at the Cleveland Museum of Art, curates an exhibition of thirty-four works dating from 1982 to date in *Paper Now: Bent, Molded, and Manipulated.*

Artist David Hockney unveils his "home-made prints," made from photocopies produced on Canon PC25, Canon NP 3525, and Kodak Ektaprint 225F copiers.

Jim Dine Prints 1977–1985, a catalogue raisonné by Ellen G. D'Oench and Jean E. Feinberg (New York: Harper & Row), is published in association with an exhibition organized for the Davison Art Center, Wesleyan University.

1987 Tandem Press, a nonprofit fine art press, is established as a self-supporting printmaking studio affiliated with the Department of Art at the University of Wisconsin, Madison.

Tyler Graphics: The Extended Image is the title of the exhibition at the Walker Art Center to celebrate the 1983 acquisition of the Tyler Graphics Ltd. archive. The exhibition is curated by Elizabeth Armstrong, who is also editor of the accompanying two-volume catalogue that contains a catalogue raisonné of Tyler's print publications from 1974 to 1985.

Riva Castleman curates an exhibition for the Museum of Modern Art entitled *Crown Point Press for Twenty-Five Years.*

Charles Kuralt's network television program *Sunday Morning* on CBS features a ten-minute segment on artist Chuck Close and the Crown Point Press etching program in San Francisco and its woodcut program in Japan.

Crown Point initiates a similar woodcut program in China this year, first in Beijing at the Rong Bao Zhai workshop, then later expanding to workshops in Shanghai and Hangzhou.

The Prints of Ellsworth Kelly: A Catalogue Raisonné 1949–1985 by Richard Axsom (New York: Hudson Hills Press in association with the American Federation of Arts), is published in conjunction with an exhibition of the prints that travels throughout the United States from September 1987 to January 1990.

Susan Tallman's article, "Independent Print Publishers: The New Breed," in the November-December issue of the *Print Collectors Newsletter,* identifies new publishers who work exclusive of any particular print shop or gallery. Among them are Mark Baron of Baron/Boisanté Editions, Joe Fawbush of Joe Fawbush Editions, Raymond Foye of Raymond Foye Editions, Matthew Fraser of This History, Delano Greenridge, Ilene Kurtz of Editions Ilene Kurtz, Julie Sylvester of Edition Julie Sylvester, and Peter Blum, who began Peter Blum Edition in 1980 and remains the model for this type of publishing.

fig. 17

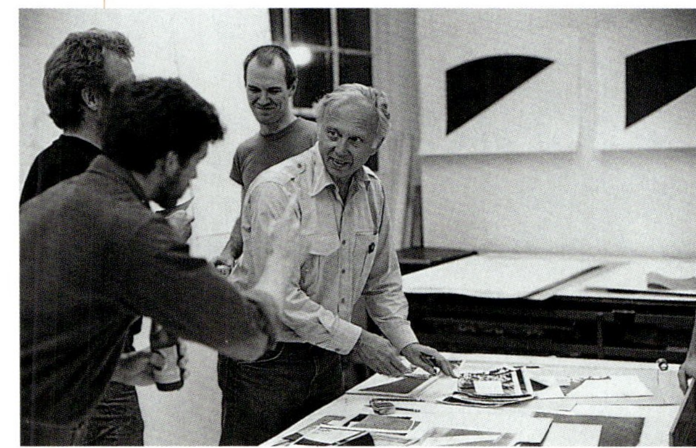

fig. 16 Joe Wilfer (left) with artist Chuck Close (right) and printer Ruth Lingen (background) at the Spring Street Workshop, working on the handmade paper-pulp edition *Susan,* 1988.

fig. 17 Ellsworth Kelly working at Gemini G.E.L. with Bill Padien, Patrick Foye, and Ken Farley, 1983.

1988 The Walker Art Center acquires a large group of Jasper Johns prints to form a complete holding of the artist's work to date. Curator Elizabeth Armstrong will produce *Jasper Johns: Signs and Symbols,* an exhibition that will travel throughout the United States in celebration of Johns's significant contributions to contemporary printmaking.

Johns' screenprint *Flags I* (1973) fetches $242,000 at the November auction at Christie's, New York, a record for a contemporary print sale. Four days later, another impression of *Flags I* will sell for $275,000 at Sotheby's. In May 1989, *Flags I* will sell for $308,000 at Christie's. The surge in prices for Johns's prints at auction is fueled in part by the popularity of his work among Japanese art collectors, who are in turn spurred by the strong yen. Japanese bidders are often the major buyers of Johns's lots offered for sale at auctions in 1988 and 1989, paying record prices. At the Sotheby's Tokyo sale in November 1989, *Flags I* will sell for YN 50,600,000 or $404,000.

Committed to Print, a survey of twenty-seven years of political printmaking from in the United States, is organized by Deborah Wye at the Museum of Modern Art, New York, with an accompanying catalogue.

Aldo Crommelynck, a legendary master printer in Paris with a forty-year career at his Atelier Crommelynck, sets up a New York etching studio in association with Pace Prints' Spring Street Workshop.

Aldo Crommelynck: Master Prints with American Artists is an exhibition of ninety works by thirteen artists presented at the Whitney Museum of American Art's Equitable Center branch, including works by Jim Dine, Chuck Close, Richard Bosman, and Jasper Johns.

1989 *First Impressions: Early Prints by Forty-Six Artists* is the catalogue by curator Elizabeth Armstrong for the exhibition at the Walker Art Center. Among the artists surveyed are many who had been making prints since the 1960s, such as Jasper Johns, Robert Rauschenberg, Roy Lichtenstein, and Andy Warhol, and also artists who have received acclaim for their prints made in the last decade, including Susan Rothenberg, Eric Fischl, Jennifer Bartlett, and Richard Bosman.

The 1990s

1990 The contemporary print market crashes at the Sotheby's and Christie's New York spring auctions with record numbers of unsold lots. However, an impression of *Flags I* sells for $209,000 at Sotheby's. By November, even the Johns's print market is affected, an impression of *Flags I* remaining unsold at Christie's with a $280–300,000 estimate. In May 1991, *Flags I* is unsold again at Sotheby's, even with a lower estimate of $200,000.

The Art Institute of Chicago mounts a major survey of ULAE editions celebrating its 1982 acquisition of the ULAE archive and the 1989 publication *Universal*

fig. 18

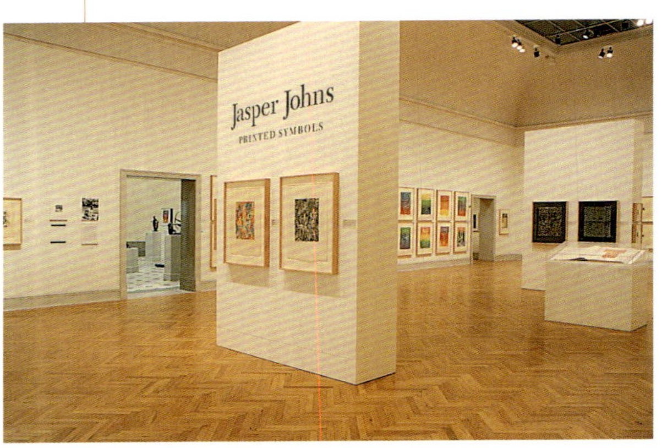

fig. 18 An installation of the traveling exhibition *Jasper Johns: Printed Symbols* at the California Palace of the Legion of Honor, San Francisco, 1990.

Limited Art Editions: The First Twenty-Five Years by Esther Sparks (Chicago:Art Institute of Chicago; New York: Harry N. Abrams).

The Prints of Robert Motherwell: A Catalogue Raisonné 1943–1990 (New York: Hudson Hills Press), introduced by Stephanie Terenzio and catalogued by Dorothy Belknap, is published and documents 431 prints. The text by Terenzio also includes extensive interviews of twelve printers and publishers with whom Motherwell has collaborated.

As part of its thirtieth anniversary celebrations, Tamarind Institute, Albuquerque, hosts a symposium focusing on the role of the printer as collaborator in the creation of fine art prints. Tamarind also initiates a suite of prints in which twenty-four artists contribute black-and-white prints in a 12 by 12 inch format. The suite, *Artists's Impressions*, is completed and released in 1992.

The Unique Print: 70s into 90s is the title of an exhibition of eighty-nine works by seventy-four American and European artists curated by Cliff Ackley at the Boston Museum of Fine Arts that further explores some themes seen in his 1986 exhibition, especially unique variants and monotypes.

1991 The Fine Arts Museums of San Francisco acquire the Crown Point Press archive through purchase and gift. The archive consists of an impression from each edition made at Crown Point since its inception in 1962, working proofs, drawings, and technical materials, and an agreement to provide an impression from each edition published into the future. By 1997, the archive's 3,700 works are housed at the Achenbach Foundation for Graphic Arts at the California Palace of the Legion of Honor.

1992 The Landfall Press archive is established at the Milwaukee Art Museum with more than six hundred editioned prints and three thousand drawings, proofs, plates, stones, and other materials. The archive will grow as the museum is given Landfall's annual publications, and is documented in the 1996 catalogue for the exhibition *Landfall Press: Twenty-Five Years of Printmaking.*

Ink, Paper, Metal, Wood: How to Recognize Contemporary Artists' Prints, a 62-page handbook by Kathan Brown, is published by Point Publications, San Francisco. The handbook serves as the catalogue for an exhibition of eighty prints organized by Crown Point that will travel throughout the United States from 1993 to 1995.

1994 *Hot Off the Press: Prints and Politics*, edited by Linda Tyler and Barry Walker, is the first issue of the Tamarind papers in book form. The issue explores through various essays the effectiveness of prints as an expressive visual medium for current social and political issues throughout history.

The Prints of Roy Lichtenstein: A Catalogue Raisonné 1948–1993 by Mary Lee Corlett, with an introduction by Ruth E. Fine (New York: Hudson Hills Press), is published in conjunction with a retrospective of Lichtenstein's prints at the National Gallery of Art, Washington, D.C.

At Yale University, the Print Catalyst Program is introduced by Rochelle Feinstein, professor of painting and printmaking. The program introduces a skilled printmaker to an artist who rarely makes prints, or is untried at printmaking. They make prints in a one-day collaboration and discuss the process with student observers. By 1999 the program will be host to two collaborations annually, including Louise Fishman with Nancy Bressler, Nicola Tyson with Jennifer Melby, Lisa Yuskavage with Greg Burnett, and Dan Walsh with Garner Tullis.

1995 The International Print Center New York (IPCNY), a nonprofit membership organization for the advancement of printmaking, is founded in New York. Focused exclusively on the fine art print as a medium, the group will promote its cause through lectures, symposia, exhibitions of historical and contemporary prints, an information center with library, and a website.

1996 *Thinking Print: Books to Billboards, 1980–95* is an exhibition and catalogue organized by Museum of Modern Art curator Deborah Wye, exploring the role of prints, deluxe and inexpensive books, and editioned multiples during a fifteen-year period. The survey includes some established printmakers such as Diebenkorn, Lichtenstein, Oldenburg, and Rauschenberg, but primarily focuses on a new generation of artists, including those working in traditional workshop printing and publishing such as Bill Jensen, Terry Winters, Elizabeth Murray, Susan Rothenberg, Francesco Clemente, Kiki Smith, and also those artists working in alternative forms such as Felix González-Torres, Barbara Kruger, and Jenny Holzer.

Ink, paper, metal, wood: Painters and Sculptors at Crown Point Press by Kathan Brown (San Francisco: Chronicle Books) is published, a greatly expanded version of her 1992 handbook in its detailed explanation of printmaking processes, particularly etching, and in-depth portraits of the artists she has worked with at the press.

The Le Roy Neiman Center for Print Studies is founded at Columbia University with a $6 million endowment from Mr. Neiman. The center will be fully operational in 1998 and will include studios for printmaking and a number of graduate fellowships.

The Print Collector's Newsletter ceases publication after a twenty-six-year run. A new bimonthly journal, *On Paper*, premieres its first issue in September–October with Faye Hirsch as editor. The publication will change its name to *Art on Paper* in September–October 1998.

Frankenthaler: A Catalogue Raisonné. Prints 1961–1994 by Pegram Harrison (New York: Harry N. Abrams, Inc.), is published and includes entries for 235 of Frankenthaler's prints and monotypes.

1997 *Thirty-Five Years at Crown Point Press: Doing Prints, Making Art* (San Francisco: Fine Arts Museums of San Francisco; Berkeley: University of California Press) is published on the occasion of two exhibitions. Coauthored by Karin Breuer, Ruth E. Fine, and Steven Nash, the book is the catalogue for *Thirty-Five Years at Crown Point Press*, an exhibition of two hundred prints from the Crown Point Press Archive at the Fine Arts Museums of San Francisco that opens in October at the California Palace of the Legion of Honor. A smaller version of the exhibition is shown in June at the National Gallery of Art, Washington, D.C., with prints from the San Francisco archive and the National Gallery's "OK to Proof" Crown Point collection.

The Corcoran Gallery of Art, Washington, D.C., presents *Proof Positive: 40 Years of Contemporary American Printmaking at ULAE, 1957–1997*, an exhibition with catalogue by Jack Cowart, Tony Towle, and Sue Scott, which provides an illustrated overview of ULAE's historic years to 1982 under the direction of Tatyana Grosman, and also a valuable artists' chronology of editions produced at ULAE from 1983–1996 under the direction of Bill Goldston.

Printed Stuff: Prints, Posters, and Ephemera by Claes Oldenburg. A Catalogue Raisonne 1958–1996 (New York: Hudson Hills Press), introduced by Richard Axsom and catalogued by David Platzker, is published in conjunction with the traveling exhibition *Claes Oldenburg: Printed Stuff*, organized by the Madison Art Center, Madison, Wisconsin.

The Museum of Modern Art, New York, presents the first of its exhibitions in the series *New Concepts in Printmaking*. Peter Halley's experiments in printmaking and computer-generated installations are mounted in an interactive gallery that is intended to challenge the idea of the

fig. 19

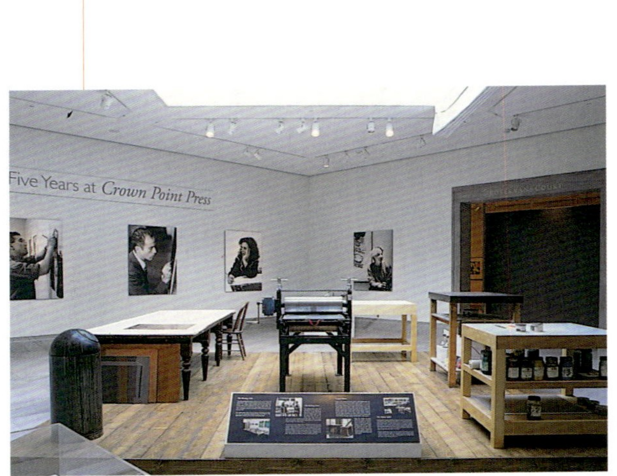

uniqueness of the work of art. Halley's art is generated from a computer disk (that will be acquired by MOMA), instead of traditional printmaking methods.

The American submission to the 22nd International Biennial of Graphic Art in Ljubljana, selected by University of South Florida gallery director Margaret Miller and Jade Dellinger, is made up of works employing digitial technology. *(re) Medititation: The Digital in Contemporary American Printmaking* includes works by ten artists—John Baldessari, David Hockney, Robert Rauschenberg, Frank Stella, Doug Aitken, David Humphrey, Alfredo Jaar, Diana Thater, Dani Tull, and Pae White.

The Whitney Museum produces its first portfolio in conjunction with the 1997 Whitney Biennial, with prints and photographs by four Biennial artists—Wendy Ewald, Paul McCarthy, John Schabel, and Sue Williams. The portfolio is organized by Julie Sylvester.

1998 *PhotoImage: Printmaking 60s to 90s* is an exhibition with catalogue by Cliff Ackley at the Boston Museum of Fine Arts.

Process and Collaboration: Contemporary Printmaking 1960 to the Present is presented by New York University's School of Continuing Education over three days in June. Sessions include panel discussions on prints in the 1990s, including digital prints.

Collective Impressions, a symposium at the Tamarind Institute, Albuquerque, investigates collaborations in printmaking with presentations by artists and their printer/publishers such as Dottie Attie/Solo Impression, Enrique Chagoya/Segura Publishing Co., Roberto Juarez/Tamarind Institute, Will Mentor/Hamilton Press, and Judy Pfaff/Tandem Press.

Artist Terry Winters produces *Graphic Primitives*, a portfolio of nine woodcuts printed at Two Palms Press, New York. For the prints, Winters scans drawings into the computer where he digitally manipulates them. The digitized drawings are then used to program laser cuts of the woodblocks, which become the print matrices. *Graphic Primitives* are included in the catalogue raisonné of his graphic work, *Terry Winters Prints 1982–1998* by Nancy Sojka (Detroit: Detroit Institute of Arts, 1999).

ArtByte/The Magazine of Digital Arts launches its first issue in April–May as a supplement to *Art on Paper*. Bill Jones is the editor of the journal that will feature articles on developments in digital technology and new media from artists' perspectives. To commemorate the publication, *Art on Paper* offers an Iris monoprint by Peter Halley, "Cell with Smokestack," at a discount to subscribers.

1999 *Pop Impressions Europe/USA: Prints and Multiples from the Museum of Modern Art,* an exhibition of ninety works curated by Wendy Weitman, examines printmaking's pivotal role in the Pop Art movement and the rise of the multiple during the 1960s.

Edward Ruscha Editions 1959–1999 (Minneapolis: Walker Art Center) is a catalogue raisonné by curator Siri Engberg to accompany the exhibition of the same name that premieres at the Walker Art Center. The catalogue and exhibition document Ruscha's editioned work, including prints, books, photographs, multiples, and other special projects.

Artist Fabian Marcaccio creates a giant scale (17 by 84½ feet) digital print at Muse X Editions, Los Angeles, for the Gorney Bravin + Lee gallery space in New York. He will reuse the digital files to produce a reconfiguration of the print panels for an exhibition in Stuttgart, Germany.

2000 Kenneth Tyler, who founded Gemini G.E.L. in 1966 and Tyler Graphics Ltd. in 1974, announces his retirement after thirty-seven years as a printer and publisher. There is a special auction at Sotheby's in May of prints from the Kenneth Tyler and Tyler Graphics collections, accompanied by a catalogue with an appreciation by Pat Gilmour.

fig. 19 Installation of the exhibition *Thirty-five Years at Crown Point Press* at the California Palace of the Legion of Honor, San Francisco, 1997. The installation featured a workshop for printmaking demonstrations by printers from Crown Point.

fig. 20

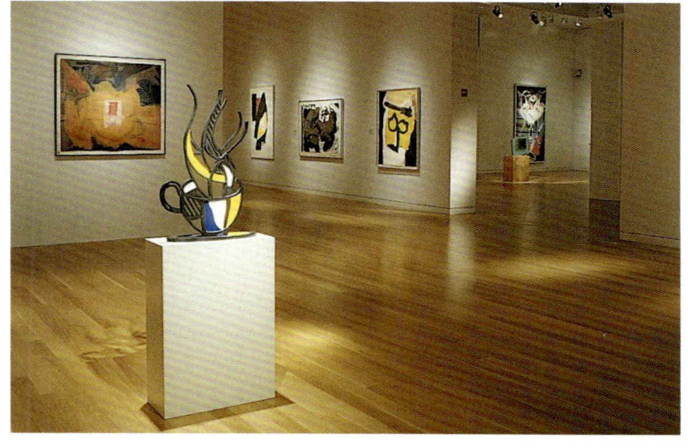

fig. 20 The Kenneth Tyler and Tyler Graphics collections, 6 May 2000; the Tenth Floor Exhibition Galleries at Sotheby's New York.

With the exception of fifty loans from the collection of Harry W. and Mary Margaret Anderson, all prints in this exhibition are from the Anderson Graphic Arts Collection at the Fine Arts Museums of San Francisco. Works marked by a star [⋆] are from the Anderson's personal collection and will not travel beyond the exhibition at the Palm Springs Desert Museum.

Measurements are given in inches, height preceding width. Plate size refers to the plate mark on the sheet. Image size refers to the printed image on the sheet when there is no plate mark, as in a lithograph, woodcut, or screenprint.

•

Published catalogues raisonnés are shown in abbreviated form at the end of the documentation of a print. The catalogues used in this checklist are:

Axsom, Richard H. *The Prints of Frank Stella: A Catalogue Raisonné 1967–1982*. New York: Hudson Hills Press; Ann Arbor: The University of Michigan Museum of Art, 1983.

Axsom, Richard H. *The Prints of Ellsworth Kelly: A Catalogue Raisonné 1949–1985*. New York: Hudson Hills Press in association with the American Federation of Arts, 1987.

Axsom, Richard, and David Platzker. *Printed Stuff: Prints, Posters, and Ephemera by Claes Oldenburg. A Catalogue Raisonné 1958–1996*. New York: Hudson Hills Press; Madison, Wisconsin: Madison Art Center, 1997.

Corlett, Mary Lee. *The Prints of Roy Lichtenstein: A Catalogue Raisonné 1948–1993*. New York: Hudson Hills Press; Washington D.C.: National Gallery of Art, 1994.

D'Oench, Ellen G., and Jean E. Feinberg. *Jim Dine Prints 1977–1985*. New York: Harper & Row, Publishers, 1986.

Engberg, Siri. *Edward Ruscha Editions 1959–1999: A Catalogue Raisonné*. Minneapolis: Walker Art Center, 1999.

Field, Richard. *Jasper Johns: Prints 1960–1970*. Philadelphia: Philadelphia Museum of Art, 1970.

Field, Richard. *Jasper Johns: Prints 1970–1977*. Middleton, Connecticut: Wesleyan University, 1978.

Glenn, Constance W. *Time, Dust: James Rosenquist. Complete Graphics 1962–1992*. New York: Rizzoli International, 1993.

Guillemin, Chantal. Catalogue raisonné in *Richard Diebenkorn: Etchings and Drypoints 1949–1980*. Houston: Houston Fine Art Press, 1981.

Harrison, Pegram. *Frankenthaler: A Catalogue Raisonné. Prints 1961–1994*. New York: Harry N. Abrams, Inc., 1996.

Hoppe-Sailer, Richard. *Richard Serra: Das druckgraphische Werk/Prints—A Catalogue Raisonné 1972–1988*. Bochum, Germany: Galerie m, 1988.

Krens, Thomas, ed. *Jim Dine Prints 1970–1977*. New York: Harper & Row in association with Williams College, 1977.

Lembark, Connie W. *The Prints of Sam Francis: A Catalogue Raisonné 1960–1990*. New York: Hudson Hills Press, 1992.

Maxwell, Rachel Robertson. *Susan Rothenberg: The Prints. A Catalogue Raisonné*. Philadelphia: Peter Maxwell, 1987.

Sheehan, Susan. *Robert Indiana Prints: A Catalogue Raisonné 1951–1991*. New York: Susan Sheehan Gallery, 1991.

Sojka, Nancy. *Terry Winters Prints 1982–1998: A Catalogue Raisonné*. Detroit: The Detroit Institute of Arts, 1999.

Terenzio, Stephanie, and Dorothy C. Belknap. *The Prints of Robert Motherwell: A Catalogue Raisonné 1943–1990*. New York: Hudson Hills Press in association with the American Federation of Arts, 1991.

ULAE. *The Prints of Jasper Johns 1960–1993: A Catalogue Raisonné*. West Islip, New York: Universal Limited Art Editions, 1994.

Checklist

1
WAYNE THIEBAUD
b. Mesa, Arizona 1920
Gum Machine, 1964,
pl. 9 from the portfolio *Delights*, 1965
Etching
$3\frac{15}{16}$ x $3\frac{7}{8}$ in. (plate); $12\frac{7}{8}$ x $16\frac{7}{8}$ in. (sheet)
Edition: 22/100
Printed by Kathan Brown
Published by Crown Point Press
1996.74.473.9

2
WAYNE THIEBAUD
b. Mesa, Arizona 1920
Lemon Meringue, 1964,
pl. 10 from the portfolio *Delights*, 1965
Etching
$3\frac{15}{16}$ x $4\frac{7}{8}$ in. (plate); $12\frac{7}{8}$ x $16\frac{7}{8}$ in. (sheet)
Edition: 22/100
Printed by Kathan Brown
Published by Crown Point Press
1996.74.473.10

3
SAM FRANCIS, ed.
San Mateo, California 1923–1994
Santa Monica, California
1¢ Life, by Walasse Ting, 1964
Unbound book of sixty-two lithographs
(three in black and fifty-nine in color)
Artists: Pierre Alechinsky, Karel Appel, Enrico Baj, Alan Davie, Jim Dine, Oyvind Fahlström, Sam Francis, Robert Indiana, Alfred Jensen, Asger Jorn, Alan Kaprow, Kiki Kogelnik, Alfred Leslie, Roy Lichtenstein, Joan Mitchell, Claes Oldenburg, Mel Ramos, Robert Rauschenberg, Reinhoud, Jean-Paul Riopelle, James Rosenquist, Antonio Saura, Kimber Smith, K.R.H. Sonderborg, Walasse Ting, Bram van Velde, Andy Warhol, Tom Wesselmann
$16\frac{1}{16}$ x $11\frac{5}{15}$ in. (each page)
Edition: 33/100 from the Special Paris Edition
Printed by Maurice Beaudet, Paris
Published by E. W. Kornfeld, Bern
1996.74.1

Illustrated:
SAM FRANCIS
Pink Venus Kiki, with the poem "Black Stone"
by Walasse Ting, 1964
Color lithograph, Lembark L. 82

4
ROBERT MOTHERWELL
Aberdeen, Washington 1915–1991
Provincetown, Massachusetts
Summertime in Italy (with blue), 1965–1966
Color lithograph
$22\frac{1}{4}$ x $17\frac{1}{4}$ in. (image); 30 x 22 in. (sheet)
Edition: 12/100
Belknap 24
Printed by Irwin Hollander
Published by Hollanders' Workshop
1996.74.311

5
RICHARD DIEBENKORN
Portland, Oregon 1922–1993
Berkeley, California
Pl. 18 from the portfolio
41 Etchings Drypoints, 1965
Etching and drypoint
8 x $9\frac{1}{2}$ in. (plate); $17\frac{3}{4}$ x $14\frac{3}{4}$ in. (sheet)
Edition: 4/25
Guillemin p. 118
Printed by Kathan Brown
Published by Crown Point Press
1996.74.76.18

6
RICHARD DIEBENKORN
Portland, Oregon 1922–1993
Berkeley, California
Pl. 26, 1964, from the portfolio
41 Etchings Drypoints, 1965
Aquatint, drypoint, and etching
$10\frac{7}{8}$ x $8\frac{3}{8}$ in. (plate); $17\frac{3}{4}$ x $14\frac{3}{4}$ in. (sheet)
Edition: 4/25
G. p. 119
Printed by Kathan Brown
Published by Crown Point Press
1996.74.76.26

7
RICHARD DIEBENKORN
Portland, Oregon 1922–1993
Berkeley, California
Pl. 31 from the portfolio
41 Etchings Drypoints, 1965
$6\frac{7}{8}$ x $5\frac{3}{4}$ in. (plate); $17\frac{3}{4}$ x $14\frac{3}{4}$ in. (sheet)
Aquatint and etching
Edition: 4/25
G. p. 119
Printed by Kathan Brown
Published by Crown Point Press
1996.74.76.31

8
RICHARD DIEBENKORN
Portland, Oregon 1922–1993
Berkeley, California
Pl. 33 from the portfolio
41 Etchings Drypoints, 1965
Aquatint, etching, and drypoint
$11\frac{3}{4}$ x $9\frac{3}{4}$ in. (image); $17\frac{3}{4}$ x $14\frac{3}{4}$ in. (sheet)
Edition: 4/25
G. p. 120
Printed by Kathan Brown
Published by Crown Point Press
1996.74.76.33

9
JOSEF ALBERS
Bottrop, Germany 1888–1976
New Haven, Connecticut
White Line Square III, from the series
White Line Squares, 1966
Color lithograph
$15\frac{11}{16}$ x $15\frac{3}{4}$ in. (image); 21 x 21 in. (sheet)
Edition: 44/125
Printed by Bernard Bleha
Published by Gemini G.E.L.
1996.74.10

10
JOSEF ALBERS
Bottrop, Germany 1888–1976
New Haven, Connecticut
White Line Square IV, from the series
White Line Squares, 1966
Color lithograph
$15\frac{11}{16}$ x $15\frac{3}{4}$ in. (image); 21 x 21 in. (sheet)
Edition: 44/125
Printed by Bernard Bleha
Published by Gemini G.E.L.
1996.74.11

11
AD REINHARDT
Buffalo, New York 1913–1967
New York, New York
Untitled #5, from the portfolio
10 Pieces, 1966
Color screenprint
$16\frac{1}{16}$ x 10 in. (image); $21\frac{3}{4}$ x $16\frac{13}{16}$ in. (sheet)
Edition: 167/250
Designed and produced by Ives-Sillman, Inc.
Printed by Sirocco Screenprint, Inc.
Published by Wadsworth Atheneum
1996.74.419.5

12
AD REINHARDT
Buffalo, New York 1913–1967
New York, New York
Untitled #6, from the portfolio
10 Pieces, 1966
Color screenprint
12 x 12 in. (image); $21\frac{3}{4}$ x $16\frac{13}{16}$ in. (sheet)
Edition: 167/250
Designed and produced by Ives-Sillman, Inc.
Printed by Sirocco Screenprint, Inc.
Published by Wadsworth Atheneum
1996.74.419.6

13
ROBERT RAUSCHENBERG
b. Port Arthur, Texas 1925
Booster, 1967
Color lithograph and screenprint
72 x 36 in. (image and sheet)
Edition: 6/38
Printed by Kenneth Tyler, assisted by
Robert Bigelow
Published by Gemini G.E.L.
1996.74.401

14
CY TWOMBLY
b. Lexington, Virginia 1928
Untitled I, 1967–1974
Open-bite aquatint and aquatint
$23\frac{9}{16}$ x $28\frac{1}{4}$ in. (plate); $27\frac{9}{16}$ x $40\frac{5}{8}$ in. (sheet)
Edition: 5/19
Printed by Donn Steward
Published by Universal Limited Art Editions
1996.74.484

15
FRANK STELLA
b. Malden, Massachusetts 1936
Irving Blum Memorial Edition, from the *Star of Persia Series*, 1967
Lithograph printed in metallic silver on English vellum graph paper
$25\frac{3}{4}$ x $31\frac{3}{4}$ in. (sheet)
Edition: 10/16
Axsom 3
Printed by James Webb
Published by Gemini G.E.L.
1996.74.457

16
FRANK STELLA
b. Malden, Massachusetts 1936
Ifafa I, from the *V Series*, 1968
Color lithograph
$16\frac{1}{4}$ x $22\frac{3}{8}$ in. (sheet)
Edition 13/100
A. 21
Printed by James Webb and Charly Ritt
Published by Gemini G.E.L.
1996.74.441

17
FRANK STELLA
b. Malden, Massachusetts 1936
Ifafa II, from the *V Series*, 1968
Color lithograph
$16\frac{1}{4}$ x $22\frac{3}{8}$ in. (sheet)
Edition 13/100
A. 22
Printed by James Webb and Charly Ritt
Published by Gemini G.E.L.
1996.74.442

18
FRANK STELLA
b. Malden, Massachusetts 1936
Quathlamba I, from the *V Series*, 1968
Color lithograph
$16\frac{1}{4}$ x $28\frac{7}{8}$ in. (sheet)
Edition: 13/100
A. 25
Printed by Charly Ritt and Bruce Lowney
Published by Gemini G.E.L.
1996.74.447

19
FRANK STELLA
b. Malden, Massachusetts 1936
Quathlamba II, from the *V Series*, 1968
Color lithograph
$16\frac{1}{4}$ x $28\frac{7}{8}$ in. (sheet)
Edition: 13/100
A. 26
Printed by James Webb, Dan Gualdoni, and George Page
Published by Gemini G.E.L.
1996.74.448

20
CLAES OLDENBURG
b. Stockholm, Sweden 1929
Untitled [geometric mouse], from the portfolio *Notes*, 1968
Color lithograph
$22\frac{11}{16}$ x $15\frac{3}{4}$ in. (sheet)
Edition: 31/100
Platzker 55.6
Printed by James Webb
Published by Gemini G.E.L.
1996.74.349

21
ROBERT INDIANA
b. New Castle, Indiana 1928
One, from the portfolio *Numbers*, 1968
Color screenprint
$23\frac{7}{16}$ x $19\frac{5}{8}$ in. (image);
$25\frac{9}{16}$ x $19\frac{5}{8}$ in. (sheet)
Edition: 46/125
Sheehan 46
Printed at Domberger KG
Published by Edition Domberger and Galerie Schmela
1996.74.192.1

22–31
JASPER JOHNS
b. Augusta, Georgia 1930
Black and White Numeral Series, 1968
Figure 0, lithograph printed in black and transparent gray, $27\frac{5}{8}$ x $22\frac{1}{4}$ in. (image); 37 x 30 in. (sheet)
Figure 1, lithograph printed in black and transparent brown gray, $27\frac{1}{4}$ x $21\frac{7}{8}$ in. (image); 37 x 30 in. (sheet)
Figure 2, lithograph printed in black and transparent gray, $27\frac{5}{8}$ x $21\frac{7}{8}$ in. (image); 37 x 30 in. (sheet)
Figure 3, lithograph printed in black and transparent brown gray, $27\frac{1}{2}$ x 21 in. (image); 37 x 30 in. (sheet)
Figure 4, lithograph printed in black and transparent gray, $27\frac{3}{8}$ x $21\frac{3}{8}$ in. (image); 37 x 30 in. (sheet)
Figure 5, lithograph printed in black and transparent flat gray, $27\frac{3}{8}$ x $22\frac{5}{8}$ in. (image); 37 x 30 in. (sheet)
Figure 6, lithograph printed in black and transparent gray, $27\frac{5}{8}$ x $21\frac{1}{4}$ in. (image); 37 x 30 in. (sheet)
Figure 7, lithograph printed in black and transparent gray; decal of Mona Lisa transferred to the black stone, $27\frac{1}{8}$ x $21\frac{3}{8}$ in. (image); 37 x 30 in. (sheet)
Figure 8, lithograph printed in black and transparent brown gray, 28 x 22 in. (image); 37 x 30 in. (sheet)
Figure 9, lithograph printed in black and transparent gray, $28\frac{3}{8}$ x $22\frac{1}{4}$ in. (image); 37 x 30 in. (sheet)
Edition: 22/70
Field 94–103; ULAE 44–53
Printed by Charly Ritt, James Webb, and Kenneth Tyler
Published by Gemini G.E.L.
1996.74.194-203

32–41
JASPER JOHNS
b. Augusta, Georgia 1930
Color Numeral Series, 1968–1969
Figure 0, color lithograph, $27\frac{5}{8}$ x $22\frac{1}{4}$ in. (image); 37 x 30 in. (sheet)
Figure 1, color lithograph, $27\frac{1}{4}$ x $21\frac{7}{8}$ in. (image); 37 x 30 in. (sheet)
Figure 2, color lithograph, $27\frac{5}{8}$ x $21\frac{7}{8}$ in. (image); 37 x 30 in. (sheet)
Figure 3, color lithograph, $27\frac{1}{2}$ x 21 in. (image); 37 x 30 in. (sheet)
Figure 4, color lithograph, $27\frac{3}{8}$ x $21\frac{3}{8}$ in. (image); 37 x 30 in. (sheet)
Figure 5, color lithograph, $27\frac{3}{8}$ x $22\frac{5}{8}$ in. (image); 37 x 30 in. (sheet)
Figure 6, color lithograph, $27\frac{5}{8}$ x $21\frac{1}{4}$ in. (image); 37 x 30 in. (sheet)
Figure 7, color lithograph $27\frac{1}{8}$ x $21\frac{3}{8}$ in. (image); 37 x 30 in. (sheet),
Figure 8, color lithograph, 28 x 22 in. (image); 37 x 30 in. (sheet)
Figure 9, color lithograph, $28\frac{3}{8}$ x $22\frac{1}{4}$ in. (image); 37 x 30 in. (sheet)
Edition: 14/40
F. 104–113; ULAE 59–68
Printed by Charly Ritt, Dan Freeman, and James Webb
Published by Gemini G.E.L.
1996.74.204-213

42★
BARNETT NEWMAN
New York, New York 1905–1970
New York, New York
Untitled Etching #1, 1968–1969
Etching and aquatint
$14\frac{1}{2}$ x $23\frac{1}{4}$ in. (plate); $22\frac{1}{2}$ x $31\frac{3}{4}$ in. (sheet)
Edition: 19/28
Printed by Donn Steward
Published by Universal Limited Art Editions
Collection of Harry W. and Mary Margaret Anderson
1969.100

43
LEE BONTECOU
b. Providence, Rhode Island 1931
Thirteenth Stone, 1968–1972
Lithograph
$22\frac{3}{8}$ x $28\frac{5}{8}$ in. (sheet)
Edition: 6/22
Printed by Frank Akers
Published by Universal Limited Art Editions
1996.74.42

44
ROY LICHTENSTEIN
New York, New York 1923–1997
New York, New York
Cathedral #1, from the *Cathedral Series*, 1969
Color lithograph and screenprint printed in yellow and white
$41\frac{13}{16}$ x 27 in. (image); $48\frac{1}{2}$ x $32\frac{1}{2}$ in. (sheet)
Edition: 13/75
Corlett 75
Printed by Robert de la Rocha
Published by Gemini G.E.L.
1996.74.238

45
ROY LICHTENSTEIN
New York, New York 1923–1997
New York, New York
Cathedral #2, from the *Cathedral Series*, 1969
Color lithograph and screenprint printed in red and blue
$41\frac{13}{16}$ x 27 in. (image); $48\frac{5}{16}$ x $32\frac{3}{8}$ in. (sheet)
Edition: 13/75
C. 76
Printed by Stuart Henderson
Published by Gemini G.E.L.
1996.74.23

46
ROY LICHTENSTEIN
New York, New York 1923–1997
New York, New York
Cathedral #3, from the *Cathedral Series*, 1969
Color lithograph and screenprint printed in blue
$41\frac{13}{16}$ x 27 in. (image); $48\frac{1}{2}$ x $32\frac{1}{2}$ in. (sheet)
Edition: 13/75
C. 77
Printed by Stuart Henderson
Published by Gemini G.E.L.
1996.74.240

47
ROY LICHTENSTEIN
New York, New York 1923–1997
New York, New York
Cathedral #4, from the *Cathedral Series*, 1969
Color lithograph and screenprint printed in red and blue
$41\frac{13}{16}$ x 27 in. (image); $48\frac{3}{8}$ x $32\frac{3}{8}$ in. (sheet)
Edition: 13/75
C. 78
Printed by Charly Ritt
Published by Gemini G.E.L.
1996.74.241

48
ROY LICHTENSTEIN
New York, New York 1923–1997
New York, New York
Cathedral #5, from the *Cathedral Series*, 1969
Color lithograph and screenprint printed in yellow and black
$41\frac{7}{8}$ x 27 in. (image); $48\frac{5}{8}$ x $32\frac{1}{2}$ in. (sheet)
Edition: 13/75
C. 79
Printed by Dan Freeman
Published by Gemini G.E.L.
1996.74.242

49
ROY LICHTENSTEIN
New York, New York 1923–1997
New York, New York
Cathedral #6, from the *Cathedral Series*, 1969
Color lithograph and screenprint printed in blue and black
$41\frac{13}{16}$ x $27\frac{1}{16}$ in. (image);
$48\frac{5}{16}$ x $32\frac{5}{16}$ in. (sheet)
Edition: 13/75
C. 80
Printed by Dan Freeman
Published by Gemini G.E.L.
1996.74.243

50
CLAES OLDENBURG
b. Stockholm, Sweden 1929
Profile Airflow, 1969
Cast-polyurethane relief over lithograph
33½ x 65½ x 4 in. (overall)
Edition: 15/75
P. 59
Lithograph printed by Richard Wilke
Polyurethane fabricated at CalPolymers
Published by Gemini G.E.L.
1996.74.353

51
JASPER JOHNS
b. Augusta, Georgia 1930
High School Days, from the series *Lead Reliefs*, 1969
Sheet-lead relief with mirror
23 x 17 in. (overall)
Edition: 9/60
F. 118, ULAE 72
Printed by Kenneth Tyler
Published by Gemini G.E.L.
1996.74.216

52
JASPER JOHNS
b. Augusta, Georgia 1930
The Critic Smiles, from the series *Lead Reliefs*, 1969
Sheet-lead relief, cast gold, and tin leaf
23 x 17 in. (overall)
Edition: 9/60
F. 119, ULAE 73
Printed by Kenneth Tyler
Published by Gemini G.E.L.
1996.74.218

53
JASPER JOHNS
b. Augusta, Georgia 1930
Flag, from the series *Lead Reliefs*, 1969
Sheet-lead relief
17 x 23 in. (overall)
Edition: 9/60
F. 120, ULAE 74
Printed by Kenneth Tyler
Published by Gemini G.E.L.
1996.74.214

54
JASPER JOHNS
b. Augusta, Georgia 1930
Light Bulb, from the series *Lead Reliefs*, 1969
Sheet-lead relief
39 x 17 in. (overall)
Edition: 9/60
F. 121, ULAE 75
Printed by Kenneth Tyler
Published by Gemini G.E.L.
1996.74.217

55
JASPER JOHNS
b. Augusta, Georgia 1930
Bread, from the series *Lead Reliefs*, 1969
Sheet-lead relief and embossed rag paper, hand painted by the artist
23 x 17 in. (overall)
Edition: 9/60
F. 122, ULAE 76
Printed by Kenneth Tyler
Published by Gemini G.E.L.
1996.74.215

56
ANNI ALBERS
Berlin, Germany 1899–1994
Orange, Connecticut
Blue Meander, 1970
Color screenprint
19⁷⁄₁₆ x 16 in. (image); 27¾ x 23⅞ in. (sheet)
Edition: 65/75
Printed by Sirocco Screenprint, Inc.
Published by Brooke Alexander Inc.
1996.74.3

57
ROY LICHTENSTEIN
New York, New York 1923–1997
New York, New York
Peace through Chemistry II, from the *Peace through Chemistry Series*, 1970
Color lithograph and screenprint
31⅞ x 57½ in. (image); 37⅜ x 63 in. (sheet)
Edition: 10/43
C. 97
Printed by Charly Ritt and Adolph Rischner
Published by Gemini G.E.L.
1996.74.250

58★
ROY LICHTENSTEIN
New York, New York 1923–1997
New York, New York
Untitled Head I, 1970
Solid brass on a brass-plated steel base
25⅝ in. (height)
Edition: 9/75
Fabricated by Kenneth Tyler, Jeff Sanders, and Herbert Tomkins
Published by Gemini G.E.L.
Collection of Harry W. and Mary Margaret Anderson
1970.030

59★
ROY LICHTENSTEIN
New York, New York 1923–1997
New York, New York
Untitled Head II, 1970
California English walnut wood
30 in. (height)
Edition: 9/30
Fabricated by Kenneth Tyler, Jeff Sanders, and Herbert Tomkins
Published by Gemini G.E.L.
Collection of Harry W. and Mary Margaret Anderson
1970.031

60
HELEN FRANKENTHALER
b. New York, New York 1928
Lot's Wife, 1971
Color lithograph
Upper section, 41¾ x 36 in.; center section, 48½ x 36 in.; lower section, 45¼ x 36 in. (image); 135½ x 36 in. (overall)
Edition: 8/17
Harrison 32
Printed by Fred Akers and David Umholz
Published by Universal Limited Art Editions
1996.74.137

61
ROBERT MOTHERWELL
Aberdeen, Washington 1915–1991
Provincetown, Massachusetts
The Black Douglas Stone, 1970–1971
Color lithograph
44⅜ x 19⅝ in. (image); 48 x 32 in. (sheet)
Edition: 2/18
B. 73
Printed by Ben Berns
Published by Universal Limited Art Editions
1996.74.317

62
ROBERT RAUSCHENBERG
b. Port Arthur, Texas 1925
Cardbird II, from the *Cardbird Series*, 1971
Cardboard, tape, steel staples, photo-offset lithograph, and screenprint
54 x 33½ in. (overall, irregular)
Edition: 10/75
Printed by Jeff Wasserman and Richard Ewen
Published by Gemini G.E.L.
1996.74.403

63
CLAES OLDENBURG
b. Stockholm, Sweden 1929
Ice Bag—Scale B, 1971
Programmed kinetic sculpture, yellow nylon, fiberglass, and mechanical movement
40 in. (height) x 48 in. (diameter)
Edition: 10/25
Fabrication supervised by Kenneth Tyler and Jeff Sanders assisted by Lou Faibish, Frank Doose, Pete Hoefer, Paul Muff, Bud Rogers, Frank Arnott, and Myron Judson
Published by Gemini G.E.L.
1996.74.354

64★
CLAES OLDENBURG
b. Stockholm, Sweden 1929
Geometric Mouse—Scale C, 1971
Black anodized aluminum
24½ x 20 in. (face), 9 in. (ears)
Edition: 10/120
Fabricated by Kenneth Tyler, Jeff Sanders, Lou Faibish, and Frank Doose
Published by Gemini G.E.L.
Collection of Harry W. and Mary Margaret Anderson
1971.055

65
FRANK STELLA
b. Malden, Massachusetts 1936
River of Ponds IV, from the *Newfoundland Series*, 1971
Color lithograph
31⅞ x 31⅞ in. (image); 38 x 38 in. (sheet)
Edition: 20/70
A. 53
Printed by Ron McPherson
Published by Gemini G.E.L.
1996.74.466

66
FRANK STELLA
b. Malden, Massachusetts 1936
Bonne Bay from the *Newfoundland Series*, 1971
Color lithograph and screenprint
31⅞ x 63¾ in. (image); 38 x 70 in. (sheet)
Edition: 10/58
A. 55
Printed by Stuart Henderson and Jeff Wasserman
Published by Gemini G.E.L.
1996.74.465

67★
JASPER JOHNS
b. Augusta, Georgia 1930
Decoy, 1971
Color lithograph
41 x 29 in. (sheet)
Edition: 21/55
F. 134, ULAE 98
Printed by Bill Goldston and James V. Smith
Published by Universal Limited Art Editions
Collection of Harry W. and Mary Margaret Anderson
1971.123

68
JASPER JOHNS
b. Augusta, Georgia 1930
Fool's House, 1971
Color lithograph
44 x 29 (sheet)
Edition: 10/67
F. 154, ULAE 109
Printed by Serge Lozingot
Published by Gemini G.E.L.
1996.74.22.1

69
JASPER JOHNS
b. Augusta, Georgia 1930
Two Flags (Black), 1970–1972
Lithograph
25 x 20 in. (image); 31½ x 23 in. (sheet)
Edition: 16/40
F. 165, ULAE 121
Printed by Bill Goldston
Published by Universal Limited Art Editions
1996.74.220

70
MARISOL [MARISOL ESCOBAR]
b. Paris, France 1930
Diptych, 1971
Lithograph in 2 parts
$47\frac{3}{4}$ x $31\frac{5}{8}$ in. (top sheet);
$47\frac{3}{4}$ x $31\frac{5}{8}$ in. (bottom sheet)
Edition: 3/33
Printed by Zigmunds Priede
Published by Universal Limited Art Editions
1996.74.279-280

71
NATHAN OLIVEIRA
b. Oakland, California 1928
Untitled, pl. VII from the portfolio
To Edgar Allan Poe, 1971
Lithograph
$30\frac{3}{16}$ x $22\frac{3}{8}$ in. (sheet)
Edition: 4/30
Printed by Nathan Oliveira
Published by Yankee Press
1996.74.368.7

72
BRUCE NAUMAN
b. Fort Wayne, Indiana 1941
War, 1971
Color lithograph
$22\frac{1}{2}$ x $28\frac{1}{4}$ in. (image and sheet)
Edition: 10/100
Printed by Paul Hamilton at Cirrus Editions
Published by Castelli Graphics and the Nicholas Wilder Gallery
1996.74.328

73
SAM FRANCIS
San Mateo, California 1923–1994
Santa Monica, California
Spleen (Red), 1971
Color lithograph
35 x $78\frac{3}{4}$ in. (sheet)
Edition: 10/27
Lembark L. 130
Printed by James Webb
Published by Gemini G.E.L.
1996.74.116

74
ELLSWORTH KELLY
b. Newburgh, New York 1923
Mirrored Concorde, 1971
Chromed steel sculpture on oak base
$22\frac{3}{4}$ x $26\frac{1}{2}$ x 10 in. (overall sculpture);
$28\frac{1}{2}$ x $25\frac{3}{4}$ x $13\frac{1}{2}$ in. (overall base)
Edition: 10/12
Fabricated by Kenneth Tyler, Jeff Sanders, Lucius Hudson
Published by Gemini G.E.L.
Anderson Graphic Arts Collection, gift of Harry W. and Mary Margaret Anderson
1999.134

75
RICHARD SERRA
b. San Francisco, California 1939
Du Common, 1972
Lithograph
$51\frac{1}{2}$ x $40\frac{1}{2}$ in. (sheet)
Edition: 10/59
Hoppe-Sailer 4
Printed by Ron Olds
Published by Gemini G.E.L.
1996.74.432

76
ROBERT MOTHERWELL
Aberdeen, Washington 1915–1991
Provincetown, Massachusetts
A la pintura/To Painting, by Rafael Alberti, 1968–1972
Unbound book of 24 pages with 19 aquatints and/or sugar-lift aquatints, most with etching, soft-ground etching, and/or line-block printing; one etching; one soft-ground etching
In a white Formica-laminated box with a Plexiglas top designed by the artist
$25\frac{9}{16}$ x $37\frac{15}{16}$ in. (each sheet),
28 x 40 x 6 in. (box)
Edition 15/40
B. 82–102
Printed by Donn Steward
Published by Universal Limited Art Editions
1996.74.319.1-24

Illustrated:
Untitled ["Red/Rojo 8–11"], B. 95, 1971.

77
RON DAVIS
b. Santa Monica, California 1937
Double Slice, 1972
Inkless intaglio on color lithograph
$20\frac{1}{4}$ x $39\frac{1}{2}$ in. (sheet)
Edition: 10/65
Printed by Serge Lozingot
Published by Gemini G.E.L.
1996.74.71

78★
JIM DINE
b. Cincinnati, Ohio 1935
Frédéric Moreau, from the series *Flaubert Favorites* (Edition A), 1972
Lithograph on handmade Nepalese paper, Williams 98
$24\frac{7}{8}$ x $18\frac{7}{8}$ in. (sheet)
Edition: 4/8
Printed by Bill Goldston and James V. Smith
Published by Universal Limited Art Editions
Collection of Harry W. and Mary Margaret Anderson
1972.07804

79
RICHARD ESTES
b. Kewanee, Illinois 1932
Grant's, from the series *Urban Landscapes I*, 1972
Color screenprint
14 x $20\frac{1}{2}$ in. (image); $19\frac{1}{2}$ x $27\frac{1}{2}$ in. (sheet)
Edition: C/A–Y
Printed by Luitpold Domberger at Domberger KG
Published by Parasol Press Ltd.
1996.74.107

80
RICHARD ESTES
b. Kewanee, Illinois 1932
Danbury Tile, from the series *Urban Landscapes I*, 1972
Color screenprint
15 x 20 (image); $19\frac{1}{2}$ x $27\frac{1}{2}$ in. (sheet)
Edition: C/A–Y
Printed by Luitpold Domberger at Domberger KG
Published by Parasol Press Ltd.
1996.74.108

81
RICHARD ESTES
b. Kewanee, Illinois 1932
Seagram Building, from the series *Urban Landscapes I*, 1972
Color screenprint
14 x 22 in. (image); $19\frac{1}{2}$ x $27\frac{1}{2}$ in. (sheet)
Edition: C/A–Y
Printed by Luitpold Domberger at Domberger KG
Published by Parasol Press Ltd.
1996.74.111

82
RICHARD ESTES
b. Kewanee, Illinois 1932
560, from the series *Urban Landscapes I*, 1972
Color screenprint
$15\frac{5}{16}$ x $23\frac{3}{16}$ in. (image);
$19\frac{1}{2}$ x $27\frac{1}{2}$ in. (sheet)
Edition: C/A–Y
Printed by Luitpold Domberger at Domberger KG
Published by Parasol Press Ltd.
1996.74.112

83
HELEN FRANKENTHALER
b. New York, New York 1928
Crete, 1969–1972
Color etching and sugar-lift aquatint
$13\frac{7}{8}$ x $18\frac{5}{8}$ in. (plate); $22\frac{1}{2}$ x 27 in. (sheet)
Edition: 4/18
H. 34
Printed by Donn Steward
Published by Universal Limited Art Editions
1996.74.135

84
HELEN FRANKENTHALER
b. New York, New York 1928
Connected by Joy, 1969–1973
Color etching and sugar-lift aquatint on Jeff Goodman handmade brown paper
14 x 19 in. (plate); $16\frac{1}{2}$ x 21 in. (sheet)
Edition: 8/27
H. 39
Printed by Donn Steward
Published by Universal Limited Art Editions
1996.74.136

85
ED MOSES
b. Long Beach, California 1926
Wedge Series: No. 5, 1973
Color lithograph on silk tissue
$24\frac{1}{4}$ x $18\frac{3}{8}$ in. (image and sheet)
Edition: 10/50
Printed by Ed Hamilton
Published by Cirrus Editions
1996.74.297

86
ROY LICHTENSTEIN
New York, New York 1923–1997
New York, New York
Bull I, from the *Bull Profile Series*, 1973
Line-cut
27 x 35 in. (sheet)
Edition: 10/100
C. 116
Printed by Ron McPherson
Published by Gemini G.E.L.
1996.74.254

87
ROY LICHTENSTEIN
New York, New York 1923–1997
New York, New York
Bull II, from the *Bull Profile Series*, 1973
Color lithograph and line-cut
$22\frac{15}{16}$ x 33 in. (image); 27 x 35 in. (sheet)
Edition: 10/100
C. 117
Printed by Ron McPherson and Bruce Porter
Published by Gemini G.E.L.
1996.74.255

88
ROY LICHTENSTEIN
New York, New York 1923–1997
New York, New York
Bull III, from the *Bull Profile Series*, 1973
Color lithograph, screenprint, and line-cut
$24\frac{1}{16}$ x $32\frac{1}{16}$ in. (image); 27 x $35\frac{1}{16}$ in. (sheet)
Edition: 10/100
C. 118
Printed by Dan Freeman and Ron McPherson
Published by Gemini G.E.L.
1996.74.256

89
ROY LICHTENSTEIN
New York, New York 1923–1997
New York, New York
Bull IV, from the *Bull Profile Series*, 1973
Color lithograph, screenprint, and line-cut
$23\frac{7}{16}$ x $33\frac{5}{8}$ in. (image); 27 x 35 in. (sheet)
Edition: 10/100
C. 119
Printing by Ron McPherson and Ron Olds
Published by Gemini G.E.L.
1996.74.257

90
ROY LICHTENSTEIN
New York, New York 1923–1997
New York, New York
Bull V, from the *Bull Profile Series*, 1973
Color lithograph, screenprint, and line-cut
$23\frac{1}{16}$ x 33 in. (image); $27\frac{1}{16}$ x $35\frac{1}{16}$ in. (sheet)
Edition: 10/100
C. 120
Printing by Ron McPherson and Jim Webb
Published by Gemini G.E.L.
1996.74.258

91
ROY LICHTENSTEIN
New York, New York 1923–1997
New York, New York
Bull VI, from the *Bull Profile Series*, 1973
Color lithograph, screenprint, and line-cut
$25\frac{1}{16}$ x 33 in. (image); 27 x 35 in. (sheet)
Edition: 10/100
C. 121
Printing by Ron McPherson and Bruce Porter
Published by Gemini G.E.L.
1996.74.259

92
ELLSWORTH KELLY
b. Newburgh, New York 1923
Black Curve I (White Curve I), 1973
Lithograph with graphite
26 x 26 in. (image) 34 x 34 in. (sheet)
Edition: 10/49
A. 100
Printed by Serge Lozingot
Published by Gemini G.E.L.
1996.74.235

93★
ED RUSCHA
b. Omaha, Nebraska 1937
Evil, 1973
Color screenprint on woodgrain veneer, perfumed with Cabochard by Grès
$19\frac{7}{8}$ x $29\frac{11}{16}$ in. (sheet)
Edition: 10/30
Engberg 70
Printed by Jane Aman
Published by Cirrus Editions
Collection of Harry W. and Mary Margaret Anderson
1973.051

94
DAVID HOCKNEY
b. Bradford, England 1937
The Master Printer of Los Angeles, 1973
Color lithograph and screenprint
48 x 32 in. (sheet)
Edition: 10/27
Printed by Kenneth Tyler and Jeff Wasserman
Published by Gemini G.E.L.
1996.74.179

95
DAVID HOCKNEY
b. Bradford, England 1937
Celia, 8365 Melrose Ave., Hollywood, 1973
Lithograph
$47\frac{1}{2}$ x $31\frac{1}{2}$ in. (sheet)
Edition: 10/46
Printed by Serge Lozingot and Kenneth Tyler
Published by Gemini G.E.L.
1996.74.178

96
JAMES ROSENQUIST
b. Grand Forks, North Dakota 1933
Off the Continental Divide, 1973–1974
Color lithograph
42 x 78 in. (sheet)
Edition: 12/43
Glenn 69
Printed by Bill Goldston and James V. Smith
Published by Universal Limited Art Editions
1996.74.426

97★
ROBERT RAUSCHENBERG
b. Port Arthur, Texas 1925
Link, 1973–1974
Handmade paper, pigment, screenprint, tissue, and paper pulp
25 x 20 in. (overall)
Edition: 16/29
Screenprint printed by Jeff Wasserman, Gary Reams, Richard Ewen, and Marie Porter
Papermaking and collaboration by Kenneth Tyler and the Moulin à Papier Richard de Bas, Ambert, France
Published by Gemini G.E.L.
Collection of Harry W. and Mary Margaret Anderson
1974.04302

98
ROBERT RAUSCHENBERG
b. Port Arthur, Texas 1925
Preview, from the *Hoarfrost Editions*, 1974
Photo-offset lithograph, newsprint and screen-print transfers, and collage, on silk chiffon and silk taffeta fabric
69 x $80\frac{1}{2}$ in. (overall)
Edition: 19/32
Printed by Charly Ritt and Robert Knisel
Published by Gemini G.E.L.
1996.74.413

99
JOE GOODE
b. Oklahoma City, Oklahoma 1937
Untitled, State II, 1974
Color lithograph on two sheets of paper
$28\frac{3}{8}$ x $40\frac{1}{2}$ in. (image); 30 x $41\frac{1}{2}$ in. (sheet)
Edition: 10/25
Printed by Ed Hamilton
Published by Cirrus Editions
1996.74.157

100
WILLIAM T. WILEY
b. Bedford, Indiana 1937
Mr. Nobody, 1975
Color lithograph
$42\frac{5}{16}$ x $31\frac{1}{16}$ in. (sheet)
Edition: 10/45
Printed by Lloyd Baggs
Published by Cirrus Editions and Hansen-Fuller Gallery
1996.74.486

101
LOUISE NEVELSON
Kiev, Russia 1900–1988
New York, New York
Dawnscape, 1975
Cast paper pulp
$27\frac{3}{4}$ x $30\frac{1}{2}$ in. (sheet)
Edition: Archive proof
Printed by Garner Tullis and Ann McLaughlin at the Institute for Experimental Printmaking (later Experimental Workshop)
Published by Pace Editions, Inc.
1996.74.330

102★
ELLSWORTH KELLY
b. Newburgh, New York 1923
Colored Paper Image V, 1976
Colored pressed paper pulp
$46\frac{1}{2}$ x $32\frac{1}{2}$ in. (sheet)
Edition: AP V of 19 variations
Papermaking by John and Kathleen Koller at HMP
Paper coloring by the artist, assisted by Kenneth Tyler and John Koller
Published by Tyler Graphics Ltd.
Collection of Harry W. and Mary Margaret Anderson
1978.064

103★
JASPER JOHNS
b. Augusta, Georgia 1930
Corpse and Mirror, 1976
Color screenprint
$42\frac{5}{8}$ x 53 in. (sheet)
Edition: VI/VIII
F. 211, ULAE 169
Printed by Takeshi Shimada, Kenjiro Nonaka, and Hiroshi Kawanishi
Published by the artist and Simca Print Artists
Collection of Harry W. and Mary Margaret Anderson
1981.067

104
FRANK STELLA
b. Malden, Massachusetts 1936
Sinjerli Variation IV, from the *Sinjerli Variations Series*, 1977
Color lithograph
32 x $42\frac{1}{2}$ in. (sheet)
Edition: AP
A. 116
Printed by Bruce Porter and John Campione
Published by Petersburg Press
1996.74.472

105
FRANK LOBDELL
b. Kansas City, Missouri 1921
6.22.77 I, 1977
Color monotype
$22\frac{5}{8}$ x $17\frac{1}{8}$ in. (image); $29\frac{5}{8}$ x $22\frac{1}{4}$ in. (sheet)
1996.74.271

106
SAM FRANCIS
San Mateo, California 1923–1994
Santa Monica, California
A Fixed Course of Changes #3, 1977
Color monotype with oil paint, watercolor, and embossing
$28\frac{1}{2}$ x $22\frac{1}{4}$ in. (image and sheet)
Published by Experimental Workshop
1996.74.123

107
CHUCK CLOSE
b. Monroe, Washington 1940
Self-Portrait, Black on White, 1977
Etching
$44\frac{1}{2}$ x $35\frac{5}{8}$ in. (plate); $54\frac{1}{8}$ x $40\frac{3}{4}$ in. (sheet)
Edition: 8/35
Printed by Patrick Foy at Crown Point Press
Published by Pace Editions, Inc.
1996.74.65

108★
JASPER JOHNS
b. Augusta, Georgia 1930
Savarin, 1977
Color lithograph
45 x 35 in. (sheet)
Edition: 45/50
F. 259
Printed by Bill Goldston and James V. Smith
Published by Universal Limited Art Editions
Collection of Harry W. and Mary Margaret Anderson
1977.007

109
JOSEPH ZIRKER
b. Los Angeles, California 1924
Untitled, 1978
Color monotype on vacuum-formed paper
$14\frac{5}{8}$ x $18\frac{1}{4}$ in. (image and sheet)
1996.74.490

110
MATT PHILLIPS
b. New York, New York 1927
Untitled, 1979
Color monotype
$16\frac{7}{8}$ x 21 in. (image); 18 x 22 in. (sheet)
1996.74.376

111
NATHAN OLIVEIRA
b. Oakland, California 1928
Seated Shaman Woman, 1978
Color monotype with hand coloring by the artist
$19\frac{15}{16}$ x $17\frac{7}{8}$ in. (image); $26\frac{1}{8}$ x $22\frac{1}{4}$ in. (sheet)
1996.74.372

112
MARY FRANK
b. London, England 1933
Untitled, 1978
Color monotype
$31\frac{3}{4}$ x $35\frac{1}{4}$ in. (sheet)
1996.74.133

113–124★
JOSEPH GOLDYNE
b. Chicago, Illinois 1942
Produce/A Portfolio of Twelve Monotypes, 1978
Portfolio of 12 color monotypes
$6\frac{3}{4}$ x $4\frac{7}{8}$ in. (each image);
$11\frac{1}{4}$ x 15 in. (each folio sheet)
Collection of Harry W. and
Mary Margaret Anderson
1978.025

125–136★
JOSEPH GOLDYNE
b. Chicago, Illinois 1942
Produce Series, 1978:
Pink Asparagus Huddle
Arrangement with Blackberry
Aubergine Passing at Dusk
Flame Lettuce
Composition Featuring Banana
Watermelon Section, Mit, Ball
Grapes and Guadagnini
Diagonal Husk
Poires Hollandaise
Falling Apple Meadow
Squash Icon
Winter Onion II
12 color monotypes (cognates of the monotypes from the *Produce* portfolio) with watercolor additions by the artist
$6\frac{3}{4}$ x $4\frac{7}{8}$ in. (each image);
11 x $7\frac{1}{2}$ in. (each sheet)
Collection of Harry W. and
Mary Margaret Anderson
1978.026.01-12

137
TOM HOLLAND
b. Seattle, Washington 1936
Eddy I, 1979
Color monotype on silk
24 x 20 in. (sheet)
Printed by Lee Altman
Published by 3EP, Ltd.
1996.74.191

138
JASPER JOHNS
b. Augusta, Georgia 1930
Periscope I, 1979
Color lithograph
50 x 36 in. (sheet)
Edition: 35/65
ULAE 200
Printed by Serge Lozingot
Published by Gemini G.E.L.
1996.74.232

139
WAYNE THIEBAUD
b. Mesa, Arizona 1920
Boxed Balls, pl. 6 from the portfolio
Recent Etchings I, 1979
Color aquatint and drypoint
$24\frac{1}{2}$ x 19 in. (plate); $29\frac{3}{4}$ x $22\frac{3}{4}$ in. (sheet)
Edition 29/50
Printed by Stephen Thomas at Crown Point Press
Published by Parasol Press Ltd.
1996.74.478

140
WAYNE THIEBAUD
b. Mesa, Arizona 1920
Palm Ridge, pl. 7 from the portfolio
Recent Etchings I, 1979
Color aquatint and soft-ground etching
$16\frac{5}{8}$ x $13\frac{1}{4}$ in. (plate); $29\frac{1}{2}$ x $22\frac{3}{4}$ in. (sheet)
Edition 29/50
Printed by Stephen Thomas at Crown Point Press
Published by Parasol Press Ltd.
1996.74.477

141
PHILIP GUSTON
Montreal, Quebec 1913–1980
Woodstock, New York
Studio Corner, 1980
Lithograph
32 x $42\frac{1}{2}$ in. (sheet)
Edition: 27/50
Printed by Serge Lozingot
Published by Gemini G.E.L.
1996.74.169

142
JENNIFER BARTLETT
b. Long Beach, California 1941
At Sea, Japan, 1980
Color woodcut and screenprint on 6 sheets
$22\frac{1}{2}$ x $104\frac{1}{4}$ in. (overall);
$22\frac{1}{2}$ x $16\frac{3}{4}$ in. (each sheet)
Edition: AP IV/IX
Printed by Simca Print Artists
Published by the artist and Simca Print Artists
1996.74.29

143
MICHAEL MAZUR
b. New York, New York 1935
Calla Lily Diptych, 1980
Color monotype (cognate)
$41\frac{9}{16}$ x $29\frac{1}{2}$ in. (sheet)
1996.74.294

144
MIKLOS POGANY
b. Budapest, Hungary 1946
Untitled, 1981
Color monotype with pastel additions by the artist
$49\frac{3}{4}$ x $38\frac{1}{16}$ in. (sheet)
1996.74.393

145★
RICHARD DIEBENKORN
Portland, Oregon 1922–1993
Berkeley, California
Large Bright Blue, 1980
Color spit-bite aquatint and soft-ground etching
24 x $14\frac{3}{8}$ in. (plate); 40 x 26 in. (sheet)
Edition: 22/35
G. p.111
Printed by Lilah Toland
Published by Crown Point Press
Collection of Harry W. and
Mary Margaret Anderson
1980.043

146
RICHARD DIEBENKORN
Portland, Oregon 1922–1993
Berkeley, California
Spreading Spade, 1981
Color aquatint, spit-bite aquatint, and drypoint
18 x 19 in. (image); $36\frac{3}{8}$ x $30\frac{7}{8}$ in. (sheet)
Edition: 20/35
Printed by Nancy Anello
Published by Crown Point Press
1996.74.87

147
KENNETH NOLAND
b. Asheville, North Carolina 1924
Chevron, 1981
Color monotype
$29\frac{5}{8}$ x $25\frac{1}{8}$ in. (sheet)
Published by Experimental Workshop
1996.74.339

148
VIJA CELMINS
b. Riga, Latvia 1939
Strata, 1982
Mezzotint
$29\frac{1}{2}$ x $35\frac{1}{4}$ in. (sheet)
Edition: 10/37
Printed by Doris Simmelink
Published by Gemini G.E.L.
1996.74.58

149
JONATHAN BOROFSKY
b. Boston, Massachusetts 1942
Molecule Men, 1982
Screenprint
$96\frac{1}{2}$ x $79\frac{3}{4}$ in. (sheet)
Edition: 8/12
Printed by Ron McPherson, Robert Sexton, and Ernie Garcia
Published by Gemini G.E.L.
1996.74.44

150
JIM DINE
b. Cincinnati, Ohio 1935
Fourteen Color Woodcut Bathrobe, 1982
Color woodcut
$77\frac{1}{2}$ x 42 in. (sheet)
Edition: 32/75
D'Oench/Feinberg 112
Printed by Garner Tullis at Experimental Workshop
Published by Pace Editions, Inc.
1996.74.102

151
JIM DINE
b. Cincinnati, Ohio 1935
The Apocalypse/The Revelation of Saint John the Divine, 1982
Bound book of 29 woodcuts
$14\frac{13}{16}$ x $11\frac{1}{8}$ in. (each page)
Edition: 10/50
D/F. 141
Published by The Arion Press, San Francisco
1996.74.103

Illustrated:
The Voice of the Bridegroom and of the Bride (D/F. 141x), in ch. 18:23.

152
JIM DINE
b. Cincinnati, Ohio 1935
Double Venus, 1983
Color monotype
63 x 36 in. (image and sheet)
Printed by Toby Michel at Angeles Press
Published by Pace Editions, Inc.
1996.74.104

153
CHARLES ARNOLDI
b. Dayton, Ohio 1946
Untitled, 1983
Color monoprint
$59\frac{7}{8}$ x 50 in. (sheet)
Published by New City Editions
1996.74.25

154★
LADDIE JOHN DILL
b. Long Beach, California 1943
Untitled, 1985
Vacuum-cast paper relief, hand painted by the artist
30 x 48 in. (overall)
Paper cast by Charles Hilger
Published by 3EP, Ltd.
Collection of Harry W. and
Mary Margaret Anderson
1985.032

155
DAVID GILHOOLY
b. Auburn, California 1943
Selbstbildnis mit Tod, from the series *3–A*, 1983
Monoprint etching
$22\frac{1}{2}$ x $30\frac{1}{8}$ in. (sheet)
Printed by Ikuru Kuwahara
Published by 3EP, Ltd.
1996.74.147

156
ROBERT ARNESON
Benicia, California 1930–1994
Benicia, California
Robert Arneson, from the series
Five Guys, 1983
Woodcut
$21\frac{3}{16}$ x $14\frac{3}{8}$ in. (image);
$31\frac{5}{16}$ x $24\frac{13}{16}$ in. (sheet)
Edition: 11/25
Printed by Will Foo and John Stemmer
Published by Experimental Workshop
1996.74.20

157
ROY LICHTENSTEIN
New York, New York 1923–1997
New York, New York
View from the Window, from the
Landscape Series, 1985
Color lithograph, woodcut, and screenprint
$76\frac{9}{16}$ x $30\frac{9}{16}$ in. (image);
$79\frac{9}{16}$ x $33\frac{5}{8}$ in. (sheet)
Edition: 10/60
C. 215
Printed by Alan Holoubek, Ron McPherson,
Totti DiAngelo, James McGowan, and
Anthony Zepeda
Published by Gemini G.E.L.
1996.74.269

158
DAVID HOCKNEY
b. Bradford, England 1937
Caribbean Tea Time, 1985–1987
Double-sided four-panel folding screen with front
printed in color lithograph with hand coloring
and collage; the back in color screenprint
$84\frac{5}{8}$ x $134\frac{1}{2}$ in. (overall)
Edition: 1, unnumbered, of 36
Printed by Kenneth Tyler, Lee Funderburg,
Tom Strianese, Michael Herstand, and
Roger Campbell
Published by Tyler Graphics, Ltd.
1996.74.184

159★
SUSAN ROTHENBERG
b. Buffalo, New York 1945
Stumblebum, 1985–1986
Color lithograph
$86\frac{1}{2}$ x $42\frac{1}{2}$ in. (sheet)
Edition: 5/40
Maxwell 26
Printed by Keith Brintzenhofe, Bill Goldston, and
Douglas Volle
Published by Universal Limited Art Editions
Collection of Harry W. and
Mary Margaret Anderson
1989.007

160
JUDY PFAFF
b. London, England 1946
Manzanas y Naranjas, 1987
Color woodcut
$56\frac{3}{8}$ x $69\frac{1}{2}$ in. (image and sheet)
Edition: 4/15
Printed by Lawrence Hamlin
Published by Crown Point Press
1996.74.375

161–164★
TERRY WINTERS
b. Brooklyn, New York 1949
4 prints from the portfolio of 11, *Folio*, 1986:
Folio, Title Page
Folio One
Folio Two
Folio Three
Color lithographs
Sojka 9–12
31 x 22 in. (each sheet)
Edition: 16/39
Printed by Keith Brintzenhofe
Published by Universal Limited Art Editions
Collection of Harry W. and
Mary Margaret Anderson
1989.011

165★
JASPER JOHNS
b. Augusta, Georgia 1930
The Seasons (Spring), 1987
Color sugar-lift aquatint, spit-bite aquatint,
drypoint, etching, and scraping and burnishing
26 x 19 in. (sheet)
Edition: 45/73
ULAE 238
Printed by John Lund, Hitoshi Kido, and
Craig Zamiello
Published by Universal Limited Art Editions
Collection of Harry W. and
Mary Margaret Anderson
1988.00701

166★
JASPER JOHNS
b. Augusta, Georgia 1930
The Seasons (Summer), 1987
Color sugar-lift aquatint, spit-bite aquatint,
drypoint, etching, photogravure, and scraping
and burnishing
26 x 19 in. (sheet)
Edition: 45/73
ULAE 239
Printed by John Lund, Hitoshi Kido, and
Craig Zamiello
Published by Universal Limited Art Editions
Collection of Harry W. and
Mary Margaret Anderson
1988.00702

167★
JASPER JOHNS
b. Augusta, Georgia 1930
The Seasons (Fall), 1987
Color sugar-lift aquatint, spit-bite aquatint,
drypoint, etching, and scraping and burnishing
26 x 19 in. (sheet)
Edition: 45/73
ULAE 240
Printed by John Lund, Hitoshi Kido, and
Craig Zamiello
Published by Universal Limited Art Editions
Collection of Harry W. and
Mary Margaret Anderson
1988.00703

168★
JASPER JOHNS
b. Augusta, Georgia 1930
The Seasons (Winter), 1987
Color sugar-lift aquatint, spit-bite aquatint,
drypoint, etching, and scraping and burnishing
26 x 19 in. (sheet)
Edition: 45/73
ULAE 241
Printed by John Lund, Hitoshi Kido, and
Craig Zamiello
Published by Universal Limited Art Editions
Collection of Harry W. and
Mary Margaret Anderson
1988.00701

169
RICHARD DIEBENKORN
Portland, Oregon 1922–1993
Berkeley, California
Blue with Red, 1987
Color woodcut
$33\frac{3}{4}$ x 23 in. (image); $37\frac{1}{4}$ x $25\frac{1}{2}$ in. (sheet)
Edition: 2/200
Printed by Tadashi Toda
Published by Crown Point Press
1996.74.92

170
ELIZABETH MURRAY
b. Chicago, Illinois 1940
Up Dog, 1987–1988
Color lithograph on 14 pieces of Arches paper
attached to a Japanese paper backing and
formed into an irregular shape
$45\frac{1}{2}$ x $46\frac{1}{2}$ in. (overall, irregular)
Edition: 5/62
Printed by Keith Brintzenhofe, Douglas Volle,
and Richard Dawson
Published by Universal Limited Art Editions
1996.74.325

171
PAT STEIR
b. Newark, New Jersey 1940
Waterfall, 1988
Color aquatint, spit-bite aquatint, soft-ground
etching, etching, and drypoint
45 x $35\frac{1}{2}$ in. (plate); $53\frac{3}{8}$ x $41\frac{1}{8}$ in. (sheet)
Edition: 47/60
Willi 32
Printed by Brian Shure
Published by Crown Point Press
1996.74.440

172
SEAN SCULLY
b. Dublin, Ireland 1945
Sotto Voce, 1988
Color aquatint
$27\frac{3}{4}$ x $41\frac{3}{4}$ in. (plate); $41\frac{1}{4}$ x $51\frac{3}{4}$ in. (sheet)
Edition: 23/40
Printed by Brian Shure
Published by Crown Point Press
1996.74.429

173
ELLSWORTH KELLY
b. Newburgh, New York 1923
Purple/Red/Gray/Orange, 1988
Color lithograph
$51\frac{3}{4}$ x $225\frac{1}{2}$ in. (sheet)
Edition: 10/18
Printed by James Reid, Claudio Stickar, Diana
Kingsley, Maggie Parr, and Andrew Rubin
Published by Gemini G.E.L.
1996.74.236

174
ROBERT RAUSCHENBERG
b. Port Arthur, Texas 1925
Bellini #5, 1989
Color photogravure
59 x $38\frac{1}{4}$ in. (sheet)
Edition: 13/50
Printed by Shelly Beech, Richard Dawson, and
Hitoshi Kido
Published by Universal Limited Art Editions
1996.74.418

175★
JASPER JOHNS
b. Augusta, Georgia 1930
Between the Clock and the Bed, 1989
Color lithograph
$26\frac{1}{4}$ x $40\frac{1}{4}$ in. (sheet)
Edition: 35/50
ULAE 246
Printed by Douglas Volle, Bruce Wankel, and
Bill Goldston
Published by Universal Limited Art Editions
Collection of Harry W. and
Mary Margaret Anderson
1989.042

176★
JASPER JOHNS
b. Augusta, Georgia 1930
The Seasons, 1989
Sugar-lift aquatint, spit-bite aquatint, drypoint,
etching, open-bite etching, and scraping and
burnishing
$26\frac{3}{4}$ x $58\frac{1}{4}$ in. (sheet)
Edition: 45/54
ULAE 244
Printed by John Lund, Craig Zammiello, Hitoshi
Kido, and Keith Brintzenhofe
Published by Universal Limited Art Editions
Collection of Harry W. and
Mary Margaret Anderson
1989.021

177★
JASPER JOHNS
b. Augusta, Georgia 1930
The Seasons, 1989
Sugar-lift aquatint, spit-bite aquatint, drypoint, etching, open-bite etching, photogravure, and scraping and burnishing
$38\frac{7}{8}$ x $25\frac{1}{2}$ in. (plate); $46\frac{3}{4}$ x $32\frac{1}{2}$ in. (sheet)
Edition: 18/59
ULAE 247
Printed by John Lund, Craig Zamiello, and Shi Ji-hong
Published by Universal Limited Art Editions
Collection of Harry W. and Mary Margaret Anderson
1989.042

178★
JASPER JOHNS
b. Augusta, Georgia 1930
The Seasons, 1990
Sugar-lift aquatint, spit-bite aquatint, drypoint, etching, open- bite etching, and scraping and burnishing on chine collé
Variously sized plates in cruciform configuration; $50\frac{1}{4}$ x $44\frac{1}{2}$ in. (sheet)
Printed by John Lund, Shi Ji-hong, Hitoshi Kido, Craig Zammiello, and Keith Brintzenhofe
Edition: 12/50
ULAE 249
Published by Universal Limited Art Editions
Collection of Harry W. and Mary Margaret Anderson
1990.031

179
JENNIFER BARTLETT
b. Long Beach, California 1941
The Four Seasons: Autumn, 1990
Color screenprint
$31\frac{3}{4}$ x $31\frac{3}{4}$ in. (image); 33 x $34\frac{3}{4}$ in. (sheet)
Edition: 11/62
Printed at Simca Print Artists
Published by the artist and Simca Print Artists
1996.74.32

180
JENNIFER BARTLETT
b. Long Beach, California 1941
The Four Seasons: Winter, 1991
Color screenprint
$31\frac{9}{16}$ x $31\frac{9}{16}$ in. (image); 33 x $34\frac{3}{4}$ in. (sheet)
Edition: 11/62
Printed at Simca Print Artists
Published by the artist and Simca Print Artists
1996.74.33

181★
JENNIFER BARTLETT
b. Long Beach, California 1941
The Four Seasons: Spring, 1992
Color screenprint
$31\frac{1}{4}$ x $31\frac{1}{4}$ in. (image); 33 x $34\frac{3}{4}$ in. (sheet)
Edition: 11/62
Printed at Simca Print Artists
Published by the artist and Simca Print Artists
Collection of Harry W. and Mary Margaret Anderson
1992.014

182★
JENNIFER BARTLETT
b. Long Beach, California 1941
The Four Seasons: Summer, 1993
Color screenprint
$31\frac{1}{4}$ x $31\frac{1}{4}$ in. (image); 33 x $34\frac{3}{4}$ (sheet)
Edition: 11/62
Printed at Simca Print Artists
Published by the artist and Simca Print Artists
Collection of Harry W. and Mary Margaret Anderson
1994.004

183★
BILL JENSEN
b. Minneapolis, Minnesota 1945
For Alice, 1990–1991
Color spit-bite aquatint, sugar-lift aquatint, and scraping and burnishing
$14\frac{3}{8}$ x $14\frac{1}{4}$ in. (plate), $22\frac{1}{2}$ x $21\frac{3}{4}$ in. (sheet)
Edition: 24/45
Printed by John Lund, Shi Ji-hong, and Keith Brintzenhofe
Published by Universal Limited Art Editions
Collection of Harry W. and Mary Margaret Anderson
1991.018

184★
CHRISTOPHER BROWN
b. Camp Lejeune, North Carolina 1951
Forty Flakes, 1991
Color aquatint and soft-ground etching
30 x 30 in. (image); 42 x 41 in. (sheet)
Edition: 25/55
Printed by Pamela Paulson
Published by Crown Point Press
Collection of Harry W. and Mary Margaret Anderson
1991.032

185★
ELIZABETH MURRAY
b. Chicago, Illinois 1940
Her Story, by Anne Waldman, 1988–1990
Unbound book with 13 illustrations, each a color lithograph with etching
$11\frac{3}{8}$ x $17\frac{3}{4}$ in. (each page)
Edition: 19/74
Printed by Douglas Volle, Keith Brintzenhofe, John Lund, Hitoshi Kido, Nancy Mesenbourg, Shi Ji-hong, and Bruce Wankel
Published by Universal Limited Art Editions
Collection of Harry W. and Mary Margaret Anderson
1991.002

Illustrated:
Pl. 11, with the poem "Glacial men. . . ."
$5\frac{13}{16}$ x $4\frac{1}{2}$ in. (plate)

186★
JASPER JOHNS
b. Augusta, Georgia 1930
Green Angel, 1991
Color spit-bite aquatint and sugar-lift aquatint on Barcham Green paper
$25\frac{5}{8}$ x $18\frac{1}{4}$ in.; 31 x $22\frac{1}{2}$ in. (sheet)
Edition: 27/46
ULAE 253
Printed by John Lund, Shi Ji-hong, and Craig Zammiello
Published by Universal Limited Art Editions
Collection of Harry W. and Mary Margaret Anderson
1991.019

187★
ROBERT THERRIEN
b. Chicago, Illinois 1947
Untitled [hangman], 1993
Color aquatint
$26\frac{1}{2}$ x 20 in. (sheet)
Edition: 12/25
Printed by Chris Sukimoto and Derek Isono
Published by Simmelink/Sukimoto Editions
Collection of Harry W. and Mary Margaret Anderson
1993.014

188★
ROBERT THERRIEN
b. Chicago, Illinois 1947
Untitled [red chapel], 1993
Color aquatint
$26\frac{1}{2}$ x 20 in. (sheet)
Edition: 12/25
Printed by Doris Simmelink
Published by Simmelink/Sukimoto Editions
Collection of Harry W. and Mary Margaret Anderson
1993.014

189
KIKI SMITH
b. Nuremberg, Germany 1954
My Blue Lake, 1995
Color lithograph and photogravure
$43\frac{1}{2}$ x $54\frac{3}{4}$ in. (sheet)
Edition: 23/41
Printed by Craig Zammiello
Published by Universal Limited Art Editions
Museum purchase, Anderson Graphic Arts Collection, gift of Michael Wilsey and the Lucille Brugh Memorial Fund
1997.143

190
ROY LICHTENSTEIN
New York, New York 1923–1997
New York, New York
Landscape with Poet, 1996
Color lithograph and screenprint
$90\frac{1}{2}$ x $36\frac{1}{8}$ in. (sheet)
Edition: 30/60
Printed by James Reid, Eric Donato, Paul Gellman, Robert Meyer, Claudio Stickar, and Matthew Thomason
Published by Gemini G.E.L.
Museum purchase, Anderson Graphic Arts Collection, gift of the Harry W. and Mary Margaret Anderson Charitable Foundation, Judith Clancy Fund, Achenbach Graphic Arts Council, and Dr. and Mrs. Donald Heyneman Fund
1997.36

191★
DEBORAH OROPALLO
b. Hackensack, New Jersey 1954
Rails, 1996
Color woodcut and etching
30 x 28 in. (sheet)
Edition: 3/45
Printed by Will Foo, Nicole Mackinley, and John Stemmer
Published by Experimental Workshop
Collection of Harry W. and Mary Margaret Anderson
1997.002

192★
TERRY WINTERS
b. Brooklyn, New York 1949
Multiple Visualization Technique, 1998
Color sugar-lift aquatint, spit-bite aquatint, and open-bite etching
$43\frac{3}{4}$ x $33\frac{3}{4}$ in. (plate); 53 x 42 in. (sheet)
Edition: 6/41
S. 144
Printed by Shi Ji-hong and Craig Zammiello
Published by Universal Limited Art Editions
Collection of Harry W. and Mary Margaret Anderson
1999.055

Presses and Publishers

3EP, Ltd., Palo Alto, California

Angeles Press, Los Angeles

The Arion Press, San Francisco

Brooke Alexander Inc., New York

Castelli Graphics, New York

Crown Point Press, San Francisco (formerly Oakland)

Cirrus Editions, Ltd., Los Angeles

Edition Domberger, Stuttgart/Filderstadt, Germany

E. W. Kornfeld, Bern, Switzerland

Experimental Workshop, San Francisco (now Emeryville, California) (formerly Institute for Experimental Printmaking)

Galerie Schmela, Düsseldorf, Germany

Gemini G.E.L., Los Angeles

Hansen-Fuller Gallery, San Francisco

Hollanders' Workshop, New York

Ives-Sillman, Inc., New Haven, Connecticut

New City Editions, Venice, California

Nicholas Wilder Gallery, Los Angeles

Pace Editions, Inc., New York

Parasol Press Ltd., New York

Petersburg Press, New York and London

Simca Print Artists, New York

Simmelink/Sukimoto Editions, Marina del Rey, California (now Middletown, New York)

Sirocco Screenprint, Inc., New Haven, Connecticut

Tyler Graphics, Ltd., Mount Kisco, New York (formerly Bedford Village, New York)

Universal Limited Art Editions, West Islip, Long Island

Wadsworth Atheneum, Hartford, Connecticut

Yankee Press, Stanford, California

The Anderson Graphic Arts Collection Sharing Program at the Fine Arts Museums of San Francisco

In 1996 the Harry W. and Mary Margaret Anderson Charitable Foundation presented a significant portion of their extensive collection of contemporary prints to the Fine Arts Museums of San Francisco. This collection, known as the Anderson Graphic Arts Collection, consists of 656 works (574 prints and multiples, and 82 monotypes) by major American artists. The collection spans over thirty years of print production from 1962 to 1996, surveying the American printmaking renaissance with outstanding examples of print processes—woodcut, intaglio, lithography, screenprint, and monotype—from major American fine art presses. "Sharing our collection by making it available to the public has always been important to us," noted Mr. Anderson in 1996 with the announcement of the gift. "The Fine Arts Museums will provide excellent exhibition and educational programs for the Anderson Graphic Arts Collection."

In keeping with the Andersons' wishes, since 1997 the Fine Arts Museums have provided an ongoing series of exhibitions from the Collection as well as interpretative publications and programs in order to share this important educational and art historical resource with museum audiences. The Fine Arts Museums are also dedicated to pursuing an active collective sharing program, which makes the Anderson Graphic Arts Collection accessible as a resource to museums and galleries throughout the western United States. Individual loans, self-organized exhibitions, or exhibitions previously presented at the Fine Arts Museums are available to small and mid-sized institutions, with no rental or participation fees.

The Fine Arts Museums welcomes requests for loans from the Anderson Graphic Arts Collection. A complete checklist as well as a visual directory in CD-ROM form are available by writing to Collection Curator, Anderson Graphic Arts Collection, Fine Arts Museums of San Francisco, 100 34th Avenue, San Francisco, CA 94121.

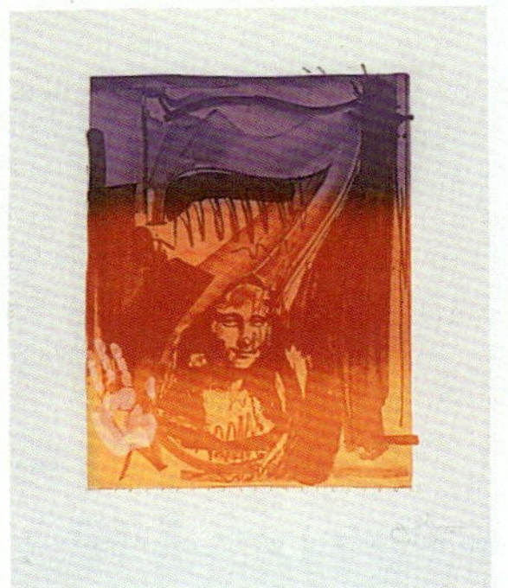

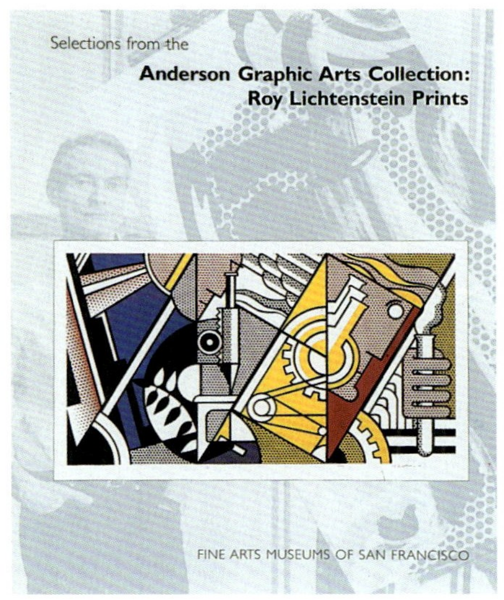

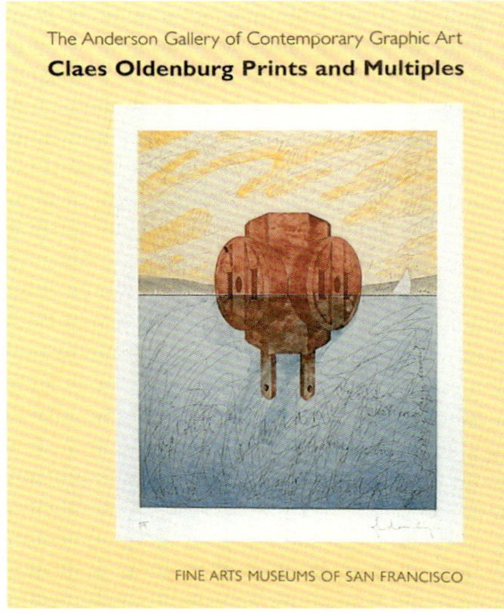

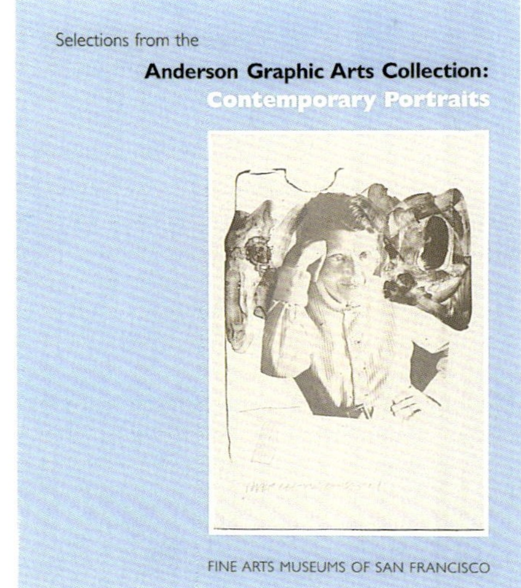

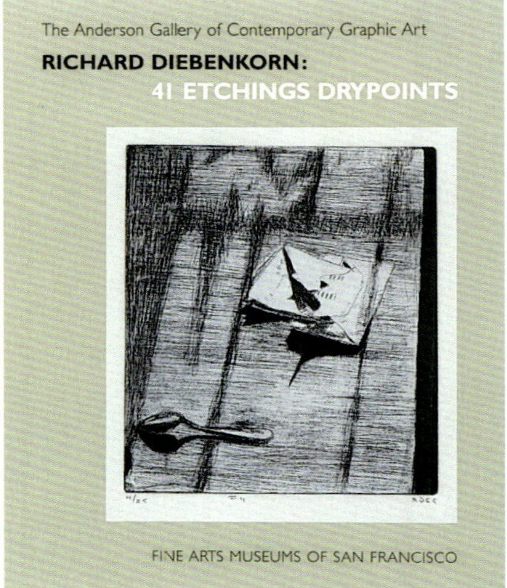

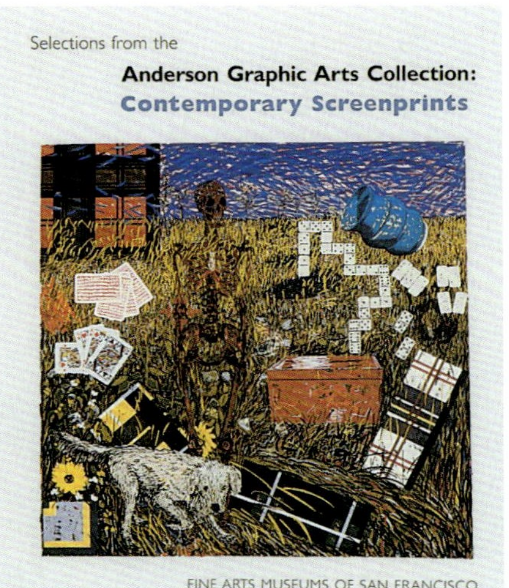

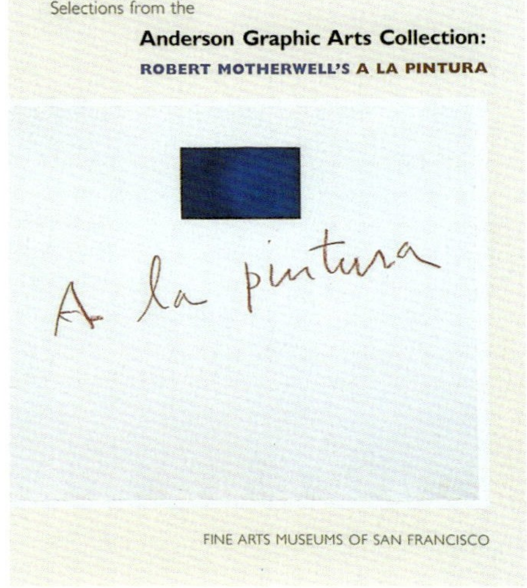

A selection of brochures from exhibitions presented in the Anderson Gallery of Contemporary Graphic Art, which are available for loan through the Collection Sharing Program.

Index

A listing of artists represented in the exhibition and illustrated in *An American Focus: The Anderson Graphic Arts Collection*

Page numbers in boldface refer to illustrated works

Photography Credits

Journey to the New.
Four Decades of Print Collecting
Page 10, Joseph McDonald
Fig. 1 Leo Holub
Fig. 2 Malcolm Lubliner; courtesy Malcolm Lubliner
Page 19 Scott Sibley, Photo International

All works in the *Catalogue of the Exhibition* were photographed by Joseph McDonald, with the exception of cat. 62 and cat. 173.

Permission to reproduce works was granted by the following:

Anni Albers, cat. 56
© 2000 The Josef and Anni Albers Foundation/Artists Rights Society (ARS), New York

Josef Albers, cat. 9, 10
© 2000 The Josef and Anni Albers Foundation/Artists Rights Society (ARS), New York

Robert Arneson, cat. 155
© Estate of Robert Arneson/Licensed by VAGA, New York, N.Y.

Richard Estes, cat. 78–81
© Richard Estes/Licensed by VAGA, New York, N.Y./Marlborough Gallery, N.Y.

Sam Francis, cat. 3, 73, 106
© 2000 The Estate of Sam Francis/Artists Rights Society (ARS), New York

David Hockney, cat. 158
© David Hockney/Tyler Graphics Ltd.

Robert Indiana, cat. 21
© 2000 Morgan Art Foundation Ltd./ Artists Rights Society (ARS), New York

Jasper Johns, cat. 22–41, 51–55, 66–68, 103, 108, 140, 166–169, 175–178, 186
© Jasper Johns and ULAE/Licensed by VAGA, New York, N.Y.

Ellsworth Kelly, cat. 74, 92, 102, 173
© Ellsworth Kelly

Roy Lichtenstein, cat. 44–49, 57, 58, 59, 86–91, 157, 190
© Estate of Roy Lichtenstein

Marisol [Marisol Escobar], cat. 70
© Marisol/Licensed by VAGA, New York, N.Y.

Robert Motherwell, cat. 4, 61, 76
© Dedalus Foundation, Inc./Licensed by VAGA, New York, N.Y.

Bruce Nauman, cat. 72
© 2000 Bruce Nauman/Artists Rights Society (ARS), New York

Louise Nevelson, cat. 101
© 2000 Estate of Louise Nevelson/Artists Rights Society (ARS), New York

Barnett Newman, cat. 42
© 2000 Barnett Newman Foundation/Artists Rights Society (ARS), New York

Kenneth Noland, cat. 147
© Kenneth Noland/Licensed by VAGA, New York, N.Y.

Robert Rauschenberg, cat. 13, 69, 97, 98
© Untitled Press, Inc., and Gemini G.E.L./Licensed by VAGA, New York, N.Y.

Robert Rauschenberg, cat. 174
© Untitled Press, Inc., and ULAE/Licensed by VAGA, New York, N.Y.

Ad Reinhardt, cat. 11, 12
© 2000 Estate of Ad Reinhardt/Artists Rights Society (ARS), New York

James Rosenquist, cat. 96
© James Rosenquist/Licensed by VAGA, New York, N.Y.

Susan Rothenberg, cat. 159
© 2000 Susan Rothenbert/Artists Rights Society (ARS), New York

Richard Serra, cat. 75 and cover
© 2000 Richard Serra/Artists Rights Society (ARS), New York

Frank Stella, cat. 15–19, 64, 65, 104
© 2000 Frank Stella/ Artists Rights Society (ARS), New York

Robert Therrien, cat. 187, 188
© 2000 Robert Therrien/Artists Rights Society (ARS), New York

Wayne Thiebaud, cat. 1, 2, 139, 140
© Wayne Thiebaud/Licensed by VAGA, New York, N.Y.

William Wiley, cat. 100
© William Wiley/Licensed by VAGA, New York, N.Y.

A Chronology of Printmaking in America

Figs. 1, 2, 5, 6, 7, 11, 18, 19 Joseph McDonald

Fig. 2 Courtesy Museum of Modern Art, New York

Fig. 3 Jo Fielder Photography; courtesy Universal Limited Art Editions

Fig. 4 Marvin Silver; courtesy Tamarind Institute

Figs. 7, 8, 9 Malcolm Lubliner; courtesy Malcolm Lubliner

Fig. 10 Harry Westlund; courtesy Cirrus Editions, Ltd.

Figs. 12, 14, 15 Kathan Brown; courtesy Crown Point Press

Fig. 13 Jill Sabella; courtesy Tyler Graphics, Ltd.

Fig. 16 John Back; courtesy Pace Editions, Inc.

Fig. 17 Courtesy Gemini G.E.L.

Fig. 20 Courtesy Sotheby's

Front Cover:
Richard Serra, *Du Common* (detail), cat. 75

Page 2:
Ad Reinhardt, *Untitled #5* (detail), cat. 11

Page 4, from top to bottom:
Roy Lichtenstein, *Cathedral #5* (detail), cat. 48
Ellsworth Kelly, *Colored Paper Image V* (detail), cat. 102
Terry Winters, *Folio One* (detail), cat. 162
Kiki Smith, *My Blue Lake* (detail), cat. 189

Page 6:
The Anderson Gallery of Contemporary Graphic Art at the California Palace of the Legion of Honor, San Francisco, 1997

Pages 8–9:
Jasper Johns, *Two Flags (Black)* (detail), cat. 69

Published on the occasion of the exhibition

An American Focus: The Anderson Graphic Arts Collection
organized by the
Fine Arts Museums of San Francisco
California Palace of the Legion of Honor
M. H. de Young Memorial Museum

California Palace of the Legion of Honor
7 October to 31 December 2000

Palm Springs Desert Museum
17 January to 21 March 2001

Albuquerque Museum
7 October 2001 to 6 January 2002

The catalogue is published with the assistance of the Andrew W. Mellon Foundation Endowment for Publications.

First published in paperback by the Fine Arts Museums of San Francisco. Distributed in paperback and cloth by the University of California Press, Berkeley, Los Angeles, and London.

LIBRARY OF CONGRESS CATALOGING-IN-PUBLICATION DATA

Breuer, Karin.
An American focus: the Anderson Graphic Arts Collection/Karin Breuer.
p. cm.
Published in conjunction with an exhibition organized by the Fine Arts Museums of San Francisco and held at the California Palace of the Legion of Honor, 7 Oct. – 31 Dec. 2000, the Palm Springs Desert Museum, 17 Jan. – 21 Mar. 2001, and the Albuquerque Museum, 7 Oct. 2001 – 6 Jan. 2002.
Includes bibliographical references and index.
ISBN 0-520-22761-1 (cloth: alk. paper) – ISBN 0-520-22763-8 (pbk.: alk. paper)
Prints, American – Exhibitions. 2. Prints – 20th century – United States – Exhibitions. 3. Anderson Graphic Arts Collections (Fine Arts Museums of San Francisco) – Exhibitions. 4. Prints – Private collections – California – San Francisco – Exhibitions. 5. Fine Arts Museums of San Francisco – Exhibitions. I. Fine Arts Museums of San Francisco. II. California Palace of the Legion of Honor. III. Palm Springs Desert Museum. IV. Albuquerque Museum. V. Title.

NE508 .B67 2000
769.973'09'04574794—dc21 00-032580

Printed and bound in Italy

Produced by the Publications Department of the Fine Arts Museums of San Francisco.
Ann Heath Karlstrom, director of publications and graphic design
Karen Kevorkian, senior editor
Book and cover design by Tracey Shiffman, Los Angeles
Printed and bound at Mondadori Printing, Verona, Italy

This publication is typeset in Futura, designed by Paul Renner and first issued by the Bauer Foundry in 1927. The stock is Biberist Furioso Matt, 170 g. The endpapers are Zanders Efalin, Bütten finish, 120 g. The hardcover edition is bound with Van Heek Scholco, Dubletta cloth. Both editions were printed on a Heidelberg Speedmaster CD 102.